Witness for Humanity

Lilly and Clarence Pickett at Waysmeet
with Hannibal II and Heavenly Hobo
on Clarence's 65th birthday
19 October 1949

Witness for Humanity

A Biography of Clarence E. Pickett

by

Lawrence McK. Miller

Pendle Hill Publications
Wallingford, Pennsylvania

For information, please address Pendle Hill Publications
338 Plush Mill Road
Wallingford, Pennsylvania 19086-6099
1-800-742-3150

Library of Congress Cataloging-in-Publication Data

Miller, Lawrence McK.
  Witness for humanity: the biography of Clarence E. Pickett/by Lawrence
McK. Miller.
      p. cm.
  Includes bibliographical references and index.
  ISBN 0-87574-934-8
    1. Pickett, Clarence, 1884-1965. 2. Quakers--United States--Biography.
  3. American Friends Service Committee--Biography. I. Title.

BX7795.P55 M55 1999
289.6'092--dc21
[B]

99-045120

To the staff and committee members of the
American Friends Service Committee:
past, present, and future

The red and black star was first used when it was stenciled onto bales of relief goods shipped by British Friends to France during the Franco-Prussian War in 1870 and 1871. Both British and American relief units used the symbol in World War I. It has since become a widely recognized identificantion of Quaker Service in domestic and international programs of the Religious Society of Friends.

Contents

Photographs

Foreword

Friends—and many others for whom the name of Clarence Pickett evokes reverence—have been waiting for this book for thirty years. To some still living, Clarence was a friend and mentor. To those younger, he is a legend. To all, he is remembered as one of the greatest Quakers of the twentieth century. A definitive biography is long overdue, and we are much indebted to Lawrence McK. Miller for finally filling the void with this meticulously researched and lucid record of a life lived with beauty and grace, a life that touched the marginalized and the mighty, a life that made a difference.

Larry Miller is well suited to his task. He is a Friend himself, with a long record of service to the Religious Society of Friends, as general secretary of the national association, Friends General Conference, and as a staff member in a number of programs of the American Friends Service Committee. In these pages the reader will follow Clarence from his boyhood on a Kansas farm through his formative educational and teaching years, to his warm friendship with Franklin and Eleanor Roosevelt, his leadership of the American Friends Service Committee, and his interaction with distinguished American and United Nations leaders in later years. We follow, too, his spiritual growth toward a powerful and persuasive witness to the social gospel.

Clarence Pickett touched and inspired those around him. He shaped many lives, including mine. The two years I served as his assistant during his tenure as AFSC's executive secretary were among the richest of my life. His humor, his great warmth, and his joyousness never failed to lift and encourage. A room brightened when he entered it. A world brightened when he talked about it. One could not miss his transparent faith in the immanence of a loving God whose power to redeem was beyond question or limit. One had a sense that Clarence's life was a continual meeting for worship.

Quaker educator and author, Rufus Jones, commenting on Clarence Pickett as executive secretary of the American Friends Service Committee, once said, "He is made in heaven for the job." That remark recalls for me the reverence with which Laurens Van der Post, the distinguished South African writer and philosopher, spoke about the people of the Kalahari Desert, at once among the world's most primitive but also among the most perfectly attuned to the world around them. Van der Post saw a man sitting high in a tree and asked if he might speak to him. "No, you can't," he was told. "He's very busy. He's making a cloud." Clarence Pickett could make a cloud. He could also engage a world leader. Truly he walked in the Light.

—Stephen G. Cary

Acknowledgments

I should first express appreciation for the wealth of written material Clarence Pickett generated during his lifetime, primarily his journal running to five thousand single-spaced typewritten pages. He began this record of his "doings and thoughts" (as he himself phrased it) in 1933 in his fourth year as executive secretary of the American Friends Service Committee (AFSC), noting that his work was bringing to him such a multitude of experiences and contacts that he wanted to record some of them for his future reference. "Perchance it may be that my children," he wrote on 1 January 1933, "may care to look them over some time." With some few exceptions very late in his life, Clarence Pickett's journal covers his activities, thoughts, and feelings every day of his life as a staff member of the Service Committee, up to just two weeks before his death. Lilly Pickett, his wife, completed the journal by describing the days of his last illness and the hour of his passing.

I also wish to express appreciation for his autobiographical account of his twenty-two years as executive secretary of the American Friends Service Committee, entitled *For More Than Bread*, and published by Little, Brown and Company in 1953. Apart from a brief preface, the autobiography did not cover the years prior to his assumption of the executive secretaryship or the fifteen years of inspiring service he gave on behalf of the Committee after becoming honorary secretary and then executive secretary emeritus.

Apart from Clarence Pickett's journal and his book *For More Than Bread*, there is available in the well-organized archives of the American Friends Service Committee under the able oversight of archivist Jack Sutters what I have referenced as the "Clarence Pickett papers." These papers include all of the letters that he and Lilly Dale Peckham wrote to each other during their courtship of five years; Clarence's notes for the courses he took at Hartford Theological Seminary; his correspondence with relatives and personal friends; and materials relating to the many organizations in which he was involved.

The archives embrace, chronologically since the Committee's formation in 1917, the minutes of board and committee meetings, correspondence relating to its programs, and AFSC statements and publications. Included in these files are Clarence Pickett's correspondence, first as executive secretary, then as honorary secretary and executive secretary emeritus. In the endnotes this correspondence is simply designated as being in the "AFSC archives."

Supplementing the Pickett papers in the AFSC archives is a relatively small cache of personal papers and photographs in the custody of his daughter, Carolyn Pickett Miller, my sister-in-law, who was consistently helpful in making these materials available along with her personal copy of the journal. Of particular value are the several hundred letters her father and mother received on the occasion of his retirement in 1950 as executive secretary of the AFSC. Closely related to my sister-in-law's sustained interest in the book project was the skilled contribution my brother, G. Macculloch (Cully) Miller, made in readying for the printer photographs made available to me by the family and by the AFSC.

A number of institutions have been singularly cooperative in providing documentary materials. They include the archives of Penn (now William Penn) College; Iowa Yearly Meeting of Friends; Canadian Yearly Meeting; and the Samuel Paley Library at Temple University. The staff of the Franklin D. Roosevelt Library in Hyde Park, New York, were immeasurably helpful. Thomas D. Hamm, archivist at the Lilly Library of Earlham College, made it possible for me to gain information about the Pickett and Macy families and more importantly about Clarence Pickett's vital role in the life of Earlham College during his six years as a member of the faculty.

Finally, closer to home, was the year after year assistance I received from the staff of Magill Library of Haverford College, principally those in charge of the Quaker Collection. I am indebted to Betsy Brown and Diana Peterson for their unfailing support. My research took me to a lesser extent to the Friends Historical Library at Swarthmore College.

In any literary enterprise of this sort there are individuals who stand out among those giving counsel. I wish to single out Ralph Pickett, who is the only remaining family member who recalls life in the Kansas farm community where Clarence Pickett grew up. Ralph remains sharp in his memory and suggestions. Gretta Stone, a member of my own Friends meeting, Doylestown, faithfully critiqued the entire manuscript and did some advance editing. My daughter, Janice Miller, edited some of the first completed chapters, those used for my proposal to potential publishers.

I interviewed in person or by phone—in most cases tape recording the conversations—forty persons (some now deceased) who had worked closely with Clarence Pickett. Listing them here, I express my appreciation for the invaluable insights they gave me about the subject of my biography: Rosaline Albert, Margaret Bacon, Martin Barol, Elise Boulding, Stephen Cary (author of the foreword), Bronson Clark, Rebecca Clark, Eleanor Stabler Clarke, Spencer Coxe, Nancy Duryea, Earle Edwards, Jean Fairfax, Barrett Hollister, Lewis Hoskins, Deborah Miller Hull, Patricia Hunt, Elizabeth Jensen, Mary Hoxie Jones, Jack Kavanaugh, Wayne and Gertrude Marshall, Elizabeth Mansfield, Hugh Middleton, Cully and Carolyn Miller, Jennifer Miller, Barbara Moffett, George Oye, Robert and Phyllis Painter, Kellogg Peckham, Ralph Pickett, Charles Read, Armand Stalnaker, Dorothy Steere, Gilbert White, Dan Wilson, and Mildred Young. There were other colleagues and friends who wrote to share remembrances.

It was Rachel Pickett Stalnaker, the Picketts' older daughter, who died before the work of this biography was initiated, who in 1964 (the year before he died, as it turned out) had the forethought to station her father in front of a tape recorder and to encourage him to talk as long as he wished about his life story. This was then transcribed. Subsequently, in 1972, Quaker historian and author Margaret Hope Bacon interviewed Lilly Pickett and made the recording and transcript of those conversations available to me. Both of these oral histories have been precious resources.

I wish to pay tribute to Teresa Jacob Engeman, my personal secretary, who, month after month after month, from the beginning to the end of this undertaking, transcribed the dictation of my hand-written drafts and then, with loyalty and good cheer, transcribed the dozen revisions of the manuscript. Her enthusiasm for the project never faltered, even as I failed to receive positive replies from publishers to whom I had sent my book proposal.

Those serial rejection letters, received over a spread of two years, happily led me to direct my attention to Pendle Hill, a highly-respected Quaker publishing house associated with the adult center for study and contemplation. Now that I have had the pleasure of working with Pendle

Hill's editor, Rebecca Mays and her two associates, Eve Beehler and Holley Webster, I recognize how fortunate it has been to have an editor and a team who were personally and deeply interested in the Pickett biography. It has been an inspiration to collaborate with them.

Finally, I wish to express appreciation for the devoted assistance of my wife, Carol. All the research at a distance from home—in Glen Elder, Kansas; Oskaloosa, Iowa; Richmond, Indiana; and Hyde Park, New York—was done in tandem. She read and critiqued the entire manuscript at an early stage. And beyond this assistance has been her willingness to have a third person living with us, albeit someone who passed on thirty years ago. But what a blessing it has been to have Clarence Pickett's spirit so close at hand. We give thanks for that presence.

—Larry Miller

Chapter 1

Boyhood in Kansas

I didn't know we were poor

IT WAS 1884. HULDA MACY PICKETT was forty-two years old. She and her husband, Evan, had already brought eight children into the world, three sons and five daughters, and they assumed and hoped that her childbearing years were over. The previous year the youngest daughter, three-year old Eva, had died of pneumonia. As the other children later recalled, their father spoke "very tenderly to us of the beautiful place where our Eva had gone to be with Christ."[1]

But Hulda Pickett soon realized she was expecting another child. As Minnie Pickett Bowles, one of the older daughters, remembered it, "Mother said, 'At first I resented having once more to go through that painful experience, for I had grown weak; then I realized this was of God, and I decided to put the very best of my whole life into this child and pray that he might carry on what I might never be able to do.' Then and there, Mother gave this coming one into the hands of God for all time and future work."[2] This remembrance was confirmed by Clarence Pickett himself in his later years. He tells of the day when his mother, then well over eighty years old, told him in confidence of the bitterness she had felt and the spiritual struggle which she went through when she learned she was once again pregnant. "But finally she came to the firm resolve to purge her spirit of all resentment, to look forward cheerfully to the arrival of a new child, and to pray that he might be a devoted and useful member of the Kingdom of Heaven on earth, in which she so profoundly believed."[3]

Hulda Macy Pickett, Clarence's mother

Clarence Evan Pickett was born on Sunday, 19 October 1884 on the family farm in Cissna Park, Iroquois County, Illinois. As an adult, Clarence always enjoyed telling about his arrival. It was "rather unexpected. My older brother went off on horseback to the nearest town, which was six miles away, and got the doctor. The doctor came, but I was already on hand before he got there, so I only cost five dollars. If he'd had to really see me arrive, he would have charged ten dollars for the privilege. This may be a mythical story, I don't know, but that's the way I remember my mother telling me. The reason I say it might be mythical is that my wife tells almost the identical story about her birth in northwest Iowa."[4]

Both of Clarence Pickett's parents came from a long line of Quaker ancestors. Hulda's forebears went back to Thomas Macy of Nantucket, the family that included the Macy who started the Macy Department stores.[5] She was the daughter of Alva and Mary Lewis Macy and was born in Economy, Indiana, on 25 September 1841. She was one of a large family of children. Her father died early, leaving a heavy responsibility on the older children and her mother. This early training prepared Hulda well for the sizable family she and Evan Pickett were to have.

Evan Pickett was born on 1 January 1839 and was the first son of John and Mary Hadley Pickett. The Picketts migrated from Pennsylvania to North Carolina, then later, along with many other North Carolina Friends who were opposed to slavery, to Indiana, a "free state." When Evan was not yet two years of age, both of his parents and their second son died of typhoid fever within two weeks of each other. Evan was taken into the home of his maternal uncle, Edward Hadley, and his wife, Elizabeth (known as "Lizzie"). Evan lived with his aunt and uncle until manhood.

Evan Pickett and Hulda Macy were married in Wayne County, Indiana on 25 March 1862.[6] Evan was a member of West Union Monthly Meeting in Mooresville in Morgan County, Hulda of Springfield Monthly Meeting in Wayne County.[7] In accordance with Indiana Yearly Meeting's book of discipline, strict procedures existed regarding the mar-

Evan Pickett, Clarence's father

riage of members, one of the requirements being the need to obtain written approval of the members' meetings. It is of passing interest, perhaps a sign of a rebellious spirit, that Evan and Hulda "married out of meeting," meaning that they did not seek nor receive permission to marry from their respective meetings. Presumably they were married by an appropriate county official. Each of them was formally condemned by his or her respective meeting for this conduct.[8] But the discipline of Indiana Yearly Meeting had a provision stating that "offenders . . . who incline to make acknowledgment of their offenses"[9] could formally apologize to the monthly meeting for the misconduct and ask to be continued as a member. Both Evan and Hulda were excused and permitted by their meetings to remain as members. Hulda then transferred her membership to the West Union Meeting in November 1863.[10]

The young couple settled on a farm in Morgan County, southwest of Indianapolis. Their first two children were born on that farm, Charles Edward in January 1863 and Mary Alice one year later. Then, with the

Clarence Pickett at two years of age

ending of the Civil War in April 1865, the Pickett family moved to the Quaker community in Cissna Park, Illinois.[11] It was on the family farm in Cissna Park where the other seven Pickett children were born.

In 1887, when Clarence was three years old, the Pickett family decided to move from the damp climate of Illinois to the dry climate of Kansas. According to Minnie Pickett Bowles, the decision followed an epidemic of influenza in the community. "My father did not make a good recovery, and it was the doctor's decision that he must seek a drier climate."[12]

Evan went to look for a farm in Glen Elder, in north central Kansas, where an uncle, a Hadley from his mother's side of the family, resided. He decided to purchase a farm in Mitchell County from Alfred and Christina Newsom in a Friends settlement called Pleasant Valley in the southwest corner of what was known as Section 32. Beginning in 1854 the federal government had mapped the Kansas territory, dividing the land into endlessly repeated squares, or sections. Each section consisted of 640 acres, or one square mile. The Picketts' property consisted of a quarter-section containing 160 acres "more or less," as the warranty deed put it.[13] The "less" in fact were the 14.4 acres that the Newsoms had sold in 1881 to the Glen Elder Friends Meeting for the purpose of establishing a cemetery and building a Quaker high school, called an "academy." Also, in the extreme southeast corner of the property there was a public elementary school, the Pleasant Valley School. Meetings for worship and business of the Glen Elder Meeting were held in the Pleasant Valley schoolhouse until the construction of the academy.

Clarence Pickett remembered nothing about life in Illinois or the trip westward. It is reasonable to assume that the Pickett family made the entire journey by train, probably via Chicago and Kansas City. The Central Branch Union Pacific Railroad Company had completed an extension of its line westward from Beloit, Kansas, to Glen Elder (eleven miles) and then to Cawker City (an additional six miles) in 1879. Young Clarence must have been fascinated by what he saw out the train window on the flat, rural stretches of land across Illinois and Missouri. He knew that accompanying them in another car, along with all of their household possessions, were three horses, one stallion and two mares. These were Percherons, a French breed of draft horse. His father, a great lover of horses, was determined, as Clarence put it in later years, "to improve the quality of horses in the community to which we were moving. Looking back over the years, I am sure he had a great deal of satisfaction in knowing that the idea of what a horse could be was quite changed by the fact that these fine thoroughbred livestock had serviced their neighbors in a way that lifted the whole level of the quality of horseflesh in the community."[14] So remembers Clarence Pickett, but his brother, John—thirteen years older and the only sibling who stayed on in the community and in 1910 purchased 160 acres just east of where he grew up—felt that the Percherons did not stand the heat well.[15]

The Pickett family arrived in Glen Elder, Kansas, on 6 March 1888.[16] Although Clarence Pickett's father had previously visited Glen Elder, Hulda and the children had not. Their first impressions of Mitchell County, the Solomon River Valley, and Glen Elder must have been important ones. Unlike many other parts of Kansas, the landscape can best be described as undulating. The Solomon River, with its many tributaries, flowed into the county from the northwest corner, and passed through it in an easterly direction. As an account written in 1883 described it, "The river is quite a rapid stream in this county and furnishes many mill privileges along its course. . . . The soil is a rich loam, and in the valleys very deep. Twenty-five per cent of the county is bottom land, and a little over two per cent is native forest. . . . Many acres of bluegrass are now in good growing condition in the county, but it is quite difficult to make any tame grass take root in the wild ground. The most general, and for all purposes the most profitable, crop is corn. Wheat and rye are also a favorite with many, and in 1882 the yield of all these cereals was large."[17]

Glen Elder itself was a thriving business community. It was one of the older towns in Mitchell County. According to a centennial edition of

The Pickett Family, Glen Elder, Kansas, c. 1888
Back row: Charles, Mary, John
Middle row: Minnie, Evan, Hulda, Ida
Front row: William, Clarence, Carrie

a local newspaper, "It was said at the time that if a pin was stuck in the ground in the center of her beautiful square [a square that exists to this day], and a circle drawn around it, that it would take in the most beautiful country under the sun, capable of producing millions of dollars in crops. . . . The wheat yields were surprising. . . . By 1890 Glen Elder had four hotels, two newspapers, two millinery shops, five grocery stores, two livery stables, two lumber yards, a cheese-processing plant, two saloons, and two banks."[18]

Farming in Kansas during the last two decades of the nineteenth century and first decades of the twentieth was a matter of horsepower and wheeled machinery.[19] Corn was the leading crop, but the Pickett farm also produced wheat and oats and raised hogs, cattle, horses, and chickens. There were fruit trees and a big garden. According to Clarence, early in his life he "was learning to handle horses, milk cows, feed hogs, to cultivate crops, to endure heat, and keep up courage when the hot wind destroyed the corn crop and consequently our hope of emerging from debt. It was expected that every third crop would be lost because of drought. I didn't know we were poor, and I guess we weren't, compared to the neighbors, if that's the way one estimates poverty. We certainly had plenty to eat and we had something to wear, and I even had a school to go to. So I have no memory of unpleasant experiences, really, because of shortage of food or water. Water was, of course, an object. In the long dry spells our well sometimes got pretty low, and the question was whether we would have to go to the river to get water. That wouldn't have been so good, because the water wouldn't have been very pure. But it never did completely fail us, I'm glad to say."[20]

"My father was afflicted with rheumatism almost as long as I can remember.[21] He was so crippled that he couldn't do an ordinary day's work in the field, but he took upon himself to grow chickens and sell eggs to the little grocery store nearby. We almost never spent cash for groceries; we took our eggs in and traded them and got a due bill. You used these due bills as cash to pay for groceries as you needed them. Of course, we didn't buy very much in the way of groceries. Salt, pepper, sugar, never any meat, never any bread, certainly never anything to make bread of. We grew that. It was a good life. Although I'm not here idealizing it, because I know it had many limitations."[22]

Clarence's place as the youngest of eight surviving children appears to have been a determining factor in his personal growth. Clarence Pickett felt that "it was almost like living with uncles and aunts, older people."[23] While there were children the same age on neighboring farms, he did not have many children to play with as a young boy. "All of us had so many things to do. . . . There was always so much of interest to do that was useful in getting the chores done about the farm, and the barn, and the pasture, and the house, that we didn't have a great deal of time to spend playing. And the neighboring boys were not close at hand. They didn't very often come to see us."[24] But it is reasonable to suppose that Clarence and other boys would climb in the cottonwood trees and swim on a hot summer day at the confluence of the Solomon River and Granite Creek, less than a mile from his home.

In later years, Clarence Pickett looked back on his childhood as one that was similar to that of a one-child family. "My brothers and sisters were so much older that I really was like their own children, their own child, and I suppose that does leave some kind of mark on one's development."[25] While he viewed this as a disadvantage, his family and friends in later years quite possibly saw it as one of the reasons for his emotional and mental good health. He was surrounded in his childhood by loving parents and siblings.

Being actively involved in the local Quaker meeting was important in the life of the Pickett family.[26] A common practice in the eighteenth and nineteenth centuries was for lay ministers to visit meetings. These were Friends, both women and men, who had been designated as ministers by their own monthly meetings—a title and role reserved for those members who were seen as having spiritual sensitivity and a gift for ministry. With the permission of their home meeting, in the form of a minute agreed upon at a business meeting (and sometimes including provision for the care of the family staying behind), these Friends would travel extensively to other meetings, staying in homes in the community being visited.

Clarence Pickett noted in later years that his parents' house "was the largest one in the community and, therefore, the visiting minister usually stayed with us. I can recall at least a score of men and women who became members of our household for a few days, or for as much as two months, who came from various parts of the country as concerned Quakers to nourish the growing life of the spirit in the scattered groups and colonies of Friends in the western prairies."[27]

Among all the visits, that of Henry Stanley Newman, editor of *The Friend,* an English Quaker magazine, was of special significance to Clarence: "On Monday mornings we always did the family washing, and as a growing boy my job was to run the washing machine. Never shall I forget how surprised and gratified I was when this distinguished and somewhat austere Friend from England helped me run the washing machine on Monday morning after his speaking to us at our meeting for worship the preceding day. As we alternated in turning the handle, he talked to me about life in England and of the orphanage that he had helped to establish, about the Quaker schools in England, and the Quaker meetings. And, when he went away, I am sure there was planted deep within me a feel for spiritual maturity which I had not known before."[28]

Clarence Pickett looked back at his home as a "devout one." "We had prayers and Bible reading at every breakfast time [a practice in respect to Bible reading he was to follow as his own children were growing up]. When wheat harvest and threshing time came around, it was always a

The Pickett Family, Glen Elder, Kansas, c. 1898
Back row: Ida, William, Carrie, John, Mary, Charles
Front row: Evan, Minnie, Clarence, Hulda

temptation to question whether we might not forgo Bible reading and prayer during this special harvest season, because we had so many hired hands about. But as far as my memory goes, no such accommodation was made, nor was it simply my father offering a formal prayer on behalf of his family, but encouragement was given to any or all children or visitors to participate in the act of petition to a God Who was concerned with our welfare."[29]

For Minnie Pickett, sixteen years older than Clarence, one particular visitor had a convincing effect upon her life. She recalled in her later years how, when she was only fifteen, she had been deeply moved by the preaching of a Quaker minister to take what she called "a decisive step with a new life beginning. From that time I had a new responsibility to *live* the Christian life."[30] Indeed, in 1893 she went to Japan under the auspices of the Women's Mission Board of the Philadelphia Yearly Meeting to teach in the Tokyo Friends Girls School. This was, for her youngest brother, Clarence, a window to the world that would be important in his development. He was nine years old when she left for a five-year term of Christian service. He would always remember how they had hitched up two big work horses to a heavy lumber wagon and driven three and a half miles to Glen Elder to put his sister on the train when she started on her long trip to the West Coast and then across the Pacific Ocean.[31] And Minnie Pickett proved to be a great letter writer. Clarence Pickett said of these five years: "One of my most vivid memories is my family receiving letters rolled up, long rolls of rice paper on which very beautiful descriptions of life in Japan were written. And it was a great day when we got a letter from Minnie. All the family would gather together, and we would read the letter with fascination. The mystery and the glamour, and buoyancy of her life as revealed in these letters, I am sure, tended to turn my mind in the direction of some form of social-religious service, and toward new horizons."[32]

Other early windows to the world derived from the fact that Clarence's father subscribed to the newspaper, the *Prairie Farmer,* and to *The People's Sentinel,* one of the Glen Elder weeklies. In addition to local news, social notes, columns on livestock and horticulture, and patent medicine ads, *The People's Sentinel* regularly featured a section on page two entitled "News of the Week: Interesting items gathered from all parts of the world, condensed into a small space for the benefit of our readers." As he grew older, this section greatly interested Clarence. The family also subscribed to the magazine, *The Friends Review,* which included a summary of foreign news in each weekly issue and, beginning in 1894, its successor, *The American Friend,* was published under the editorship of Rufus Jones, a man with whom Clarence Pickett was to be intimately related in later years. His early exposure to these publications would prove to be influential in his personal development.

As Clarence's brothers and sisters left, one by one, to establish homes of their own, his help on the farm became increasingly important and demanding. But there were then more opportunities to interact on a one-to-one basis with his parents. He recalled his mother telling him one day, as they worked together in the garden, that she hoped he would be a missionary. "This was her conception of the life which called for the fullest dedication to religious service. I'm sure that this comment from my mother . . . had as deep an influence on me as any other one thing that happened. I never became a missionary in the formal sense, but I

saw that I had an inward response to the real concern she was expressing. She wanted me to work with human beings, for their betterment."[33]

For the Pickett family it was a definite advantage to have the (Quaker)
Grellet Academy based on the edge of the section of land they had
purchased. Built in 1881, it was a one-story building with seats for forty
students. The academy (named after Stephen Grellet, an itinerant Quaker
minister early in the nineteenth century), was under the care of Glen Elder
Monthly Meeting and was also used by the Meeting for its two weekly
meetings for worship. The requirements to enter the Academy, apart from a
reasonably good academic standing, were "a good moral character and cheer-
ful obedience to the rules of the institution. The use of intoxicating liquors
was strictly forbidden. Pernicious literature, dancing, card playing, and all
such things detrimental to good scholarship were [to be] laid aside. . . ."[34]
Consistent with the historic Quaker emphasis on the equality of men and
women, Grellet Academy was coeducational.

In light of these strict standards, it is interesting that one of Clarence
Pickett's few recorded recollections of his father related to the issue of
dancing. He recalled going with his father, on a Fourth of July evening,
to see the fireworks in Glen Elder. "My father allowed me to stand by a
platform that was erected in the town square to watch the social dancing. I have a notion that he may have enjoyed it quite as much as I. But
of course, we did not participate."[35]

In 1899 Clarence completed his eight years of schooling in the
Pleasant Valley school on the edge of the Pickett property. His parents
had fully expected that, after leaving the district grade school, he would
enroll in the Grellet Academy, where several of his siblings had studied.
But that opportunity did not materialize. The academy building was
destroyed by fire in 1895, one of the years during which Evan Pickett
was president of the Board of Trustees. Since there was now a three-
year public high school in Glen Elder, the academy was not rebuilt, and
it was on the site of the destroyed academy that the Glen Elder Meeting
built a church.

Therefore, in the autumn of 1899, Clarence Pickett began commuting
between home and Glen Elder, at first by horse and basket cart and
then by bicycle, "the pride and joy of my life."[36] "It was here that my
[personal] contact with the wider world was begun. The principal was
the former head of the Grellet Academy, Elam Henderson, a Quaker
minister from New England, a man of quiet, gentle spirit, who seemed

to me to have remarkable knowledge and culture."[37] Many years later, in 1919, this same Elam Henderson took Clarence Pickett's place as pastor of the Toronto, Canada, Friends Meeting.

Clarence Pickett also especially remembered another one of his teachers "who was very well trained and particularly put emphasis on speaking and writing English correctly."[38] This emphasis was consistent with what Clarence was experiencing at home. As Minnie Pickett Bowles recollected, "My father was a great reader, and very careful of our grammar. As we grew up we naturally picked up colloquial words and expressions which we heard at school. If these words did not meet our father's high standards of good English, he would never let it pass without explaining to us why we should never use such a word: then he would teach us the proper word to use."[39]

Clarence finished the three years of high school at the end of June 1902. As the local paper described it, "The graduating class consisted of six members—three boys and three girls—the class not being as large as in former years. The exercises were held in the Glen Elder Christian Church and included a debate: 'Resolved, that England's war with the Boers was just,' with Clarence Pickett in the affirmative and a classmate, Vernon Taylor, taking the negative position. Just above the platform was arranged, in large letters, the class motto, 'GROWING, NOT DRIFTING,' which presented an appropriateness."[40]

Once graduated from Glen Elder high school, Clarence Pickett was invited to be the teacher in the little public school that he had attended. He earned $35 a month, which enabled him to start saving for college. As he retrospectively recalled it, ". . . from somewhere came not so much a specific decision but the assumption that of course I would go to college."[41] And for the next three years, Clarence worked towards this goal, not only teaching school but also taking over the burdens of the farm operations. His father was increasingly an invalid from rheumatism and his older brothers had married and no longer lived at home. His life, however, was not all work and no play. During the summer of 1904 he went to St. Louis for the World's Fair, called the Louisiana Purchase Exposition in celebration of the area's one hundredth year in the Union.[42] And in March of 1905, *The People's Sentinel,* in its regular gossip section entitled "Grellet Items," reported in detail on the sixteenth birthday party of a neighbor, Ida Slaven. In the party games that evening Clarence Pickett won a prize and tied for another.[43]

During these years he had an indelible experience of his father's sense of integrity. "We still owed $2,500 on the farm, a big debt in those days. My secret hope was to be able to get away to college when the debt was paid. We had grown a fine crop of hogs for the market, and together with other income, it looked as though at last we were going to be able to eliminate the mortgage. The hogs were almost ready for market when one Sunday morning I went out to feed them and found one dead. Once cholera has started in a drove of hogs, it is likely that it will take the whole lot. A common practice, when the disease first appeared, was to rush all the well hogs to market, hoping to get them to the packers without too much loss. Whether the contamination of hog flesh was transferable to those who ate the diseased meat was an open question, but my father feared that it might jeopardize the health of the people who bought the meat.

"Without a moment's hesitation, therefore, he resolved not to run that risk, and sent me to the nearby village where I routed out the railway station man (no trains ran on Sundays) and got him to telegraph to Kansas City for a new cure for hog cholera [probably the treatment developed by de Schweinitz and Dorset in 1903]. The net result was that we saved a number of the hogs that were infected with the disease, but we had to fatten them all over again. With that additional expense, all profits were gone. My plans for getting off to school had to be postponed. But the memory of that quick and accurate moral judgment of values on the part of my father always stayed with me as a contribution far more valuable than anything I would have gained by entering college one or two years earlier than I did." [44]

At last, in 1905, the mortgage was paid off. His father also rented out some of the land to lighten the work load. More importantly, Clarence's brother, John, who had purchased a farm less than a mile down the road, was taking increasing responsibility for his parents' farm in addition to his own.[45] As Clarence Pickett observed, "This opened the way for me to fulfill my cherished ambition."[46] "No member of our family had enjoyed the privilege of college training. But the contacts with visiting ministers who stayed in our home, the experience of my sister and that of one of the boys in our community who had gone to college, all had conspired to develop in me a hunger to know something of what is called higher education."[47] The fact that his brother-in-law, Gilbert Bowles, had gone to Penn College, a Quaker institution, in Oskaloosa,

Iowa, and that the College had a department (Penn Academy) enabling students to take a fourth year of high school were deciding factors in selecting Penn for Clarence's further education.

The "Grellet Items," in *The People's Sentinel,* featured his departure for the Academy in the second week of September 1905, probably on the 6:40 a.m. train.[48] He was met the next morning in Oskaloosa by a Penn College senior, Clarence McClean. Years later Clarence observed, "Little did I suppose that I would later marry the girl whose company he [McClean] had kept for several years."[49]

With the exception of the course in German (he never did master a modern language), Clarence Pickett excelled at the academy and graduated with ten other students in June 1906. He returned to Glen Elder that summer, and, sadly, it was during that vacation that his father passed away on 6 August 1906. "He died . . . without a struggle, just peacefully left,"[50] as Clarence Pickett remembered it. The obituary in the local paper stated that, "No other man will be more greatly missed from our neighborhood than Mr. Pickett. He was a true Christian and took Christ as his example in his everyday walk of life. He always identified with only those things which meant the uplifting of mankind. His kind and gentle way endeared him to the hearts of all."[51]

On Friday, 7 September 1906 Clarence Pickett left Glen Elder[52] to enter Penn College in Oskaloosa. It signaled the close of his life on a Kansas farm, his mother leaving soon thereafter to live with her daughters. At twenty-two years of age, he was poised to take full advantage of the four college years.

NOTES

1. Bowles family papers, Haverford College, Haverford, PA: Magill Library, Quaker Collection.

2. Bowles family papers.

3. Louis Finkelstein, ed., *Thirteen Americans: Their Spiritual Autobiographies* (New York: Institute for Religious and Social Studies, 1953), 1.

4. Clarence Pickett taped recollections, 1964.

5. Ralph H. Pickett (son of John Alva Pickett, one of Clarence's brothers), letter to author dated 28 September 1993.

6. Index to marriage records, Wayne County, 1860-1920, vol. 2, Earlham College, Richmond, IN: Lilly Library.

7. In the Religious Society of Friends (Quakers), the local congregation is typically called a "monthly meeting," with members meeting once a month to transact their business. Some monthly meetings in the 19th century (and in rare cases today) had several subordinate "preparative meetings," each with its own meeting house. Each monthly meeting is associated with a regional "quarterly meeting," at which members of the constituent local congregations come together for worship and business every three months. Quarterly meetings are in turn in association with one another through a "yearly meeting," often on a statewide basis, with members of the local congregations gathering annually for several days of worship and business. It is the yearly meeting that issues, from time to time, a book of discipline setting forth statements of faith and practice for its constituent meetings. West Union Monthly Meeting was part of White Lick Quarterly Meeting of Indiana Yearly Meeting. Springfield Monthly meeting, made up of four preparative meetings (Springfield, West River, Nettle Creek, and Flat Rock) was part of Whitewater Quarterly Meeting, also of Indiana Yearly Meeting. The Macy family worshipped at the Springfield meeting house in Economy, just northwest of Richmond, Indiana.

8. Willard C. Heiss, ed., *Abstracts of the Records of the Society of Friends in Indiana* (Indianapolis: Indiana Historical Society, 1962-1977), vol. 2.

9. 1819 Discipline of Indiana Yearly Meeting: "It is the judgment of the Yearly Meeting, that offenders, whether under dealing [manner of conduct], or disowned [removed from membership], who incline to make acknowledgment their offenses, shall prepare the same in writing ought to be shewn if under dealing, to the committee appointed in their case; or if disowned, to the overseers. And if the purport is judged to be suitable to the occasion, the party may present it to the Monthly Meeting, and stay 'til it is read, and after time given for a solid pause, should withdraw before either that or any other business is proceeded upon. The meeting is then to consider the case, and appoint two or more Friends to inform the party of the result."

10. Heiss, *Abstracts,* vol. 2.

11. The records show that on 8 May 1865, Evan and Hulda and the two children were granted certificates of transfer from West Union Monthly Meeting to Vermilion Monthly Meeting in Illinois. However, soon after the Picketts' arrival, Quakers in Cissna Park and vicinity established a new meeting, Ash Grove Monthly Meeting. The Picketts' membership was transferred to Ash Grove.

12. Bowles family papers.

13. Mitchell County Courthouse records, Beloit KS.

14. Pickett taped recollections, 1964.

15. Ralph Pickett (John Pickett's son), interview 27 March 1993.

16. William E. Connelley, *History of Kansas State and People* (Chicago: American Historical Society, 1928), 2410.

17. "Glen Elder, Kansas, Celebrates One Hundred Years of History," Glen Elder Centennial Edition, the Beloit, KS *Daily Call,* 9 August 1979.

18. *Daily Call,* 9 August 1979.

19. Federal Writer's Project of the Works Project Administration for the State of Kansas, *The WPA Guide to 1930s Kansas* (Lawrence, KS: Univ. of Kansas, 1984), 68.

20. Clarence E. Pickett, *For More Than Bread* (Boston: Little, 1953), vii.

21. Just north of where Evan Pickett lived, on the other side of the Solomon River (and consequently relatively inaccessible to him), was the Waconda Spring, a mineral pool about fifty feet in diameter set in a curious limestone basin. The healing waters were sacred to generations of Native Americans. A Waconda Spring Sanitarium was established in 1906, specializing in the treatment of acute and chronic rheumatic illnesses. In 1936 Ripley's *Believe It or Not* noted that the spring was 600 miles from the sea, yet the water rose and fell just as in the case of the ocean. The spring, along with farm land north and south of the Solomon River, including the former Pickett homestead, was purchased during the 1960s by the Bureau of Reclamation of the U.S. Department of the Interior to allow for the building of the Glen Elder Dam and the formation of the 20-square-mile Waconda Lake.

22. Pickett taped recollections, 1964.

23. Pickett taped recollections, 1964.

24. Pickett taped recollections, 1964.

25. Pickett taped recollections, 1964.

26. In Illinois it was Ash Grove Monthly Meeting until 1880 when members of Ash Grove transferred to Watseka Monthly Meeting. Then, after the move, it was Glen Elder Monthly Meeting. Certificates of transfer of membership were received from the Watseka Meeting by the Glen Elder Meeting on 25 August 1888.

27. Finkelstein, *Thirteen Americans,* 7.

28. Finkelstein, *Thirteen Americans,* 7.

29. Finkelstein, *Thirteen Americans,* 4.

30. Bowles family papers.

31. Finkelstein, *Thirteen Americans,* 5.

32. Finkelstein, *Thirteen Americans,* 5.

33. Pickett, *Bread,* viii.

34. Hazel Thompson, *Glen Elder Friends Church, 1879-1979.*

35. Pickett taped recollections, 1964.

36. Pickett taped recollections, 1964.

37. Pickett taped recollections, 1964.

38. Pickett taped recollections, 1964.

39. Bowles family papers.

40. *The People's Sentinel,* 3 July 1902.

41. Finkelstein, *Thirteen Americans,* 5.

42. According to Armand Stalnaker, Pickett's son-in-law, taped phone interview, 10 October 1993.

43. *Sentinel,* 23 March 1905.

44. Finkelstein, *Thirteen Americans,* 3. Another lesson in integrity came from a great uncle, William Pickett, who lived in a Quaker community in southern Kansas. Clarence Pickett claimed throughout his life that it was a true story. "William Pickett was a truck gardener, and lived near a coal mining town where he sold much of his produce to the miners and their families. Every Saturday afternoon he traveled to the mining village to collect for the vegetables he had sold on previous days, and in doing so passed through a woods on his way to and from the town. For some time a gang of thieves had been using the woods as cover to rob travelers, so William Pickett decided to hide $40 of the $47 he was carrying under a bag in the wagon. Predictably, while passing through the woods, he was stopped by the thieves and ordered to hand over all of his money. 'Is that

all you have?' they asked. 'That,' he responded, 'is all I have on me.' The thieves let him continue on his way, but William Pickett started to meditate on what had occurred and he became troubled about how honest he had been. Finally he decided to return to the scene of the crime. He drove back, tied his horse to a tree, and tried to find the thieves. Eventually he found them, and told them the story. The thieves were so startled by this unexpected turn of events that they handed back the $7 they had previously taken from him." Confirmed by Jack Kavanaugh, director, AFSC Publicity Department (1946-53) in telephone interview, 21 July 1999.

45. 23 September 1993 letter from Ralph Pickett (John's son).

46. Pickett taped recollections, 1964.

47. Pickett, *Bread,* vii.

48. Timetable, Missouri Pacific Railroad, National Railway Historical Society, Philadelphia.

49. Letter to Stacy McCracken, 12 September 1947, family papers, courtesy of Carolyn Pickett Miller.

50. Letter dated 20 January 1910 to Lilly Peckham, commenting on her grandfather's death.

51. *Sentinel,* 6 August 1906.

52. *Sentinel,* 13 September 1906.

Chapter 2

PENN COLLEGE

On the escalator going up

IN HIS ADOLESCENT YEARS AT HOME IN KANSAS, and then his years at Penn College, an institution strongly identified with Iowa Yearly Meeting, Clarence Pickett's life was influenced by the Orthodox Gurneyite persuasion among Friends. They considered themselves to be the only true Friends in America, just as Friends from the other two traditions, Hicksite and Wilburite, saw themselves as the only true Friends. The chasms between these traditions were deep and wide, but occasionally there would be marriages overriding the divisions. Indeed, Clarence's sister, Minnie, married a Wilburite Friend, Gilbert Bowles, a member of North Branch Monthly Meeting of the breakaway conservative "Kansas Yearly Meeting of Friends" established in 1879. It was not until after World War I that bridges between the traditions began to form, particularly among younger Friends. Pickett was to play a significant role in building these bridges.

Many of the changes and separations had already taken place within the Religious Society of Friends by the time he went to college. The Quaker movement, characterized by some historians as the radical wing of the Reformation, originated in England in 1652. Its founder and leader was George Fox, who in his individual religious journey rebelled against many of the forms and practices of the Christian churches of the day, both Catholic and Protestant. He appealed strongly to "seekers," persons who, like himself, were dissatisfied with the existing churches and who were particularly turned off by the hypocrisies they saw, the inconsistencies between faith and practice.

Fox intended to reform the whole Christian church, but, as was the case with other such reform efforts, the Children of Light, as Friends were at first called, slowly became a sect. What distinguished them in the early and rapid days of growth was a deep respect for the sanctity of each individual, variously described as the indwelling Spirit, the Inner Light, or the inward Christ. Pastors and priests, the sacraments, music and programmed worship services, and buildings designated for such services, were seen as negative and unnecessary components of religion. On the positive side was the development of unprogrammed meetings for worship, held in any location, in which each person (women and men alike) was free to minister in accordance with the leading of the Spirit. And paralleling this democratic form of worship were the "testimonies" that grew out of and became an integral part of their religious convictions. These were the refusals to participate in war, to take oaths, and to doff their hats before nobility. There were "concerns" for the care of prisoners (based in part on their own experience in English prisons), for equality, and for simplicity in speech and dress.

Both because of a fervency to spread the Quaker message and because of persecution in England, the Quaker movement spread to the American colonies. William Penn and his followers became firmly implanted in Pennsylvania, as were their convictions regarding right and peaceful relationships with Native Americans, religious liberty, and the treatment of criminal offenders. Racial equality gradually became a major concern, and by 1784 slaveholding and membership in the Religious Society of Friends were deemed incompatible. The abolition of slavery became an issue to which many Friends devoted their attention. For Quakers in the southern states the opening of the Northwest Territory as free territory was a godsend, and whole meetings migrated to states in the west that were established as free from slavery. The Picketts and Macys were among those Friends.

Yet, despite a degree of unity in respect to the style of worship and the testimonies, doctrinal divergencies were developing within the Society and crystallizing in the early years of the nineteenth century. In part they reflected differences between city and country Friends. The right place of authority within meetings was also at issue. These differences were serious enough to result in separations, beginning first in 1827 within Philadelphia Yearly Meeting, then quickly followed by divisions in New York, Ohio, Baltimore, and Indiana Yearly

Meetings. On one side were the Orthodox Friends, on the other side the Hicksite Friends, named after Elias Hicks, a Long Island farmer. The separation pulled meetings and even families apart, leaving a bitterness on both sides.

But this was not to be the only separation among Friends. With the exception of the yearly meeting in Philadelphia, a second separation, eighteen years later, took place among Orthodox Friends. This is known as the Wilbur-Gurney separation of 1845, named after two leading Friends, John Wilbur, a New England Quaker who combined a Christocentric theology with conservative quietist traditions, and Joseph John Gurney, a scholarly and magnetic English Friend firmly devoted to evangelical Christianity.

All three of these branches of Friends initially held to the traditional unprogrammed meetings for worship, what Quakers have called waiting in expectant silence. It was assumed that any member of the meeting might be led to speak out of the depths of worship. However, under frontier conditions there were unique forces at work. Farm families might be living at a considerable distance from the meetinghouse and find it difficult to attend meetings for worship and business. Transportation was by horse and cart over poor roads. Christian revivalists from other denominations were an attraction, especially for younger Friends. Revivals included music and singing, not permitted in the traditional meetings for worship. There was an increasing interest in Bible schools and foreign missions. In general, it was the Gurneyites who were open to new ideas and new forms of worship, and they came to be seen and labeled as the Progressives.

As Elbert Russell, the noted Quaker historian, has explained the changes:

> The new methods spread almost at once to many places, and within a few years the revival became general in the Orthodox "Gurneyite" meetings. Under their influence silence in the meetings for worship was superseded by public testimony and prayer; young people took part; and the Bible was more frequently read in them. The young and eager leaders of the revival movement were vigorously opposed to the older, quietist methods which they regarded as the cause of the static and unspiritual condition of the Religious Society of Friends.

> Many of the older customs, such as the plain speech and dress, the emphasis on silence and worship, the habit of rising during prayer,

the wearing of men's hats in meetings, the "plain" names of the days of the week and the months, and marriages after the order of Friends, were generally discontinued within the decade. Other new methods were imported by the revivalists. Singing was introduced because many of the leaders coming from other denominations felt that there could not be a revival without singing, and after years of hesitation musical instruments were brought into the meetinghouses also.[1]

Clarence Pickett experienced these changes as he was growing up in the Glen Elder Friends Meeting. "We were a little colony of Quakers, but we had some sense of responsibility for the people on the periphery of the community, whose habits sometimes showed up in objectionable ways. Now and again we would hear of drinking and dancing parties, quite unknown to our community. A professional minister came along, imbued with the revivalist spirit of that time. He held a series of revival meetings in our community, and some of the people of whom we had been critical were 'converted' and joined our Meeting. This expansion of interest and responsibility led to an important step. We employed the revival minister to be our pastor. I saw this process going on and welcomed it as a genuine progress."[2]

Aware of his Quaker background and having attended Penn Academy the previous academic year, Clarence Pickett was fully prepared to enter into the life of Penn College. In a matter of days, on the urging of Stacey McCracken, an upperclassman with whom Clarence kept in touch throughout their lives, Clarence Pickett joined the Brightonian Literary Society, one of several "societies and associations" on campus. He also soon became active in the Young Men's Christian Association (YMCA) and, as chairman of the Employment Bureau, was a member of the YMCA cabinet.

There were twenty-five students in the freshman class. Clarence Pickett himself, in reflecting on the college in later years, characterized it as a "struggling little institution, with the poorest of buildings and facilities."[3] "Speaking generously," he said, in writing to his alma mater twenty years after his graduation, from the perspective of having attended Hartford Theological Seminary for three years, Harvard Divinity School for one year, and having taught for five years at Earlham College, "a small campus, modest buildings and inadequate library and laboratories were hers. But her [Penn's] idealism far outshone her bricks and mortar."[4]

The spirit of Penn College during the early years of this century largely reflected the achievements of Absalom Rosenberger, a young Quaker attorney from Wichita, Kansas who was president from 1890 to 1910, the year Clarence Pickett graduated. A broad practical program of education motivated by Christian purposes was Rosenberger's aim. He desired that every student, by graduation time, should have arrived at the place of personal commitment to Christian ideals in his chosen field of service.[5] The Rosenberger period of Penn's history was marked by the establishment of a number of new

Clarence Pickett at Penn College, 1909

departments of instruction and a corresponding increase in the number of teachers. A new gymnasium was constructed in 1907, spurring the development of athletic programs. Departments of Music and Art were added. The Department of Psychology and Education was split into two separate departments. All in all, during the Rosenberger administration the number of faculty members was increased from eight to twenty-eight.

The faculty most impressed Clarence Pickett. "Few in numbers, overcrowded often with classes, they were persons well-intentioned and well-trained, who were living examples of self-giving lives," wrote Pickett. "Their character and breadth also brought to the institution, conservative arts college though it was, an atmosphere of freedom, which encouraged the student to search for truth and report freely his findings; which made one want to explore, to go further, to create. It stimulated me, it awakened a curiosity which I hope has never died."[6]

Quite specifically, Pickett in future years paid tribute especially to three of his teachers. There was Stephen Hadley "who always seemed to me a paragon of learning, who through the instruments of calculus and astronomy instilled the concept of accuracy and precision in thinking, and who always left the impression with me that it was possible to develop the same accuracy in moral and spiritual judgments. Without being arrogant, he seemed to have endless assurance of the rightness of the decision which he reached, which was a good counterbalance to the age of relativity I was soon to encounter."[7] Halfway through Clarence Pickett's years at Penn, Stephen Hadley also began serving as Dean of the College.

Then there was Rosa Lewis, his English teacher. She was strict about the kind of writing her students produced and the penmanship they used. Pickett credited her with taking students like himself "with a rather dull regard for most poetry" and enabling them to appreciate Browning and Wordsworth. "Her beauty of appearance, her charm of manner, her effectiveness in speech, her personal interest in her students, at least illustrated what life might be."[8] The record shows that he consistently got an A in the courses she taught.

Finally, Clarence Pickett singles out William Berry, teacher of classical languages. Unlike his marks in German and French, Clarence's grades were excellent in Latin, Greek, and Hebrew. He recollected in thinking back on his college years, how studying Hebrew was the beginning of understanding what it was to study the Bible critically: "Professor Berry did not have to point out to us that there were two very different stories of the creation in the Book of Genesis. We discovered it ourselves, and wondered how it could all happen. . . . There was great fear on the part of many devoutly religious people that a critical study of the scriptural text would destroy faith. I have always been grateful that my approach to that problem was through the instrument of language. I cannot see how anyone can study the Hebrew text without coming away from it with a deepened sense that what we have is not a piece of literature mechanically produced, but one which grows out of the long, hard struggle of a group of God's children to find the way to moral conduct and spiritual appreciation through many failures and some successes, and over thousands of years."[9] Clarence Pickett's admiration for William Berry did not diminish over the years. In 1934, in a letter to President William Dennis of Earlham College, Pickett strongly recommended Berry for the position of Professor of Religion.

In the 1906-07 academic year at Penn College, Clarence's freshman year, there were three terms, fall, winter, and spring. In succeeding years there were two semesters of equal length, with "recitations" and examinations for the first semester coming at the end of January. In each freshman year term students took English and five other subjects, including, in Clarence Pickett's case, courses in Greek, Latin, and German, the latter two being subjects he had taken the previous year in the academy. Geometry and trigonometry filled out the curriculum. The record also shows that in the spring term he took a course on "missions," probably an elective. From firsthand family experience Clarence already knew something about missions. By his first year at Penn College his sister Minnie (having been in Japan for five years prior to her marriage) and her husband, Gilbert Bowles, were already jointly serving in Japan under the Women's Mission Board of Philadelphia Yearly Meeting, with the focus of their activities the Friends Girls School and Tokyo Friends Meeting.

Clarence was also becoming increasingly aware of the Student Volunteer Movement (SVM). The movement circulated in colleges and seminaries across the United States and Canada a pocket-size Declaration Card for signature, which read, "It is my purpose, if God permit, to become a foreign missionary." At Penn College and other Christian colleges, it was the Young Men's Christian Association (YMCA) and the Young Women's Christian Association (YWCA) that promoted the Declaration in addition to being responsible for Bible study and devotional meetings.

As he looked back at his college years, Pickett said, "Of all the extra-curricular activities, none excepted, I believe it would be fair to say that the most highly respected group on the campus was this little band of students who anticipated being missionaries. The evangelization of the world in this generation was the great cry being sounded throughout the Christian world. There was a strong sentiment in our college for sharing in this great enterprise. Little did we know, however, that the evangelization of the world was needed about as much at home as anywhere. But the inevitable happened. Those who belonged to our Student Volunteer Movement discovered this to be true."[10]

In the middle of his freshman year at Penn Clarence was exposed to interpretations of the Quaker faith that were at variance with those understandings to which he was accustomed in his home meeting in Glen Elder and in Kansas Yearly Meeting. Rufus Jones, professor of philosophy at Haverford College in Pennsylvania and later to be a close associate in the work of the American Friends Service Committee, gave a series of lectures on Quakerism, emphasizing the contribution

Clarence Pickett, Cecil Peckham, and
Wendell Farr, Penn College c.1910

of the Religious Society of Friends in the "modern world." For the first time Clarence was hearing a prominent Quaker leader state, as *The Penn Chronicle* reported it, that "Religion consisted not in dogma, but in the soul's experience. It included daily life, making every moment and act sacred. 'Mind the light of Christ within you.'" Rufus Jones concluded the lecture series with a challenge to the student body: "What we need to make religion prevail is a band of young men and women ready to give up their lives for a real, genuine religion."[11]

Clarence Pickett's life in his college years was to all outward appearances, and in most inward respects, a model of progress upward, but there was one feature that was stubbornly problematical. This was his relationship to Lilly Dale Peckham, a junior he had met when he was a freshman. The story of his first date, as Clarence himself told it, reveals his competitive spirit:

> I met this young Iowa girl early in my stay at Penn. I was awfully shy, and couldn't think how in the world I'd ever get to know her. She was tall and slender and beautiful, a little older than I. She had a great many friends, and how I was to break through these barriers and get to know her was a great puzzle to me. Well, one of my classmates, Charlie Moore, and I, were making a little extra money by cleaning the carpets of Dr. Pierson. The way we did it was to hang the carpet on a clothesline in the back yard and beat it. Charlie and I beat that carpet long and hard, and in the process he revealed to me that he was going to make a date with Lilly Peckham to take her to some social event that was about to occur. I didn't say a word, but I made a resolution that, knowing that he had this intention, I was going to beat him to it. So I did, and got the date.[12]

Like Clarence Pickett, Lilly Peckham came from a large family. Born in 1882, she was the third child and first daughter of Hamilton Nathan and Adrienne Rogers Peckham. Her father and mother were true pioneers. After their marriage they rented five hundred acres of land (the Dan Miller farm) in Union, Iowa for a period of two years. "They lost their hearts to this beautiful spot of earth," wrote one of their daughters.[13] Then they moved with their son, Errol, to a quarter section of unbroken prairie land in Calhoun County in western Iowa. "They lived there for nine years in a little four-, then five-room frame cabin nestled in the bluestem prairie grass."[14]

Lilly Dale Peckham
Freshman at Penn College, 1905

During those years, in the tiny front bedroom of the cabin, four more children were born, the third being Lilly Dale. The story of her birth prior to the arrival of the doctor matches Clarence Pickett's story, and the amount paid the doctor was the same—five dollars.

Hamilton and Adrienne Peckham then moved to New Providence, Iowa, to be close to a Quaker academy (high school) and then later they purchased the Dan Miller farm in Union, the realization "of their greatest desire and wildest dream."[15] By this time their youngest child, Letha, a daughter, had been born. Here they remained for twenty years, during which time the children grew up. All of the children remained Methodist except Lilly and Errol who became Friends.

They were determined that if at all possible their children would, first of all, go to high school, and then to college. As Lilly remembered it, "The plan was that as soon as a child was ready for high school, he should start, and that mornings and evenings, weekends and vacations, he [or she] should make a hand with work on the farm. After graduation from high school the boys were to make full-time hands year-round on the farm until they were twenty-one years of age. They would then start to college. During their college years they were to carry the best-paying job available, which they could manage and still have time for their college studies."[16]

Towards the end of his life, in recollecting on his contacts with the Peckham family, Clarence Pickett remembered Lilly's father as "an awesome person, huge in stature [he was over six feet tall and weighed over two hundred pounds] with a great, red beard [Lilly would always describe it as 'auburn'] and an ample supply of hair on his head, a firm voice and a masterly approach to his business, which was farming, and farming on a sizable scale. He had what seemed to me a big farm [500 acres] and he had four boys, all of them bigger than I and all of them together making a powerful team. I was a little overawed by the whole situation, but I've always been glad that I didn't allow the dominance of the male part of the family to scare me off. The mother was a delightful, petite woman, not without firmness, and not without deep concern for her daughter, but very gentle and very appreciative."[17] Clarence Pickett viewed Lilly Peckham at the time as being in "a little higher strata in society" although she insisted she was not.[18]

During the spring recess in 1908, towards the close of Clarence Pickett's sophomore year and Lilly Peckham's senior year, Clarence and Lilly decided to go to a revival meeting in Marshalltown, Iowa led by the great evangelist, Billy Sunday. Clarence traveled on a special Iowa Central Railroad train up from Oskaloosa, and Lilly came south on a chartered train from Union. "We spent the day together at that revival meeting. In the evening, when it came time to go home, there were two trains standing at the platform in Marshalltown, one going north to Union where Lilly lived, the other going south to Oskaloosa. The two trains started very, very slowly. I stood beside the train as it moved north, and said to myself, "Should I go north, or shall I go south?" Finally I went north, and that night I asked Lilly if she would venture to marry me. She never said she would, but she never said she wouldn't. . . . I came away feeling that that important matter was making progress at least."[19]

Just as soon as classes were over, in June 1908, Clarence Pickett and classmate Alexander Purdy (the two men were to be lifelong close friends) journeyed to Lake Geneva, Wisconsin, to attend a Student

Volunteer Movement conference at the YMCA camp. Clarence and Lilly were writing at length to each other, the beginning of four years of weekly correspondence punctuated by remarkably few opportunities to see each other. Clarence was excited by the conference. He said it was "all I could expect. John R. Mott is one of the greatest speakers I have ever heard, I know."[20] Clarence noted that the Life Work Meetings were developing a "missionary trend." He met a YMCA secretary from Tokyo who knew Gilbert Bowles. Clarence was clearly feeling the pressure to become a foreign missionary. But not all of his attentions were focused on vocational plans. To Lilly he wrote, "Alex [Purdy] and I were down by the lake last evening, and for a long time watched the shimmer of the water in the moonlight. It was simply beautiful. Just one streak of bright red as far as a fellow could see. I would have given most anything I felt like to have had you here and to have taken a boat ride."[21]

Then he headed for Union for a brief visit with Lilly, and then on to Colorado Springs to spend the summer with his mother and his sister, Ida, to find work, and to be on hand when Gilbert and Minnie Bowles and their young children came from Japan on furlough. The visit with Lilly was a difficult one for both of them. While in their last time together at Penn College before vacations began, he had promised not to press for a decision, he was hoping that Lilly would give him a favorable response to his marriage proposal. But Lilly was not yet ready. "I'm sorry to disappoint you when this letter comes by not telling you what I would like to, and what you so much want to know," she wrote at the end of June, "but I simply can't. Now really I've tried, for you know it hurts me if I hurt you, but my questioning, wondering and doubting heart will not let me. 'Tis because of such a heart that I was always so quiet, sad, and serious when we talked of our relation to one another."[22]

Their lives that summer differed markedly in respect to personal satisfactions. Clarence landed a job outdoors with a ranchman, "working with men who don't appreciate things which I do at all, it seems. The swearing is something fierce, but they have learned that I'm a Christian, and respect me for it."[23] In the evenings he especially enjoyed seeing his sister, Minnie. "It seems to me that seven years of separation [he had seen Minnie and her husband last when they went to Japan as a couple in 1901], service and development has only drawn us closer. . . . The children are, every one, as dear as can be. They talk Japanese when they are playing, but English to other people."[24]

Lilly Peckham, on the other hand, was stuck on the farm in Union with her brother, Hubert, and her sister Letha who was concentrating on music lessons. Their parents were off traveling in states further west, looking for a new place to live, having decided to sell the farm. "It is dreadfully hot," Lilly Peckham complained.[25] She was cooking and washing, not only for the immediate family, but for a half dozen hired hands—haymakers, thrashers, corn-pickers. "I have been baking bread and picking over cherries like a good girl," she wrote in July.[26] "I shall be glad when the folks [her parents and other brothers] begin to gather home here. I shall appreciate them not only for their company but for their help as well. The work has been so hard for me that I am as much worked down now as I have been for a long time."[27] Indeed, the way she was feeling was preventing her from making plans for the autumn. "I feel so strange to not be making arrangements either to go to school or to teach this fall."[28]

Two critical issues were standing in the way of the Pickett-Peckham love relationship, the one darting in and out, the other a dark shadow. Both issues were clouding the future. But to a considerable extent the circumstances of their respective lives, the patience and love that each increasingly showed each other, and their inclination to keep talking, and "visiting" (through letter writing), proved to be the way they overcame these obstacles.

The first barrier related to Clarence Pickett's interest in foreign missionary service. There were pressures *within* him and around him to sign the Student Volunteer Movement Declaration Card, a statement of a definite life purpose. He was greatly influenced by his sister Minnie's choice. At the end of January 1909 the question of whether to sign the Declaration was coming to a head because the international secretary of the Student Volunteer Movement was coming to the Penn Campus. Clarence knew that the SVM secretary would urge upon him the claims of the pledge. "You know how it seems clearer to me as time goes on that this is my work," he wrote Lilly. "I'm afraid you grow weary with my often asking you your attitude as to this, but as a close friend and one who knows me, I want to know if you think I'd better sign it. I know there's an 'inner chamber' into which no one else but myself can enter to decide this finally, but you can come closest of any friend on earth, I feel. I know this bears also a personal message of what may be the consequences between us."[29]

In February of 1909, Clarence Pickett's junior year at Penn, Lilly Peckham finally was able to articulate fully her feelings about living abroad. "Personally," she said in a letter to him, "I do *not* want to go to the foreign field, and have always had a perfect dread of it. . . . Rather, with what seems to be clearness and ease of conscience, my final answer to you is this: I *will* go if God will give me the grace to be true to such a promise, and only His grace can do it, and provided we later decide to spend our lives together, and also provided that that finally proves to be your field of service."[30]

In still later correspondence it became clear that she was, among other things, thinking of the risks of giving birth to children in a foreign country, in the absence of family members and up-to-date medical care. Clarence Pickett tried to quell her fears in this particular regard by telling her of the experiences of Friends at the mission in Ramallah, Palestine, but she was not convinced. Clarence did not sign the pledge in that year, or later, but the subject continued to come up, even after they were engaged.

The second obstacle was an earlier relationship Lilly Peckham had had. This was her love affair with and her engagement to Clarence McClean, whom Lilly had known since both of them were children. He was the senior who had met Clarence Pickett at the train the morning he arrived from Glen Elder, Kansas, to enter Penn Academy. McClean entered Penn College in 1902, while Lilly's entrance took place in 1904. They overlapped for two years, McClean graduating in June 1906. The college records indicate that in his senior year Clarence McClean was active in the YMCA, sang as a bass in the College glee club, and played center field on the baseball team. "He was her first and all-consuming beau," observed Clarence Pickett many years later.[31]

Some time before his graduation, McClean and a classmate, Bertrell Stewart, developed a love relationship and were subsequently married. Lilly Peckham was bitter about what had happened. Five years later, following a disparaging story she had heard about Clarence McClean, Lilly wrote her new Clarence, "How happy I am to think that I am yours instead of the false C. McC. . . . I could not but help feel so sorry for Bertrell, even if she did hurt me more than I can tell and schemed her best to steal from me the one who had claimed my love. I'm *glad* she got him. What I suffered then will probably be small as compared with what she will suffer through the years to come, and has through the years since their wedding."[32] It was this traumatic experience that left Lilly Peckham with a "questioning, wondering and doubting heart."

During the Christmas holidays of 1908, Clarence visited Lilly at her home in Union. She was also on vacation from her teaching job in a local school. They talked about whether their relationship should continue. They both realized, and had so expressed it to each other in letters, that the longer the relationship continued, the more hurtful would be the ending of it if that should happen. Their last moments together before he left were tense and clouded. She referred, in the first letter she wrote to him after the visit, to the "hardened, distant look that he gave her." Then this: "I think you know pretty well now, but I will tell you this, that your life has come nearer to filling the vacant place left in my life by the loss of a few years ago than I could have believed was possible at that time. You know what seals my lips and makes it almost impossible for me to talk of these things which come so close to where I really live. . . . I hope I did not treat you so heartless and unkind that you can never forgive me."[33] "How can I *know*?" she asked in a subsequent letter. "I know, all too well, that constantly putting it off will only increase the day of sorrow, should it come. I have tried to know, but it seems I can't understand. Can't you find out whether it is right or wrong for us to keep company longer or not?"[34]

Their lives differed sharply in terms of day-to-day satisfactions. Lilly Peckham, only tutoring one or two children in a "dinky old school house," was usually lonely and gloomy. Clarence Pickett was buoyantly happy, now at the close of his junior year at Penn, with a full load of courses, participating in intercollegiate debates, and providing leadership within the YMCA. He was having a "jolly" time, as he put it. He was involved in "capers." Referring to a skit, he commented that he had laughed until his sides almost ached. He was revealing a sense of humor and an enjoyment of others for which he became well-known throughout his lifetime.

In May, Clarence managed to get to Union to visit with Lilly. The subsequent correspondence reveals that, while he continued to look for expressions of affection and commitment, she was still feeling blocked by her experiences "with other men." In a letter to her dated May 22, Clarence Pickett wrote frankly about feeling "pretty blue" and faced the problem with characteristic courage and clarity:

For I'm afraid, Lilly, that if we should go on and become closer friends, and then break, that it might break your life entirely, and that held me back and made me do as I did. You see, if I should go on as though I didn't think about such things, and then they should come, I would be guilty of a terrible crime against you, such a crime as I am not ready to shoulder. Now, if after what I've said, you want us to keep company, if you can feel that it is right and that I am not leading you only to fool you, I would like to do so. I know I acted cold, but it certainly was not because you didn't appeal to me as you have formerly.

As I recall it now, never, or very seldom have you and I been especially affectionate toward each other when we were together, but that we have done it partly because one was trying to console the other. I think this is all right sometimes, but it seems to me that it would mean more if I could do so simply because I loved you and was expressing joy rather than sorrow in the heart. I promise you this, that if ever I'm permitted to see you again as I have, we'll leave that part (the sorrow) out so far as possible. I know it's hard on you. I know also that it's hard on me. I feel that a certain amount of the affection is proper, but as an expression of love and not of sorrow. Surely our courtship should be one of pleasure instead of sorrow. [35]

But a change *was* taking place in their relationship. Clarence Pickett was deeply in love with Lilly Dale Peckham, and what was to be characteristic of him throughout his life, he was both persistent and patient in overcoming obstacles, in this instance the distrust Lilly had carried over from her earlier love affair. Clarence Pickett's decision not to sign the Student Volunteer Movement pledge pushed aside the other major hurdle, although he did not give up entirely the prospect of serving abroad.

Shortly before he set off to engage in door-to-door selling when classes were over in the spring of 1909, he made a quick visit to Union. "How different you looked when I left, from the week before," he wrote her. "Did Letha or Hubert notice it? I just spoke to your mother and father Monday morning, and they were wonderfully surprised to see me. . . . Glad I can say, with you—happily yours."[36]

The summer correspondence reveals Lilly's increased yearning for Clarence as she slaved away on the family farm. Clarence reminded her that yearly meeting time was approaching and that summer would soon be over. And then Lilly, to Clarence after his return to Penn College in

September: "You have seemed different to me since the last time that you were here—more free with me, I guess it is, that gives me more liberty. I do not know what has caused the change but perhaps you do."[37]

Clarence Pickett and Lilly Peckham were now eagerly waiting for each other's letters and replying immediately. And the subjects covered varied from the nuances of their own relationship to what was happening to parents and siblings, to the love affairs of mutual acquaintances, to what was taking place at the College in Clarence Pickett's senior year. As early as October he brought up in a letter the question of what he would do after graduation. "I haven't decided what next for me, but it looks rather like a year in the east at school."[38] He sought her thoughts and feelings on this crucial decision.

In December 1909 Clarence visited Union over the Christmas holidays, and Lilly visited Oskaloosa (in part to meet Clarence's mother, and sister Ida, who were then residing in Oskaloosa). In January 1910 their letters to each other revealed a deepening commitment. "You are dealing with a corner of my heart and life that has never been open to anyone before," he wrote. "And I hope that I may come some day, no, that *we* may someday, unfold a new corner in your heart, if we haven't done so already, which will bring you a *new* freedom."[39] Looking back many months later, he recalled the significance of the New Year's visit. "How stammeringly yet how sincerely I told you for the first time *all* my heart."[40] Salutations and endings in their letters were unmasking their inner feelings: "My dearest one"; "Yours lovingly, Clarence"; "Very tenderly yours, Lilly Dale."

Clarence entered fully and enthusiastically into the courses and extracurricular activities of his senior year. He continued to serve on the YMCA cabinet. He was elected business manager of *The Penn Chronicle,* and he sang as a tenor in the widely acclaimed Penn College glee club, for which he was the business manager. In reflecting on and praising Penn College many years later, he wrote: "It talked not about adaptation, but attempted to cultivate the fundamental values of life, and put a high premium on the significance of men as God's children. While there was some feeling of being on the escalator going up and the kind of predestination of success, there was no illusion that success came without dedication and hard work."[41]

It was over the Christmas holidays in 1909 that Clarence Pickett finally decided what he was going to do in life. Having by this time

determined not to sign the
missionary pledge, three possibilities seemed available to him:
teaching, farming, and the
ministry. "I cannot claim that
a voice from heaven directed
me," he wrote late in life, "and
I cannot say why, but I chose
the ministry. It was partly because two ministers of great
skill and of fine character
crossed my path, Ellison R.
Purdy, who was minister of the
Quaker meeting at Oskaloosa,
Iowa, while I was in college
there, and Charles M.
Woodman, who visited our
community during my college
career and spoke very much to
my condition. . . . In all honesty it perhaps ought to be said

Lilly Dale Peckham
Oskaloosa, Iowa, 1907

that the fact that one could get a scholarship in a theological seminary,
whereas such opportunities in other fields were not then as well known,
may have had some influence."[42]

Lilly Peckham gave her "promise" to Clarence Pickett on 28 April
1910. While Peckham family members saw this as an "engagement"
(and freely wrote about it as such within the family)[43] no formal engagement could be announced until a date of marriage was established.
Neither of them was openly talking about an engagement, although
many persons assumed that there was "an intended" in his life, and
Lilly Peckham's most intimate friends knew of the "promise." The
date for the wedding was uncertain because of Clarence Pickett's
decision to go to Hartford Theological Seminary, a decision that
might delay the marriage for from one to three years. Furthermore,
with the Peckham farm in Union sold, Lilly Peckham decided to take
off for Salem, Oregon, with her good friend and classmate, Blanche
Ford, who had accepted a call to be pastor of the Salem Friends
Meeting. Lilly was to assist her and seek an opportunity to teach school.

The unsureness of the wedding date became a bone of contention and the geographic distance between them made it financially impossible for them to see each other. A continent between them, they kept each other informed of their respective activities, thoughts, and feelings by writing long letters every couple of days. Lilly Peckham's life was noticeably restricted to her voluntary role as a pastor's assistant and to her schoolteaching. Clarence Pickett's life was bursting with new experiences. Little could she imagine the implications of his liberal seminary experiences. Nor, for that matter, could he know what intellectual and spiritual developments lay ahead for him.

NOTES

1. Elbert Russell, *The History of Quakerism* (New York: Macmillan, 1943), 427.

2. Louis Finkelstein, ed., *Thirteen Americans: Their Spiritual Autobiographies* (New York: Institute for Religious and Social Studies, 1953), 6.

3. Finkelstein, *Thirteen Americans,* 7.

4. S. Arthur Watson, *William Penn College: A Product and A Producer* (Oskaloosa: William Penn College, 1971), 91. Penn College was renamed William Penn College in 1933.

5. Watson, *Penn College,* 237.

6. Watson, *Penn College,* 237.

7. Finkelstein, *Thirteen Americans,* 7.

8. Finkelstein, *Thirteen Americans,* 8.

9. Finkelstein, *Thirteen Americans,* 8.

10. Finkelstein, *Thirteen Americans,* 8-9.

11. *The Penn Chronicle,* Feb. 1907.

12. Pickett taped recollections, 1964.

13. "The History of the Peckhams and the Rogers," compiled by Lilly Dale Peckham Pickett, 1961, 17, family papers, courtesy of Carolyn Pickett Miller.

14. "History," 17.

15. "History," 17.

16. "History," 18.

17. Pickett taped recollections, 1964.

18. Tape recording of remark made by Pickett on the occasion of his 80th birthday, 19 Oct. 1964, AFSC archives.

19. Pickett taped recollections, 1964.

20. Pickett-Peckham correspondence, 17 June 1908, Pickett papers, AFSC archives.

21. Pickett-Peckham, 17 June 1908.

22. Pickett-Peckham, 30 June 1908.

23. Pickett-Peckham, 30 July 1908.

24. Pickett-Peckham, 23 July 1908.

25. Pickett-Peckham, 4 Aug. 1908.

26. Pickett-Peckham, 30 July 1908.

27. Pickett-Peckham, 4 Aug. 1908.

28. Pickett-Peckham, 4 Aug. 1908.

29. Pickett-Peckham, 24 Jan. 1909.

30. Pickett-Peckham, 16 Feb. 1909.

31. Pickett Journal, 7 June 1947, AFSC archives.

32. Pickett-Peckham, 26 May 1911.

33. Pickett-Peckham, 3 Jan. 1909.

34. Pickett-Peckham, 27 Jan. 1909.

35. Pickett-Peckham, 22 May 1909.

36. Pickett-Peckham, 30 May 1909.

37. Pickett-Peckham, 1 Oct. 1909.

38. Pickett-Peckham, 3 Oct. 1909.

39. Pickett-Peckham, 23 Jan. 1910.

40. Pickett-Peckham, 1 Dec. 1910.

41. Finkelstein, *Thirteen Americans,* 9.

42. Finkelstein, *Thirteen Americans,* 9.

43. Pickett-Peckham, 9 July 1910.

Chapter 3

THE SEMINARY YEARS

Just ripe for what Hartford had to offer

IN DECEMBER 1909, DURING THE FIRST SEMESTER of Clarence Pickett's senior year at Penn College, Hartford Theological Seminary pressed him to come to the seminary in the next academic year. "From what Mr. [Carleton] Wood, at present studying with us [as a Quaker postgraduate student] has said regarding you," Dean Melancthon Jacobus wrote, "I am anxious to do anything I can to bring Hartford's advantages before you."[1] Professor Jacobus was also pursuing Clarence's best friend, Alexander Purdy, and stated that the seminary had already received an application from Lilly Peckham's brother Errol. Errol, however, changed his mind because of his impending marriage and postponed his entrance to the following year.

The seminary offered Clarence Pickett a scholarship of $250 for the year, covering all expenses, including tuition, board and room, books, and a small spending allowance. Penn College, in forwarding a transcript of his courses and grades, noted that his average grade was 95, second only to the straight A's that Alex Purdy received.

While the seminary scholarship was generous, Clarence Pickett needed additional funds for transportation and recreational expenses. One possible source of income for a seminary student was to work as a part-time pastor. With over fifty meetings, most of them pastoral, New England Yearly Meeting was always on the lookout for pastors, full time or part time. As early as September 1909, Thomas Wood, general superintendent of the Evangelistic and Church Extension Committee of the

Yearly Meeting, got in touch with Pickett "concerning available young men for service in New England."[2] Clarence Pickett in his reply disclosed the fact that he and Alexander Purdy were giving thought to entering Hartford Theological Seminary in the autumn. Thomas Wood immediately answered, "laying before them the needs and the character of the work in New England."[3]

When Clarence Pickett submitted his application for admission to the seminary in May 1910, he immediately received a letter of acceptance. Then he wrote Thomas Wood and expressed interest in serving for the summer as pastor of the Westport Friends Meeting in Central Village, Massachusetts. This was a community with historic Quaker roots, with the first Friends having arrived from England in the mid-1600s and with New England Yearly Meeting of Friends having been established in 1660 in Newport, Rhode Island.

Westport Meeting, in common with most other New England meetings, had responded in the late nineteenth century to the same pressures for change that influenced Clarence Pickett's home meeting in Kansas. In 1872 the sliding partitions dividing the meetinghouse to allow for separate men's and women's business sessions, the galleries (the facing benches), and fireplaces were removed. Carpets, cushions on the simple benches, and stoves were installed. However, by 1910 there still was no electricity in the Westport meetinghouse. An organ was allowed, first for the Sunday evening service, and then also for the morning meeting.

Finally, with new life in evidence and increased community activities, the meeting felt in 1907 the need to have a paid pastor. Coincidentally, that pastor, who served for a year and a half, was Wilbur Thomas, who was later to become Clarence Pickett's predecessor as executive secretary of the American Friends Service Committee. In 1910, when Pickett arrived in Central Village, there was a total membership of thirty-seven, with only twenty-four of these residents.[4]

Traveling all the way by train, first by coach to Chicago, and then eastward "in a splendid New York Central sleeper," and stopping off to go up to Niagara Falls, Clarence Pickett arrived at Moses Brown School in Providence, Rhode Island just in time for the annual sessions of New England Yearly Meeting, the 250th consecutive time the yearly meeting had met. He viewed the proceedings as "a great success. It seems to be on the verge of a great revival. There is so much freedom allowed one, more than I had expected."[5]

While Clarence Pickett surely knew where Central Village was located and may have been drawn to that opportunity because of its proximity to the Atlantic Ocean (less than two miles away), he was not prepared for the beauty of the surroundings. "I wish you could get just a glimpse of the country here," he wrote Lilly Peckham. "It is so beautiful. Not that farms look nice. They do not, but forests and lanes, everything is rustic and beautiful. They pay so much more attention to that here than with us."[6]

Clarence Pickett was also impressed with the "great wealth" he found within New England Yearly Meeting. "Several millionaires, and many near that stage. Money flows much more freely than with us," he wrote Lilly, comparing the circumstances with Kansas and Iowa Yearly Meetings. "Yesterday I received six dollars and fifty cents for going out [to preach] . . . to a very humble meetinghouse built in 1701, in which for 200 years not a single Sabbath service has been missed. I was taken to dinner by a very wealthy Friend, a cotton manufacturer in Fall River, who lived in an elegant suburban home. The beautiful thing about it," Clarence observed, "is that when one is taken in by these people, they treat you O so kindly. You cannot help loving them. Their wealth has not in the least injured them."[7]

It was right after the conclusion of the sessions of New England Yearly Meeting that Clarence Pickett took up his post as pastor of the Friends Meeting in Central Village, close to the state line with Rhode Island and including members from across that boundary. He was warmly welcomed, but he felt "scared of the task, for it seemed so big and so different for me," he wrote Lilly Peckham. "Then I think of *Him* back of me, and your prayers and confidence, and I said, 'No, I'll fight it through.'"[8] He decided that his first Sunday morning sermon would be on "The Work of Being a Christian," and that at the first Sunday evening service he would speak on "Our Nation: A Part of God's Plan."

It was not long before he identified his summer objectives in the meeting: to get the men interested, to improve the activities for the young people, and to improve the singing. "They are a *terrible* lot of singers," he wrote. "They are almost all related, and they happen not to be a family of singers."[9] He was beginning to realize that most Quakers, with their traditional rejection of music, were not good candidates for a choir. Even whistling a tune was deemed to be improper in some Quaker families up to the end of the nineteenth century.

Within a few weeks Clarence was thoroughly enjoying himself, with "pleasant new experiences" piling up one on another. On the Fourth of July he made his initial trip to the beach with four families, seeing the Atlantic Ocean and enjoying "sea bathing" for the first time. He was often playing tennis. "I play more than I want to, but I feel like it is giving me a hold on the young people which I couldn't get in any other way, so I play quite often."[10] He had his first boat ride on Narragansett Bay. He went to see the U.S. Atlantic fleet in Newport. "Although I am a Quaker minister," he wrote, "I should like very much to see the gunboats [actually, sixteen battleships]."[11] On the same trip he saw the "palaces and castles" of the multimillionaires who had summer residences in Newport. "I was almost disgusted to see so much wealth simply thrown to the birds when there's so much need of it to be put to real use."[12]

The tasks in the meeting for which he took responsibility were without limit. He organized a Young People's Society, he paid pastoral calls on members of the meeting, some of them invalids, many simply inactive in the life of the meeting. On his return one day from a pastoral visit, always by bicycle, he saw a man starting to put a load of hay in his barn. "I saw he needed another man badly, so I stopped and helped him. I found he had formerly been a Friend, but had drifted away. He had not been to church for years, but promised me to come some time."[13]

Every Sunday pastor Pickett gave two sermons, one at the morning service, a second in the evening. One theme was personal freedom, showing how the Christian life was a truly free life as opposed to "the life of sin." "At least half my audience were not Christians, and they were particularly attentive," he said on one occasion.[14] He began a series of addresses on Sunday evenings on "The Social Significance of the Teachings of Jesus," a subject he was to emphasize throughout his pastorates and was to teach many years later at Earlham College in Indiana. Through the summer, attendance at Sabbath services increased.

All in all, it was an effective time for Clarence. The people of Central Village loved him; he loved them. On a weekend visit he made in October, after beginning his studies at Hartford Seminary, he was pleased with their reception of him. "The people here really seem to be glad to see me again, and especially Earl Wood, 'my Timothy" [referring to the disciple and companion of the Apostle Paul]. He has a holiday this week from the office [on] Wednesday, and plans to come up to Boston to be with me there. He was down this afternoon, and we had a good long talk. I am to have the extreme pleasure next Sunday of extending the right hand of fellowship to him into our little church. "You cannot know," he wrote Lilly Peckham, "how much good it does me to have such a fellow come over to our side [from a non-religious home]."[15]

Earl Wood, a young man at the time, viewed his becoming a member of the Friends Meeting as his "conversion." Forty years later, on the occasion of Clarence Pickett's retirement as executive secretary of the American Friends Service Committee, Earl Wood wrote the Committee about the experience:

> The work of Clarence E. Pickett with the American Friends Service Committee is so well known by all his friends that I need not say anything about that. Perhaps many of them do not realize that even in his student days his work began. Friends of Westport Monthly Meeting at Central Village, Massachusetts, remember his service as minister of their meeting. His work and the influence of his ministry is still alive in our meeting. I would like him to know that what little I am now doing is the direct result of that ministry.[16]

It was on Tuesday, 20 September that he journeyed from Central Village by train to Hartford to enter the seminary. He was particularly looking forward to seeing Alex Purdy, fresh from having visited with Lilly Peckham in Iowa. The two Quaker students were assigned to Hosmer Hall in adjoining suites, each with a bedroom and study. Clarence was pleased to learn that the dormitory was entirely under student management, "no profs around to be afraid of."[17] He was pleased also about the practice of a student, every evening after supper, leading "family devotions," and then on Monday nights there was the holding of a class prayer meeting. These devotional meetings supplemented the more formal chapel services.

Clarence Pickett plunged immediately into Bible study that was in sharp contrast to the approach found among Orthodox Friends and other evangelistic Christians. After hearing initial lectures by Professors Melancthon Jacobus and Edward Nourse (men Clarence viewed as deeply spiritual), he could write to Lilly Peckham that they had "already opened up a new vision of the way to study Scriptures and interpret them."[18] In his three years at Hartford he was to complete no less than twenty Bible study courses, almost all of them under these two professors, with a strong emphasis on the New Testament.

The approach that was so appealing was called "Biblical criticism," part of what became known as "modernism" within the Christian church. As Shirley Jackson Case, a noted New Testament scholar, was to put it two decades later, "One who sincerely desires to have Jesus win the respect of men today must recognize that his reputation cannot thrive in the intellectual atmosphere of the twentieth century if it is unable to endure the white light of historical research."[19] Pickett noted that for him this "higher criticism" made the Scriptures "infinitely more meaningful and made God more real."[20]

At the end of his first academic year at Hartford, Clarence Pickett sought to be listed as a "recorded minister" by Oskaloosa Friends Church to which he had transferred his membership from the Glen Elder Meeting. Designation as a recorded minister would give him status as he visited other meetings and would be a prerequisite if he were to seek full time employment as a pastor of a Friends Church. The process of obtaining this designation was fully spelled out in the 1902 Book of Discipline of the Orthodox Iowa Yearly Meeting, both in respect to doctrinal beliefs and decision-making procedures. His cousin, Stephen Hadley, who was dean at Penn College, replied to Pickett's inquiry, quoting in part from the Book of Discipline: "The question of acknowledging your gift in the ministry was brought before our local meeting on ministry and oversight. It was favorably reviewed and was forwarded to the Quarterly Meeting on Ministry and Oversight. After a season of deliberation, the Quarterly Meeting on Ministry and Oversight appointed a committee (of which I am chairman) to consider the subject; to obtain information that the person has received spiritual gifts; as to his manner of life; his doctrinal views; his mental capacity; and his general qualification for the ministry."[21]

Recognizing that the whole process would have to be done by correspondence rather than on a face-to-face basis, Stephen Hadley then asked Clarence Pickett to answer questions outlined in the Book of Discipline. There were nine queries. Pickett evidently decided not to get into doctrinal disputes with the members of his meeting, but there were two points about which he expressed his growing liberalism. He noted that he believed in the spiritual resurrection of Jesus Christ rather than the physical resurrection. And in respect to the "Holy Scriptures," he stated, "I believe that the Scriptures were given to us through the lives of men inspired of God. That these men interpreted the spiritual truths imparted to them by means of the scientific and historical conceptions of their times, hence are not always scientifically or historically true, but the message which they intend to teach is true."[22]

It was in respect to these points that Clarence Pickett seemingly took the risk of not being approved as a recorded minister. But, as it turned out, in accordance with the slow process of determining the fitness of a Friend to be recorded as a minister, Clarence Pickett's answers to the queries were given "seasoned deliberation," first by the appointed committee and subsequently by various quarterly meetings and local meeting bodies. It was on 1 April 1912 that he was recorded as a minister of the gospel by Oskaloosa Monthly Meeting of the Religious Society of Friends.

This same issue of the interpretation of the Quaker faith also came up in correspondence between Clarence Pickett and Lilly Peckham that same academic year at seminary. She wrote, on 15 January 1911, that the Salem Friends Meeting had been having splendid [revival] meetings. "Mr. Hayes is an unusual[ly] clear and forceful teacher and preacher. My, but he has attacked the school of higher education most fearfully. So often and so hard it has really troubled me lest you should be led aside from God's truths. . . . I do believe you ought to be on your guard."[23]

Clarence Pickett responded promptly to her letter. He expressed deep regret about Mr. Hayes' condemnation, realizing that the preacher would have no use for the seminary. Clearly what hurt Clarence deeply was the possibility of a misunderstanding between himself and Lilly. Wrote Clarence: "It would be an extremely sad condition if I were to go here two or three years and not be changed, not have my belief changed on some things, for I certainly don't feel infallible. But it surely is a fact, evinced more and more every day, that each change makes one's faith and confidence in the love and mercy of God stronger."[24]

It is significant that Clarence Pickett attached a 3x5 card to the January 15 letter from Lilly Peckham, stating, "This letter caused me very severe pain in what I fear bespoke of lack of confidence. I believe, however, that I can answer it in the spirit of love."[25] This was another disclosure of his marked need for Lilly's emotional support. Indeed, in the final paragraph of his long response, he said, "I feel I must have your confidence to do the best work. . . . It is from you, my dearest, that I have always received the deepest encouragement and confidence, and it is with you that I hope to carry the true spirit of Christ into the world."[26] Repeatedly, in subsequent letters, Lilly assured him of her confidence in him, but added, "I felt anxious lest your faith and belief in some of the vital truths of Christianity should be shaken, and that you might lose the true secret of beauty and power in your life."[27]

Quite apart from the full load of seminary courses, Clarence Pickett had a variety of educational experiences while at Hartford. He read Upton Sinclair's *Jungle,* a novel based on the shocking conditions in Chicago meat-packing houses, and urged Lilly Peckham to read it. As part of a sociology course the class visited the slums of Hartford, "as bad here as in New York, they say." He and Lilly, over a period of months, read William Allen White's recently published novel, *A Certain Rich Man,* the story of a poor boy who sets out to make his millions any way he can get them, and who then finds that his riches have brought him more sorrow than happiness.

And then, of a trip to a Boston Symphony Orchestra concert he and Alex Purdy attended, Pickett wrote: "It was so far beyond any music of that kind I have ever heard, that there is little comparison."[28] He had his "first at theater," [*sic*] seeing Shakespeare's *Merchant of Venice.* One of his reactions deserves mention: "This one thing kept coming up to me," he wrote Lilly. "A feeling of *pity* for the players. Of course, in the love parts, certain expressions of affection are essential, and though they are modest about it as the play would allow, yet it certainly cannot but spoil them for the real, heartfelt expression of love and affection when they so repeatedly feign it to those whom they do not love at all."[29]

Word had reached the Fall River, Massachusetts, Meeting of Clarence Pickett's very acceptable pastoral services at the Westport Meeting in Central Village. Fall River soon asked him to come every week for Sunday services during the school year. He was intrigued about working in the heart of a city of one hundred thousand people and agreed to begin at the end of October. Every weekend he left Hartford on Saturday afternoon by train directly for Fall River, returning Sunday afternoon via New Haven. He realized he was undertaking a heavy schedule. For the first time in his life he was earning a little bit above his expenses. His monthly income, counting scholarship and wages, amounted to $73.40, with expenses totaling about $53, leaving $20 clear each month.

Increasingly he described his Sundays at Fall River as "happy . . . and blessed." He was taking a course in homiletics at the seminary. "I find it intensely interesting to work on sermons, though I always shrink from delivering them until I get started, then I'm usually all right. I write my sermons all the time now, not very good Quaker method, is it? I do it for the sake of style. I only use a very brief outline in the pulpit, but I think it is a great help to write out your thoughts in concise form."[30] Further-more, he was discovering that in the preparation of a sermon he would direct the sermon content at himself as much as at the intended congrega-tion. For example, a sermon on sincerity forced him to examine himself in this respect. On another occasion a sermon "took hold of me so when I was preparing it I found myself all nerved up, and tears in my eyes."[31]

As the school year progressed, it was becoming clear to both Clarence and Lilly that for financial reasons they would not be able to see each other in the coming summer. Their letters to each other spoke about the loneliness each was experiencing. "My heart aches when I think I shall not see you this summer,"[32] Clarence wrote. "I just feel I can't stand it sometimes." They talked in their correspondence about the future home they would have. Clarence was very clear on more than one occasion as to what role he wanted for Lilly. When the Salem, Oregon, Friends Church was growing, he realized that Lilly Peckham might become a paid assistant to Blanche Ford, the pastor, with whom she was living. "I have no objections to your being thus employed if you *won't preach*. I draw the line there."[33] And then in another letter: "I'm glad you don't take to preaching. In fact, I never feared you would; but it isn't at all in the desire of my heart to have a companion who is a public orator. Far from it. I hope, if I am called upon to do public work, that I can some day be one to be admired by you, but the home is what we want mutu-ally to make the great center of our lives, I feel, and so much of that depends upon you, my dear."[34]

In Salem, Lilly Peckham's life was a full one, with her health improv-ing. Over the past several years her "side" had been bothering her, the pain at times worse than on other days. The doctor she consulted did not know the cause of the trouble. She was making pastoral calls with Blanche and taking responsibility for leading Christian Endeavor meetings in the Church. She was working on a mission study class among the young people, using for study the new book by John R. Mott, *The Decisive Hour of Christian Missions*. Clarence frequently brought up the possibility of missionary work abroad, but Lilly continued to feel unenthusiastic about overseas missions, even educational work in Japan where Gilbert and Minnie Bowles were serving. "I just can't hope [for work with the Bowles] when I consult my personal feelings about it. When I dream of the cozy, happy home that I want ours to be, I just can't put it in Japan. . . .[35] Her wishes in respect to employment were clearly centered on teaching, *but* not abroad. She demonstrated this clear preference by agreeing in January to teach third grade at the South Salem School.

It was in May 1911 that Clarence Pickett learned of the opportunity to work for the summer at Spring Street Presbyterian Church Neighborhood House, a settlement located on the lower west side of New York City. It consisted mostly of noisome slums in an area between Varick Street and the Hudson River docks that would later be rehabilitated as part of Greenwich Village.[36] A classmate of his had served there the previous year and recommended it as a great chance to get a view of the work which is being done for the poor and foreigners in the great city. The seminary was offering a scholarship for two months, July and August. The minister of the Church was H. Roswell Bates, who had served as pastor since 1901 and who had started the settlement house in 1905.[37] Bates, well-known as a college teacher and leader of student conferences, contended with his inadequate budget by coaxing young college graduates with clerical ambitions to work for him for a small salary on the grounds that the experience was valuable. Dozens of collegians had got their first taste of what was called "active Christian service" in this way. Norman Thomas, later to be a candidate for president of the United States under the Socialist party emblem and a man whom Clarence Pickett admired and voted for, was one of those volunteers in the 1906-07 academic year. The experience at Spring Street affected Thomas' whole life, turning him against the law career which he had contemplated and moving him into church work and politics.

Bates was characteristically persuasive in recruiting Pickett for the summer of 1911. He explained how the church and its neighborhood house confronted "the great social and economic problems of the city, such as the assimilation of the immigrant, [the need for] the living wage, proper housing, efficient education of the working classes, the development of cooperative enterprise, the saloon, and white slavery."[38] Clarence quickly agreed to accept the position. "It will be much more strenuous work than at Fall River for those two months, "he wrote Lilly, "but it is exactly the chance I have wanted, so I won't mind the work. I will go down just after [New England] Yearly Meeting. . . . The work will be chiefly with vacation school, gathering in children and teaching them some industrial work and telling them Bible stories. Besides this, there is assisting in the pulpit on Sunday, visiting poor, sick people, looking after some bums who have been converted, etc. With it all I expect to see some of the city and get into its life a little bit."[39]

On Tuesday, 4 July 1911, Clarence Pickett took a Fall River Line steamer with about eight hundred passengers aboard, directly to downtown New York. "I had a splendid sleep last night on the boat," he wrote. Arriving at 7:00 a.m., he traveled from the wharf by horsecar to Spring Street in time for a Vacation Bible School conference at 10 o'clock. It was in the midst of the worst heat wave that the East Coast had had for many years. *The New York Times* (which he purchased for one cent) reported that the weatherman saw no promise of relief in the near future. "Deaths number about 175 in New York City alone," he wrote.

Summer volunteers slept out on the roof of the Neighborhood House, eight stories high. "But the poor people all about us who have such bad rooms in which to sleep," wrote Clarence, "are certainly to be pitied. Today at our conference one lady dropped from her seat, stricken with heat. Our janitor was taken away to the hospital last night, prostrate. In going only a few blocks I saw six horses dead or dying in the street from heat."[40]

Clarence Pickett's day off was typically a Saturday, and he and the other workers would go out into the country for rest and recreation. His Saturday trips included going to: the Caroline Country Club for settlement workers in Hartsdale, New York; a visit to the largest ocean liner, the *Olympic*, bluffing his way to get on board; Roswell Bates' summer home in Bronxville, New York, owned by Bates' millionaire father-in-law; the Bronx park and zoo; the James Woods', members of the Twentieth Street Friends Meeting, who lived in Mount Kisco.

During this summer in New York Clarence Pickett especially felt the lack of feminine company. Earlier in the year he had written Lilly Peckham about the one occasion, Washington's Birthday party, when men at the seminary were allowed to bring ladies to seminary functions. He spoke about the great oversupply of "fair maidens" and noted that there were some "dandies" among them, he felt a "passing pleasure" to be with them, but recognized that his heart was with her. With his outgoing nature Clarence relished talking to girls and "jollying a little," but his relationship to Lilly and the generally conservative atmosphere of the seminary made it inappropriate to loosen up.

Early in 1911 Lilly Peckham had written that she wanted to have a ring on her finger, to make her status clear, especially in respect to male admirers. Like Clarence, she was not openly talking about their engagement. Clarence was somewhat miffed that it was Lilly who was taking the initiative in respect to an engagement ring, but then came to see her point of view. He purchased a "little diamond," and mailed it to her in time for her to wear it for the first time on April 28, the first anniversary of the day of the "promise." He described it as "the seal of their pledge to each other and the outward sign of an inward reality."[41]

However, when Clarence Pickett went to Spring Street he did not say anything about his engagement, although he had Lilly's picture on his bureau. Among the volunteers was Margaret Juliet Shearer, a 1910 graduate of Bryn Mawr College. "She is certainly an intensely interesting and likable person," he wrote Lilly, using exactly those same words again in a subsequent letter. "Reared in wealth, she is intensely practical. She is quite an enthusiastic student volunteer, yet is by no means a 'pious Betty'."[42] Towards the end of August, with the Vacation Bible School closed, Clarence, "Miss Shearer," and another volunteer, "Miss Hull" (he had, earlier in the summer, characterized her as "slightly on the ragtime order") stretched the usual Saturday day off into Monday, spending extra time at the Bates' summer home. A week later Clarence reported to Lilly that Margaret Shearer had sprained her ankle when the Spring Street crowd went to Coney Island. After Labor Day those left at Spring Street were Clarence Pickett, Margaret Shearer, and Marian Savage, the resident manager, "a tall, slender Wellesley girl, very *proper* and yet is becoming more and more open to admit friends into her life."[43]

There were ample times to be with Margaret before Clarence left New York on 22 September for Providence, Rhode Island, again on an overnight steamer, "a little lonely for Spring Street," as he wrote Lilly. "I look back to it as one of the shrines where I offered up my little and received very much. I think I regard this as my very best summer yet."[44]

Upon his return to Hartford, Pickett recognized his need for rest, "for my nerves have been troubling me some lately."[45] He turned down the request of Fall River Friends to return as a student pastor. He only agreed to take on a Bible study class at the Hartford YMCA. In mid-October he wrote Lilly that his work at the YMCA was strenuous, "but I'm standing it splendidly. My nerves seem to be getting back almost normal now [*sic*] and I do enjoy the work."[46] He was disciplining himself to get one or two hours of exercise every day, playing tennis or basketball.

But a return to normalcy did not come quickly. At the end of October he wrote about an attack of "neuralgia," (medically defined as pain caused by irritation of, or damage to, a nerve). He went to see a doctor, who ordered him to do as little work as possible. "I'm sleeping fairly well now that the neuralgia is over, though sometimes I get too nervous for that." Then he reported on "a very peculiar day," a Sunday:

> Just after breakfast I felt so nervous I couldn't be still, so despite the rain I started out to walk. I walked eight miles out in the country, getting home by trolley just in time for dinner. Then after supper I walked about five miles further. I didn't attend any service—couldn't bear the thought of being confined in a room. It is terribly hard for me, when I'm feeling that way, to think of you as I so often do when I'm all right. I can't seem to fix my mind on anything very well. My devotions go to pieces pretty badly, too. [47]

Clarence Pickett characterized the whole incident as "a close call." He blamed his nervous condition on not having any vacation after being at Spring Street, although in earlier correspondence with Lilly Peckham he had said he was taking a brief holiday before returning to seminary.

When Roswell Bates, minister of Spring Street Presbyterian Church, wrote to the Seminary expressing the hope that Clarence Pickett could come again the following summer on a scholarship, Dr. Jacobus, dean of the Seminary, explained that it was against policy to give a second scholarship to the same student, then added:

> Much as he [Pickett] enjoyed his work with you, and as well as he accomplished it, it reduced him in health to a very low point. In fact, it pretty well exhausted him, and I question whether, if the way was otherwise clear, it would be altogether wise for him to attempt the same sort of work another year. He should have work this summer that would in every way be recuperative for him, as it will be the last vacation he has before he goes out into his full and complete life service.[48]

Apart from Clarence Pickett's experience of nervous exhaustion and Lilly Peckham's anxiety about his health, two interrelated concerns dominated their correspondence during the autumn of 1911. Clarence was once again being attracted to the idea of being a missionary in the foreign field. At this same time Clarence sent to Lilly one of

the Declaration Cards of the Student Volunteer Movement for Foreign
Missions. Lilly expressed irritation and deep misgivings in her reply:

> I'm sorry you sent those volunteer cards and asked me to sign one.
> Clarence, can't such decisions as that be left now until we get to-
> gether? As you keep asking of me these various things, and I answer
> one way or another, I don't feel satisfied, and I do not think you do. In
> fact, they make me more and more dissatisfied all the time, 'til some-
> times I think—I mustn't say it.[49]

That hint from Lilly that perhaps they should give up on their
relationship may have been a turning point for the better. He began to
appreciate more fully Lilly's situation of uncertainty: what would she
do when Blanche Ford got married in the spring of 1912? What work
was Clarence going to take up upon graduation? And when would she
and Clarence be getting married? Where would they be setting up their
home after marriage? And how would it be financially possible for her
to join Clarence in Hartford as he was suggesting, assuming that her
parents would approve of the move? "Dear Lilly," he wrote on 21 December, "I see that I have not thoroughly realized your position, and it is
constantly coming in upon me how terribly hard it is to keep in close,
sympathetic touch without frequent visits. We must, however, get something settled definitely soon, and I am going to do what I can during this
vacation."[50]

Just before Christmas Clarence screwed up his courage (as he put it)
to talk with Dr. Jacobus, dean of the seminary, at Jacobus' house,
telling him "our exact condition," and asking for his advice. "He talked
simply like a big brother to me," Clarence wrote Lilly, "and I certainly
felt better after it was all over." Clarence determined that "it would be a
big mistake not to complete the three years of seminary. I consider my
studies sacred—that is, I feel I have here a God-given opportunity to
prepare for our life work."[51] He reviewed all the advantages of being
together, spoke about the courses available to students, principally
women, at the seminary-affiliated School of Religious Pedagogy and
the probable availability of a scholarship for her to go to the School.

In subsequent letters, he went into the financial details: $4.50 per
week for board and room ($135 for the academic year) plus $100 for all
other expenses. To pay these expenses, he anticipated that his income
would be $3.00 a week for teaching at night school, which for nine

months would bring in $120. Lilly Peckham had figured that she would have $100 remaining from her school work in Oregon, but there was an outstanding pledge to Penn College of $125. Clarence Pickett suggested that they both postpone paying their pledges to the college, accruing interest to be paid on those pledges for a year or more. The pledges were not fully paid off until 1939, following Clarence's receipt of the Bok Award in Philadelphia.

With the financial problem seemingly solved, Lilly Peckham's brother Errol, persuaded his parents to approve of the idea of her coming east to live in Hartford, with Errol and Mary Peckham as chaperones. Indeed, the Peckham parents went the second mile and said that Lilly should not worry about finances. Finally, it became a certainty that she would come to Hartford in the autumn of 1912. Clarence Pickett, often having felt depressed about the impasse in regard to the immediate future, was now saying that the blues had been driven "sky high."

With the crucially important visit with Dean Jacobus out of the way, and with post-Christmas Day letters sent to Lilly, Clarence Pickett and Alex Purdy set out for a visit to the Spring Street settlement house over the New Year's weekend. His letters to Lilly about the weekend focused principally on his and Alex's visit to the all-night missions in the Bowery on Saturday night, 30 December. "Alex and I prayed with about a dozen men who came up to be saved. I think out of all with whom I worked, one seemed really sincere. It is awfully inspiring to get down there now and then and see souls in action. I don't think I'm fitted for that kind of work very well, but I do love to get a touch of it."[52] The visit to Spring Street renewed a feeling of inadequacy in respect to mission work of that type. He expressed scorn for men who were preaching damnation and hellfire to anyone, including committed Jews, who was not Christian, calling these preachers "fanatics."

It is not known whether Margaret Shearer was at Spring Street at the time of the visit. It is more likely that she was at home in Carlisle, Pennsylvania for the holidays. What is known is that all during the autumn, when she was still at Spring Street, Clarence was corresponding with her. It was only after his New Year's weekend visit to Spring Street— and possibly knowing for sure that Lilly Peckham would be coming east in the autumn—that he wrote both to Margaret Shearer and to Marian Savage, the very "proper" resident manager, about his engagement to Lilly.

In February, Marian wrote him a long letter, addressing him as "My dear Evan," using his middle name which evidently had become popular during the summer at Spring Street:

> When I heard of your engagement I was very much astonished, for it seemed to me very unnatural that you had not said anything of it last summer. It seemed especially strange to me that you had never told Margaret of it, for I know that you had talked with her very intimately about everything else— or at least about a great many things that were very personal and close to your inward self—and it seems to me that the first thing a man would do in a friendship of that kind would be to speak of his fiancée. I know that a good many people remarked upon your marked attentions to Margaret last summer, and I know, too, that you have written her very often since then. . . . I do not think it quite honorable for a man who is engaged to one girl to be quite as intimate with another girl as you have been with Margaret unless *both girls* understand the matter fully.[53]

And from Margaret Shearer a few days later: "I think it is fine that you are engaged. I must confess I had heard of it, but of course didn't know whether it was rumor or the real thing. It surprised me, because it is unusual for it to be possible to be a good friend of another girl when one is engaged. Even more difficult than for a girl to have a friendship that is real with another man. It seems to me it would have been more dignified and wise to announce it last summer. The friendship would have been formed just the same, whether you were an engaged person or not, but I think it would have been a less personal one."[54]

There is no record of Pickett's replies to these letters. He did keep in touch with Spring Street over the years and noted in his journal that the church property, near the entrance to the Holland Tunnel under the Hudson River, was put up for sale in 1963, the last religious service being held on Sunday, 29 December of that year.

On 1 March 1912 Clarence Pickett wrote Lilly Peckham about a whole new turn of events. An English Friend at the seminary, Jack Hoyland, obtained a scholarship for Clarence at the Quaker Woodbrooke Settlement for Social and Religious Work in Birmingham, England, proposed attending a Young Friends conference at Swanwick, and secured ocean passage for both Clarence Pickett and Alex Purdy.[55]

There can be little doubt that the opportunity to go to Woodbrooke and to visit with English Quakers was a turning point in Clarence Pickett's

career, because it moved him towards service with the Religious
Society of Friends on a domestic basis. The days at Central
Village and Fall River, and then
Spring Street, and now more
recently his association with
Elmwood Congregational
Church in Hartford, were push-
ing him towards becoming a
full-time Quaker pastor.

It was not until September
that Clarence Pickett and Lilly
Peckham saw each other for the
first time in over two years, in
Clinton Corners, New York,
where Errol, Lilly's brother, was
pastor for the summer at the
Friends Church. Clarence's one-
line-per-day diary records some
of those vacation days: "We look

*Clarence Pickett, student at Hartford
Theological Seminary, 1913*

forward to a happy week together. She seems much like in former years
except stronger." "Good visit with L.D.P." "L.D.P. and I go to Poughkeepsie to see the Binfords. Have a pleasant evening. Return in auto."
"On Lake Upton with L.D.P." "Hear Errol preach a good sermon."[56]

On 23 September Clarence and Lilly went to Poughkeepsie to take a
Day Line boat to New York, arriving at Spring Street in time for dinner.
He clearly wanted her to touch base with that part of his recent life that
had had such a far-reaching impact. The next day they toured New York
and then took the four o'clock train for Hartford. Clarence Pickett and
Lilly Dale Peckham were now united and in a very real sense starting
their lives together, albeit not as a married couple and not in a home of
their own. Two important decisions were facing them: where he would
serve as pastor following graduation, and when and where the wedding
would take place

Clarence Pickett's third year at Hartford Theological Seminary was
dominated by some of his most challenging courses of study. He took
courses on the English Reformation and on Christian mysticism, both

of which were particularly relevant to him as a Quaker. He also plowed through Dogmatics I, II, and III under Dr. William Douglas Mackenzie, president of the Seminary and author of the recently-published book, *The Final Faith.* "In that volume," wrote Pickett in later life, "this huge, stalwart Christian theologian sought to prove that Christianity was the one, only, and final faith. I had never been dealt with quite on that scholarly basis, and it was excellent discipline. Since then I have come to know many great spirits whose dogma was less emphatic, but whose grasp of the reality of the spiritual life has led me further than any dogma, however clearly reasoned. I now find *The Final Faith* an inward experience much more than an outward expression. I find some of Dr. Mackenzie's book very unsatisfying to me, but he did give me a good, strong anchor from which my mental and spiritual explorations could go forth."[57]

Clarence Pickett's thesis was "A Comparison of the Mysticism of Bernard of Clairvaux with that of the Prophet Jeremiah." There were nine chapters with an introduction and a conclusion. Drawing upon the writings of William Hocking, Friedrich von Hugel, William Inge, Evelyn Underhill, Robert Vaughan, and (Quaker) Rufus Jones, Pickett paid tribute to the scholars who were bringing mysticism to the forefront of Christian thought. "Instead of viewing these mystics as interesting archeological specimens of a past, brighter age, we come to them with bared heads and docile minds, bidding them teach our dumb spirits their secrets, and to turn our blinded eyes toward the 'way home.'"[58]

Clarence Pickett's everyday, one-line diary for the academic year principally notes the activities he and Lilly Peckham shared and some of the decisions they made. In January 1913 they decided not to go to Japan. In the same month Rufus Jones, whom Clarence Pickett had visited earlier in the month in Haverford, began the four Carew lectures at Hartford on "The Spiritual Reformers." Clarence and Lilly went together to a concert by the Boston Symphony Orchestra. Looking ahead, with Mary Peckham's help, they figured out what it would cost two persons to live as a couple for one year, total expenses coming to $743. They discussed the date of their wedding, went to a Shakespearean play (a first for Lilly), and visited together in Fall River and Central Village.

Of prime importance to both of them was finding employment for Clarence after graduation and establishing a home as a married couple. He was seeking a position as pastor in a Friends meeting. The options were many. Letters were received from meetings and churches in Greens-

Lilly Dale Peckham on her wedding day,
25 June 1913

boro (North Carolina), Brooklyn, Minneapolis, South China (Maine), Manchester (New Hampshire), and Toronto. He subsequently made weekend visits for interviews and was offered opportunities to preach in Toronto, Greensboro, and Brooklyn. These meetings then issued formal "calls" with specifics about salaries and living arrangements. Toronto, Canada particularly appealed to him and Lilly. Rufus Jones was favoring Toronto, and the Rogers brothers, affluent and "weighty" members of that meeting, were aggressive in reaching out to Clarence and Lilly. In March, the Picketts decided upon Toronto Meeting, in part because of its proximity to Pickering College (a Quaker secondary school), the opportunity to become acquainted with Canadian Friends, and probably because the meeting had made the best financial offer.

Clarence graduated from Hartford Theological Seminary with a Bachelor of Divinity degree on 28 May 1913. The following day he and Lilly went to Toronto and chose the meeting parsonage as the place for their first home. They continued on to Fremont, Iowa, to visit Clarence Pickett's mother and sister Ida. It was the first time he had seen them in three years.

On Wednesday, 25 June the wedding was in the evening at the home of Lilly's parents. The occasion served as a general reunion for the widely scattered Peckham family, with brothers and sisters of the bride coming in from Idaho, Hartford, and Iowa Falls. Penn College President David Edwards conducted a modified form of the traditional Quaker ceremony. Just before the ceremony Lilly's sister Letha sang de' Hardelot's "All for You," and then, as the local newspaper reported, "to the solemn strains of Lohengrin's Wedding March, played by Miss Jeanette Hadley, the bride and bridegroom entered, attended by the brother and sister of the bride. . . . The party made a pleasing picture against the dark background of palms and roses. The ceremony closed with ring pledges. A delicious three-course supper was served for the thirty guests, and after spending an hour of social pleasure with their friends, Mr. and Mrs. Pickett were most unexpectedly whizzed away in a waiting automobile."[59]

In less than a month Clarence and Lilly Pickett would be settling into a new and challenging life together in Toronto, Canada.

NOTES

1. Jacobus to Pickett, 9 Dec. 1909, Pickett papers, AFSC archives.

2. Thomas Wood to Pickett, 7 Sept. 1909, Pickett papers, AFSC archives.

3. Thomas Wood to Pickett, 16 Nov. 1909.

4. Minutes of the 1910 Yearly Meeting of Friends for New England, Haverford College, Haverford, Pa.: Quaker Collection, Magill Library.

5. Pickett-Peckham correspondence, 27 June 1910, Pickett papers, AFSC archives.

6. Pickett-Peckham, 27 June 1910.

7. Pickett-Peckham, 27 June 1910.

8. Pickett-Peckham, 30 June 1910.

9. Pickett-Peckham, 22 July 1910.

10. Pickett-Peckham, 4 July 1910.

11. Pickett-Peckham, 16 Aug. 1910.

12. Pickett-Peckham, 16 Aug. 1910.

13. Pickett-Peckham, 11 July 1910.

14. Pickett-Peckham, 11 July 1910.

15. Pickett-Peckham, 26 Aug. 1910.

16. Earl Wood to AFSC, as quoted in letter of 25 Apr. 1950 from Alice A. Macomber, correspondent for Westport Monthly Meeting, Pickett papers, AFSC archives.

17. Pickett-Peckham, 23 Sept. 1910.

18. Pickett-Peckham, 25 Sept. 1910.

19. Shirley Jackson Case, *Jesus Through the Centuries* (Chicago: Univ. of Chicago Press, 1932), 10.

20. Pickett-Peckham, 28 Sept. 1910.

21. Hadley to Pickett, 8 June 1911, AFSC archives.

22. Pickett undated notes, AFSC archives.

23. Pickett-Peckham, 15 Jan. 1911.

24. Pickett-Peckham, 20 Jan. 1911.

25. Undated, AFSC archives.

26. Pickett-Peckham, 27 Jan. 1911.

27. Pickett-Peckham, 27 Jan. 1911.

28. Pickett-Peckham, 28 Feb. 1911.

29. Pickett-Peckham, 3 Mar. 1911.

30. Pickett-Peckham, 13 and 17 Nov. 1911.

31. Pickett-Peckham, 25 Jan. 1911.

32. Pickett-Peckham, 25 Oct. 1910.

33. Pickett-Peckham, 5 Nov. 1910.

34. Pickett-Peckham, 7 Nov. 1910.

35. Pickett-Peckham, 12 Nov. 1910.

36. W. A. Swanberg, *Norman Thomas: The Last Idealist* (New York: Scribner's, 1976), 17.

37. 1811-1931, The One Hundred and Thirtieth Anniversary, Old Spring Street Presbyterian Church, Spring and Varick Streets, New York City, Presbyterian Church (USA): Dept of History, Philadelphia, 1931.

38. Swanberg, *Norman Thomas,* 17.

39. Pickett-Peckham, 3 June 1911.

40. Pickett-Peckham, 7 July 1911.

41. Pickett-Peckham, 15 April 1911.

42. Pickett-Peckham, 13 July 1911.

43. Pickett-Peckham, 20 July 1911.

44. Pickett-Peckham, 15 Sept. 1911.

45. Pickett-Peckham, 22 Sept. 1911.

46. Pickett-Peckham, 18 Oct. 1911.

47. Pickett-Peckham, 30 Oct. 1911.

48. Jacobus to Bates, 1 Feb. 1912, Pickett papers, AFSC archives.

49. Pickett-Peckham, mid-December, 1911.

50. Pickett-Peckham, 21 Dec. 1911.

51. Pickett-Peckham, 24 Dec. 1911.

52. Pickett-Peckham, 1 Jan. 1912.

53. Savage to Pickett, 9 Feb. 1912, Pickett papers, AFSC archives.

54. Shearer to Pickett, 19 Feb. 1912, Pickett papers, AFSC archives.

55. Pickett-Peckham, 1 Mar. 1912.

56. Pickett sunrise diary, 15-22 Sept. 1912, family papers, courtesy of Carolyn Pickett Miller.

57. Finkelstein, *Thirteen Americans,* 10.

58. Thesis presented to the faculty of Hartford Theological Seminary for the degree of Bachelor of Divinity by Clarence Evan Pickett, 1 March 1913.

59. *Oskaloosa Daily Herald,* 29 May 1913.

Chapter 4

QUAKER PASTOR IN TORONTO

To work myself out of a job

CLARENCE AND LILLY PICKETT'S HONEYMOON began after a one-day visit as a married couple with his mother and sister. Their travels began with an overnight trip by train to Chicago and then by boat on the Lake Michigan steamer, the *Missouri*, to Leland, Michigan. From there they traveled up to Northport on the west shore of Grand Traverse Bay. "Began our vacation by sleeping late. Lilly tired but happy," Clarence wrote in his diary. For two weeks they loafed, hiked, swam in and boated on Northport Bay; then they returned to Leland to take the *Missouri* north to Harbor Springs and on into Lake Huron. Their destination was Collingwood, Ontario on Georgian Bay.

They were met by Albert Rogers, of the Toronto Meeting, for transport by automobile to the thirteen-room pastorate. The congregation welcomed them the following day with a reception and shower. Clarence Pickett preached his first sermon as pastor on 20 July, choosing as his text, "The Son of Man Came to Seek and Save That Which Was Lost." He also participated in the evening worship service and on Wednesday, the evening prayer meeting.

Clarence was immediately fitting himself into what were termed "the regular appointments and stated meetings" of the meeting. It was not long before he was making suggestions for change. His summer with English Friends, and then his occasional visits to the Philadelphia area where no pastoral meetings existed, had planted in his mind some questions about the "pastoral system" of which he was now a part.

Reflecting in later years on his Toronto pastorate, Pickett claimed that his ambition was "to work myself out of a job. It seemed to me that the recovery of a general sense of responsibility for the conduct of the meeting by the total congregation was the goal that I ought to seek. I felt in Toronto that I made almost no progress in that direction, but I am happy to say that over the years which succeeded my service there, this transition has taken place in that group of worshippers. For the most part, it seemed to me that the congregation tended to become more dependent upon the minister rather than less, the longer I stayed with it, and that therefore my ambition was one that could never be realized."[1]

Clarence Pickett's first twelve months of service at the Toronto Friends Meeting were relatively uneventful. He and Lilly were enjoying life as a married couple. His diary indicates that he regularly assisted with the cleaning of the house and in doing the laundry. He was gradually becoming involved in the Toronto community. In November he accepted membership in the Presbyterian Ministers Association. He preached at the Central Prison and the reformatory. The Rogers families would regularly give Clarence and Lilly tickets to concerts of the Toronto Symphony Orchestra. It was not until late in 1913 that Clarence Pickett spent his first night away from home on a brief trip with Joseph Rogers to Welland, Ontario.

In the summer of 1914 Clarence and Lilly spent their vacation in the lake district of northern Ontario, possibly at "Go-Home Bay," a Rogers summer house. "I don't think we've ever had as nice a summer as we had that summer," he said in late life. "So far as we knew, the world was calm and going on quite peacefully, and yet, after we had been away about three weeks, we came home to find soldiers drilling in the streets of Toronto, offering themselves to join the British army to fight the Germans."[2] Canada promptly enacted military conscription with little attention given to the place of the conscientious objector. Exempted from military service were "clergy and ministers of religion and certain members of the Mennonites and Doukhobors [those who fled Russia in objection to conscription] promised exemption by the Dominion in 1873 and 1898."[3]

Members of the Religious Society of Friends in Canada and elsewhere were quite clear about the Society's traditional stand in respect to participation in war. The books of discipline of the three yearly meetings in Canada uniformly quoted from the Declaration of Friends to Charles II in 1660 on the occasion of being accused of involvement in a violent uprising of the Fifth-Monarchy Men:

> We utterly deny all outward wars and strife and fightings with outward weapons, for any end, and under any pretence whatsoever. And this is our testimony to the whole world. The spirit of Christ, by which we are guided, is not changeable, so as once to command us from a thing as evil, and again to move unto it; and we do certainly know, and so testify to the world, that the spirit of Christ, which leads us into all Truth, will never move us to fight and war against any man with outward weapons, neither for the kingdom of Christ, nor for the kingdoms of this world.[4]

Books of discipline from the very earliest days of the Society included "queries," which were questions directed to individual members and to meetings as a corporate body, and which were regularly read at business meetings. In the case of Canada Yearly Meeting of Friends the query relating to the peace testimony was as follows: "Do you maintain the Christian principle of peace and consistently refrain from bearing arms and from performing military service as incompatible with the precepts and spirit of the Gospel?"[5]

Although Friends in Canada, as well as in the United States, were surprised by the outbreak of war in Europe in August 1914, they were not totally unprepared. The monthly issues of *The Canadian Friend* indicate some attention to peace questions, but clearly foreign missions and the issue of temperance took precedence. Prior to the war, Canada Yearly Meeting had a peace committee of only four members. By 1917 the committee membership had been increased to eleven, with Albert Rogers as chairman. It is noteworthy that the August 1913 issue of *The Canadian Friend* carried a carefully-researched article by Friend Arthur Dorland on the peace movement, the adoption of military conscription in Australia and New Zealand, the push by the Canadian Defense League for universal military training, and the complacency of Friends in regard to these developments. And in that same summer, somewhat prophetically, Canada Yearly Meeting in a "Memorial to the Government and People of Canada" warned against the disasters that would come from the build-up of naval and other armaments by "the great civilized peoples" of the world. "Can it be denied," the resolution said, "that at any previous time was there such a narrow space between a terrible cataclysm of war and the adoption of general arbitration in its stead?"[6]

It was within the context of these statements of apprehension, but with relatively weak attention to the issues by the vast majority of Friends, that Clarence Pickett returned from his summer vacation to a Toronto and a country full of the fever of war. Press and pulpit promoted the conviction that this was a war that had been forced upon France and England—and, by association, all countries within the British Empire— and that the Allies were in the right. It was this war spirit that Pickett, as the somewhat untried pastor of the largest Quaker meeting in Canada, had to face.

Beginning in January 1915, *The Canadian Friend* came under the editorship of Clarence Pickett. Its place of publication was shifted from Newmarket, Ontario to Toronto. The motto under previous editor, John Webb, was "Conservative enough to retain the fundamental principles of Quakerism, liberal enough to meet the needs of the twentieth century." In the first issue under his editorship, Clarence wrote: "We cannot feel that this any longer expresses our ideal. It would be far nearer the mark if we should say: 'Progressive enough to retain the fundamental principles of Quakerism. Conservative enough to meet the needs of the twentieth century.'" His editorial explained the change:

> The cry for world peace, the demand for liberty of thought, the insistence upon simplicity of worship, the return of the emphasis in religion to the mystical, the placing of social responsibility upon the Church— these and others were the fruits of early Quaker character. We have been too conservative to live up to these high ideals. We must be progressive if we would retain the fundamental principles of Quakerism.
>
> But with the needs of the twentieth century, with war raging rampant, poverty stalking about, hatred and injustice unchanged, one is tempted to forget that a quiet conservatism which acts slowly and thoughtfully, always in the councils of the Father, is the surest method of progress.[7]

The monthly issues of *The Canadian Friend* immediately began to include more news and articles about the war. Late in his life Pickett was to say, in regard to the issue of conscientious objection to war at that time, "We found solutions for two or three of our young men [one of them, Goldwyn Gregory, joined the Friends Ambulance Unit in France], but by and large I never felt that we quite got that issue worked out so that it was a clear testimony to ourselves and to others that war was inconsistent with the Christian life, and that therefore, whatever the consequence, we couldn't participate in it."[8]

Even though Clarence Pickett was a strong proponent of the Quaker peace testimony and of the component of that testimony that called for conscientious objection and some alternative service, he was careful not to dictate to young Friends the course they should take. If they did join the Canadian contingent of the British Expeditionary Force, he kept in touch with them by mail, always aware that the letters would be censored. His private files contain letters from these men, such as a letter dated 3 March 1915 from Albert Mellody, 10801-C Company, 4th Battalion, 1st Infantry Regiment. Attached to the letter is a newspaper notice that Private Mellody died of wounds.

Usually letters from the field were written on YMCA stationery in England, the letterhead boldly stating, "For God, for King, and for Country, YMCA H.M. Forces on Active Service." One Toronto Meeting member, in answer to a letter from Clarence Pickett, wrote back that he was pleased to receive the letter and the kind wishes of his pastor. "I am indeed sorry I did not come to see you before I left Canada, but I did not want you to know I had joined the Army. I tried three times to join, including the Medical Corps, but could not pass, and the Artillery I succeeded in getting into. I know the principal [sic] of the Friends is peace, but all my chums joined and I was left, so I thought I would follow."[9]

In November 1915 Clarence and Lilly Pickett experienced a very personal loss. Lilly Pickett was pregnant. As Clarence Pickett recorded it in his one-line diary, "Lilly has trouble inwardly and has to go to bed. Called Dr. Adams. Threatened miscarriage." Then two days later, "Lilly loses child at once. She is disappointed, yet gets along remarkably well. Doctor announces to us that an operation will be necessary." Three days later, "Lilly's operation successful." And then, another three days later, "Lilly getting along well."[10] Her sister Letha came to visit later in the month. Then, to complete the year in respect to personal setbacks, Clarence Pickett was knocked down by an automobile the day before Christmas, and Lilly Pickett contracted measles and was very ill.

The year 1916 began with no letup in the war, and the cry for patriotism on the home front intensified. In February Pickett agreed to stay on as pastor in Toronto. Increasingly, Pickett was giving greater attention in the pages of *The Canadian Friend* to events and issues relating to the war. He gave a full account of the proposed World Conference of All Friends to be held in Great Britain as soon as the war ended. The purpose of the Conference was "to consider and restate the testimony of the Religious Society of Friends regarding war and international relations generally."[11] Included would be the implications of the testimony in individual and social life. London Yearly Meeting had already appointed a committee on "War and the Social Order."

In May Pickett was approached by a committee of the board of management of Pickering College to determine if he would consider being principal, beginning in the 1917-18 academic year. "Pickering College" was a misnomer because it had always been "a resident school for boys and girls," since its establishment in 1841 as Friends Seminary in West Lake Township, Prince Edward County, Ontario.

Although he was offered the position in May, Clarence Pickett did not give the board of management his decision until late January of the next year. A happy upcoming event was dominating the Picketts' lives. Lilly Pickett was again pregnant, and to their great satisfaction, Rachel Joy Pickett was born on 6 January 1917. Just two weeks later Clarence Pickett resigned from his position as pastor of the Toronto Friends Meeting and as editor of *The Canadian Friend,* both effective 1 July, and accepted the principalship of the Quaker boarding school.

These plans and expectations, however, were radically altered when, in April 1917, the Military Hospital Commission in Canada approached the board of management of the school with a proposal that Canada Yearly Meeting make the school available for the accommodation of disabled soldiers, particularly for difficult mental cases which required care of a special kind. Canadian Friends saw this as an opportunity for service in wartime. "Canada Yearly Meeting accordingly offered Pickering College with its land and all its equipment to the Military Hospital Commission, to be used by them free of rent until the end of the War, or until such time as permanent hospitals for the insane could be erected and equipped."[12]

The closing of Pickering College as a residential school for an indefinite period of time introduced uncertainties into the Picketts' lives. And the unavailability of the school principalship was coincident with the United States declaration of war on Germany on 6 April. It was U.S. entry into the war that was particularly responsible for Clarence Pickett's decision not to rescind the resignation from the pastorate of Toronto Meeting despite the Meeting's strong wish to have him continue there.

As soon as word got out that Clarence Pickett would not be heading Pickering College, letters started coming in from Friends in the United States urging him to fill one or more vacant positions. Greensboro Meeting again sought him as pastor. Portland (Maine) Meeting reached out to him for the same purpose. The American Friends Board of Foreign Missions urged him to consider the claims of work in the Jamaica field. The American Friends Bible School Board of the Five Years Meeting wanted him to head up that Board. And William Berry, one of his favorite teachers at Penn College and now clerk of Oskaloosa Monthly Meeting, pressed him to become pastor of the Oskaloosa Friends Church in Oskaloosa. This request was seconded in a letter from his friend Ora Carrell, field secretary to the boards of Iowa Yearly Meeting. "The opportunity that would be afforded you in the Meeting and city [Oskaloosa], including our College and Yearly Meeting, is most excellent. And, Clarence, *you* are splendidly fitted for the work. . . . We *need* you—and *want* you—and *hope* you will come!"[13]

It was this call from his own college meeting in his own country that tipped the scales in favor of going to Oskaloosa following the close of Canada Yearly Meeting sessions on 4 September 1917. He agreed to give his first sermon in Oskaloosa on 16 September. Little could Clarence and Lilly Pickett have known how upset the Oskaloosa community would become over his views in respect to the war.

NOTES

1. *Thirteen Americans: Their Spiritual Autobiographies,* ed. By Louis Finkelstein (New York: Institute for Religious and Social Studies, 1953), 10-11.

2. Pickett taped recollections, 1964.

3. The Militia Service Act of 1917, from unidentified Canadian newspaper article, 5 Jan. 1917, Pickett papers, AFSC archives.

4. Philadelphia Yearly Meeting of the Religious Society of Friends, *Faith and Practice: a Book of Christian Discipline* (Philadelphia: Philadelphia Yearly Meeting, 1997), 76.

5. Discipline of the Canada Yearly Meeting of Friends (1903), 57, Haverford College, Haverford, PA: Magill Library, Quaker Collection.

6. Minutes of 1913 Canada Yearly Meeting of Friends, 23, Haverford College, Haverford, PA: Magill Library, Quaker Collection.

7. *The Canadian Friend* 10, no. 7 (Jan. 1915): 1.

8. Pickett taped recollections, 1964.

9. Pickett papers, AFSC archives.

10. Pickett, sunrise diary, 4 and 6 Nov. 1915, family papers, courtesy of Carolyn Pickett Miller.

11. *The Canadian Friend* 12, no. 8 (Feb. 1917): 1-3.

12. Arthur G. Dorland, *The Quakers in Canada, A History* (Toronto: Ryerson Press, 1968), 285.

13. Carrell to Pickett, 4 June 1917, Pickett papers, AFSC archives.

Chapter 5

WITNESS IN OSKALOOSA

Supporting the war is just what I cannot do

SOON AFTER CLARENCE ASSUMED HIS RESPONSIBILITY as pastor of the College Avenue Friends Church, he was emphasizing four lines of development: a more thorough understanding and application of the principle of Christian stewardship—applied to life and possessions; development of a greater sense of responsibility of the entire membership for the meetings for worship, a goal similar to what he had hoped to achieve in Toronto; establishment of more effective contact with neighbors within the Oskaloosa community; and broader interest in the application of the principles of Jesus to world problems.

During this time he gave a great deal of attention to the young men of the meeting who were subject to the draft, noting that forty-two of them had entered some phase of war work. As was the case in Toronto, he followed many of them by correspondence after they left, pointing out how their service had given to the meeting "a broader sympathy and a wider interest in world affairs." "I earnestly hope," he said to meeting members, "we may constantly remember them in prayer and by letter, and be loyal to them."[1]

Ten members of the meeting had taken the conscientious objector position and were working with the Friends Reconstruction Unit in France under the American Friends Service Committee that had been organized in Philadelphia on 30 April 1917. The unit also received financial support from the meeting and garments for distribution. Pastor Pickett concluded his first annual report with these words: "The future looms large, with problems and possibilities. These can be realized, however, only in the most complete consecration to the will of God. His kingdom can come in our midst whenever we will let it break in through us."[2] This was a proclamation Clarence Pickett was to set forth throughout his lifetime, reflecting his spiritually-based optimism.

As had been the case in Toronto, Pickett was soon making some suggestions for change in the schedule of services at the meeting. In October, he suggested that the time of the Sunday vesper service be moved from 8:00 p.m. to 4:00 or 4:30 p.m., making it possible to hold weekly Young People's Christian Endeavor meetings immediately following the afternoon service. There was no change in the hours of the Sunday morning Bible school and meeting for worship, 9:45 and 11:00 respectively, nor in the Thursday evening prayer meeting. The advantage of the new schedule was that it made Sunday evenings available for Clarence and Lilly Pickett to invite meeting members and college students to their home, "after all events of the day were over, where we conducted a kind of round table seminar on the issues of war and peace."[3]

The Selective Service Act of 1917 was passed on 18 May. It contained a clause exempting from combatant service in the armed forces any man who was a member of ". . . any well-organized religious sect or organization . . . whose existing creed or principles forbid its members to participate in war in any form, and whose religious convictions are against war or participation therein."[4] The exemption was provided only for members of recognized peace churches (Church of the Brethren, Religious Society of Friends, and Mennonites), and the exemption was from *combatant* service only. No alternative service of a civilian nature or under civilian direction, was mentioned in the law.

The government hoped that conscientious objectors would at least accept noncombatant service within the armed forces. Almost a year after the draft began, the Medical Corps, the Quartermaster Corps, and engineer service were officially considered noncombatant. But there were drafted men in the Army cantonments whose consciences would not allow them to perform noncombatant military service of any kind. In October 1917 a ruling came from the War Department ordering these men to be segregated from the other soldiers in camp and placed under officers especially selected for their tact and consideration. "With reference to their [COs'] attitude of objecting to military service, the men are not to be treated as violating military laws . . . but their attitude in this respect will be quietly ignored, and they will be treated with kindly consideration."[5]

In an atmosphere of rigid interpretation of loyalty and of intolerance for opposition to the war Clarence and Lilly Pickett began their service in Oskaloosa in mid-September 1917. Small-town sentiments in the United States were quite different from the diversity of opinions tolerated in the larger cities. Oskaloosa was not Toronto, Canada. Furthermore, Penn College faculty members and students and members of the Oskaloosa Friends Meeting were closely interrelated. The college was an integral part of the Oskaloosa community, with all of the usual interdependencies of town and gown. Penn College decided not to have on campus a unit of the Student Army Training Corps.

Clarence Pickett's inaugural sermon at the College Avenue Friends Church on Sunday morning, 16 September was soon followed by an opportunity to address Penn College students in the college chapel. He compared the wartime conditions in Canada in the early days of the conflict with present times in the United States, "illustrating how wartime slogans of one, two, or three years ago were obsolete now."[6] A week later he attended the weekly Tuesday noon luncheon of the Oskaloosa Commercial Club. A discussion of the school election to be held the following Monday, and a progress report from the chairman of the Liberty Loan Committee of Mahaska County were the two items of business. "The Rev. Clarence Pickett of the Friends Church was introduced and made a brief speech," noted the *Daily Herald*.[7]

Just two days later, the *Daily Herald* had a lead story on the second Liberty Bond sales campaign. "Proud Mahaska's head was raised a little higher, and the gleam in his eyes has become brighter today, as the result of the successful Liberty Loan meetings and patriotic rallies held Wednesday evening."[8] Every day the *Daily Herald* had front page stories on the progress of the campaign—and on the morally imperative reasons for purchasing the bonds. Mahaska County's allotment was $1,304,625, considered by the campaign committee and the newspaper to be "an enormous sum." "To raise the full amount, everyone must subscribe. . . . There'll be no slacking in Mahaska County. . . . Through patriotic rallies and personal solicitation, the amount will be subscribed."[9] The rate of interest was four percent beginning 5 November 1917. The national goal for the second Liberty Loan drive was $5 billion.

As the deadline approached for the raising of the Mahaska County allotment, 21 October was designated as Liberty Loan Sunday with pastors and ministers requested to preach patriotic sermons. The county committee mailed information to all clergypersons for the preparation of these sermons. We do not know what Pastor Pickett preached on Sunday, 21 October, but he certainly did not equate religious commitment with the buying of bonds. For one thing, he knew that there were as many Christians on the other side of the war front as on the Allied side.

Finally, 28 October was designated by Oskaloosa as "Go to Church Sunday," following President Wilson's proclamation setting that Sunday "as a day of prayer for the success of the American arms in the war."[10] At the Friends Church Clarence Pickett made the pulpit address, and at the vesper service the popular former president of Penn College, Absalom Rosenberger, now president of Whittier College, attracted a big attendance. Rosenberger at the time was a member of the Collegiate Anti-Militarism League as were a number of other highly-placed Quakers in the educational world.

On 24 October, just three days before the end of the Liberty Loan campaign of 1917, the *Daily Herald* carried a news release from Washington reporting that "English and American Friends, conscientious objectors to war . . . are now cooperating with the American Red Cross and have become a powerful factor in remedying the evils of war. Both the British and American governments have recognized the legitimacy of the Friends 'conscientious objection' and the present plan for cooperation with the Red Cross has been worked out with the approval of the War Department. One reconstruction unit of a hundred men, who have been training at Haverford, Pennsylvania since the middle of July, will soon be in France."[11]

It was precisely for this opportunity—to enable Quaker COs to join units of British Friends in relief work behind the lines in France—that the American Friends Service Committee (AFSC) had been organized in Philadelphia the preceding April, stating "We are united in expressing our love for our country, and desire to serve her loyally. We offer our services to the Government of the United States in any constructive work in which we can conscientiously serve humanity."[12] Bringing together under a single organizational umbrella American Quakers from the three branches within the Religious Society of Friends, the Committee was immediately confronted with the many individual situations being encountered in Army cantonments by Quaker COs, with the commanders of these camps not having clear directions from the War Department in Washington as to what to do with religious objectors.

A sentiment prevailed both in the War Department and among the camp officers that COs were fundamentally seeking an easy way out of combatant service and could be coerced or enticed into noncombatant positions under military orders. Therefore, the AFSC and its cooperating yearly meeting committees needed to help Quaker COs understand that compromising (to the extent of accepting noncombatant service in the armed forces) would undermine the efforts to convince the War Department in Washington that according to the Society's principles, conscientious objection meant objection to the whole military organization and that the only viable solution was for Quaker COs to be granted a deferred classification in order to work in France.

The reality of the situation faced by the individual objector meant that agonizing decisions had to be made as to just when to register his objection: refusal to put on a uniform and to carry a rifle were standard points of objection for most men, but was washing the dishes in the camp kitchen cooperating with the military? saluting an officer? what about weeding the flower beds, or cleaning out the stables?

As early as November 1917 the AFSC was saying that, "The two most vital things to be accomplished in establishing the status of Friends at national army cantonments is [sic], first, to have the man himself be thoroughly clear in his own mind and conscience, and, second, to make sure that the commanding officers thoroughly understand the force and intent of Form 174 [noncombatant certificate] and the order issued from Washington that such persons shall be segregated and not punished for nonperformance of military duty."[13]

But regulations established in Washington were frequently either unknown or ignored. In spite of the Army's official policy of "kindly consideration," there were brutalities in the treatment of conscientious objectors in the camps, where they were subject to unauthorized hazing, often of a serious nature, at the hands of other men. Some COs were forced into uniform, beaten, immersed in latrines, prodded with bayonets, and threatened with execution. Clarence had a letter from Paul Michener at Fort Flagler in the state of Washington illustrating the difficulties: "We were called before the major who, after looking the matter up, said we were sent to him as soldiers, that he had no orders to segregate us, that Form 174 meant nothing to him, and that we could take the regular work or go to the guard house. We chose the guard house, of course, and were promptly sent there."[14]

Clarence Pickett believed that he had a pastoral responsibility to both those who had decided to join the armed forces and those who were objectors. He had a particular interest in those young Friends who were endeavoring to uphold the testimony of Friends in regard to participation in war. He reserved Sunday evenings for informal meetings at his home for anyone who wished to discuss issues of war and peace. Wrote Clarence: "We didn't talk about Germany and Great Britain. We talked about whether we should allow ourselves to be drawn into the fanatical attitude that was assumed by the community in which we lived, that we must, in order to show that you are a real American, stand by the boys as they go to war, and support it with your finances. I never took the attitude of trying to persuade any boy to take the conscientious objector position. We did, however, try to see what that testimony had been in times past and what it seemed to us to be now and to raise the personal question, 'What would I, as an individual, do?'"[15]

Leroy Reynolds, one of the students involved in these discussions, was to write Clarence a year later from Camp Taylor, Kentucky, where he was taking the CO stand: "I want you to know that the things we studied together last winter seem more true the farther I go. It has given me a more satisfactory basis of faith than I had before."[16] Still another student of that period, Forrest Comfort, wrote Clarence Pickett thirty years later:

> My thoughts go back to 1918, when on the verge of a hasty move to volunteer for military service, I went to say goodbye to you. You didn't tell me to wear my sword as long as I could [referring to an anecdote well known to Friends about George Fox's advice to William Penn]. You did say, "What's your hurry, Forrest?" While thinking that question through I joined in discussion groups in your home. I have never been tempted to enter into any war activity since that time. I was only one of the 70 or 80 fellows who were influenced in your home and other contacts to be interested in the way of life which does away with the causes of war.[17]

Pleased with the work of the one hundred COs who were in the Reconstruction Unit in France, the American Red Cross decided to give American Friends the chance of supplying an additional three hundred men for civilian relief in France. The problem that the AFSC faced was that despite this call for additional men the Secretary of War, Newton Baker, did not promise that this work would be viewed by the government as noncombatant service for drafted men. The AFSC could not afford to send men to France who might subsequently be caught up in the second and subsequent drafts. Finally, in March 1918 the needed favorable ruling was obtained from the War Department.

Clarence Pickett was in frequent correspondence with the AFSC regarding Quakers in Camps Dodge, Gordon, and Pike. The men would ask him to recommend them for service in France. They were eager to be released for service abroad. Wrote Raymond Mendenall: "We now live in segregation with Mennonites, Brethren, and, as our commander Lieutenant Manahan aptly describes them, 'The Other Birds.'"[18] Mendenall was cooperating to a minimal extent, "acting during the evenings and rush hours practically as a secretary. It does not seem to have occurred to them up there that I can sweep floors."[19] What he wanted was hospital work within the Friends Reconstruction Unit in France.

Clarence Pickett's Sunday evening study groups for men and women continued right through the 1917-18 winter and into the spring. On 6 April 1918 the third Liberty Loan Campaign was launched from Washington, DC. Not having responded to the second campaign, Clarence took the initiative to write to the Mahaska County Liberty Loan Campaign Committee on 9 April. In a letter dated 11 April, Clarence received a reply from the chairman of the Mahaska County Committee indicating that it was expected that he would subscribe voluntarily, with no specific amount suggested.[20]

As before, in the earlier campaigns, the buying of the bonds or stamps was inextricably bound up with the notion of loyalty, and, as the campaign was drawing to a close in the early autumn, Clarence came under intense pressure to prove his loyalty. The minister of the Episcopal church, who had been so successful in obtaining liberty loans from his own congregation, called at the Pickett home and asked Clarence to prove his loyalty by buying a war savings stamp. Pickett's own recollections of the incident, recorded close to the end of his life, revealed its seriousness:

> He said, I suppose your salary isn't very much, just buy one or two of these stamps to prove you're loyal. Well, I said to him, I don't mind the 25¢ or even the 50¢ or more than that, but to do this to prove that I am in

favor of this war and supporting it is just what I can't do. He at once grew red in the face and angry and swore at me, and the next Monday morning at the Ministerial Association meeting, he got the Association to throw me out. He was called back to Virginia not long after, and the Ministerial Association took me back in after he had gone, but that little incident impressed itself on the young men and their girlfriends as showing that this issue that we had been discussing, of participation in war, was not just a passing issue with me, but had to be acted upon personally.[21]

But this incident was not the end of Pickett's troubles. Three leading members of the Friends Meeting offered to buy a $50 bond for him so that the meeting would not come under attack for being disloyal. Clarence told them of his sympathy for them personally in not wanting to see the meeting ostracized by the community, but the stakes were too high for him. It was a matter of deep principle for him. He could not accept the $50 bond from them. Happily, all of them backed away from the request, and, as was so often the case in his lifetime, all of them remained intimate friends of his and, as he put it, "I think we all grew through the experience."[22]

Even that confrontation, however, did not draw the issue to a close. One night the parsonage was defaced with large slashes of yellow paint (the color clearly signifying cowardice). "They stayed there a long time," Clarence later recalled. "I wasn't particularly anxious to get them removed, because I thought it was probably a good thing for the community, the Quaker community, to be made somewhat conspicuous by the thoughtful attitude it was trying to take on this issue in a community of neighbors, many of whom didn't share our point of view, but to whom we could bear testimony by simply letting the yellow painted crosses stay on the house until the fever was over."[23]

As to Clarence Pickett's view of the Oskaloosa incident and his decision not to erase immediately the yellow markings, his references to the experience may not have altogether captured the full dimensions of the time. We do know that those days of community hostility were especially stressful for Lilly Pickett. On 25 October 1918 a daughter was "stillborn."[24] The child was to have been named Betty. Said Carolyn Pickett Miller, "My mother blamed the loss of the child on the stress of that period."[25] These were dark days indeed for Clarence and Lilly. As one personal friend wrote, "We were saddened over the great sorrow that came to you because of that awful anticlimax after those doubtless many weeks of joyous expectation."[26]

Clarence was taking a keen interest in the commissions that were set up by American Friends to prepare for the postwar Peace Conference of All Friends called by London Yearly Meeting. Henry Cadbury at Haverford College, in correspondence with Clarence, was noting that "there is very little, much too little, work being done for the Peace Conference after the war."[27] Often with financial support from the Philadelphia Yearly Meetings, Clarence traveled to Philadelphia for meetings regarding the postwar conference (the dates for which were set for 22-29 August 1919), for meetings of the American Friends Service Committee relating to the reconstruction work in France, and for Young Friends gatherings at nearby Westtown School.

Henry Cadbury was particularly encouraging Clarence to come east for these meetings. As soon as Clarence learned of the furor at Haverford College regarding a letter Henry Cadbury had written on college stationery to a Philadelphia paper, he wrote a letter of sympathy. Cadbury, assistant professor of Biblical studies at Haverford, and later to become a professor at Harvard University's divinity school, had said in part in the published letter:

> As a Christian and patriotic American, may I raise one cry of protest in your columns against the orgy of hate in which the American press and public indulges on the receipt of peace overtures from the enemy. Whatever the immediate result of the present German request for an armistice, the spirit of implacable hatred and revenge exhibited by many persons in this country indicates that it is our nation which is the greatest obstacle to a clean peace and the least worthy of it.[28]

Cadbury offered to resign, but the board of managers of the College preferred to grant him a leave of absence for the balance of the academic year, his resignation to be finally accepted or refused later in the year. Cadbury wrote Pickett as follows: "Your letter of sympathy was needed and *appreciated*, and I hear you are having troubles of your own. Well, let's 'stick it.' Of course, I don't wish to defend myself. I was said to be intemperate and indiscreet. But as thee says, we mostly err on the other side. I am impressed with how different the penalties are for missing the golden mean on its two sides. Overcaution rarely gets what thee and I get. I am most concerned to convert it all into good—with thy assistance and friendship. Many thanks for thy help."[29]

Whatever may have been the reservations of some Oskaloosa Meeting members (and especially those associated with Penn College) about Clarence Pickett, the pastoral committee of the meeting decided in September 1918 to recommend to the monthly meeting that he "be continued as our pastor without time limit. Either party desiring change shall give two months notice before the relationship is severed."[30] The monthly meeting agreed. But within six months, on 5 March 1919 the following communication was presented to Oskaloosa Monthly Meeting by pastor Pickett: "With grateful appreciation for a short period of service with you, I hereby tender my resignation as pastor, to take effect not later than June 1, 1919."[31]

The resignation was unexpected. Clarence Pickett explained that some time earlier a call had been presented to him to act as secretary of the Board of Young Friends Activities of the Five Years Meeting, and that only the overwhelming sense that this service was the call of God had led to his decision. The resignation was referred to the pastoral committee and subsequently accepted by the meeting.

Clarence Pickett was now released to work in all yearly meetings of the Five Years Meeting— Baltimore, California, Canada, Indiana, Iowa, Kansas, Nebraska, New England, New York, North Carolina, Oregon, Western, and Wilmington (Ohio)—and free to cross the boundaries of the separations into Hicksite and Conservative yearly meetings in the interest of a more unified and dynamic Religious Society of Friends. The base of operations would be Richmond, Indiana, where he and Lilly would live for the next ten years.

NOTES

1. Pastor's report for 9-1/2 months, 15 Sept. 1917 to 30 June 1918, Iowa Yearly Meeting archives, Oskaloosa, IA.

2. Pastor's report.

3. Pickett taped recollections, 1964.

4. American Friends Service Committee, *An Introduction to Friends Civilian Public Service,* Chapter 8, "American Conscientious Objectors in World War I," (Philadelphia, PA, 1945),37.

5. *Introduction,* 38.

6. *Oskaloosa Daily Herald,* 3 Oct. 1917.

7. *Herald,* 10 Oct. 1917.

8. *Herald,* 11 Oct. 1917.

9. *Herald,* 12 Oct. 1917.

10. *Herald,* 27 Oct. 1917.

11. *Herald,* 24 Oct. 1917.

12. Statement, 30 Apr. 1917, AFSC archives.

13. Furnas to Pickett, Pickett papers, 3 Nov. 1917, AFSC archives.

14. Michener to Pickett, 6 Jan. 1918, Pickett papers, AFSC archives.

15. Pickett taped recollections, 1964.

16. Reynolds to Pickett, 10 Aug. 1918, Pickett papers, AFSC archives.

17. Comfort to Pickett, 10 May 1950, on the occasion of Pickett's retirement as executive secretary of the American Friends Service Committee. Family papers, courtesy of Carolyn Pickett Miller.

18. Mendenall to Pickett, 25 March 1918, Pickett papers, AFSC archives.

19. Mendenall to Pickett.

20. Mahaska County Committee to Pickett, 11 Apr. 1918, Pickett papers, AFSC archives.

21. Pickett taped recollections, 1964.

22. Pickett taped recollections, 1964.

23. Pickett taped recollections, 1964.

24. Certificate 443, 2 Nov. 1918, Record of Births, Mahaska County, as reported by Dr. L. A. Rodgers.

25. Interview with Carolyn Pickett Miller, 26 Apr. 1993.

26. W. Carleton Wood to Clarence and Lilly Pickett, 24 Dec. 1918, Pickett papers, AFSC archives.

27. Cadbury to Pickett, 26 Nov. 1918, Pickett papers, AFSC archives.

28. *Philadelphia Public Ledger,* 12 Oct. 1918, as quoted in Margaret Hope Bacon, *Let This Life Speak: The Legacy of Henry Joel Cadbury* (Philadelphia: Univ. of Pennsylvania Press, 1987), 44.

29. Cadbury to Pickett, 9 Nov. 1918, Pickett papers, AFSC archives.

30. Minutes of Oskaloosa Monthly Meeting, 11 Sept. 1918, Iowa Yearly Meeting of Friends archives, Oskaloosa, IA.

31. Minutes of Oskaloosa Monthly Meeting, 5 Mar. 1919.

Chapter 6

PACESETTER FOR YOUNG FRIENDS

*Consecration of life to a discovery
of a Christian social order*

WITH THE EXTENSIVE ATTENTION HE HAD GIVEN to teenage and young adult Friends during his pastorates in Toronto and Oskaloosa, Clarence Pickett was fully acquainted with both the history of the Young Friends Movement and its contemporary emphases. Organizationally it was one of the boards of the Five Years Meeting of Friends, called the Board of Young Friends Activities. It had been created at the sessions of the Five Years Meeting in 1912, but it was not until April 1914 that the new board was fully functioning with a field secretary. That secretary was Thomas E. Jones, a young Friend himself, who later in life was to distinguish himself first as president of Fisk University and then as president of Earlham College.

The Young Friends Movement was an expression of new life within the Religious Society of Friends, at first in Ireland, then soon after in England, Australia, and the United States. The Movement was on the cutting edge in securing a greater sense of identity for Friends, notwithstanding the advantages to Quakers of being involved in interdenominational movements. These young Friends felt that they had a message and witness to put forth within the wider circles of Christian endeavor. The young Friends emphasized the importance of studying the history of their religious society and formed active fellowship groups within meetings. Typically, these groups would find themselves preferring to worship in accordance with the traditional unprogrammed style of worship, not requiring the leadership of a pastor, the method adhered to by Hicksite and Conservative Quakers.

When Clarence Pickett moved into the secretaryship of the Board of Young Friends Activities in June 1919, the program was well-established and demanding. For example, in the months remaining in that year, in addition to the Young Friends General Conference at Earlham in late July, he visited North Carolina and Wilmington (Ohio) Yearly Meetings and in each case was invited to speak. In October he attended meetings for worship and business of the young Friends of the Hicksite Baltimore Yearly Meeting at their invitation. Wrote Clarence: "There were four hundred present, about half young Friends and half older. They knew practically nothing of the Young Friends Movement, the Five Years Meeting, etc. More serious than this, they need an awakening to the life of service. There is tremendous power, unusual culture, and plenty of wealth. I feel we must respond to all calls upon us from these Friends when they open the way for our message. The few from their number who were at the last summer's conference are evidently the hope of the whole group."[1]

Also in 1919, Pickett visited in Kansas Yearly Meeting, writing in his report, "It is evident that the membership, especially the younger group, have far outgrown in education and vision their pastoral leadership. In many cases this leads to some impatience among the young life, and a harsh demand for orthodoxy and standpatism by pastors."[2] Once again Clarence Pickett was experiencing the considerable variance between the Biblical literalism and doctrinal narrowness of some evangelical Quaker Christians with his own liberal and open religious convictions. These pastors surely must have also been critical of his interest in working with Hicksite and Conservative Friends. He was to contend with the criticisms throughout his lifetime of those who today would be called "right wing" Christians, but he never denigrated their sincerity and religious commitment.

In the 1920 calendar year the lines of activity of the Young Friends Board remained basically the same as in the previous year. There were Life Service missions to the eight Friends colleges within the Five Years Meeting, leading up to a virtual vocational guidance bureau at the office in Richmond, and resulting in voluminous correspondence with Quaker students in all of the colleges. Working closely with *The American Friend,* the Board issued literature for the use of local meeting Christian Endeavor societies and was responsible for four special supplements in the magazine. The program of reaching out to those Friends in the teaching profession blossomed, the list growing to six hundred teachers, most of whom were working in public schools. Clarence Pickett noted in his annual report that in some yearly meetings there had been criticisms and misunderstandings, but "these one must expect if he undertakes to go forward with an aggressive policy of righteousness. It has always [been] so."[3]

Clarence Pickett's dominant interest was in the application of the Quaker faith to the social problems of the day. This interest was very much reflected in the eleventh Young Friends General Conference held in early July 1920 on the Earlham College campus. For the lecture series Clarence had obtained Paul Jones, secretary of the Fellowship of Reconciliation and a bishop who had been defrocked on the initiative of the Salt Lake (Utah) diocese of the Episcopal church during the war because of his pacifism. The two themes that Jones emphasized in his lectures were the sacredness of personality and the call to service. A socialist in his thinking, Jones spoke to the need in the industrial and international fields for new leadership. The message of the Conference reflected the impact of the lectures. Acknowledging the calls for workers in the more traditional missions both abroad and at home, the message broke new ground for young Friends."From the great world outside comes a multitude of calls to a newer, but no less fundamental service. Insistent are the demands that we avail ourselves of every opportunity to study and remedy the existing social conditions, which tend continually to produce misery, stunted personality, and great wealth for the few at the expense of the many."[4]

With the Earlham Conference over and with his wife and child going to Caldwell, Idaho, to spend the rest of the summer with Lilly's parents, Clarence made final preparations for his participation in the Conference of All Friends in London on the peace testimony and in the follow-up International Conference of Young Friends at the Jordans Friends Meeting House twenty miles outside of London. English Friends were hoping that there would be four hundred delegates at the London conference from American yearly meetings representing all three Quaker branches, Orthodox, Hicksite, and Conservative. In the end, 330 American Friends attended, these Friends being selected in accordance with yearly meeting quotas based on the number of members in a yearly meeting.

Having himself been selected, Clarence Pickett, working through his Board and through the American Friends Service Committee, took a particular interest in making sure that young Friends were generously included among the delegates. His Board hoped that at least fifty Young Friends from within the Five Years Meeting would be present at the London conference, and then at the Jordans gathering. While it was expected that the delegates would have credentials and financial assistance from their yearly meetings, English Friends asked the American Friends Service Committee to appoint some at-large delegates. The AFSC, engaged as it was with young Friends, particularly conscientious objectors such as those at work in Europe, felt that it was important to have some student Friends present from each of the Quaker colleges. As Bernard Walton, one of the associate secretaries of the AFSC stated it, "It is the feeling [within the AFSC] to make the work of the Conference count for the most, it should include a large number whose peace work will be in the future rather than in the past."[5]

Clarence Pickett left Richmond with some other delegates for the All-Friends Conference on 28 July 1920 with a stopover in Philadelphia. En route he realized that he had left behind his passport, steamship ticket, and income tax statement. "Needless to say, the situation produced some little agitation" he wrote, "and, as soon as we arrived in Philadelphia, I burnt up the telephone and telegraph wires trying to get word to Richmond about my predicament."[6] His alert secretary had discovered the documents and sent them on a later train in the care of another delegate.

He crossed the Atlantic on the White Star, *Baltic,* with about seventy-five other Friends bound for the London conference. The entire group of Friends on board had opportunities to meet together to discuss Commission reports that had been prepared in advance of the London conference, and to have meetings for worship "after the manner of Friends" referring to the traditional, unprogrammed form of worship. Reported Clarence: "I'm sure it would have been impossible to have told Hicksy [the Hicksite Quakers] from Doxy [the Orthodox Friends]. There were, if they had then counted up accurately, many variations of the Friendly theme represented, but it is doubtful if, under the shadow of the London Conference, any one remembered to inquire into his neighbor's peculiarities of thought or worship."[7]

On landing in Liverpool, Clarence and five other Friends did some sightseeing in the region prior to traveling to London. English Friends arranged for the hospitality of all foreign Friends in private homes in or near London. The first session of the Conference, open to the public, was held at the Methodist Central Hall, which had a capacity of two thousand. Rufus Jones lectured on "The Nature and Authority of Conscience." The hall was full. "It was excellent," said Clarence, "though a bit scholarly for some of our Friends, I'm sure."[8]

The London Conference closed on 22 August. Its final message was addressed "To Friends and Fellow-seekers." While it spoke of "Christ's way of life and His standard of values," it was far from a doctrinal, let alone a fundamentalist, statement. Addressed as it was primarily to the Religious Society of Friends itself, the message called Friends to self-examination and action.

> The world today is in sore need. Does it not rest in part with us whether its pains are to be the agonizing of a dying civilization or the birth pangs of a new and fairer life in which justice shall dwell? Have not we who call ourselves Christians been more than others responsible for the ruin and wreckage of human life which are left by war, for the oppression of the weaker races by the strong, for the evils within our social and industrial order which are still dwarfing and marring the lives of men?[9]

Clarence Pickett was then immediately involved with English Friends in final preparations for the International Young Friends Conference at Jordans Meeting. "All day Monday," he wrote Lilly, "I was captain of a squad of men who were getting the barn, riding room, women's rest room, cloakroom, and two recreation tents in order, so had no leisure. Then Tuesday, yesterday, was the day when we received people who came into the Conference, and so we've come on into Wednesday. Most of the crowd came about noon yesterday. They are now here, four hundred and twenty strong. . . . We have representatives from Great Britain, Ireland, France, Switzerland, Germany, Austria, Scandinavia, Japan, China, India, South Africa, Australia, New Zealand, and America (including Canada). These various groups were introduced, and one person spoke for each group. There were ninety-one Americans."[10] Wrote Clarence:

> One of the most touching scenes I've ever seen was when the chairman called for those from His Majesty's late enemy countries who are not, and never have been, our enemies. There was a burst of applause when five men and two women, including one man from Austria, arose. Then one German woman arose, and in a most tender and beautiful address of

ten minutes spoke in response. It even brought tears to stolid English eyes, and was quite too much for me.

The Germans are a fine lot, par excellence . . . the little mingling I've done with these young Germans makes me feel that its just another case of those subjected to military defeat being the real victors.[11]

As soon as the Jordans conference was over, Pickett went at once back to London and, under prior arrangement with his Board and the American Friends Service Committee, took off for Germany via Dover, Ostend (Belgium), and Cologne (in British occupied territory), and thence to Berlin. The following day he had his first opportunity to observe the child-feeding in Germany undertaken by Friends. Quakers were feeding children in three hundred places in the city of Berlin alone, and in Germany in fifteen different cities. Six hundred thousand children, soon to grow to over one million, were receiving one meal a day, largely through the schools.[12]

Clarence Pickett's quick tour of American Friends Service Committee operations in Germany at AFSC's expense was a measure of his growing relationship to the Committee. It was his involvement during the war as a visitor to Quaker COs in Army cantonments and the promotion of the opportunities for COs in the AFSC's Reconstruction Unit in France that first brought him into sympathetic contact with the Committee and its staff. And then there was his particular interest in the famine situation in Russia and his willingness to serve on an investigation committee. That opportunity never materialized, but in March 1921 he received a telegram from Wilbur Thomas. WE NOW NEED YOU IN RUSSIA HAVE A CALL FOR SECRETARY FOR MOSCOW IMPORTANT POSITION UNLIMITED OPPORTUNITY URGE YOU ACCEPT AND PLAN TO GO AT YOUR EARLIEST CONVENIENCE.

A follow-up letter from Thomas explained that the Committee was asking Clarence Pickett to "head up the office work, do some typewriting, and take charge of the office affairs as they [the field workers] travel about the country. It is a most responsible position, requiring a person of tact, one able to think clearly, also one who can keep his mouth shut. . . . Rufus [Jones], chairman of the Committee, and I have talked it over and others who know you are assured that you are the one."[13]

On the back of the letter Clarence Pickett scribbled two possible telegraphic replies: "Home obligations will likely prevent going to

Moscow;" and "Interested and think might get away from present work but home obligations will likely prevent going to Moscow."[14] It is not known which telegram he finally sent, but clearly he was not prepared to leave Lilly and little Rachel for a long-term assignment in war-torn Russia. Nor, it can be assumed, would he have seen this position, at least as Thomas described it in his letter, as responsible and important as the work that he was doing. Holed up in Moscow, he would have been completely out of touch with those concerns and issues within the Religious Society of Friends in America to which he was dedicated and for which he was considered by many to be a moving force.

In August 1921, Clarence Pickett had another request from Wilbur Thomas, Pickett to be an assistant secretary with responsibility for home service work. The two of them entered into rather extensive correspondence about just what the job would entail and how it might be coordinated with Clarence Pickett's position in the Five Years Meeting. Clarence Pickett agreed to spend the month of December 1921 in the Philadelphia office to set up the Home Service Department and to enable young Friends, especially those graduating from Quaker colleges, to have an opportunity to give a year of service in some kind of work in the United States on the same basis as those persons going to Europe. By early 1922 a Home Service Committee within the AFSC was established, with Clarence Pickett as part time field secretary. This work was integrated into his responsibilities under the Board of Young Friends Activities, with the AFSC making occasional payments to the Board for his services.

Clarence Pickett continued to be criticized for the program content and his leadership of the annual Young Friends Conferences held at Earlham College. In response to news that a member of the Greensboro, North Carolina, meeting had publicly stated in 1921 that the Young Friends Conference was unsound, he wrote an exceedingly forthright letter, saying in part:

> To say that the Conference is unsound when you have not been here, and when at the time you made the criticism the Conference had not even been held, and in the face of the fact that at least 99% of the people who attended the Conference, I should say, are led to a deeper experience of God in their lives, seems to me to be judging both falsely and without facts before you. It is a serious thing to criticize the religious faith and expression of anyone, and I hope that you understand that to say what you have said does that very thing.[15]

In respect to one of these gatherings at Earlham College, a California Friend asked whether an advocate of socialism was placed on the program deliberately. "I presume that those who are concerned," Pickett replied, "have in mind William Simkin. He definitely disavows any inclination towards socialism, but is rather concerned only with seeking to establish a type of life here which is definitely christian [*sic*] in all respects."[16] Then the same correspondent asked whether he, Clarence Pickett, had advocated the Socialist platform.

Clarence replied forthrightly, revealing that he had voted for Eugene Debs, the Socialist candidate for president. "I could not conscientiously vote for either of the major parties," he wrote. "I thoroughly disapproved of the candidates [Warren G. Harding, Republican, and James M. Cox, Democrat] and the platform on which they stood. I therefore sought the best possible way to protest, and I felt that a vote for the Socialist Party was the most vigorous protest that I could render."[17] He noted how carefully he had studied the platform of the Socialist party and the extent to which he had inquired into the life and character of Eugene Debs.

Clarence had made it clear when he became executive secretary of the Board of Young Friends Activities that he would serve only through the next sessions of the Five Years Meeting, 8-11 September 1922. Early in the year he was giving thought to what the next step would be for him. It was complicated by the happy circumstance of Lilly Pickett expecting another child in May. New England Yearly Meeting was trying to draw him back to their region, preferably as secretary of the Yearly Meeting's Board of Young Friends or alternately as pastor at the Moses Brown School.

Especially in light of the coming of a second child in the family, Lilly Pickett was undoubtedly hoping that there could be some respite from Clarence's frequent absences from home. The continuation of Young Friends Board responsibilities and the AFSC Home Service work was calculated to keep him on the run, away from home, much of the time. It is not surprising, therefore, that he gave fresh consideration to the proposal he had received some years earlier from president David Edwards of Earlham College to join the faculty of the College, enabling him to continue his relationship with young people.

His closest friend, Alexander Purdy, having continued on at Hartford Theological Seminary to obtain a Ph.D., was Professor of Biblical Literature and Church History at the College and was in addition the College pastor. The Purdy and Pickett families visited each other frequently in Richmond. They surely must have discussed at length the work of the 1920 Joint Committee of Indiana and Western Yearly Meetings to "investigate the Religious, Scholastic, and Sanitary conditions of Earlham College."[18] It was these two yearly meetings that had jurisdiction over Earlham. Reporting in March 1921, the Joint Committee by majority vote cleared the College of failing to follow the fundamental principles of the Friends Church and the 1887 Richmond declaration of faith as published in the Uniform Discipline. The report noted that the method of Bible study was historical or scientific in contrast to the approach under which literal meanings are ascribed to the Scriptures.[19]

The report to the Trustees must have been judged reasonably satisfactory by Alexander Purdy, but, possibly because of the stress of the investigation and anticipated continuing tensions between the College and the more orthodox Friends in the two yearly meetings, Purdy accepted an invitation from Hartford Theological Seminary to join the faculty as Professor of Practical Theology, beginning in the 1923-24 academic year. He taught at Hartford until 1960.

This left the way open for Clarence Pickett to apply for the position that Purdy was vacating. The terms of Clarence Pickett's appointment were spelled out in a letter from President Edwards to him in September 1922, and the College's annual catalogue listed him as Professor of Biblical Literature and Church History (elect). He was also appointed College pastor. This decision by the College enabled him to take a year of graduate study, this time at the Harvard Divinity School, with scholarship assistance from the School and the Society for the Promotion of Theological Education.

He and his family, now four of them, with Carolyn Hope Pickett (born 5 May 1922) only three months old, moved to Cambridge, Massachusetts, and lived for the academic year in a cramped apartment in Cambridge. Without working towards a particular degree, Clarence took two courses in the Old Testament, one in the New Testament, and a fourth, "Philosophy of the State." He also audited "Beginnings of Church History" and a social ethics course, "The Study of Character in Difficulties." Every Sunday he journeyed to the Moses Brown School in Providence to be in charge of meetings for worship at the school. Even with this commitment, and with other occasional responsibilities at Young Friends gatherings along the eastern seaboard, Clarence Pickett was more able than in the immediately preceding years to be a family man at home with his wife and children. This relationship was to prevail through the six succeeding years at Earlham.

NOTES

1. Pickett papers, AFSC archives.

2. Pickett papers, AFSC archives.

3. Report of executive secretary to the Young Friends Board for calendar year 1920, Earlham College, Richmond, IN: Lilly Library archives.

4. *The American Friend* (new series) 8, no. 29 (15 July 1990): 645.

5. Pickett papers, AFSC archives.

6. Clarence E. Pickett, Trip report: Europe Oct. 1920, family papers, courtesy of Carolyn Pickett Miller.

7. Clarence Pickett to Lilly Pickett, 15 Aug. 1920.

8. Pickett, Trip report, 1920.

9. The [London] Friend 60, no. 35 (27 Aug. 1920): 535.

10. Clarence Pickett to Lilly Pickett, 25 Aug. 1920.

11. Clarence Pickett to Lilly Pickett, 25 Aug. 1920.

12. Trip report, 1920.

13. Thomas to Pickett, 3 Mar. 1921, Pickett papers, AFSC archives.

14. Thomas to Pickett, 3 Mar. 1921.

15. Pickett to Nathan Andrews, 7 Sept. 1921, Pickett papers, AFSC archives.

16. Pickett to Harry Keates, 10 Dec. 1920, Pickett papers, AFSC archives.

17. Pickett to Keates, 10 Dec. 1920.

18. *Earlham College Bulletin* (new series) 4, no. 2 (April 1921): 1-14. Earlham College, Richmond, IN: Lilly Library archives.

19. *Bulletin*, 1921.

Chapter 7

EARLHAM COLLEGE PROFESSOR

*To release the creative life that lies latent
in its students*

LILLY PICKETT WOULD LOOK UPON THE YEARS at Earlham College as "the happiest years of our married life. The family was all together, Clarence stayed at home, and everybody came home for lunch."[1] They had purchased a large house, having rented a half-house the previous years in Richmond. She was contrasting, of course, those six years at the college during which he was Professor of Biblical Literature and Church History with the three years that he was Young Friends Secretary and the years beginning in September 1929, when he worked for the American Friends Service Committee. This is not to suggest that Clarence Pickett was turning down engagements away from Richmond. Indeed, he welcomed such opportunities.

Earlham College was the outgrowth of the educational enterprise which characterized the pioneer Quaker settlers of eastern Indiana and western Ohio. It was opened as a school of advanced grade in 1847. In 1859 it was organized as a college. Its earliest officers and teachers were men and women from New England, whose refinement, force of character, and scholarly attainments gave the school from its beginning an enviable reputation throughout the Ohio Valley.

From the very beginning, consistent with Quaker traditions, it was coeducational. It was (and still is today) under the auspices of the Religious Society of Friends, as represented by Indiana and Western

Yearly Meetings. During Clarence Pickett's years these two yearly meetings, along with the Alumni Association, appointed members to the board of trustees. In summary, its stated purpose was to offer the advantages of a liberal education in an atmosphere that was "stimulating, scholarly, democratic, and thoroughly Christian."[2] But in his final academic year at the institution, Pickett saw the aims of the College in more expansive terms. "The aim of Earlham College," he wrote to an interested party, "should be to *release* the creative *life* that lies latent in its students; to give it direction as it develops; and to assist in hooking it up to some load that needs carrying."[3] He noted that this aim was in part based on "absolute honesty and sincerity as the atmosphere they [the students] breathe in the school . . . and frequent contacts with stimulating personalities outside our group who can help in the release of creative life."[4]

From the time of his very first semester in the 1923-24 academic year Clarence Pickett taught a formidable array of courses. Every year he taught Old Testament history, with special attention to the development of social and religious ideas; The Life and Teachings of Jesus; Biblical Literature; Modern Social Problems and the Teaching of Jesus (an elective). Then in alternate years, he taught Christian Fundamentals, History of Friends, History of the Christian Church, Religions of the World, and the preparation and delivery of sermons. Clarence's course on social problems, a study of the practicability of the Christian life under modern social conditions, was his most popular course, open to all students, not only those working towards a degree in his Department of Biblical Literature and Church History. In fact, even in his first year of teaching this course, seventy-one students registered, and he had to hold it in two sections, even though he was not "thoroughly satisfied with the way in which this course is worked out."[5]

Clarence served on various faculty committees: for two years, the committee on freshman advisors; two years on the personnel committee; and in his final year, 1928-29, the standing committee for public lectures. This committee on outside speakers tied in the most with his position as pastor of the college. He actively brought to the campus to speak at chapel services (compulsory during his first academic year), to YMCA and YWCA meetings, and to his own classes, leaders, Friends and non-Friends, who could challenge students and who provided an example of lives full of religious faith. Among these was his own brother-in-law, Gilbert Bowles, the foundation stone for the College's increasing interest in sending a student to Japan; the theologian Reinhold Niebuhr; Rufus Jones, the eminent Haverford College professor of philosophy; Alexander Purdy from Hartford Theological Seminary; Edgar Goodspeed, the Biblical scholar; Paul Hutchinson, editor of *The Christian Century*; Garry August, a Jewish rabbi; and Friend Thomas Kelly, who became professor of philosophy at Earlham in the fall of 1924. Clarence Pickett himself provided most of the sermons at the College services, customarily speaking from notes neatly handwritten on an index card.

During his years at Earlham College Pickett continued to keep in touch with the Home Service office of the American Friends Service Committee, to correspond with young Friends, and to counsel on the campus with students regarding their future plans. He was the hub of information for Friends, young and old, who were looking for vocational and avocational opportunities to apply the Quaker testimonies on peace and social justice. Many of these Friends, such as Hugh Moore from Winston-Salem, North Carolina; Elizabeth Marsh, his successor as secretary of the Board of Young Friends Activities of the Five Years Meeting; his brother-in-law Errol Peckham; and Clay Treadway, working at the Southland Institute (a Quaker school for African-Americans in Arkansas), eventually were drawn into the orbit of the American Friends Service Committee when Clarence became its executive secretary in 1929. He was a magnetic force around which the lives of many younger Friends revolved and developed. He always seemed to be available for Young Friends Conferences and for individual consultations.

During Clarence's first academic year at Earlham the College decided to have a summer school, with a number of the faculty members to be involved and the timing not to conflict with the Young Friends Conference. As it developed, the summer session ended in early August, making it possible for the Pickett family to go to Buck Hill Falls, Pennsylvania, for a vacation. The Buck Hill Falls community had begun as a summer colony for Hicksite Friends in 1901. In that same year an independent local meeting of Friends was established, independent in the sense that it was not formally related to any quarterly or yearly meeting. The colony grew to embrace one hundred and fifty or more cottages and the Buck Hill Falls Inn, which had a capacity for four hundred guests. A large percentage of the summer residents were non-

Friends. The meetings for worship were held at the Inn. While most of those attending were Hicksite Friends, there were also Orthodox Friends and persons of other denominations.

Clarence Pickett headed up an international house on the Buck Hill Falls grounds, with accommodations for a host and hostess family and seven guests. During the summer of 1928, as many as thirty-six guests from sixteen different countries stayed at the house for varying periods of time. As Clarence and Lilly Pickett expressed it in an article in *The American Friend*, "Certainly the world has flowed in and out of our doors . . . the Friendly approach to religion, basing it on an experience rather than on forms or creeds, and our fundamental belief in the quality of godlikeness in men, draw men of all faiths and beliefs into a family of love, whether Mohammedan, Jew, Hindu, or Christian."[6] This program at Buck Hill Falls not only enriched Clarence Pickett's relationships with persons of other faiths and from different countries, it also put him in touch with the many American organizations that were reaching out to foreign students.

Quite apart from the summer programs at Buck Hill Falls, there was another movement, centered in Philadelphia, which was of interest to Clarence. This was Woolman School (named after the revered New Jersey Quaker abolitionist, John Woolman) which was born as a concern of the Advancement Committee of Friends General Conference, an association of six Hicksite yearly meetings. The concern was to have a longer course of training for religious workers than could be provided in short summer schools. The school opened in January 1915 in a three-story house in Swarthmore, Pennsylvania, with the understanding that Swarthmore College would later be interested in taking over the house. At its first session, eleven students, mostly women, were taught courses on the Bible, Quakerism, religious education, psychology, and social welfare and reform.[7]

In 1917 the Advancement Committee sought ways to have the school serve a wider group than one branch of Friends. The Whittier Fellowship Committee, an informal group representing all branches of Friends, was asked to name a representative board of managers. This was done, and the school was turned over to this board in the summer of 1917, in time to provide a residence for fifteen trainees for reconstruction work with the American Friends Service Committee in France. But the problems of finding students and money remained acute for Woolman School.

In 1925 Swarthmore College expressed a wish to take over the house. It looked as if the school would then be homeless, but Mary Lippincott, owner of an estate in Wyncote, a suburb east of Philadelphia, offered her property to the school, convinced that racial and economic relations were the most challenging problems facing the Religious Society of Friends, and that Woolman School was attempting to deal with them creatively.

In that same year the school asked Alexander Purdy to be the full-time director of studies. He declined the appointment and suggested Clarence Pickett as "the person best fitted for the place, in my judgment, certainly far better fitted than I."[8] But Purdy did not encourage his close friend to accept the appointment unless he had a very strong concern to do it. Purdy saw that the director, in addition to teaching responsibilities, "will be compelled to help raise money, recruit students, travel, in short do in a small way the work of a college president."[9] Having taught at two of the summer schools held in Swarthmore, Purdy noted the extent to which the whole project called for a pioneering spirit. "To study and at the same time to experience racial, international, interreligious problems is exceedingly stimulating," he said.[10]

Clarence Pickett gave the request from the Woolman School board serious consideration, traveling to Philadelphia for three days of consultations and interviews, and staying with his close friends, Paul and Betty Furnas, who were much involved in the project. Clarence did not immediately turn down the offer. In the spring of 1926 he was asked by Caroline Norment, the acting director, to give three lectures at the summer school, during those weeks that the Pickett family was to be at Buck Hill Falls. This he agreed to do, but at the same time said that he did not feel free to ask the Woolman School board to keep the door open for him as a possible director of studies. In subsequent years he sustained a strong interest in the school as it went through a time of metamorphosis, eventually resulting in the birth of Pendle Hill, the adult center for study and contemplation which became a thriving institution, based in Wallingford, a suburb west of Philadelphia. Drawn as he must have been to the pioneering features of the Woolman School venture, Clarence must have seen the disadvantages of uprooting his family, with Rachel already in school, for a move to Philadelphia. Yet in another four years he would be making precisely that move, to head the American Friends Service Committee.

There is little doubt that Clarence Pickett, even in 1925, was beginning to experience the discomforts of being a theological liberal and a peace and justice activist within the yearly meetings, Indiana and Western, that had jurisdiction over Earlham College. As a case in point, it was probably Clarence, as pastor of the college and head of the religion department, who suggested that Harry Emerson Fosdick be invited to give the baccalaureate sermon in June 1925. Dr. Fosdick, by that time as author of *The Manhood of the Master* and the "three meanings"— *The Meaning of Prayer, The Meaning of Faith, and The Meaning of Service*—was one of America's outstanding exponents of liberal Christianity. It was in May 1922 that he stood in the pulpit of the First Presbyterian Church in New York as that church's minister (even though he was a Baptist) to preach one of the most far-reaching sermons of his career, "Shall the Fundamentalists Win?" He had already declared "belief in the Virgin birth nonessential, the inerrancy of the Scriptures incredible, the Second Coming of Christ from the skies an outmoded phrasing of hope."[11] With financial aid from John D. Rockefeller, Jr., a dedicated Christian liberal who was later to finance the building of Riverside Church with Fosdick as its first minister, the sermon was distributed to every ordained Protestant clergyman in the country and was reprinted in *The Christian Century* and *The Baptist.* Certainly Quaker pastors, although not formally ordained, would have read the sermon and discussed it with fundamentalists of other denominations.

In spite of the dissatisfaction his services as professor and pastor at Earlham College were engendering among fundamentalist Friends, Clarence made remarkable contributions to the lives of his students. Apart from the commendations he received from ex-students throughout subsequent years, the archival material on his sermons is equally revealing. Week after week after week it was Clarence Pickett who gave the sermon at the college's Sunday chapel services. The record in the Earlham College bulletins reveals that many of them focused on the life of Jesus, viewed by Pickett as a radical, "not in the sense of one who waves a red flag and creates confusion, but radical as explained by its real meaning, which is 'root'."[12] Said Pickett:

> It was with purpose that he [Jesus] identified himself with John the Baptist, for he realized that he would be better able to carry his message if he were linked up in the beginning with a radical religious movement. . . .

During his days of temptation in the wilderness, Jesus decided upon his method. Ideas of using force and magic came to him, but he put them aside and planned instead to win men with a message of love and good will. . . . Jesus identified himself with the needy and the sinful.[13] Jesus placed the emphasis not on the dim, distant future but on the glowing, ever-present today, with its many and varied perplexities."[14]

Clarence Pickett, often using a scriptural text, always emphasized the personal applications of religious truths over theological abstractions. "We can no longer preach religion. We must no longer force our thoughts on others. We must live our Christianity and live true to our convictions. Life is incomplete unless it is shared."[15] He would repeatedly cite examples of great souls and their influence on others, such as the impact Tolstoy had upon the life of Jane Addams, the American social worker. He noted how Mahatma Gandhi was plumbing the depths of the significance of the life of Jesus. In a sermon entitled "Shall this Christmas Count for Good?" he referred to Gandhi's profound influence upon Jan Christian Smuts of South Africa.

Pickett urged students and others to read the Bible daily and to commit passages to memory. He recommended the Weymouth, Moffatt, and Goodspeed translations and the American Revised Version. He was frequently asked for his recommendation of books that would promote an understanding of the Bible and of Quaker faith and generally aid the devotional life. He would suggest, of course, relevant books by Rufus Jones and Henry Cadbury (fast becoming one of the foremost Biblical scholars in the country), but his recommendations went far beyond the limited field of Quaker writers. Frequently on his list would be Rudolph Otto's *The Idea of the Holy*, George A. Barton's *Jesus of Nazareth*, Luther Weigle's *Training the Devotional Life*, and Ernest F. Scott's *The First Age of Christianity*. Always the intent of his wide-ranging suggestions was to urge the correspondent to become a seeker after truth and to link up intellectual searching with both individual and social moral issues.

Clarence Pickett made a deep impact upon many students. Writing twenty-five years later, Leslie Shaffer, one of his students and a person who in his own life distinguished himself, commented on Pickett's influence:

It seems like a long time since those days at Earlham when you interpreted to your classes Quaker history and the lives of the Old

Testament prophets. I have always been grateful for the manner in which you made those religious reformers vivid to me, especially Amos. He seems as real as though I had met him personally.[16]

And this from yet another one of his students, Stanley Hamilton:

I shall long remember studying Modern Social Problems with Clarence as instructor, visiting the social agencies, the county jail, the various churches in Richmond, and also the slums north of the tracks. I had a social conscience before coming to Earlham, but I am very sure that Clarence polished it up a great deal.[17]

Early in his years at Earlham College he had determined that race relations, specifically the relations between whites and blacks, was a crucial moral issue. For their records, the Mitchell County, Kansas, schools asked teachers to indicate whether there were "colored" children in their classes. It would appear that there were none in the actual classes of which Clarence was a member, nor were there any in the classes he taught. But at Penn College there was a black in his graduating class. It is not clear whether she was an American or a Jamaican. Iowa Yearly Meeting since 1881 had had a mission in Jamaica, and it is quite possible that she was Jamaican.

As pastor of Earlham College, Pickett was understandably drawn into interracial matters. As a key member, then chairman, of the Southland Committee under the Board of Home Missions of the Five Years Meeting, he already had some experience in this field. The Southland Institute was an elementary and high school "for Negroes" in Arkansas, founded and operated with a missionary emphasis. In the mid-'20s Pickett was involved in the devolvement of Quaker responsibility for the Institute.

Replying to a letter from Esther Morton Smith, chairperson of the Race Relations Committee of the Orthodox Philadelphia Yearly Meeting, he described the situation at the College shortly after assuming his position at Earlham. "We have this year two colored boys as students at Earlham, one of whom is a senior living in the boys' dormitory."[18] He pointed out that "both in courses with Professor [Homer] Morris in Sociology, and in Modern Social Problems in the Biblical Department, race relations are frankly discussed. . . . It is here that the most constructive thinking is done."[19]

He reported on the occasional meetings of Richmond's interracial committee, with much of the impetus for these meetings coming from college faculty members. He noted that "the activity of the Klan is a good deal in evidence in the state of Indiana."[20] Answering a letter to the chairperson of the Interracial Committee, Pickett replied positively to the request of an African American stenographer for a job in Richmond, but he was unsuccessful in breaking the color line on her behalf.

At the college itself he became much involved in the plight of Harold Ballysingh, a student from the Jamaica Friends mission, who experienced no prejudice at the college, but in Richmond was grossly discriminated against in respect to lodging, employment, and eating at restaurants. In correspondence regarding a second Jamaican student, Clarence wrote, "I think we all ought to be more ardent in our efforts to change the general attitude on the matter of race, but, of course, you understand that we cannot prevent Harold Ballysingh, nor anyone else who is dark, from coming up against embarrassing and difficult situations."[21]

As much as the board's Committee on Religious Instruction, President David Edwards, key faculty members, and students may have approved of the college's courses in religion and its pastor, there were Friends within the two yearly meetings, Western and Indiana, who felt that the college was seriously out of step with the doctrines of Friends. They were Friends of the mind of Albert Copeland, who had objected vigorously to the invitation to Harry Emerson Fosdick. "Fundamentalist" in their beliefs, they found solid support for their views in a lengthy statement, the Richmond Declaration of Faith, which had been adopted by orthodox yearly meetings in 1887.

These Friends also tended to be conservative politically. Pickett's outspoken views on a whole range of issues, such as the World Court, race relations, and industrial problems, were generally at variance with the opinions of Christian fundamentalists. In spite of Rufus Jones' open support of presidential candidate Herbert Hoover, himself a Quaker,[22] in 1928, Clarence Pickett supported Norman Thomas, the candidate for the Socialist Party, seeing the Republican Party "tied up with privilege and prosperity as a dead weight of conservatism."[23]

It is likely that two articles by Clarence Pickett which appeared in successive issues of *The American Friend,* 23 February and 1 March 1928, contributed materially to the erosion of support for him among fundamentalist Friends. The first compared the democracy of the Spirit that characterized the early Christian church with "the unholy marriage of a capitalist social order with the [present day] church. Prosperity first, which became her slogan, led to a belief that God was with the prosperous. . . . One of the most tragic facts of the world in which we live is that our so-called Christian civilization has been so successful in convincing the world of its superiority. . . . Undue emphasis upon dogma, legalistic religion, and institutionalism have supplanted Christianity as a joyous fellowship of friends in quest of God and of life."[24]

The second article, first published in *The Christian Century,* and entitled "What Worries the Quaker," was as hard-hitting as the first. He compared the idealism of the Society in the war and post-war years—its pacifism and projects of good will in Europe—with the present day lack of protest and experimentation in respect to the acquisitive American society:

> The whole war setting conspired to make the case of the pacifist conspicuous and dramatic. He was called to bear his testimony before generals, majors, judges, advocates, and tribunals. He was rooted up out of his home environment and released to show a practical idealism at work in a war-torn world. In camp and in France, his very clothing marked him off from others. And whereas he might cherish the same love for a warless world as his soldier brother, his method of securing that world was quite as important as his goal. The method itself brought reconciliation. Then he returned to America. It was an America pleading for normalcy. He sought his place in a competitive business world, "red with tooth and claw." For the most part he fitted into that world with slight and usually ineffective protest.[25]

Then Clarence Pickett deals with the causes of Quaker impotence. First, was the nature of the Quaker constituency. He saw the Religious Society of Friends as not generically a church but rather a fellowship, ideally made up of men and women cemented by a common view of life. But he notes that the Society has in fact become a church, the Friends Church, with most members not seeing deeply into the inner meaning of the peace testimony. "The fact that war debauched personality, that race prejudice and modern factory systems do the same thing, were not deep-seated convictions with great numbers of Friends."[26]

Secondly, he noted the divisions among Friends, the legacy of the nineteenth century separations. And, "as our third handicap I would place our lack of knowledge of our historic view of God and man. Too many Quakers are Calvinists. . . . The Puritan Calvinist often speaks through the modern Quaker ministry with its doctrine of selfish salvation, its appeal to materialism, and the support of capitalism. . . . The rainy-day old-age care-of-family nest-to-be-feathered view of life so religiously entrenched in our social order, holds us. . . . Loss of prestige, loss of membership, loss of money, personal suffering, lie down the pathway for the Quaker who will release moral and religious forces in an acquisitive, militaristic, race-prejudiced society."[27]

This forthright criticism of the Religious Society of Friends must have shocked many Quakers in both pastoral and unprogrammed meetings. While the article seemed to be directed especially at the fundamentalist churches, many members of the meetings holding to the traditional form of worship, yet espousing a more liberal theology, would have seen themselves accurately portrayed in what he said. As he stated, "The promotion and actual work of the war and postwar service was due to the vision of a very small percentage of the Society."[28] It was the American Friends Service Committee that had gathered these Friends into this widely acclaimed witness, with generous financial support from all segments of the Society's membership.

Despite the favorable report of the board of trustees' Committee on Religious Instruction in 1927, it is clear that during the 1928 calendar year there was an erosion of support for reappointing Clarence Pickett to the positions he held at Earlham College. By the beginning of January 1929 no definite decision had been made by the trustees.

Following the board of trustees' meeting in February, Clarence Pickett was given to understand, "that there was considerable disturbance on the part of some Western Yearly Meeting Friends and the board members, about my connection with Earlham, and that there was probably not more than one year's tenure ahead of me. With that in mind I immediately turned my attention to two calls which were already on my desk."[29] It was not until 9 March that his supporters in Richmond sent out a "Dear Friend" letter to alumni and others:

> Earlham College is facing a crisis again. Clarence Pickett has received recently two calls to positions in the East, and the Earlham board of trustees, because of a difference of opinion within the board, has made no effort officially as yet to keep him at Earlham. Their silence is being interpreted as opposition to him, and he will decide soon whether to go or stay. Some of us fear the loss of other members of the faculty also, unless there is some vigorous expression supporting the present type of

Christian activities on the campus. There seems to be considerable chance of convincing doubtful members of the board of the value of Earlham's present distinctive religious contribution, if former students and friends of Earlham will express themselves.[30]

Clarence Pickett received many letters expressing deep appreciation for his teaching and urging him to stay at Earlham. But it was too late. He was far downstream in his consideration of the two calls in the East.

One of these was from George School, a Hicksite Quaker boarding school in Bucks County, Pennsylvania, founded in 1893. On 6 December 1928 George Walton, principal of George School, had written to a number of teachers of Bible in Quaker colleges, scouting for suggestions for "an outstanding person" to teach Bible and become director of religious life for the school. Clarence Pickett replied that he might be interested in the position himself. Having undoubtedly had contacts with Clarence Pickett at Buck Hill Falls, Walton was delighted to know of his interest, and on 1 January 1929 wrote him a long letter outlining the responsibilities, the housing options, the probable salary—$3,500, $300 more than Clarence was making at Earlham—and pointing out that the Pickett children, when eligible to enter the School, would be able to attend tuition-free. Then, on 30 January, following a meeting of the George School Committee, the position was immediately formally offered by telegram at a salary of $4,000, plus the prospect of a house on campus starting in the 1930-31 academic year. Lilly Pickett was invited to come and visit the campus.

Throughout February Clarence Pickett began to receive telegrams from school committee members, urging him to accept the appointment. Lilly and Clarence visited the school in late February. But he pleaded for additional time to make a decision, stating that Richmond Friends were urging him to delay his decision "because of a local problem."[31] Just what that local problem was is not clear. Richmond Friends may have felt that, given additional time, the trustees would shift to a position of support for him. George Walton wrote on March 8: "Both from a standpoint of George School alone as well as the best distribution of the available working force of the Religious Society of Friends, it would seem better for thee to be at George School, and this Friend [George School's second choice] to remain where he is. I want thee very much, and hope that thy decision will be in George School's favor."[32]

The second call was from the American Friends Service Committee. In the small Philadelphia Quaker world, many Friends knew that the American Friends Service Committee was engaged in a process of introspection and reorganization. In May 1928 Henry Cadbury was appointed chairperson following the resignation of Rufus Jones from that position. Then in June Jones was appointed honorary chairman. In November they both called together about forty Friends active in the work of the Committee. The gathering was "to discuss the situation that now confronts us in American Quakerism."[33] One option mentioned was "to suspend its [AFSC's] mission until a new crisis may call it into being."[34] These searching discussions continued into the next year within what came to be termed the Reorganization Committee.

A number of Friends functioned on both sides of the fence that Clarence Pickett was soon straddling. One of these was William Eves, dean of George School, who with George Walton had a tenured position at the School. He was chairman of the AFSC's Foreign Service Section and was in that capacity a member of other key AFSC committees. He was also an active member of the Woolman School board and, therefore, aware of the interest of all three institutions in Pickett.

Henry Cadbury announced publicly that Wilmer Thomas was retiring as executive secretary at the beginning of February, 1929.[35] Anna B. Griscom became acting secretary, pending the appointment of another executive secretary. Mary Hoxie Jones, daughter of Rufus Jones and Young Friends Secretary of the Orthodox Philadelphia Yearly Meeting and as such a co-opted member of the AFSC board, claimed in later life that it was she and "Uncle Henry" [Cadbury] who, in an informal conversation in Cambridge, Massachusetts, came to the conclusion that Clarence Pickett was the right man to succeed Wilbur Thomas. "Finding a successor for Wilbur Thomas was a very delicate, difficult and important task," she said.[36]

Clarence needed no introduction to anyone close to the workings of the AFSC. He was well known (although not uniformly appreciated) in all branches of the Religious Society of Friends. The fact that he had been a pastor and closely associated with the Five Years Meeting of Friends was not a barrier for those who knew him personally, heard him as a teacher, and experienced how he worked with others. Yet, considering the tensions that existed between Orthodox and Hicksite Friends across the country, it must have come as a surprise that George School, the boarding school of Hicksite Quakers *par excellence,* was so keen to have him join the faculty.

On 21 February Clarence Pickett was offered the position of AFSC executive secretary, for a three-year term at $5,000 a year. This was done in a Western Union night letter from Henry Cadbury on 21 February 1929 following a meeting of the Reorganization Committee, clearly the inner circle of those Friends who had been corporately responding to Rufus Jones' November call, and who by that date were ready to present their plan, including the name of the next executive secretary, to the whole Service Committee.

The Reorganization Committee's hope for a quick decision on Clarence Pickett's part was not realized. He already had George School's proposal in hand. It is likely that Lilly Pickett was leaning toward the more settled life style that the George School position would offer. Leaving Richmond would be a big adjustment under any circumstances. In the case of George School there would at least be the benefit of moving into a close community, with a house on campus promised at the start of the 1930-31 school year. They would be able to transfer their membership to nearby Newtown Meeting, a thriving meeting with an active First-day [Sunday] School. It was not until mid-March that Clarence and Lilly Pickett made up their minds. He telegraphed his acceptance of the AFSC offer to Henry Cadbury. He also wired his decision to George Walton: "It is with very deep regret that I feel I must decline the place at George School. Thee and the Committee have been most generous and fair, but it seems right for me to accept the Service Committee position."[37] In a follow-up letter he said, "It was, I think, the most difficult telegram I ever wrote."[38]

In less than a week, and even before Clarence Pickett's starting date, 15 June, as executive secretary, Anna Griscom, acting executive secretary of the AFSC, wrote to Clarence to inform him that she was having his name placed on the list "to receive all the minutes of the committees and all other publicity material which goes out. . . . I hope that thee won't be overwhelmed."[39] Ray Newton, secretary of the Peace Section, Margaret Jones, secretary of the Home Service Section, and Bernard Walton, chairman of the AFSC nominating committee, were soon corresponding with him.

Notwithstanding the immediate onslaught of paper and requests for advice from 20 South 12th Street where the offices of the American

Friends Service Committee in Philadelphia were based, the academic year was not at an end, and Clarence Pickett had multiple responsibilities at the college. One noteworthy event, which had a postscript in the first months of his work at the AFSC and which strongly reflected his views on race relations, was the arrangement worked out for himself, another faculty member, and about fifteen students to visit Wilberforce University, an African American church institution in Wilberforce, Ohio. The visit was made on a Sunday in May, providing an opportunity to attend the morning worship service, to have lunch as guests of the university, and then a time of discussion with some Wilberforce faculty members and students.

The visit was a great success in the opinion of both groups. Clarence Pickett wrote to his counterpart at Wilberforce, Professor Charles H. Johnson, that the fellowship together "marked a milestone in their [his students'] thinking and spiritual development, and it was a great strength to all of us. I hope that you may be able to come to us."[40] Johnson likewise expressed great appreciation for the contact with Earlham College students and faculty members and welcomed the idea of a group visiting Earlham, but he doubted that such a visit could be made in the remaining weeks of the academic year. Clarence, knowing that he would not be at the college the following year, urged Johnson to be in touch with Dean Harry Wright the following year.

In the autumn of 1929 some of the same Earlham College students did indeed propose a visit of Wilberforce students to Earlham. They were embarrassed at the reticence of the new administration under President William Dennis to permit such a return visit. Clarence Pickett felt under an obligation to write to President Dennis in support of the proposed visit. "I personally feel that it is a tragedy to break off fellowship which is so extremely valuable to students, and which prepares them for the social contacts of the world in which they are about to enter."[41]

President Dennis replied in a five-page letter, pointing out that his objection revolved around the wish of the Earlham group to be completely at liberty to discuss all aspects of race relations with the Wilberforce delegation, including interracial marriage. Dennis was unwilling to have any event "stir up a wholly unnecessary controversy just as we are trying to start a new administration of the College,"[42] pointing out that there were several African American students at the college together with some non-American students. "It must be remembered,"

he wrote, "that Earlham is now suffering from misconstruction as respects this general question of race relations. She is suffering misconstruction, both in the East and the West, from the unfortunate marriage
growing out of the association here at Earlham between a man student
from Jamaica, I believe of East Indian extraction [Harold Ballysingh],
and one of our white girl students [Marion Cowperthwaite]."[43]

Pickett replied immediately, noting that President Gilbert Jones of
Wilberforce, two or three of their faculty members, and two Earlham
College faculty members were present when the students talked with
each other. "The question of interracial marriage was raised," Pickett
wrote, "as it is sure to be in any group that frankly discusses race
questions. . . . If it is suppressed, then it is carried on in bootleg fashion,
under cover. In my judgment, it is far better to discuss the matter
openly and frankly. . . . That is what I mean by the right educational
approach: to open up the facts and acquaint students with what is really
happening racially about us, is better than to let them feel that it is a
forbidden subject.[44]

In no way would Clarence Pickett have considered the marriage of
Harold Ballysingh and Marion Cowperthwaite as "unfortunate." He
described them in later years as "rather intimate friends of the [his]
family." Harold went on to become a lawyer in Jamaica, Marion to become secretary of the Council of Social Agencies of Jamaica. Their
daughter went to the Quaker boarding school, Westtown, located west
of Philadelphia, from which both of Clarence's daughters graduated.

In this controversy at Earlham College Clarence Pickett was
expressing the strong bias for open discussion of issues, no matter how
sensitive and difficult, that characterized his life as a teacher and as a
leader of the American Friends Service Committee. In succeeding years
he would interject this approach into many troublesome issues, always
with a spirit that engendered respect and affectionate regard from those
who differed with his point of view. And there would be no holding
back from controversial issues.

NOTES

1. Margaret Hope Bacon, taped interview with Lilly Pickett, 1972.

2. 1925-26 *Earlham College Bulletin,* 11. Earlham College, Richmond IN: Lilly Library archives.

3. Ernest A. Wildman papers, 1928, Earlham College, Richmond IN: Lilly Library, Friends Collection.

4. Wildman papers, 1928.

5. Letter, Pickett to Samuel Hayworth, London Yearly Meeting, 22 May 1924, AFSC Archives.

6. "American Good Will Embassy," *The American Friend* (new series) 16, no. 38 (30 Sept. 1928): 680.

7. Carol Murphy, "The Roots of Pendle Hill," Pendle Hill Pamphlet #223 (Wallingford, PA: Pendle Hill Publications, 1979).

8. Letter, Purdy to Pickett, 13 Dec. 1925, Pickett papers, AFSC archives.

9. Purdy letter, 1925.

10. Purdy letter, 1925.

11. Robert Moats Miller, *Harry Emerson Fosdick: Preacher, Pastor, Prophet,* (New York: Oxford, 1985), 116.

12. Earlham College *Quaker Quill,* 18 Oct. 1926, Earlham College, Richmond, IN: Lilly Library, Friends Collection.

13. *Quill,* 11 Oct. 1926.

14. *Quill,* 22 Nov. 1926.

15. *Quill,* 13 June 1927.

16. Shaffer to Pickett, 4 Apr. 1950, Pickett family papers.

17. Hamilton to Pickett, 12 May 1950, AFSC archives.

18. Pickett to Esther Morton Smith, 15 Nov. 1923, Pickett papers, AFSC archives.

19. Pickett to Smith, 1923.

20. Pickett to Smith, 1923.

21. Pickett to Milo Hinkle, Ashboro Street Friends Church, Greensboro, NC, 11 Jan. 1926, Pickett papers, AFSC archives.

22. Jones to Walter Woodward, 27 Apr. 1928, Haverford College, Haverford, PA: Magill Library, Quaker Collection.

23. Pickett to William Simkin, 8 Nov. 1928, Pickett papers, AFSC archives.

24. Clarence E. Pickett, "The Church and Race," *The American Friend* (new series) 16, no. 8 (23 Feb. 1928): 131-32.

25. Clarence E. Pickett, "What Worries the Quaker," *The Christian Century* 65, no. 7 (23 Feb. 1928): 238-39.

26. Pickett, "What Worries the Quaker."

27. Pickett, "What Worries the Quaker."

28. Pickett, "What Worries the Quaker."

29. Pickett to Paul H. Douglas (later U.S. Senator Douglas), 23 Mar. 1929, Pickett papers, AFSC archives.

30. "Dear Friend" letter, 9 March 1929, Pickett papers, AFSC archives.

31. Mentioned in Walton's reply to Pickett, 8 Mar. 1929, Pickett papers, AFSC archives.

32. Walton to Pickett.

33. Letter from Rufus Jones and Henry Cadbury, 13 Nov. 1928, Haverford College, Haverford, PA: Magill Library, Quaker Collection.

34. Letter from Jones and Cadbury.

35. Minutes of the AFSC board of directors, 1 Feb. 1929, AFSC archives.

36. Taped interview with Mary Hoxie Jones, 11 Mar. 1993.

37. Quoted in Pickett to Walton letter, 23 Mar. 1929, Pickett papers, AFSC archives.

38. Pickett to Walton letter.

39. Griscom to Pickett, 27 Mar. 1929, Pickett papers, AFSC archives.

40. Pickett to Johnson, 14 May 1929, Pickett papers, AFSC archives.

41. Pickett to William Dennis, 15 Jan. 1930, Pickett papers, AFSC archives.

42. Dennis to Pickett, 5 Jan. 1930, AFSC archives.

43. Dennis to Pickett, 5 Jan. 1930.

44. Pickett to Dennis, 30 Jan. 1930, AFSC archives.

Chapter 8

FROM THE MIDWEST TO PHILADELPHIA

Little administrative experience,
but gradually I gained courage

CLARENCE E. PICKETT BECAME EXECUTIVE SECRETARY of the American Friends Service Committee on 15 June 1929, with the understanding that he would be at the office in Philadelphia one day a week until the end of August. Then on 1 September he began work on a full-time basis. The summer months enabled him to settle his affairs in Richmond, to brief himself on the details of AFSC's programs and finances, and to move with his family to the Haverford College campus where he rented, on a temporary basis, the home of Rufus and Elizabeth Jones.

Pickett knew from his own experience, from personal contacts and from an article by Henry Cadbury entitled "The Status Quo of the AFSC," (published early in 1929 in all three of the major Quaker periodicals, the *Friends Intelligencer, The Friend,* and *The American Friend*) that the AFSC was in a period of transition, indeed a time of corporate uncertainty and crisis. Since the termination of World War I emergency services in 1925, the Committee had been emphasizing the maintenance of Quaker centers in Europe, the provision of voluntary public service opportunities for young Friends, and the interpretation to Friends and society at large of the peace testimony as it applied to a variety of societal conflicts. The Reorganization Committee evaluated these objectives as it considered the future of the AFSC. Decisively rejected was the thought of maintaining "a skeleton organization for a possible future emergency or a memorial organization of service workers in the past or a mere clearing house for miscellaneous concerns."[1]

The overall objective, seen as an interpretation of Christian good will and understanding, was to prevent and correct strife between economic, social, and national groups. The new plan resembled in most respects the emphases of the immediately preceding years, a "united effort of American Quakerism along new frontiers of an emerging Christian social conscience."[2]

The Reorganization Plan noted that the Committee would cooperate to the fullest extent with existing agencies inside the Religious Society of Friends and that all work would be done under the Committee as a whole— to counteract the tendency of a section committee to respond positively to "concerns" without full consideration by the Committee and its board of directors. As the AFSC grew in scope and size—and even in 1929 there were already three branch offices—it was increasingly necessary to be speaking and acting on the basis of agreed corporate policies.

As Clarence Pickett stepped into the leadership position, the Committee had three sections (the Interracial Section having been discontinued as a separate feature in February of 1929): Home Service, Peace, and Foreign Service. There were official Quaker centers (seen as "goodwill embassies" and jointly maintained by the AFSC and Friends Service Council in London) in Paris, Berlin (with satellite centers in Frankfurt and Nuremberg), Geneva, Vienna, Warsaw, and Moscow. In addition, in the 1929-30 fiscal year, the AFSC supported a Quaker couple in Japan, Hugh and Elisabeth Borton, working with Clarence's brother-in-law, Gilbert Bowles, and gave financial aid to Harry and Rebecca Timbres in their service work at Tagore's settlement at Shantiniketan in India. Total budget for all programs, domestic and foreign, was $100,000.

The Committee itself was composed of representatives from most of the twenty-nine American yearly meetings, these appointments made annually by the yearly meetings. On the recommendation of the AFSC nominating committee, there were some appointments at large to the Committee. Twenty of these Friends served on the AFSC's board of directors. It is noteworthy that the entire Service Committee (sometimes referred to as the "general committee") would have as many as one hundred members in attendance at its monthly meetings, taking place in various Quaker meetinghouses, usually along the Eastern seaboard. These meetings were open to Friends who were not members of the Committee, and visitors had the freedom to take part in the meetings. Since there was never any voting, this arrangement could sometimes cause problems. The board of directors stated in 1929 that "These Friends should feel that their participation in the meetings is subject to the discipline necessary for the best interests of the group as a whole,"[3] this restrained and respectful approach being an essential part of the Quaker process. The board of directors had a great deal of authority and met at least once a month, almost always in Philadelphia in the Twelfth Street Meetinghouse where the offices of the Committee were located.

What dynamics of the situation did Clarence Pickett face as he assumed the full-time work of executive secretary? Perhaps the most serious challenge was the need to help bridge the differences between those Committee members and other Friends who had been in favor of his predecessor, Wilbur Thomas, continuing as executive secretary and those who had pressed for his resignation. Mary Hoxie Jones, a member of the AFSC board of directors during this time of transition, in sharing her memories with the author of this biography, noted that the division of opinion arose in part from the excellence of Thomas' service since his appointment on 10 September 1918. But, as Thomas himself expressed it in his letter of resignation in December 1928, there was not unity in the "conception of the functions of the Service Committee" and "there was not sufficient unity in the board to warrant my continuing in the work."[4] The after-effects of this forced resignation were still present as Clarence Pickett took over the helm. Clearly Pickett was aware of these difficulties when he attended in April 1929 his first meeting of the board of directors as executive secretary-elect. As the minutes recorded it, he "expressed his great desire for a close spiritual unity within the board of directors and other Friends with whom he will be working."[5]

His second challenge was the financial situation of the Committee. Operating on a total fiscal year budget of $100,000, the AFSC was frequently borrowing from allocated funds in order to cover fully its general administrative expenditures. Even before Pickett assumed the position of executive secretary, the board authorized him to secure the services of a person "to organize and direct the finances of the Committee."[6] It was Ray Newton, secretary of the Peace Section, who was particularly eager to have the Committee employ a fund-raiser, offering to take on this function himself in addition to his Peace Section responsibilities. But prior to this offer Clarence asked Midwest Friend Guy Solt, who had served for a year with the Quaker Reconstruction Unit in France following World War I, to serve as finance secretary.[7] Solt remained in this capacity for a year, moved into the task of organizing Institutes of International Relations, and then back into fund-raising, exclusively for the Peace Section, for several decades.

What Clarence Pickett brought to these challenging circumstances within the AFSC was a buoyant spirit and a genuine interest in each staff and committee member. On the occasion of his eightieth birthday he claimed that he had come to the AFSC with relatively little administrative experience. "Gradually," he said, "I gained courage."[8] But some of his colleagues began to see that in a conventional sense Pickett was not a good administrator. Blanche Tache, Pickett's secretarial assistant, recalled "that Clarence seemed to accept all engagements whenever he met anyone," and she had to call people to tell them he was already committed to another date and had to cancel or reschedule for him.[9] Wrote co-worker Eric Johnson some years later: "I came to realize that his judgments were uncannily right, and that his strength was buoyancy and eager searching for the new and vital, and that attention to administrative details would have perhaps made him more comfortable to work with, but would have made the Service Committee a more stagnant place. Clarence was constantly pumping it full of new life and giving its many-sided life direction and new meaning."[10]

Early in October 1929, with his feet hardly under his desk at 20 South 12th Street in Philadelphia, Clarence received a phone call from Norman Thomas, the unsuccessful Socialist Party presidential candidate. "I was still new to the business of being executive secretary," he wrote after his retirement from that position. "Long-distance calls to our office were not very frequent in those days. In fact, I am not sure but there was a certain sense of flattery in being called up by someone as far away as New York."[11]

Thomas, as chairman of the Emergency Committee for Strikers' Relief, was calling about the bitter strike in the textile mills of Marion, North Carolina. The facts were that textile workers had struck the previous July against low wages and long hours (about $13 per week and twelve hours a day). After nine weeks the companies granted slight improvements but, according to the workers, discriminated against union members so that many men could not get work. The strike was resumed.

On 2 October sheriff's officers, trying to prevent picketing at the gates of the Marion Manufacturing Company, shot and killed six strikers and wounded twenty others. A virtual state of civil war developed. Answering Norman Thomas, Clarence simply said, "I will see what can be done."[12]

On 17 October members of the board of directors and Home Service Section met jointly to consider a request from the Federal Council of Churches based in New York. The appeal for AFSC's involvement was presented in person by James Myers, industrial secretary of the Council, who had earlier in the month made a visit to Marion to assess the situation. He said that he had hoped that something might be done toward reconciliation, but so far he had met with no success. He stated that the immediate need was for food and clothing for the families being evicted from company houses. According to the minutes, "Mr. Myers felt very strongly that Friends are the only organization which could enter this field and administer relief impartially and be received by all groups [including the local churches]."[13]

Myers continued: "I am convinced that a situation exists at Marion which is characterized by hate, fear, suspicion, unredressed wrongs, and the immediate need of relief in the form of warm clothing, money to pay for moving. . . . "[14] There was agreement at the special meeting (all AFSC committee decisions being made by the Quaker method of seeking consensus within a religious context) that the Service Committee should respond positively to the call, and that a recommendation should be presented to the general meeting of the Committee on 24 October. It was thought that three workers should be sent if possible: one closely associated with the work of the Service Committee, and with experience in relief work; another, a Friend from North Carolina; and a third one, a nurse with experience in public health.[15]

One week later, the Service Committee, with fifty-five members in attendance, had on its agenda the proposal to accept the request of the Federal Council of Churches, with the Council to raise the relief funds and the AFSC to be responsible for the support of its workers and for overhead expenses. Clarence was obviously in favor of the project. Moving quickly, he had lined up Frank Watson, professor of sociology at Haverford College, to survey the situation and make recommendations and Lawrence Lippincott, a New Jersey Friend, to take charge of the administration of relief. Pickett saw the emergency work in Marion as an opportunity "to push his own horizons and those of the Committee further out into some of the problem areas of our country, and to form contact with the hot vein of human pressures that are called into play in the operation of our industrial structure."[16] But he knew that the AFSC general committee included Quaker businessmen who had had sad experiences in difficult negotiations with their own workers.

In the rather deliberate manner of Quaker business meetings, the corporate body seeking for the leading of the Spirit, there were those Friends in favor of the venture, and those who found it hard to believe that this was an appropriate thing for the Committee to undertake. Those who were uneasy about the proposal felt that relief to the strikers would be seen as taking sides in the dispute. However, after a thorough airing of opinions and feelings, Henry Cadbury, the chairman, stated that there seemed to be sufficient unity to approve the recommendation, with no Committee member blocking the action or wishing to *stand aside* (that is, disagreeing with the decision but unwilling to block it).

Then, following the Committee meeting, as Clarence walked upstairs from the meeting room to his office, one of the Committee members who had questioned the rightness of the move hurried to his side and said, "Thee will need something to start on, and I will write thee a check for a thousand dollars." Pickett always remembered "that act of loyalty and encouragement."[17] It was to happen over and over again in subsequent years, when Clarence would be presenting new ways of putting into effect the Quaker spirit.

In January 1930 Pickett, accompanied by James Myers of the Federal Council, made a visit to Marion . By that time Hugh Moore, pastor of the Winston-Salem Friends Meeting in North Carolina, had been *released* (allowed) by the meeting to head up the AFSC unit, replacing Lawrence Lippincott. Both a social worker and a visiting nurse had been secured. Work had begun on 15 November with assistance to two hundred families of mill workers who had gone out on strike and were shut out, not only from employment in the mills, but also from the local churches. As Pickett was always to do throughout his lifetime, he sought (invariably with success) to obtain interviews with persons on every side of a conflict. One of these visits was with R. W. Baldwin, manager of the Marion Manufacturing Company, who simply could not understand why, when they needed employment, men would refuse to work for him. "When I tried to explain to him that in my limited experience I had never seen such inadequate housing for workers, or such filth in mills anywhere, it seemed to him incredible that he should be accused of unsatisfactory provision for his workers."[18]

Profoundly affecting this program of relief and reconciliation—and other programs of the AFSC —was the stock market collapse on 24 October 1929, and the beginning of the Great Depression. The calls for domestic services increased. And the record shows that contributions held up, indeed most Quaker groups increasing their giving. The support of non-Friends, clearly identified in financial reports, decreased at first, then rose back to a level of $19,000 a year.

Even during these trying times, when economic needs and problems were coming to the fore, the AFSC Peace Committee worked steadily at its task of peace education. One imaginative program was the enlistment of college students to participate in peace caravans, usually two or three young people traveling as a team, to fulfill speaking engagements in selected American communities. The teams would venture forth in second-hand Model T Fords filled to the brim with peace literature. The departure of the caravans was preceded by an Institute of International Relations, drawing in teachers, ministers, and other community leaders.

These institutes increasingly became a central part of AFSC's peace education program, building in part on the Kellogg-Briand Peace Pact signed by the United States and fourteen other nations on 27 August 1928 and ratified by the U.S. Senate the following January. The treaty committed the signatories (eventually sixty-two countries) to renounce war as an instrument of settling international disputes and binding themselves to seek settlement of such disputes only by pacific means. As *The Christian Century* stated at the time, "With the ratification [by the United States] of the treaty outlawing war, the whole scene of international discussion has been shifted."[19]

The Service Committee was seeking to catch in its sails these winds of change. In March 1930 Clarence Pickett, aware of the possible ecumenical impacts of the Quaker peace testimony, accepted membership on the executive committee of the National Committee on the Churches and World Peace. But as much as Clarence Pickett was dedicated to the programs of the Peace Section, his energies in his first years as executive secretary flowed more into projects best described as "economics and the spirit"[20] and into the "embassies of good will" abroad, their work coming under the rubric of "foreign service."

The AFSC board of directors encouraged him to visit these foreign centers. He sailed on the North German Lloyd liner *Europa* on 29 March 1930, following the sessions of the two Philadelphia Yearly Meetings. He was impressed by the speed of the crossing—only five days, compared to the fourteen days on his first trip in 1912 during his Hartford Seminary years—and the cost, $100—only twice what he had paid eighteen years earlier. "The *Europa* is typical of the new Germany with her determination to again capture an enviable place in the commercial sun," he wrote.[21]

Bypassing England in anticipation of a later visit, Clarence Pickett's first stop after the channel crossing to Holland was a sojourn with Wilhelm Mensching and his family in Petzen, near Bückeberg in western Germany. Pickett had first met them in 1928 at the Buck Hill Falls International House. Before World War I, as a young man, Mensching had gone as a missionary to one of the German colonies in Africa. The British took over when the war came and imprisoned him and some others in India. It was during that time that Mensching learned about the teachings and work of Gandhi. He recognized pacifism as integral to the gospel he preached and the Christian faith he professed, and embraced it.

Clarence Pickett must have seen his own life mirrored in those rural parishioners with whom he met for several hours one evening. Yet Pickett and Mensching both knew that the effects of the stock market crash on Wall Street had been soon felt in Germany—and disastrously. As historian William Shirer has noted, "The cornerstone of German prosperity had been loans from abroad, principally from America, and world trade. When the flow of loans dried up, and repayment on the old ones became due, the German financial structure was unable to stand the strain. When world trade sagged following the general slump, Germany was unable to export enough to pay for essential imports of the raw materials and food which she needed. Without exports, German industry could not keep its plants going. . . . Millions were thrown out of work. Thousands of small business enterprises went under."[22] Here were the economic seed beds for the flowering of National Socialism, the rise of the Nazi party, and the ascendancy of Adolf Hitler.

One of Pickett's principal objectives in Germany was to get acquainted with German Friends, now organized into German Yearly Meeting, and to talk with "friends of Friends," students and others drawn to the principles and service activities of Quakers. For this purpose he traveled to Berlin, Frankfurt, and Nuremberg, and then to the sessions of German Yearly Meeting held at Wernigerode. Guidance in these journeys came from Gilbert and Marga MacMaster, principal AFSC representatives at the Berlin Center since 1920.

Clarence patiently sat through five days of German Yearly Meeting, including sessions of its influential executive committee, Gilbert MacMaster translating for him. His journal records key impressions: "What these [German Friends] do not have: no birthright members [those whose parents were Quakers]; no meetinghouses; no traditions; no [Quaker] schools; no invested funds. What they do have: mostly a Lutheran or Catholic background—confirmation, baptism, etc.; interest, sense of need for help; leaving the majority religiously and joining a minority; intense zeal to explore meaning of Quakerism in life. And I come away from a session with the feeling that we are here seeing one of the greatest religious experiments that any group anywhere in the world is trying out. It has already been a tremendous boost to my spirits."[23]

Clearly, Clarence Pickett was deeply impressed with the importance of German Yearly Meeting as a peace movement as well as a religious entity. He met with German Friends proposing to have a summer school somewhere near the French border so that it could serve the needs of both French and German Friends and friends of Friends. With financial support from other Friends, one German Quaker had been working with the victims of floods in France.

With the German Yearly Meeting sessions over, Clarence Pickett and Gilbert MacMaster returned to Berlin to make formal preparations for their trip to the Soviet Union via Warsaw. In Warsaw, with three hundred thousand Jews forming one-third of its population, Clarence and Gilbert met with the few active Friends in that city. In the months previous to their visit, a Quaker orphanage and center had been closed, partly due to changes required by new regulations of the Polish government and because of the difficulty of securing suitable representatives. Pickett notes in his journal the antagonism between Poland and Russia on the east and Poland and Germany on the west: "There is intense feeling about both borders, and there needs to be understanding work done between Poles and both Russians and Germans."[24]

The trip to the Soviet Union was relatively uneventful. The second- and first-class passengers on the train were mostly American engineers going to Moscow as employees of the government. "All of our fears regarding customs [at the border] were useless. At Berlin I had carefully discarded all papers which might be objectionable, but we did have two large suitcases containing $30 worth of food for ourselves and our workers [in Moscow]. Besides our own two bags, we brought in, at [Friends Service Council representative] Dorice White's request, a loudspeaker and a whole big box of other radio equipment."[25]

Quaker representatives Alice Davis and Nadia Danilevsky met the travelers, and the four of them took a Model A Ford taxi directly to the Quaker Center, where they were joined by the third representative, Dorice White. Davis and Danilevsky were serving as nurses in the Botkinsky Hospital on the outskirts of Moscow, training Russian nurses at a clinic for infant diseases. In their spare time both representatives were translating some of Tolstoy's works into English. White, in charge of the Center, largely maintained herself by teaching. With the assistance of the three representatives and the Soviet Information Service, Clarence Pickett and Gilbert MacMaster toured clinics, the Red Square, factories, schools, and government offices.

Two primary objectives in the visit to Russia were to assess ways of life under Soviet communism and to meet key officials. As to religion in the Soviet Union, Clarence noted in his journal that "the tension is now greatly relaxed by Stalin's decree. The attitude is that they shall give less attention to anti-religious acts such as closing churches, etc. and more to educating toward atheism. Three hundred of the four hundred Moscow churches [principally Russian Orthodox] are still open."[26] Clarence and Gilbert went to a morning service on their first Sunday.

Then at two o'clock that same day there was a Quaker meeting for worship at the Center. Wrote Clarence: "Those present were: Alexander Wickstead, a Quaker farm worker from England (now teaching English and writing books here), Olga Tolstoy (daughter-in-law of Count Leo Tolstoy), Dorice White, Alice Davis, Mrs. Danilevsky [Clarence always referred in his journal to her as 'Mrs. Danilevsky'], Gilbert, and myself. We sat in an impressive silence for about twenty minutes, then Alice prayed beautifully, Mrs. Danilevsky pleaded for sympathy and love toward those who persecuted, Alexander Wickstead for those in prison, both those without and those with real cause. I spoke briefly and Gilbert read a beautiful passage from Robert Barclay's letter to King Charles II in which he states Friends' attitude toward the king and his government."[27]

An important piece of business for Clarence during his Moscow visit was to think through with the three representatives the Center's program. He notes how personal contacts seemed to be about all the Center was doing. These were contacts with the Tolstoian group and with some younger people who were seeking spiritual help in the hectic life about them. He characterized these contacts as very important.

Yet, within the next twelve months the Center would be closed, not only because Friends were not granted a renewal of the lease of the premises, but also because the representatives were acutely in need of rest and recuperation. Mrs. Danilevsky, "a Russian citizen of the old order" (as Clarence often described her) secured a passport to leave the Soviet Union and a visa to enter the United States on the strength of her being accepted by Bryn Mawr College for a year's study. Alice Davis, an American citizen, having devoted six years of service in the Soviet Union, returned home. Both women seriously considered returning to the Soviet Union to work, if permitted, with their Tolstoian friends in Siberia but Mrs. Danilevsky was afraid to go back, and Alice Davis was not granted a return visa. Both women would soon be working for the Service Committee in the Appalachian coal fields. Dorice White, after home leave in England, had planned to go back to the Soviet Union in August 1930 but could not obtain the necessary visa to return.[28]

Thus the small Quaker organizational window in the Soviet Union, a channel that had begun with relief operations in the early 1920s, was closed, not to be opened again until English and American Friends began visiting in the 1950s.

Shortly before Clarence Pickett left Moscow for Berlin by train, Olga Tolstoy paid another visit to the Quaker Center. "From her," wrote Clarence, "we learned of the deep sense of tragedy felt by those who had been highly respected members of the community under the Tsar."[29] Reflecting at a later time about his days in the Soviet Union, he wrote: "Here one could see everything—fear, suffering, hope, achievement, belief in the future. But the indelible impression left on me by this all-too-short visit was of the abounding energy which had been released by the [Russian] revolution and the unqualified belief in the future of Russia on the part of nearly all the people one saw. This, of course, was 1930, and the revolution was relatively new. But I realized that here was something not to be written off as unimportant."[30]

With brief stops in Berlin and Prague, Clarence Pickett headed for Vienna. Relief work in Austria had begun in May 1919 and was now based in a town house at Singerstrasse 16, built two centuries earlier for an aristocratic Austrian family. A hostel was opened in 1924. In 1930, at the time of Clarence Pickett's visit, the Vienna Center had increasingly become a gateway to the Balkans. The AFSC representative, Emma Cadbury, had recently visited Greece and Bulgaria, while Headley and Elizabeth Horsnaill, English Friends, had visited Turkey and Romania.

As in the case of the other centers in Europe, student clubs were being sponsored. "Our clubs alone," wrote Clarence, "have [members from] all religions, all [political] parties, and all social classes. There are four hundred thousand Jews in Austria, a little state of six million. Most of them [Jews] are in Vienna, but they are certainly pretty badly discriminated against."[31] The day would come when the Quaker Center would be deluged by Jewish citizens seeking to escape from Austria.

From Vienna Clarence journeyed, via Munich, to Geneva, already as host of the League of Nations a world capital. He attended a session of the League Council and ran into old friends. On one afternoon the Center had a big tea for Clarence Pickett and Carl Heath, secretary of the Friends Service Council in London. "It was a good time to make contacts. They asked me to talk on Russia as I saw it, which I did informally. The attention which the Center is able to secure from most of the leading people about Geneva, has placed us where we have a fine responsibility to carry. . . to create something new, an international quality of life."[32] And always Clarence was interested in talking with students, noting how the theology of Karl Barth, with its confidence in and worship of a transcendent God (but with little concern for service), was gaining ground. "Certainly American speakers on matters of religion in Europe are mistrusted as too rosy, shallow, and optimistic," noted Clarence.[33]

With a stopover in Paris, to make plans for his later week's visit, Pickett next went to London for meetings of the Friends Service Council and for sessions of London Yearly Meeting. His journal includes quotations from a number of English Friends who spoke in the sessions. These reveal the wide differences in thought and action that existed among English Friends. Then he reports on what many Friends thought was a historic session of the yearly meeting. India was the subject. The poet Tagore, who was giving the Hibbert Lectures at Oxford, asked for the privilege and was invited to speak at the session. The doors had to be closed to all non-Friends, and even then the house was packed. Tagore gave an address on India and independence. Clarence noted that "it was a colorful occasion when the long-bearded, blue-velvet-robed prophet appeared and gave an address in classic English, full of feeling for the urge for independence, and the obligation of recognition of an inter-dependence built on India and England as equals, seeking to determine what that interrelationship should be."[34]

Clarence was accurately capturing in his journal entry the magnifi-cence of Tagore's appeal, which said in part:

> I find it painfully difficult to do my duty, for we want conciliation be-tween two peoples who for over a century have had a close connection and yet are separated by moral distances more difficult of overcoming than mountain or sea. The inevitable has happened. India is being ruled by a machine, and there exists the dark chasm of aloofness instead of the living touch of sympathy, and there is a disease in our political condi-tions, which can only be cured by a generous cooperation from both sides and a union of minds which know how to make proper allowances for weakness in human nature, and at the same time may keep faith in human nature.[35]

The responses of English Friends to Tagore's address revealed wide and tense differences of opinion.[36] The Indian question was taken up again at another "momentous session." Gandhi and all the top leaders of the Indian National Congress were as of this date, 26 May 1930, in prison as a result of Gandhi's march to the Arabian Sea where he and his followers illegally made salt from the sea. The boycott of foreign cloth, with its impact on English mills, had just begun.[37] After a great deal of discussion the clerk drafted a minute which the meeting later decided to have presented to the prime minister and to the press. "Sufficient to say," observed Clarence, "that in a remarkable way the minute reconciled and lifted the whole concern of widely divergent points of view to a higher level."[38] The minute was as follows:

> In response to the invitation contained in our Ninth Minute, Rabindranath Tagore has attended this session and has delivered an ear-nest, searching address on the Indian situation as seen by an Indian seer. He had contrasted Life—the free life of the individual, the free creative

life that is possible to a nation—with a machine—the machine that rules
by a system of switches and handles and wheels without the living cooperation of those ruled. Let us, the dreamers of the East and the West,
keep our faith firm in the Life that creates and not in the Machine that
constricts.[39]

Clarence Pickett was particularly interested in the India debate
because at the request of Tagore, the American Friends Service
Committee sent in September 1929 two Friends, Harry and Rebecca
Timbres, he a medical doctor and she a nurse, to do medical and social
work at Tagore's ashram, or settlement, in Shantiniketan and surrounding
villages. Following a two months' survey in the field and a study of
health work elsewhere in India, they then went to England, he to take a
course in tropical medicine and she to learn Bengali at the Quaker center at Woodbrooke. Now at the end of May 1930, Pickett had the responsibility of conferring with Tagore, Charles F. Andrews (the English
Anglican missionary who had worked with Gandhi first in South
Africa, then in India, and who made his home in Shantiniketan)[40] and
Harry Timbres about the poet's trip to America. "One is conscious while
in his [Tagore's] presence," wrote Clarence, "that a great soul is through
his rather frail body trying to reveal new and living reality to the world."[41]

It was on the voyage home on the *Europa*, from Cherbourg to New
York, that Pickett had time to reflect on the two-and-a-half months he
had been away. He affirmed what he felt to be a common goodness and
love in all people, "most of all manifest in simple people who are unspoiled by propaganda, either national, racial, or religious." He viewed
governments as, on the whole, confused and blundering, dealing with
forces the nature of which they knew little. He characterized the great
social experiment in Russia, and the small one in Vienna in housing and
education, as prophetic of something new, intelligent, and better.

As to the Quaker work ("I am prejudiced, I suppose," he said in his
report), it represented the three elements most needed in the world: social
intelligence and adventuresome spirit of discovery; an intense application of individual personal contacts, especially with people of violently
differing views; and "an emphasis on religion which looks first and
always to the inner spirit of man and finds there the love of Christ."[42]

Clarence Pickett in succeeding months continued to express enthusiasm for the Quaker centers. In a major address to Hicksite Quakers

assembled in Cape May, New Jersey less than a month after his return, he spoke about the loss of confidence in Europe in both church and government. "We should try with all our power to express the love of God in deeds, to prove that our lack of theology is not a lack of religion. We have never been good theologians. But we have a deep-lying and basic theological viewpoint, that of 'seeing God in the face of Jesus Christ,' as Paul put it. Or, in the words of St. Chrysostom, 'where shall I see God if not in the face of my brother?' It is this revelation of divinity in our lives and attitudes that is the theology of a better world."[43]

In the autumn of the same year, 1930, Clarence Pickett was directly involved with the AFSC-sponsored visit of Rabindranath Tagore to the United States. Clarence met him and his party when the *Bremen* docked and went with them to an apartment in uptown New York where he was to live. "It was one of those exciting, high moments of life," wrote Clarence. "Tagore responded partly with appreciation but also with trepidation. A limousine with driver had been furnished to bring him from the dock, and a motor escort squealed its way the full distance from lower Manhattan to the upper seventies. At the apartment we were met by newspaper reporters and photographers and movie cameramen. Tagore was rebellious and wholly unwilling to cooperate."[44]

It fell to Pickett to convince the great poet that since he was trying to place his cause before the American public, it seemed unwise to completely antagonize the press. "Finally," wrote Clarence, we were able to organize an orderly press conference, and also an opportunity for him to be properly photographed for the newsreels. . . . It was like handling a piece of delicate glass to take care of the aged saint."[45]

Pickett traveled with Tagore occasionally during the lecture tour. Tagore was unable to fulfill all of the speaking engagements the AFSC arranged for him. Nevertheless, there were some memorable occasions in connection with his visit. His first public appearance was at Carnegie Hall on 1 December. *The New York Times* gave prominent attention to the event:

> Every seat in Carnegie Hall was occupied last night and hundreds of persons lined the walls to hear Sir Rabindranath Tagore, the Indian poet and philosopher, discuss the essential dissimilarity between the East and the West. . . . About 4,000 persons were in the hall, and thousands were

turned away. Seated in a battered arm chair on the stage, and leaning forward to speak into an amplifier, Sir Rabindranath said the characteristic difference between the Orient and the Occident was that the people of the East believed in personality, while Western admiration was for sheer power. "What is the harvest of your civilization that you reap today?" he asked. "Everywhere men are suspicious of each other; all the great countries of the West are preparing for some great work of desolation, manufacturing poisons for each other's ruin."[46]

Tagore's last public appearance was on 14 December at the Broadway Theater in New York. It was billed as a recital of poetry and dance for the benefit of Tagore's International University, with the well-known Ruth St. Denis appearing as the interpretative dancer. Wrote Clarence: "To see this bronze-skinned prophet with long, white beard and flowing white robe sitting in a kind of throne chair on the platform, surrounded by children, and reading his poetry, first in his native tongue and then in English, was a sight which I am sure no one who saw it would ever forget."[47]

Just a few days later, Clarence Pickett received word that his mother, Hulda Macy Pickett, at eighty-nine years of age, had died quietly at the home of his sister Ida in Oskaloosa, Iowa. Clarence dropped everything to go to Oskaloosa and, with Ida, to accompany the body to Glen Elder, Kansas. The funeral services were held at the Glen View Friends Church on 21 December. The obituary in the Glen Elder *Sentinel* noted that "she had an unusual gift in caring for the sick, often using such occasions as opportunities for spiritual help."[48]

Much as Clarence Pickett was absorbed in foreign affairs, he was required by developments at home to focus on domestic issues. The deepening depression was urgently claiming the attention of the Friends Service Committee. The Home Service Section in January 1931 cooperated for several months with the Philadelphia Committee for Unemployment Relief in the securing of work in Protestant churches of the city, payment for these services coming from unemployment relief funds. A Quaker Economics Commission was appointed to investigate the responsibilities of Friends for helping toward a solution of economic ills. Then in the spring of 1931, quite unexpectedly, a significant request was received by the AFSC from President Herbert Hoover. It was to have consequences for Clarence Pickett far beyond the immediate challenge.

During a gala Saturday afternoon occasion at Bryn Mawr College where an award was made to Jane Addams, Grace Abbott, chief of the United States Children's Bureau, informally laid the president's request before Rufus Jones. Would the American Friends Service Committee be willing to feed the children of unemployed coal miners living in the Allegheny and Blue Ridge Mountains? [49] Clarence Pickett recalled how the following Monday morning Rufus Jones "was all aglow with this new sense of opportunity that had come to the Committee."[50]

Feeling somewhat overwhelmed as he thought of the administrative and financial responsibilities, Pickett nevertheless arranged for himself and three board members to meet at the White House with President Hoover and his associates. As Pickett remembered it, the president "spoke with a depth of understanding and appreciation which strengthened our confidence in the AFSC and in myself."[51] Hoover then offered to turn over to the Service Committee $225,000 remaining from the American Relief Administration Children's Fund provided the Committee would do its utmost to raise the additional necessary funds.

The task accepted by the Committee was to feed the undernourished children of the unemployed miners in the bituminous coal fields during the winter of 1931-32 and possibly the following winter. The maximum number of children fed at one time reached forty thousand a day, located in over five hundred communities in thirty-eight counties of the states of Maryland, Kentucky, Tennessee, Illinois, Pennsylvania, and West Virginia. "During the first year alone, the public's response to the 'universality of destitution' in the coal fields," wrote Pickett, "enabled us to carry out a $400,000 program."[52]

Bernard G. Waring, a Philadelphia businessman (one of many such Friends who were to accept the challenges of AFSC programs under Clarence Pickett's inspiring leadership), agreed to become general director of the project. And into this scene went the two women who had had extensive experience in the Soviet Union and with whom Pickett was well acquainted, Alice Davis and Nadia Danilevsky.

During the winter of 1932-33 the need for relief increased, but the situation changed somewhat due to the allotment of funds from the Reconstruction Finance Corporation to aid states in their relief activities.

Because of this allotment, many counties were able to take care of their own problems. But sixteen counties in West Virginia and Kentucky asked the AFSC to administer their allotment of funds for child-feeding, and in two cases to administer the entire relief program. Under this arrangement the AFSC was feeding approximately 25,000 children and supplementing state funds with Quaker money.[53]

But as immeasurably valuable as the relief work was in the prevention of suffering from cold, hunger, and disease, equally important to Clarence Pickett was the opportunity the project gave the AFSC to study the situation in the coal industry and to throw some light on the problem of its permanent labor surplus. He realized that vocational reeducation and subsistence living projects needed to be developed. Out of these convictions was born the Mountaineer Craftsmen's Cooperative Association which involved fifty women and men from three mine camps, the women learning to weave and the men to make furniture. Subsistence gardening was vigorously promoted.

As with many AFSC programs, these efforts were seen as "pilot projects," an opportunity to pioneer with a practical idealism. Furthermore, the work in the coal fields was to lead Clarence Pickett to new and exciting opportunities and relationships within the Roosevelt Administration.

NOTES

1. Henry J. Cadbury, "The Status Quo of the AFSC," *The American Friend* (new series) 17, no. 6 (7 Feb. 1929); *The Friend* 102, no. 32 (7 Feb. 1929); *Friends Intelligencer* 86, no 6 (9 Feb 1929): 96, 382, and 114 respectively.

2. Appendix, AFSC annual report for year ending 31 May 1929, 16.

3. Minutes of AFSC board of directors, 6 Mar. 1929.

3. Taped interview with Mary Hoxie Jones, 11 Mar. 1993.

4. Minutes of meeting of the American Friends Service Committee (general committee) held 27 Dec. 1928.

5. Minutes of meeting of the AFSC board of directors held in New Lisbon, NJ, 6-7 Apr. , 1929.

6. Minutes, New Lisbon, 1929.

7. Minutes of AFSC board of directors meeting, 10 May 1929.

8. "American Friends Service Committee, 1917-1967" (including remarks made by Pickett to a staff meeting on the occasion of his 80th birthday) tape recording, Friends Library, Philadelphia Yearly Meeting.

9. Noted in a letter dated 18 Nov. 1993 from Betty Endo, colleague and good friend of Blanche Tache.

10. In a letter on the occasion of Pickett's retirement as executive secretary in 1950, family papers, courtesy of Carolyn Pickett Miller.

11. Clarence E. Pickett, *For More Than Bread* (Boston: Little, 1953), 3.

12. Pickett, *Bread*, 4.

13. Minutes of the special meeting of the board of directors and Home Service Section, 17 Oct. 1929, 4.

14. Minutes, 4.

15. Minutes, 4.

16. Pickett, *Bread*, 16.

17. Pickett, *Bread*, 7.

18. Pickett, *Bread*, 10.

19. *The Christian Century* 66, no. 5 (31 Jan. 1929): 134-6.

20. Pickett, *Bread*, Part I.

21. Clarence Pickett, report of trip to Europe, 29 Mar.-13 June, 1930 (pages not in sequence), 3 Apr., Pickett papers, AFSC archives.

22. William L. Shirer, *The Rise and Fall of the Third Reich: A History of Nazi Germany* (New York: Simon, 1960), 136.

23. Trip report, 18 Apr.

24. Trip report, 22 Apr.

25. Trip report, 23 Apr.

26. Trip report, 25 Apr.

27. Trip report, 27 Apr.

28. *The* (London) *Friend* 70, no. 29 (18 July 1930 and 14 Nov. 1930): 663 and 1037 respectively.

29. Trip report, 29 Apr.

30. Undated addendum to 1930 trip report.

31. Trip report, 5 May.

32. Trip report, 9 May.

33. Trip report, 18 May.

34. Trip report, 24 May.

35. The (London) *Friend* 70, no. 22 (30 May 1930): 490, 492-94.

36. Trip report, 24 May.

37. Horace Alexander, *Gandhi Through Western Eyes* (Philadelphia: New Society, 1969), 62.

38. Trip report, 25 May.

39. *The* (London) *Friend* 70, no. 22 (30 May 1930): 496.

40. Alexander, *Gandhi.*

41. Trip report, 25 May.

42. "Conclusion," trip report, 13 June 1930.

43. Clarence E. Pickett, "The Place of Friends in Making a Better World," *Friends Intelligencer* 87, no. 30 (20 July 1930): 583-85.

44. Pickett, *Bread*, 92.

45. Pickett, *Bread*, 19.

46. *The New York Times*, Tuesday, 2 Dec. 1930.

47. Pickett, *Bread*, 93.

48. *Glen Elder Sentinel*, 24 Dec. 1930.

49. Pickett, *Bread*, 19.

50. Pickett, *Bread*, 19.

51. Pickett, *Bread*, 21.

52. Pickett, *Bread*, 22.

53. AFSC annual report, 1 June 1931 - 31 Dec. 1932.

Chapter 9

THE ROOSEVELT CONNECTION BEGINS

*We were caught in that net because we had some
ideas about what could be done*

CLARENCE PICKETT'S INVOLVEMENT in what was to become known as
"The New Deal" took place prior to the inauguration of Franklin D.
Roosevelt as president. FDR was calling in for consultation those persons who knew something about the Depression on a firsthand basis.
"We [the AFSC] were caught in that net," said Clarence many years
later, "because we had some ideas about what could be done about unemployed coal miners living in the mine camps. You got the president's
ear if you had concrete information of that sort, and you also got Mrs.
Roosevelt's ear."[1]

As a result, prior to the end of the 1932 calendar year, Pickett was an
overnight guest of the Roosevelts at the thirty-five-room "big house" in
Hyde Park, New York (over which FDR's mother, Mrs. James Roosevelt,
presided). At breakfast the next morning the President-elect and Eleanor
Roosevelt quizzed Clarence Pickett about what could be done in the
bituminous coal fields. The AFSC had concluded that, due to the over-
development of productive capacity during World War I, the development
of substitutes, and the mechanization of the mining process, three hundred thousand miners had only one or two days' employment a week;
two hundred thousand were entirely unemployed; and that these unemployed miners would probably never again be needed in the industry.[2]
Pickett reported to the Roosevelts on the AFSC vocational reeducation
and subsistence living projects being developed in the coal fields. It is
entirely possible that the Roosevelts had read the extensive, illustrated

article on the Quakers' work in the soft-coal fields that appeared early in 1932 in *The New York Times*.[3]

On 11 January 1933 (with President Hoover still in office) Pickett appeared before a Senate committee in Washington headed by Senators Robert L. LaFollette, Jr. from Wisconsin and Edward P. Costigan from Colorado on the matter of appropriating $500 million for federal relief. "I talked to both senators following the hearing," he said, "requesting them to provide in their bill for some funds to be spent for rehabilitation where way was open to keep people permanently off of relief, and they agreed to make this change."[4]

A week later, Clarence and Lilly Pickett drove to Morgantown, West Virginia for a conference of AFSC staff working in the coal fields. It was "a glorious drive," he noted, and Clarence marveled that they covered 310 miles in ten hours. At Morgantown they were joined by field staff members, Alice Davis and Nadia Danilevsky, and by Elliston Morris, Dan Houghton and Bill and Ruth Simkin, all four relatively young Friends. Pickett observed that "the size of the coal tragedy seems to increase each time I go to the fields. But gardening, return to farms, and revival of handicrafts are all spots—small spots—of light. Only fifty men and fifty women are really touched [by the Quaker rehabilitation project]."[5]

The turnover of administration, in this case from Republican to Democrat, took place on 4 March (it was not until 1937 that the inaugurations were on 20 January). While Clarence Pickett was clearly captivated by the Roosevelts and their interest in AFSC work in the coal fields, he also had a warm personal regard for fellow-Quaker Herbert Hoover. On the evening of Saturday, 18 February he and Lilly Pickett were guests of President and Mrs. Herbert Hoover at the White House as part of the House and Senate reception. The next morning the Picketts attended meeting for worship at the newly-built Florida Avenue Friends Meeting House. President and Mrs. Hoover were also present. Clarence Pickett and Herbert Hoover were to see each other from time to time over the next three decades, usually on matters relating to overseas relief. In an article following Hoover's death in 1964, Pickett, after listing some of Hoover's accomplishments, had this to say: "Herbert Hoover accounted well for his ninety years. As Friends we have reason to thank God for his life, which found even greater usefulness outside of public office than in."[6]

It was just at this time of changeover in administrations that Clarence Pickett had an opportunity to express in public his overall views on the crisis facing the country. The occasion was his presidential address to the annual meeting, in Detroit, of the National Church Conference on Social Work. Remembering his own years on a Kansas farm, he noted how "the early, simple efforts of a father and mother to provide food, shelter, and clothing for their families have been transferred to a great industrial machine, with the hope that profit, for some at least, might be reached in the contest. This new motive marks the difficulty. [For example] the motives that have controlled our developments in the science of health have been far from that of how widely the knowledge and information and materials for health care can be spread. I was startled recently in a reexamination of those passages in which Jesus refers to the Kingdom of Heaven to find that He does not talk about building it. . . . Rather it is something to be discovered. It is a pearl of great price, hid away, which should be the chief center of our life-long quest. . . . Society should be on the search, looking always for the Kingdom of Heaven in people."[7]

Following the inauguration, Roosevelt moved quickly to deal with the Depression in the first One Hundred Days. Among other legislative moves promoted by the new administration was the National Industrial Recovery Act, signed into law by the president on 16 June 1933. Designed to promote recovery in industry, Title I set up trade codes and placed the federal government behind the right of workers to organize and bargain collectively, free from restraint or coercion. Title II was a $3.3 billion public works program. Included in the legislation was the provision of a revolving fund of $25 million for a program of subsistence homesteading. President Roosevelt chose Secretary of the Interior, Harold Ickes, to administer the new program, and Ickes in turn delegated the job to a newly-created Division of Subsistence Homesteads within his department. Milburn L. Wilson (always called by Pickett and others in the Division, "M. L."), moved from the Department of Agriculture to become director of the Division.

Then on 22 August Secretary Ickes appointed Clarence E. Pickett Chief of the Section on Stranded Mining and Industrial Populations, in effect an assistant to Dr. Wilson. Pickett had been *liberated* (given permission) by the AFSC board of directors to give up to four days a week to this government position, even as he continued to be executive secretary of the Service Committee. Elizabeth Marsh, (who had earlier succeeded Pickett as secretary of the Young Friends movement, based in Richmond, Indiana), moved to the East, and took over the majority of the tasks of the executive secretary during his absences in Washington. But of equal importance for the flow of administration was Clarence's secretary, Blanche Cloeren (later Tache), who had been Wilbur Thomas' secretary since March 1920 and who was to remain as Pickett's secretarial assistant until his death in 1965.

Clarence Pickett's administration as assistant director of the Subsistence Homesteads Division had to do solely with the transfer of unemployed miners from coal camps to subsistence homesteads where they might find some employment on their own land and where hopefully the division might introduce new industries for cash employment. As he looked back upon the experience twenty years later, he was grateful that he did not know how many things could not be done under government regulation. "If I had known all these restrictions," he said, "I doubt whether the four homesteads for stranded miners [Arthurdale (Reedsville) and Tygart Valley, both in West Virginia, Norvelt (Westmoreland County) in Pennsylvania, and Cumberland (Crossville) in Tennessee] would ever have been built."[8]

Clarence Pickett found it particularly stimulating to work under Milburn Wilson. "M.L. was a born philosopher," wrote Pickett, "and, while sometimes one might be a little impatient for his prompt decision on some administrative matter which for the moment seemed of central concern, I learned to appreciate his ability to lean back in his chair and look with philosophic quiet on the longer-term significance of steps we were taking."[9] Clarence himself was giving attention to the fundamental objectives of subsistence homesteads. A year later he was to write on their social significance: "It was one of the basic aspirations of the subsistence homestead movement to so develop the educational, social and economic facilities that interest will be centered not primarily in income or in securing enough wealth or education to get away from the community, but in discovering the resources, joys, and satisfactions within the community itself."[10]

In terms of the needed support, the program resembled a three-legged stool. It proved to be sturdy because of three interdependent pillars. First, there were the existing Quaker workers in the coal fields, under Pickett's leadership, who had begun experimenting in the rehabilitation of the miners even before the federal government got involved in that dimension of aid. Secondly, there was federal financial support, notwithstanding the bureaucratic and legal booby traps. And, thirdly, there was the personal interest and involvement of Eleanor Roosevelt. How she became intimately engaged in some of the projects is in itself a remarkable story, evidence of the revolutionary changes she brought to the role of the First Lady. Furthermore, her involvement paralleled an increasing personal confidence in Clarence Pickett and the work of the American Friends Service Committee. The door to the White House was swinging open for him.

It was Lorena Hickok, a close personal friend of Eleanor Roosevelt and a writer working in the Federal Emergency Relief Administration (FERA), who fired up the First Lady's interest in the plight of the bituminous coal miners. Harry Hopkins, director of FERA, asked Hickok (known to all her friends as "Hick,") in the early summer of 1933 to travel as his confidential agent to report to him and to Eleanor on poverty in the United States. Hickok checked in with Clarence Pickett before she set out on her travels. He suggested that she go down to the southwestern part of Pennsylvania and into West Virginia if she wanted to see how bad things were. Clarence arranged for his brother-in-law, Errol Peckham, who was a member of the AFSC field staff, to accompany Hickok as a guide.

Pickett, Hick discovered, had not exaggerated the distress in Appalachia. She was profoundly shocked by the poverty she encountered in southwestern Pennsylvania, where both the steel mills and coal mines had virtually ceased to operate, and was absolutely appalled by what she saw and heard and smelled in West Virginia. Wrote Roosevelt biographer Kenneth Davis about Hick's visit to Scotts Run, a coal-mining community not far from Morgantown: "In a gutter, along the main street through the town, there was stagnant, filthy water, which the inhabitants used for drinking, cooking, washing, and everything else imaginable. On either side of the street were ramshackle houses, black with coal dust, which most Americans would not have considered fit for pigs. And in those houses every night children went to sleep hungry, on piles of bug-infested rags spread out on the floor. There were rats in those houses."[11]

Davis then describes the immediately subsequent events: "It was as the hottest of sparks shot into the driest of tinder that Hick's long, vividly-reported letter, written 'in a kind of state of shock' a few hours after her visit to Scotts Run, that galvanized Eleanor Roosevelt into action."[12] She and Hick got in touch with Clarence Pickett in Philadelphia and on 18 August 1933, the three met in Morgantown, West Virginia, Eleanor having driven over by herself from Washington. On that and succeeding days, neither introduced nor recognized as the First Lady, wearing a dark blue skirt, white blouse, and a white ribbon around her hair, Eleanor Roosevelt visited Scotts Run and other mining communities in company with Hickok, Pickett, and the two Quaker workers in the area, Alice Davis and Nadia Danilevsky. As she was to demonstrate over and over again in subsequent visits, even when those persons being visited knew who she was, Eleanor Roosevelt effectively communicated to the dispossessed families her compassionate feelings. As biographer Joseph Lash described it, "She listened to the miners' wives and took their babies on her lap. She went into the hovels alongside of Scotts Run, one of the worst slums in the county, where mine tipples rusted and the gully that was used for cooking and washing water also ran with sewage."[13]

Having also questioned Clarence Pickett and the two social workers on what specifically could and should be done, she returned to Washington with an abundance of horror stories and corrective ideas to pour into the receptive ears of the president and his influential political advisor and private secretary, Louis Howe, who had been an important mentor for Mrs. Roosevelt in earlier years. Both men were easily persuaded that the portion of Appalachia Eleanor visited should be the location of the first subsistence homestead project. In this manner, right then and there, Eleanor Roosevelt's favorite project, Arthurdale, was launched.

The subsistence community was named Arthurdale because the University of West Virginia, following a land survey, found the Arthur estate in Reedsville suitable for the project. It consisted of a 1200-acre tract, with a mansion, a farm, and outbuildings. On 13 October a press release from Ickes' office announced its purchase. It was intended to be the model for other subsistence homestead settlements. It was to house fifty families and later to absorb an additional one hundred families. The federal government was to buy the houses, acquire livestock, build roads, provide for electricity, bring in water, and provide farm machinery. The homesteaders would pay for their homes over a period of thirty years at a low interest rate. The principal decisions regarding the component parts of this new community were in the hands of a Projects Committee consisting of Wilson, Howe, Pickett, and Mrs. Roosevelt.

An interesting sidelight in this whole venture were the vague under-lying fears of some observers that these stranded and destitute miners might turn to violent revolution, perhaps under the influence of com-munists. Clarence himself shared in these fears. "In perspective," he wrote two decades later, "I am convinced that the efforts made in the crucial early '30s were essential, even if at points misguided and waste-ful. They demonstrated government's concern and willingness to act, they gave a new sense of confidence and hope to otherwise discouraged people."[14] When Lorena Hickok, on one of her first visits to the mining camps, inveighed against the communists, Alice Davis and Nadia Danilevsky, fully familiar with Russian communism and for the most part disillusioned with what they had experienced in the Soviet Union, told Hick that the "poor people of West Virginia were much too far beaten down, too crushed into hopeless passivity to respond actively to revolutionary propaganda."[15]

Apart from the conversations Franklin and Eleanor Roosevelt had had with Clarence Pickett in Hyde Park shortly after the election, Mrs. Roosevelt's trip to the mining areas was her first contact with the work being done by the Friends. As two of Eleanor Roosevelt's biographers were to sum up her reactions:

> She liked Pickett, whom she considered without vanity or personal am-bition, and she liked the way the Quakers validated their faith by good deeds rather than by theological disputation.[16] "I am no believer in pater-nalism," Eleanor said in a public address, "I do not like charities." The crucial need in her view was for some drastic changes in our rather settled ideas that should provide equality of opportunity for all and would pre-vent the recurrence of a similar disaster [depression] in the future.[17]

Clarence Pickett would say later that "speed was important. Some demonstration that government could act, even to the disregard of regulations, was called for. We were dealing with human misery, and there was general realization that we must not let regulations, or politicians, or our own fears, prevent our acting with promptness and reasonable adequacy."[18] On every step of the way Pickett was involved in the planning and decision-making in respect to the subsistence homesteads for miners, meeting at the White House as a member of the Projects Committee and traveling to the field with Mrs. Roosevelt. There was intense public criticism of the whole scheme.

Ever resilient in the face of this criticism, Mrs. Roosevelt headed right into the vortex of problems that had to be solved at Arthurdale: What were to be the interior essentials? How would schooling for the children be provided? Should there be a community health center? How might community self-government be developed? How could small industries be enticed to move into Arthurdale? Solutions to these problems were slowly devised. They began an ambitious school program drawing on the ideas of John Dewey and bringing in Clarence Pickett's choice, Elsie Clapp, an experienced progressive educator, to direct the school. Dewey a year later was to become a member of the advisory committee for the Arthurdale Community School. A significant contribution to the community was Clarence's success in persuading Harry Timbres, who had spent five years as a Service Committee worker at Tagore's settlement in Santiniketan in India, to serve for eight months as medical officer for the Arthurdale community of six hundred persons, in complete charge of the medical, surgical, and obstetrical work.[19]

Notwithstanding Eleanor Roosevelt's objections to charity, Arthurdale would not have developed into a pioneering community if it had not been for her personal financial contributions. These, she decided, should go through the American Friends Service Committee. In 1934 Pickett set up an Eleanor Roosevelt Transit Fund Account to which she sent her earnings from radio broadcasts, speeches, and articles. Mrs. Roosevelt then informed the Committee as to how the funds should be distributed, much of it at first to pay for services at Arthurdale which the federal government could not properly cover. For example, in 1934 she received $18,000 from six fifteen-minute radio broadcasts under commercial sponsorship, and all of these earnings went to Arthurdale—the handicraft center, the community school, and the health clinic.

Pickett's journal for 1934 chronicles the week-by-week trips to the developing subsistence homesteads, some of these journeys with an Eleanor Roosevelt entourage, and then there would be the conferences and meetings at the White House. On 8 January, at the invitation of Mrs. Roosevelt, Clarence brought to the White House for dinner Alice Davis and Nadia Danilevsky, fresh from the field. Assistant Secretary of the Interior Oscar Chapman and M.L. Wilson joined them for dinner. Clarence wrote about his impressions in a letter to Lilly:

Yesterday the president received the new ambassador from Russia
[Alexander Troyanovsky, with diplomatic relations having been established between the U.S. and the USSR the previous November] and at the
dinner table in the evening, at his left sat Nadia [Danilevsky], at his right
Alice [Davis], both semi-refugees from Soviet fury. So strange are the
fates. The president was most communicative and easy to talk with. After dinner he went upstairs, with the colored help about the house, saw a
movie, while the rest of us went into a huddle over the schools, etc. in
the homesteads. And we went full steam until 1:30 a.m.! . . . Every minute
of it was most interesting. The president was in, and took his due part in
the deliberations for about one and a half hours. . . . I feel a keen interest
in the president, a very real assurance of his mental ability and fine spirit,
but some basic misgivings.[20]

A sensitive matter in dispute within the Homesteads Division was
the race issue—whether African Americans should be admitted to homesteads in the South. "The problem was not 'the Negro,'" wrote Pickett,
"but the tensions that were intensifying around the question."[21] African
American families were among those Mrs. Roosevelt visited when
she first went to Scotts Run. She consulted Clarence Pickett about their
inclusion, and he applied discreet pressure on the Arthurdale homesteaders already selected, all white, but they voted down the idea. Eleanor
Roosevelt then asked Clarence, on her behalf, to invite to the White
House a group of African American leaders.

The meeting took place on the evening of 26 January 1934. Pickett
described it as "memorable." Those present were Mordecai Johnson,
president of Howard University; John Hope, president of Atlanta University; Robert R. Moton, president of Tuskegee Institute; Charles S.
Johnson, head of the Department of Social Science at Fisk University;
Walter White, executive secretary of the National Association for the
Advancement of Colored People (NAACP); and Charles C. Spaulding,
president of the North Carolina Mutual Life Insurance Company of
Durham, North Carolina. Clarence was deeply impressed by the unre-
strained way in which these men unburdened themselves in regard to
the predicament of African Americans in the United States, not only in
connection with this question of the homesteads, but also in terms of
the overall deep sense of frustration they felt. "No one could have entered more fully into the nature of the problem," he said, "or have
expressed more intelligently a desire to find a way to help, than did

Mrs. Roosevelt. We talked from about 8 o'clock until 12, the president came in from the Oval Room, where he had been in another meeting, and briefly entered into the spirit of our conference."[22]

The whole occasion was unprecedented in African American history. There were no decisions, but the consensus was that in the South, desegregation, desirable as it was, should have a lower priority than African American participation in the aid programs of the New Deal.

A month later Pickett made a trip with Eleanor Roosevelt to Arthurdale in its formative stage. The two of them met in the old Arthur mansion with homesteaders, discussing housing and schools. An unexpected opportunity (referred to by Quakers as an *opening*) developed. In a hurriedly scribbled letter to his wife, Clarence Pickett revealed the excitement and implications of the opportunity:

> It happened that at the [luncheon] table Mrs. Roosevelt and I sat together, and she said that she was not comfortable about our international relations, that she feared we were centering on our home problems and were missing our best service abroad. She wanted to know my feelings. I largely agreed, and mentioned the increased Navy. She said she had many letters about that and was concerned.
>
> Our conversation resulted in her asking me if I would select a small group to meet with her and the president at 4:00 on 23 February [1934] in the White House to talk about this and what might be done about it. I stalled for time, and got [Friend] Fred Libby [executive secretary of the National Council for the Prevention of War] to help me out in the selection today. I went in at her request at 5:00 today with my list, and she was going to check it with the president, then return it to me tomorrow. It looks like a rather remarkable opening to get a word in to the president, and at her solicitation. So I am thankful. We shall see how it works out. At any rate, I do pray for wise guidance! Won't thee too![23]

The meeting with President and Mrs. Roosevelt to discuss the international situation and disarmament took place Friday afternoon, 23 February. Those present, in addition to Clarence Pickett, were Harry Emerson Fosdick, minister, Riverside Church in New York; William Abbott, editor, *Christian Science Monitor,* Boston; C.C. Talbott, president, North Dakota Farmers Union,; Harold Evans, Quaker attorney, Philadelphia; Frank Aydelotte, president, Swarthmore College. Later in the year Clarence Pickett underlined his own views by mailing to Mrs. Roosevelt a copy of "Peace Costs Too Much!" by Henry W. Lawrence, which appeared in the 10 October issue of *The Christian Century,* and a paper by Frederick Libby entitled "The London Naval Conversations."

While the inauguration of Franklin D. Roosevelt resulted in almost a preoccupation by the new administration with domestic issues, portentous events in Europe were also claiming the president's attention. Adolf Hitler had been sworn in as Chancellor of Germany on 30 January 1933. The Reichstag fire on the evening of 27 February, without doubt set by the Sturmabteilung (storm troopers or Brown Shirts), provided the needed provocation to blame the communists. By decree, President Hindenberg suspended sections of the constitution which guaranteed individual and civil liberties. Elections on 5 March, with voters intimidated by truckloads of Nazi storm troopers roaring through the streets, brought to the lower house of the German Parliament a majority of Nazi Party and Nationalist Party representatives. These were to be the last democratic elections during Hitler's lifetime. There began within the Third Reich internal plots and counterplots, and within the Nazi Party itself a new and ruthless struggle for power, involving the Army, the Security Service, and Brown Shirts.

Into this political maelstrom, with ramifications for all of Europe and indeed for the United States itself, journeyed Clarence Pickett, this time with his wife, Lilly. They left Philadelphia early on 25 April 1934. By late the next evening they were settled into cabin 374 on deck D of the tourist section of the *Berengaria*, the stateroom overflowing with flowers, fruit, letters, and telegrams.

Early in the morning of 2 May, they disembarked at Cherbourg, France and immediately transferred to the boat train for Paris. Lilly Pickett, with her special and lifelong interest in gardening, was impressed with what she saw out the train window: "The countryside in France on the 2nd of May was a joy of spring beauty. The small, irregular pasture-lands separated by terraces of earth along which grew shrubs or lines of willow trees denuded of all their heavy branches, making them beautifully lacy, were just in the prime of the first spring green. Here and there on more distant hillsides would sit peasant villages with their ivy-walled and rose-roofed cottages set in a background of soft, spring green. Pictures that have tempted the brush of many an artist and made me long for the skill to preserve those dashes of beauty which were so quickly snatched away as we rode along."[24]

As much as these beautiful pastoral scenes were needed to uplift human spirits, the Picketts knew that the realities of social and economic life in France were grim in substance and tone. They were met in Paris by Mahlon and Vivian Harvey, and Henry van Etten, workers at the Friends Center. Clarence Pickett already knew that a principal task of the Center was assisting hundreds of German refugees. While Lilly toured Paris with Vivian Harvey, Clarence engaged in seemingly endless committee meetings regarding the operations and future of the Quaker center.

Their second destination was Geneva, traveling overnight in a second-class car, each choosing to save $27 by rolling up in their steamer rugs on the compartment benches. They were met in Geneva by Bertram and Irene Pickard, English Quaker representatives at the Geneva Friends Center. Again Clarence's time was filled with meetings, but he did join Lilly in some sightseeing. A high point for both of them during the Geneva stayover was meeting the daughter and grandsons of Tomas Masaryk, founding father and president of the Czechoslovakian Republic. Lilly was impressed with the high standard of living in Switzerland—"a living, happy testimony to one hundred years of peace, with no grand homes but no hovels."[25]

Clarence combined Friends Service Committee business with his interest in subsistence homesteads. At their next stop, Vienna, he called on the Department of Agriculture to discuss homesteading, following up on his 1930 visit. He visited the Leopoldau Homestead. In Prague he inquired about land settlements. In Germany he looked at the subsistence homestead at Spandau. When in Great Britain he visited land settlements in Wales and England. These findings Pickett reported to M.L. Wilson, his superior in the Division of Subsistence Homesteads at home.

Clarence Pickett did not keep a day-by-day journal of his activities and observations on this European trip, but chose to summarize his impressions, country by country, upon his return on the *Aquitania*, asking that his comments on political and social movements be seen as rather confidential. "Europe is so sensitive, especially in spots," he said, "that statements which are published should be given most careful thought. One may easily do more harm than good."[26]

He found France almost paralyzed with fear, Hitler's Germany the chief cause. In Switzerland he wondered whether the beautiful new

League of Nations building in Geneva would be completed in time to entertain the funeral of the League. "Geneva seems strangely aloof," he wrote, "far from the world of search for life, only living in the research-academic air. It is like visiting a feudal castle which is a dramatic reminder of a world which was once real."[27]

His visit to Austria was just three months after the Austrian dictator, Chancellor Englebert Dollfuss, had violently crushed socialist opposition to his authoritarian regime, leaving thousands of Austrians imprisoned or out of work. Eight thousand of these families of Social Democrats were receiving relief through the Quaker center in Vienna, with funds supplied by the International Federation of Trade Unions.

Clarence Pickett recalled years later that the Vienna center was ready to extend relief also to the families of Nazis who had been imprisoned by the government following the attempted Nazi "Putsch" in July, 1934.[28] Indeed, Rufus Jones, favoring such assistance, as usual strictly on the basis of need without reference to political or religious affiliation, secured consent from the Austrian chancellor to allow Friends to distribute relief to the estimated fifteen hundred such families in Vienna provided it could be financed through an international fund. Clarence Pickett "on his own authority," not on behalf of the committee, wrote to the International Relief Association in New York to see if it had funds that might be used for aid for these families.[29] The AFSC board, terming such assistance an unusual opportunity to express a "spirit of reconciliation," laid down specific conditions for the relief effort.[30] In part because there were no international nongovernmental sources of funds available for this relief effort, the program did not materialize.[31]

Following the visit to Czechoslovakia, Pickett noted how President Masaryk had kept his eye not on security or military development but on the needs of his people for land, houses, and the freedom to live unfettered lives. "Democracy is a strong tradition," observed Clarence, "and freedom of thought, press, assembly and worship is sacred. There are jitters now because of the Nazi bannings [condemnations] of Germans living in Czechoslovakia and because of German refugees."[32]

It is not surprising that Pickett in his trip report devotes a great deal of attention to Germany. He was aware of the Hitler movement from the time of his 1930 visit and deeply concerned about it. "Nationalism, force, unquestioning surrender to authority, and Nordic superiority are the four planks in the platform of the Nazis," he said in an address to Friends in the summer of 1932.[33] He blamed the situation on "the vicious Versailles boundaries, the exaction of reparations, the tariff barriers, long-delayed world disarmament, and financial collapse. . . ."[34] He noted in that same address how the Friends and friends of the Friends in Germany were challenging the war system, opposing the racial drive of Hitlerites against the Jews, and standing for religious liberty and freedom.

Two very personal experiences are dealt with in the trip report. The first of these deepened Clarence's awareness of how once again Jews were suffering. "I talked with one of the finest religious leaders I have ever met—a rabbi [Leo Baeck], who said, "I have to hold two, three, or four services each Saturday to accommodate in my large synagogue the crowds who want to come. And always my message is the same—let no drop of bitterness enter your hearts, no matter what comes."[35] Pickett many years later was to see Baeck again, in New York at Quaker House, there to learn of the rabbi's heroic pastoral services in a concentration camp from 1938 to 1945, during which time his wife and three children were liquidated.

The second experience of tragic proportions related to the little Quaker band in Germany: "Let me reflect it [the tragedy] through a visit to a family. The father, a distinguished lawyer, the mother a German-American of wealth, four boys. The father defended two Jews against what was obviously a travesty against justice and decency. For this he lost his right to practice. He is bewildered—his old friends shun him as though he were a leper. Meanwhile, all four sons are Nazi. They parade, greet each other when they arrive at home by 'Heil Hitler!' . . . The tragedy will kill the father and mother. What will it do to the boys?"[36]

In England, Clarence's final stop in the two-week European tour, he was comparing the measures that were counteracting the depression with those of the United States. He noted that the dole for unemployment was firmly in place. "It has maintained the dignity of home life, preserved health, and prevented political violence. I am for it. Comparing the coal fields of South Wales with our own, the condition of people and families is infinitely better. But after all, it is unemployment dole. And there has been, until recently, almost no experimenting with alternatives to unemployment. Any concession that unemployment is a normal or natural state for any able-bodied person is vicious."[37]

Then Clarence Pickett summed up his trip impressions:

The total effect of this hurried trip produces a sense that we are really in a period like the Thirty Years War, that we are seeing the death of an age of privilege and disparity of wealth, of separation between the hand and head, of the appearance of democracy—and of much that goes by the name of religion now. It is not inconceivable that a further war may be in the offing, and a longer delay in the coming of a new day of honesty, freedom, work and faith.

The peace and reconciliation forces seem so tiny and ineffective compared with those driving toward conflict. But they are deep and true. If only champions of clear thought and sacrificial devotion emerge we may be saved. It is no time for Friends to give up! In *Paradise Regained,* Milton makes Christ say as He emerged from the wilderness, "By winning words to conquer winning hearts, and make persuasion do the work of fear." Milton's sentiments had hard sledding in his day as they have today. But it is only these convictions that are adequate to today.[38]

Clarence Pickett returned home to take up again his dual set of responsibilities—in the American Friends Service Committee and in the Division of Subsistence Homesteads of the U.S. Department of the Interior. And to be present at the graduation of his oldest daughter, Rachel, from the Quaker school, Westtown. She, like her sister Carolyn six years later, then went on to Antioch College, where their father served as trustee for four terms, 1936-1948.

After their summer vacation, on 19 and 20 September 1934 Clarence and Lilly Pickett, together with Milburn Wilson and his wife, made a significant visit to Hyde Park, at the invitation of Eleanor Roosevelt. The Wilsons and Picketts drove up together, arriving for lunch at Val-Kill, the fieldstone cottage that FDR had built for Eleanor on the Hyde Park estate in 1925 in order to give her an independence she could not enjoy at the big house. Most of the afternoon was spent talking about the Arthurdale community and more particularly the community school.

Pickett and Wilson had about fifteen minutes with the president, talking about subsistence homesteads. Clarence would never forget the two-day experience. "I wish that there was a little deeper basic character involved in the group that hovers around the White House," he wrote. He had a deepening admiration for Eleanor Roosevelt. "She is a balance wheel, and a beautiful character, but in some of the people around the president there is little moral and spiritual depth, which I regret."[39]

Memorable as the Hyde Park visit was, it was only one of many such experiences with the Roosevelts that Clarence Pickett would have over the next few years. He was in and out of the White House during the Roosevelt presidency over one hundred and fifty times.

NOTES

1. Tape recording of Clarence Pickett's remarks at AFSC staff meeting on 19 Nov. 1962 following the death of Eleanor Roosevelt, AFSC archives.

2. AFSC annual report, 1 June 1931 - 31 Dec. 1932, 16-17.

3. Malcolm Ross, "When Depression Blights a Great Area," *The New York Times Magazine,* 31 Jan. 1932, 6 and 22.

4. Clarence Pickett journal, 11 Jan. 1933, AFSC archives.

5. AFSC annual report 1931.

6. Clarence E. Pickett, "Herbert Clark Hoover," *Friends Journal* 10, no. 21 (1 Nov. 1964): 490.

7. Clarence E. Pickett, "A New Deal in Motives," *The American Friend* 21 (new series), no. 29 (7 Sept. 1933): 401.

8. Clarence E. Pickett, *For More Than Bread* (Boston: Little, 1953), 44-45.

9. Pickett, *Bread,* 5.

10. Clarence E. Pickett, "The Social Significance of the Subsistence Homestead Movement," *Journal of Home Economics* 26 (Oct. 1934): 477-79.

11. Kenneth S. Davis, *FDR: The New Deal Years 1933-1937: A History* (New York: Random, 1986), 350.

12. Davis, *FDR,* 351.

13. Joseph P. Lash, *Eleanor and Franklin: The Story of Their Relationship Based on Eleanor Roosevelt's Private Papers* (New York: Norton, 1971), 393.

14. Pickett, *Bread,* 47.

15. Davis, *FDR,* 35.

16. Joseph P. Lash, as quoted in Janet Mills' "Eleanor Roosevelt's Pastoral Vision, and the Arthurdale Reality," 1984 dissertation, West Virginia University.

17. Tamara K. Haraven, *Eleanor Roosevelt: An American Conscience* (Chicago: Quadrangle, 1968), 53.

18. Pickett, *Bread*, 46.

19. Harry and Rebecca Timbres, *We Didn't Ask for Utopia: A Quaker Family in Soviet Russia* (New York: Prentice, 1939).

20. Letter dated 9 Jan 1934, Clarence Pickett to Lilly Pickett, AFSC archives.

21. Pickett, *Bread*, 48.

22. Pickett, *Bread*, 49.

23. Letter dated 12 Feb 1934, Clarence Pickett to Lilly Pickett, AFSC archives.

24. Lilly Pickett's diary letter #2, 2 May 1934, 1, family papers, courtesy of Carolyn Miller Pickett.

25. Diary letter #2, 8.

26. Clarence Pickett journal, trip report: Europe, 25 April - 7 June 1934, AFSC archives, 1.

27. Trip report, 6.

28. *Pickett, Bread*, 95.

29. Pickett to Oswald Garrison Villard, 28 Dec. 1935: AFSC archives.

30. Minutes, AFSC board of directors, 12 Sept. 1934.

31. See Hans Schmitt, *Quakers and Nazis: Inner Light in Outer Darkness* (Univ. of Missouri Press: Columbia, MO, 1997), 88-89.

32. Trip report, 6.

33. Clarence E. Pickett, "Quakerism in the Field," *Friends Intelligencer* 89, no. 36 (3 Sept. 1932): 709-11.

34. Pickett, "Quakerism," 1932.

35. Trip report, 6.

36. Trip report, 6.

37. Trip report, 7.

38. Trip report, 8.

39. Pickett journal, confidential report of visit to Hyde Park, 22 Sept. 1934.

Chapter 10

FACING UP TO RELIEF NEEDS
AT HOME AND ABROAD

*Deep down it was all one pattern, a world
in revolution but unsure of its star*

FOR CLARENCE AND LILLY PICKETT, Christmas was always a time for the immediate family to gather for the day, to open presents, and to relax. But Clarence's journal, year after year, reveals that he viewed the immediately preceding and succeeding days in December as times for work. After all, he knew that his Quaker forebears had not even celebrated Christmas, based on the belief that all days were holy. Some Quaker schools, up to the end of the nineteenth century, remained open at Christmas time in deference to this religious conviction.

Taking full advantage of the week days between Christmas and New Year's Day at the end of 1934, Clarence Pickett, AFSC vice chairman Henry Tatnall Brown, and Bernard Waring, chairmen of the Coal Committee, interviewed Myron Taylor, chairman of the board and chief executive officer of the United States Steel Corporation. They discussed the possibility of a generous contribution from the corporation as the basis for a nongovernmental rehabilitation and subsistence homestead project in the coal fields.

At a meeting on 2 January 1935 the AFSC board of directors considered the setting up of a Social Order Section and the employment of Homer Morris, "particularly to exploit the possibility of a project in the coal fields."[1] Morris, a Quaker who was professor of economics at Fisk University and on the Earlham College faculty from 1918 to 1928, had been involved, either as field director or in an advisory capacity, in the AFSC child-feeding program in Appalachia, giving him a unique opportunity to study first hand the effects of unemployment among coal miners. His findings and recommendations were published in his book, *The Plight of the Bituminous Coal Miner.*[2]

The establishment of this new section and the employment of Homer Morris required pump-priming underwriting of about $3,000 for six months. Knowing that the board would be reluctant to embrace a new program given the financial difficulties of the AFSC, Clarence Pickett had presented the need to Mrs. Roosevelt in writing, then in advance of the board meeting phoned her and obtained her agreement to contribute the full $3,000 if the board approved the program. The stage was now set for the formal establishment by the board in June of what was named the Social-Industrial Section, into which was folded the Coal Committee, the Home Service Section, and the Economics Commission.

Clarence Pickett's role in the development and management of the government subsistence homesteads, principally those that were in the coal fields, brought him increasingly closer to Mrs. Roosevelt and through her to the president. In mid-April there occurred an unusual opportunity to bring Mrs. Roosevelt closer to the Quakers and the American Friends Service Committee. Pickett made arrangements for her to attend a meeting of the AFSC general committee at the Quaker Westtown School in Chester County, Pennsylvania. Clarence and Lilly Pickett and their two daughters, Rachel (a student at Antioch College) and Carolyn, met Eleanor Roosevelt and Nancy Cook, a close personal friend of Mrs. Roosevelt, in Wilmington and took them to Arden, Delaware, for a visit to the single-tax colony (governed on the principles of Henry George), where they inspected the handcraft industries and homesteads. Then they all went to have lunch at the Picketts' large rented house in Moylan, with Homer Morris and his wife, Edna, joining the party. In the afternoon, Eleanor Roosevelt and Nancy Cook were taken to Westtown School. Mrs. Roosevelt spoke briefly to the student body and in the meetinghouse on the campus, participated in the AFSC meeting, and spoke with Clarence Pickett in a thirty-minute radio broadcast over the Columbia Broadcasting System. In her address, Mrs. Roosevelt "challenged the nation to face the fact that we are up against the end of

Carolyn Pickett, Clarence, Rachel Pickett, Nancy Cook with
Eleanor Roosevelt and Lilly Pickett on the First Lady's visit to Westtown
School for an AFSC meeting, 25 April 1935

an era. Big groups of people who refused to accept the problems of
unemployment and industrial maladjustment are the greatest stumbling
block in the path of a new and better social and economic order."[3]

In the evening Mrs. Roosevelt heard Clarence Pickett speak about
"Quakers in action," Rufus Jones on "the world-wide scope of the AFSC,"
and she herself spoke again on "why I turned to the American Friends
Service Committee with my radio funds." Pickett drove her to Philadelphia where she took the train to Washington. Newspapers the next day

gave full coverage to the First Lady's time with the "quiet folk," as the AP reporter put it. Did Clarence Pickett ever invite Eleanor Roosevelt to attend a Quaker meeting for worship? Yes, he did, in 1938 when he was to be present for a Sunday meeting for worship at the Florida Avenue Friends Meeting in Washington. She was unable to attend. Three years later he sent her a copy of the recently-published *Just Among Friends: The Quaker Way of Life*.[4]

In May, Pickett sought an opportunity for Mrs. Roosevelt to visit a coal mine. This was not an easy task because of the superstition among coal miners that the presence of a woman in a mine was an ill omen. But finally Clarence was able to arrange with the superintendent of safety at the Willow Grove mine near Neffs, Ohio for Mrs. Roosevelt, the journalist Lorena Hickok, himself, and a few others to go into and out of the mine "with hordes of cameras and newspaper people" covering the event. Indeed, it was now customary for enormous crowds to assemble when word got out that the First Lady was going to be visiting.

One stratagem used by Mrs. Roosevelt to gain some minutes of privacy for her party was to picnic for lunch alongside the road, drawing upon a large basket full of food packed in advance at the White House. Lilly Pickett, who on occasion joined her husband on the expeditions to the homesteads, recalled in later years how Mrs. Roosevelt would quite spontaneously identify a beautiful spot by the side of the road and instruct the chauffeur to stop. "A large blanket was spread with Mrs. Roosevelt and the lunch basket located in the center, and from there she served us all. I felt I should be serving the First Lady rather than being served by her, but the privilege was never granted."[5]

In January 1936 Clarence Pickett, Eleanor Roosevelt, and a dozen members of the Industrial Advisory Committee of the Department of Commerce made a visit to Arthurdale, going overnight by train in a reserved Pullman car from Washington. "Landed at Fairmont [West Virginia] at 7:30 a.m.," wrote Clarence. "There was a ten degrees below zero temperature. Then went about twenty miles for breakfast. After breakfast most of us drove up to Scotts Run and visited one or two families there. It was a terribly cold and dreary experience, but not at all as dreary for us as it was for those who have to live there."[6]

The visit to Arthurdale included a square dance in the evening at the community center, with Eleanor Roosevelt participating and Clarence Pickett an observer. Clarence arranged for the special sleeper to be transferred from Fairmont to Reedsville, enabling the party to be back in Washington by the next morning. Pickett promptly wrote to the president of the Baltimore & Ohio Railroad Company to thank him for the arrangements.

On still another trip with Mrs. Roosevelt, Clarence Pickett experienced the pace that she set for others with her. On a beautiful day in May he, Eleanor Roosevelt, and her personal secretary, Malvina Scheider, arrived by train in Mt. Sterling, Kentucky at 7:00 a.m. and were met by a White House car that had been sent out the previous day. After what Clarence described as *some* breakfast" at the home of a local physician and following a stop in Camargo for Mrs. Roosevelt to lay the cornerstone of a Works Progress Administration (WPA) school building, the party traveled (on what is today U.S. 480) to West Liberty for the dedication of a new high school. "This little town was so completely swamped with people," wrote Clarence in his journal, "that one could hardly get the sense of being in a town at all."[7]

The Roosevelt party was not able to leave West Liberty until three in the afternoon, their destination that night being Morgantown, West Virginia, 365 miles away. The Kentucky state police insisted on providing an escort of two motorcycle policemen all the way to the Ohio River border. It was slow going because much of the road was either freshly tarred or graveled. En route, in Paintsville, some teachers and their children literally flagged down the White House car, begging Mrs. Roosevelt to speak to the children; in Louisa, Kentucky a stop was made to allow time for Mrs. Roosevelt to file her newspaper column for the day and for Clarence to purchase some sandwiches and soft drinks; and in Ashland the mayor had arranged for all whistles to be blown upon the approach of the White House car. Again, the town was completely swamped with people. The First Lady spoke from the steps of the post office.

Shortly after crossing the Ohio River into Ohio, the travelers were stopped by the state police, who claimed that the headlights of the car were too bright. A very flustered officer waved them on when he read the automobile registration card. Clarence's reports on the balance of the trip capture the full flavor of the experience:

> On the whole the trip was a very calm and normal one after we got into Ohio, crossing the river near Parkersburg, West Virginia, then going to Fairmont, then on to Morgantown—and when we were within about five

miles of Morgantown we had a puncture. It was about 3:15 in the morning. The car was new and the chauffeur didn't even know where the tools were. Mrs. Scheider and Mrs. Roosevelt got out of the car and stood in the middle of the road while we pulled the seats out and got the tools. The jack was terribly stiff and hard to manage. We finally got the wheel jacked up but then the car rolled forward and let it down again. In Mrs. Roosevelt's column the next day she commented about the fact that neither of us swore [she actually said, "To use some forcible language"]. It never occurred to me to swear—I think I was too sleepy.

But we hove to, and got the wheel jacked up again and got it changed, and on into Morgantown, and made bed just about 4:00 a.m. As we left the car, Mrs. Roosevelt told the chauffeur that she wouldn't need him until 3 o'clock the next day, and to be sure to have a good sleep. As soon as we entered the hotel, she wondered whether we might be able to have breakfast at 8 o'clock the next morning so that she could get in a good day at Arthurdale, which arrangement was made. The contrast impressed me.[8]

Toward the end of July, Clarence and Lilly had the pleasure of going to Oskaloosa for a Pickett family reunion. For the first time they took the "Denver Zephyr" on the Burlington Railroad, averaging over sixty miles an hour. All were there except William, and Clarence Pickett kept hoping he would turn up. In the afternoon Clarence telegraphed William in Toledo [Ohio] asking whether he was coming, and he wired back that he was not. "That brought great sadness to us," wrote Clarence.[9] William, eleven years older than Clarence, was the brother who had left Glen Elder at a young age, feeling "the limitations so severe in Kansas that he broke away from it and went to Oklahoma."[10] One sensed that Clarence particularly wanted to keep in touch with William because of his apparent self-imposed isolation within the family. On the occasion of the reunion, Clarence was impressed with how little he had roots in the same soil as a child that other members of the family had. They all dated back to Illinois, and he to Kansas.

In early September 1937 Clarence Pickett was asked to go to Hyde Park for a conference with Mrs. Roosevelt on matters relating to the Arthurdale school. It was following this conference that Clarence had a memorable experience in respect to President Roosevelt. Pickett was invited to attend the annual meeting of the Roosevelt Home Town Club at the home of Moses Smith, a Roosevelt tenant.

The president spoke simply but effectively, saying that he was concerned about the foreign situation, and that "he would spare no pain" to prevent the United States getting into a war. "It was impressive," wrote Clarence, "to see the president of the United States, one of the largest countries in the world, sitting quite simply on the front porch of a farm house—not at all a grand one—meeting with his neighbors with a kind of fellowship that is built only where close neighborly contact is possible. Everybody present seemed to feel a desire to continue this happy and free atmosphere, and yet to be conscious of our world responsibilities.[11]

Clarence Pickett was himself feeling keenly the burden of the international situation. He had become deeply involved in the Emergency Peace Campaign. The AFSC's Peace Section had been instrumental in calling together, during 1935, a group of outstanding leaders in the peace movement to discuss plans for launching a vigorous nationwide campaign for peace, with the thought that out of the campaign would grow a more unified pacifist movement.

While the American Friends Service Committee provided much of the leadership and was the depository for contributions, an autonomous council acted as a policy-making body for the campaign. The campaign was launched on 21 April 1936 by a radio broadcast over an international hookup. Participants included George Lansbury, formerly leader of the British Labor Party and a member of Parliament, Kirby Page, author, traveler, and lecturer, and Hannah Clothier Hull, a prominent Friend, who read the prepared speech of Mrs. Roosevelt. The First Lady had agreed to speak in person, but obligations arising from the death of Louis Howe prevented her from being present.

It was Clarence Pickett who had drafted her speech but she turned it over to the president, and it was delivered in accordance with his corrections and additions. Pickett's introduction was a recital in praise of what the U.S. government had done for peace, and even in these paragraphs the president made revisions. A Pickett sentence that urged America's active involvement in international efforts to redress the grievances of the have-not nations the president allowed to remain: "We do not intend to be drawn into armed conflict," the sentence read, "but we certainly should be willing to use our resources and our unique position to bring about real results in conferences which deal with any questions remotely touching the peace of the world."[12]

The First Lady participated in the launching of the Campaign in still another way. On 22 April, throughout the country, four thousand carrier pigeons furnished by members of the International Federation of American Homing Pigeon Fanciers and the American Racing Union carried a message from Eleanor Roosevelt to mayors in towns and cities across the country:

> I am glad to take part in this Emergency Peace Program with its purpose to keep the United States out of war.
>
> The people in this country are the power behind the government. It is they who create a will to peace. When government representatives know that their people are determined that peaceful means shall be taken, and that their actions are being watched, results will be obtained. We need the same interest and sacrifice for peace now as in time of war.
>
> I hope this Campaign will arouse a sense of personal responsibility in keeping us out of war.[13]

In the two months following the opening of the Campaign, mass meetings were held in close to three hundred of the largest cities in all but one of the forty-eight states of the country. This was in turn followed by a second nationwide cycle of meetings in almost five hundred cities. The fall program culminated in an Armistice Day gathering in Madison Square Garden in New York City, at that time probably the largest peace meeting ever staged in the United States.

Clarence Pickett's role was as an active member of the campaign executive committee, and as the lead person in persuading business and other leaders to participate. Apart from his success in securing the participation of Mrs. Roosevelt, a prime example of his role and mission was his conversations with retired Rear Admiral Richard E. Byrd, the noted leader of scientific exploration trips to the Arctic and Antarctic. On 5 June 1936, in a speech at a dinner given at the Waldorf Astoria in New York in Byrd's honor by leading industrialists, scientists and educators, Byrd announced that he would "devote the rest of his life to the work of furthering peace and understanding among the peoples and nations of the world."[14]

Clarence Pickett and Ray Newton, secretary of the AFSC Peace Section, went to visit Richard Byrd on 30 September. They found Byrd to be humble in his statements about the peace cause. He told them how, out of his experience in isolation at Advance Base, deep in the interior of the Antarctic, there had come the sense of the unity of all life, and especially all human life, (a full account of which would appear two years later in his book, *Alone*[15]) and that he wanted to do something to make that a reality in present-day living. Clarence told him the story of the American Friends Service Committee and the Emergency Peace Campaign, asked him to become honorary chairman of the 1937 spring meetings, and to undertake speaking engagements.

Pickett and Newton did not obtain a definite commitment from Richard Byrd. On 19 October Ray Newton learned that Byrd was to be speaking the following day in Bloomington, Illinois. Clarence abruptly decided to take the Broadway Limited to Chicago (not realizing that his daughter Carolyn was planning to have a surprise birthday party for him that evening) and then go to Bloomington where Byrd was scheduled to give his lecture on "Antarctic Explorations." Pickett guessed that Byrd would come into Chicago for the night after finishing a lecture in Elgin and would go down to Bloomington on the afternoon train. Clarence's detective work was right on the mark. Clarence had a reserved seat in the same car in which the admiral had a compartment. He sent in his card by the porter. Byrd asked Pickett to come in. While Byrd shaved and dressed, the two of them talked—for nearly two hours.

Clarence found him full of interesting ideas. Byrd accepted the chairmanship of the sponsors for the spring meetings of the No-Foreign-War Crusade and agreed to speak at the opening of the crusade on 6 April 1937, the twentieth anniversary of the U.S. entrance into World War I. Admiral Byrd hoped that President Roosevelt would join in that broadcast, but the president was unwilling to do so. Mrs. Roosevelt gladly accepted the invitation.

The two-year Emergency Peace Campaign came to a conclusion on 31 December 1937. The campaign momentum during its first year created results which far exceeded original expectations. More than thirty thousand individuals contributed $550,000 during the two years of the campaign. Twenty regional offices were set up with seventy-one staff members. Good working contacts were organized in almost two thousand towns and cities. About ten thousand students actively participated in the campaign, some of them giving their entire summer to peace education in rural areas.

One responsibility which was increasingly engaging the American Friends Service Committee was the plight of German refugees. Virtually from the day (30 January 1933) on which Adolf Hitler was sworn in as Chancellor of Germany, German people began leaving their country in the thousands. At no time in all the years of Quaker service for refugees did the American Friends Service Committee classify these fleeing people as to religion, but it can be assumed that most of them were Jews. There were some Quaker efforts specifically aimed at Jews as they became segregated and stigmatized by the Nazis, but other non-Aryans were served on an equal basis.

In 1933 French Friends, extremely small in number, with assistance from the American Friends Service Committee and the Friends Service Council in London, were dealing with the thousands of refugees flooding Paris. The Quaker Center helped to provide heat and food in the cold, unfurnished barracks offered by the French government where refugees were herded without work or hope. In 1934 there were four thousand German refugee families in need of being placed outside Paris where they might become self-supporting. In 1935 the number was somewhat decreased, but there still remained a need for relief and rehabilitation. In 1936 other agencies joined forces with French Friends to provide for and seek permanent solutions for German refugee families.

Clarence Pickett had been drawn close to these efforts administered by the Paris center during his brief 1934 European trip. In 1935 he talked to a number of U.S. officials regarding a proposal to establish colonies for refugees in South America, but at the time with little sense of urgency. In early 1936, however, Pickett was to become fully associated with the efforts of American Jews and Christians (Catholic and Protestant) in bringing Jews out of Germany, one early plan being to take one hundred thousand younger Jewish German people away from Germany and settle them in Palestine, South America, and in other parts of the world.[16] The so-called Nuremberg Laws of 15 September 1935, depriving Jews of German citizenship and confining them to the status of "subjects," were now forcing even more thousands of Jews to seek emigration.

According to Brenda Bailey, whose Quaker parents (he German, she English) lived in Germany throughout the whole period of the Third Reich, "the first concentration camps were created in 1933 when the prisons were already overcrowded. They were mainly run by the S.A. [Sturmabteilung—storm troopers or Brown Shirts] in remote places, where their brutality would be less visible. Some political suspects and influential Jews were detained for only a few weeks, but others remained there until they died. Acts of bestiality and sadism were common, though not as routinely organized in the early years as later on. . . . In the camps, torture and degrading punishment were used not only to humiliate and extract money or information, but also to intimidate opposition in the outside community."[17]

The earliest American rescue efforts by Christians were under the auspices of the Federal Council of Churches, resulting in the formation of the American Christian Committee for German Refugees. In June 1936 Clarence attended what he termed "a weighty gathering" of fifty people called together by Harry Emerson Fosdick, minister of the Riverside Church in New York, to discuss the problem of the German refugees. Clarence was delegated to interview Herbert Hoover to see whether the former President would take a leadership role in money-raising for a rescue operation, and he wrote a long letter to Mrs. Roosevelt spelling out the details of the situation. He pointed out that about eighty thousand people had left Germany since the advent of the National Socialist German Workers' (Nazi) Party, eighty per cent of these Jews, and twenty per cent non-Jewish He noted that Jews were doing a remarkable piece of relief and relocation for their co-religionists, and were contributing thousands of dollars for the care of non-Jewish refugees. He hoped that Mrs. Roosevelt would mention in her newspaper column the extreme need of roughly twenty-five hundred non-Jewish refugees for whom the American Christian Committee was seeking financial support.[18]

Two Quaker travelers, Philadelphia businessman Robert Yarnall and Douglas Steere of the Haverford College faculty, were unable to get close enough to the situation in Germany to be personally in touch with the repression. Over a period of two years, however, two English Friends, William Hughes and Corder Catchpool, gained permission to visit many of the concentration camps, asking to see particular prisoners. "When they asked to see the punishment cells, they were shown unoccupied 'dark cubicles equipped with heavy leg irons.' . . . Hughes and Catchpool considered speaking openly about their findings in England, but realized regretfully that this would cut off the possibility of further visits. They also wanted to avoid reawakening the intense hatred of Germany which had developed in Britain during World War I."[19] And there was the need to shield German Quakers from possible repercussions.

Apart from support for the Quaker center in Paris, the year 1937 ended without any programmatic actions being taken by the American

Friends Service Committee in respect to Jews in Germany and German refugees in Europe.

The need for refugee relief in Spain, however, demanded immediate attention. After years of political turmoil following the serious impact of the Great Depression upon the lives of Spaniards, internal military forces led by General Francisco Franco inaugurated in July 1936 a brutal war against the government, an antifascist coalition (the "Popular Front") composed of democrats, socialists, and the revolutionary left. Foreign intervention complicated the civil war: the Loyalists received aid from the Soviet Union and volunteers from other countries; Nationalist forces were assisted by Germany and Italy.

It was on a Monday morning in early November 1936 when Clarence Pickett was introduced to the needs of children in Spain. Lydia Morris, a member of Germantown Friends Meeting in Philadelphia who lived from time to time in France and who had recently visited Spain, reported to him immediately upon her arrival from Barcelona. She told of ten thousand children being evacuated from Madrid and other cities in Spain, and how the English Friends, under the leadership of Alfred Jacob, an American Friend married to an English Quaker, were planning, with the help of the International Save the Children Fund, to feed children in Barcelona. "I think I shall call a little group together to discuss the situation towards the end of the week," he wrote. "It is a very tragic picture, and I had hoped that we would not have to get into a relief job there, but there is a great deal of interest in this country in it, and it may seem to be necessary."[20]

Characteristically, Pickett moved quickly on the issue. The next day he had a session in Washington with Fernando de los Rios, the Spanish ambassador, to see whether the ambassador would look favorably upon the AFSC sending funds into Barcelona (still held by the government) for relief for children. "He thought very well of it," wrote Clarence.[21] In early December Sylvester Jones, a Quaker businessman in Chicago who for many years had been a missionary in Cuba and was fluent in Spanish, agreed to investigate conditions on both sides of the fighting line. Then on successive days Clarence Pickett talked with Señora de Palencia, the Spanish ambassador to Sweden, obtaining from her letters of introduction for Sylvester Jones to the Spanish ambassadors in London and Paris; with Salvador de Madariaga, the former permanent delegate from Spain

to the League of Nations; and with Ernest J. Swift, who had just returned from a meeting with the International Red Cross.

Pickett learned from Swift how extremely bitter the war was. The
International Red Cross was finding it difficult to exchange prisoners
because most of the prisoners were being shot instead of being kept for
exchange. The Red Cross executives strongly urged the Service Committee to administer relief and said that the Red Cross would give every
facility at its command to help the AFSC.[22]

With support from other church groups such as the Mennonites, Brethren, and Unitarians, the committee's Foreign Service Section decided
to enter into relief work in Spain even in advance of Sylvester Jones'
report. A special Committee on Spain within the framework of the AFSC
was established, with members from sixteen cooperating churches and
organizations. Clarence Pickett's role centered on finding major donors,
the Committee on Spain at first setting as a goal $2,000 a month for
relief on the Loyalist side and $1,000 a month on the Nationalist side.

But given the escalation of statistics on the number of refugees, these
fund raising targets soon became insufficient. In July 1937 Pickett was
pressing the American Red Cross to participate in the relief work. "They
agreed to speak kindly of the work," he wrote, "but have thus far given
no funds."[23] He urged Mrs. Roosevelt to ask the president to call Admiral Cary Grayson, a director of the American Red Cross, and ask him
for a grant of $50,000 for Spanish relief, a request "which she
said she would try to pull off."[24] But the reality of the situation was that
the American Red Cross was a quasi-governmental organization and
inherently political. FDR did not want to lose the strongly pro-Franco
Catholic vote by taking any action that might be construed as supporting
the Loyalists. His own State Department, under Cordell Hull, tended to
see the Spanish government as dangerously leftist. Finally in October
1938 the American Red Cross gave the American Friends Service
Committee 60,000 barrels of surplus flour for relief in Spain.

In the first three months of 1939 additional shipments of wheat sent
from the United States and foodstuffs from the International Commission for the Assistance of Child Refugees in Spain, an organization English Friends had formed, enabled the Quaker workers to distribute
supplies sufficient to feed over four hundred thousand people. When
the war ended on 26 March, a civil population of three million people
had reached the last stages of exhaustion. The war had forced a half

million refugees across the snow-filled Pyrenees into France. Quaker
workers moved with them to assist Spanish women and children
scattered in colonies in France.

With the establishment of the Social Industrial Section and the assurance that Homer Morris could work full time on the rehabilitation
program, the search began for the location of an experimental subsistence homestead community entirely under AFSC auspices. After much
study and investigation, Fayette County, Pennsylvania was selected as
the most suitable area. It was determined that ninety-six of the 152 coal
mines in the County were worked out or closed down, and thirty percent of the population was on relief. Clarence Pickett asked his brother-
in-law, Errol Peckham, and Homer Morris to find some good farmland
in the county within reasonable distance of suitable roads and schools.
The search turned up some interesting history: between the Revolutionary War and the turn of the century, there had been close to a dozen
Quaker meetings in the county. The Quakers had then moved west. The
property selected for purchase, the 200-acre Isaiah Craft family farm,
turned out to be in the very heart of what had once been a heavily
populated Quaker community.

At first some assistance from the Federal government was considered to be necessary, but gradually it became evident that such aid would
not be available. Furthermore, Mrs. Roosevelt, keenly in favor of a
Quaker project, was doubting the advisability of using government
money for fear it would tie the AFSC down. Pickett realized that the
pilot project would have to rely entirely upon private financing. It was
determined, furthermore, that the project would operate on a self-help
cooperative basis, meaning that the houses would be built by the homesteaders themselves—all unemployed or partially unemployed coal
miners. Each of the carefully selected fifty families would have at least
one and a half acres of land on which to raise some of their food, keep
chickens, perhaps pigs or a cow.

It was not until the end of 1935 that plans and policies matured to
the point where Pickett could go back to his initial contacts for the
necessary substantial financing, a total of $300,000. Although his first
contact in the United States Steel Corporation had been Myron Taylor,
his primary connection was now with vice president Arthur Young. Visiting at first privately with Young, Pickett then placed before him, Edwin

Ellis (another vice president), and Thomas Moses, president of the H.C. Frick Coke Co., the request for a contribution of $35,000 a year for three years. "They were somewhat hostile at the start," wrote Clarence, "but at the end recommended a contribution, Mr. Moses being particularly enthusiastic about it."[25]

Later in that same month Clarence Pickett and Homer Morris had an interview in New York City with Myron Taylor, chief executive officer of the Corporation, and Arthur Young. Taylor invited Pickett to attend the meeting of the Corporation's finance committee the following day to present the case for a contribution. Seated around the table in the board room, with Pickett and Taylor at one end, were Arthur Young, Junius Morgan, Ralph Watson, J. Pierpont Morgan, Walter Gifford, and Thomas W. Lamont, and (at the other end of the table) Edward Stettinius (called Edgar).

For the rest of his life Clarence would remember that afternoon: "It's a long journey from Kansas to New York City. It is still farther from the secluded security of a little Quaker farm community in the Sunflower State to the board room of the United States Steel Corporation at 61 Broadway, New York."[26] As he made his presentation, Clarence already knew that Taylor and Stettinius were interested, but he was anxious about what the finance committee as a whole would decide. "I am sure Arthur Young understood my anxiety, for late that evening, after I had returned to my home, he took the pains to call me by telephone to say that the Corporation had been glad to grant my full request. Those who have had experience in raising money will know what I mean when I say that it is an almost incomparable emotion that sweeps over one when, after an effort of this sort, he finds he has been successful."[27]

Clearly, it was during Clarence Pickett's initial private conversation with Myron Taylor that Pickett had touched a sensitive conscience. One day, on another occasion Taylor revealed to Pickett something of his own inner struggle when he said, "It is not easy to be a kind of Saint Francis and at the same time an effective chairman of a giant corporation, and I should like to be both."[28] Pickett was deeply impressed by this remark, revealing possibly for the first time the almost pastoral relationship Clarence would develop with men and women in high office in the world of business and government.

Clarence Pickett was also at this time endeavoring to interest Doris Duke Cromwell, labeled by a recent biographer as "the richest girl in the world,"[29] in the homesteading movement. On 26 November 1937

Doris Duke Cromwell, her secretary Marian Paschal, and Clarence Pickett were guests of Mrs. Roosevelt for dinner at the White House and stayed overnight. Early the next morning, in two White House cars, they left for the Tygart Valley homestead in West Virginia, accompanied by Mrs. Scheider, James Cromwell (Doris's politically ambitious husband), and Congressman Jennings Randolph from West Virginia. Contending with rain and fog all the way, they did not reach Tygart Valley until late afternoon, in time, however, for a speech Mrs. Roosevelt was scheduled to make to a meeting of the homesteaders.

"All the way along we had been fighting a bevy of cameramen,"[30] wrote Clarence. One reason was the presence of the twenty-five-year-old heiress who, completely out of keeping with the mission, wore a full-length Russian mink coat and English walking shoes, and wound up signing autographs for children who thought she was a movie star. That night they attended a square dance with Mrs. Roosevelt, as usual, joining in the dancing. According to biographer Stephanie Mansfield, Doris sulked in the corner, declining all requests. "'It's been a hard day,' Doris complained. 'And, after all, this is the first time I've even seen a square dance.'"[31]

The next day was to be even more difficult for Doris Duke Cromwell when she, Mrs. Roosevelt, and Clarence Pickett spent most of the time visiting in Scotts Run, which was unusually drab and dreary.

Then the following day they all took off for the Quaker project, certainly the key part of the expedition for Clarence. "Here we had the largest attack of cameramen that we have had at all," Clarence wrote, "until Doris Duke was almost distracted by the time we had seen the project and visited one or two families in some of the derelict coal towns."[32] That afternoon Clarence rode with Mrs. Cromwell and Marian Paschal to Pittsburgh and had a good chance to talk with Doris about her difficulty in understanding the significance of all that she had seen. Clarence makes no mention of the mink coat in his journal. More noteworthy is the fact that over the years he kept in touch with her, becoming in 1946 chairman of her foundation, Independent Aid.

In 1937 the plans for the homestead project in Fayette County moved forward quickly. Pickett had raised sufficient funds from interested corporations (over the objections of some Friends who felt that the acceptance of such contributions compromised the committee's integrity[33]) to proceed with the purchase of the Craft farm for $75,000, the project henceforth to be called Penn-Craft. David Day, a Friend who had worked with Clarence Pickett on the Westmoreland government homestead project, became manager of Penn-Craft; Errol Peckham, Clarence's brother-in-law, took charge of selecting the homesteaders; and Levinus Painter, a Quaker pastor with farming experience, managed the agricultural program.

The Penn-Craft experiment was eminently successful, with the building of the stone houses on a cooperative basis stretching into the 1940s. The total cash outlay for each house was $2,000, a twenty-year loan to the owner from the AFSC at two percent interest. A knitting mill provided employment for some residents. The old farm house became a community center. More than two hundred college students (the author of this biography one of them) volunteered for a summer to help the miners quarry stone and build the houses and to provide recreation for children. Penn-Craft was the fulfillment of what a back-to-the-land community might be. In recognition of this first self-help housing project, a Pennsylvania State historical marker was dedicated on 8 November 1991, a date coinciding with the move of the first family into their completed stone house in 1939.

While there can be little doubt that Penn-Craft was based on Clarence Pickett's experience of working for the federal government on subsistence homesteads and on his enormously successful fund raising in the steel and coal industries, there were three completely unrelated projects during that same period of time that were based on the generosity of a single individual, a widow in Washington, DC, Anne Hubbard Davis. She was to make a significant impact on the work of the American Friends Service Committee during Clarence Pickett's lifetime. And the initiatives were largely hers. It was Mrs. Davis who explained the reasons for her gifts to the AFSC (and other organizations):

> My tastes were simple, and I had never longed for things I could not have and had no ambition to have a lot of money, so when my husband [Bancroft Davis] died, leaving me a large amount, I was a most surprised person, as I had never thought much about what he had, and had never been interested in business of any kind. I was only anxious to dispose of it as soon as possible before I was called to the great unknown. . . . Being, however, as I mentioned before, of an intensely economical nature, I was obliged to think of the best way to get rid of it to help the most people, and that filled my brain and heart so fully that I had no time for grief or loneliness.[34]

Waysmeet, in Wallingford, Pennsylvania
the Pickett residence from June 1937 to April 1951

Mrs. Davis' donations to the AFSC were made in quick succession. In January 1935 she talked with Clarence Pickett about giving her spacious home at 2410 Wyoming Avenue to the AFSC to be used as an international hospitality house, especially for foreign guests of color in what was at the time a racially segregated city. A provision was that she be permitted to live in a portion of the house (the third floor) until her death. Mrs. Davis established a generous trust fund to provide for the maintenance of the house. During the World War II years, the Wyoming Avenue house became, under the guidance of Clarence Pickett, the site for a monthly interdisciplinary seminar where outstanding leaders in the fields of the behavioral sciences examined the implications of their work for foreign affairs. Leading government figures were involved in these Washington Seminars.

Her second gift grew out of the need of foreign students who were meeting once a month under the auspices of the Friends Peace Committee of the Friends Meeting of Washington on Florida Avenue. They required a more adequate place to meet. Upon learning of the need from a member of the meeting, "Mrs. Davis said, 'I will give you money for a house for the students,'" reported Margaret Jones of the Friends Meeting. "She said it just like that, right out of the blue. She gave us $30,000 for a [fifteen-room] house at 1708 New Hampshire Avenue."[35] The house opened on 15 July 1937 as a residence and meeting place for students of all nationalities and races with Grace Lowry as director. Both Davis House and the International Student House moved to locations on R Street, N.W., just across the street from each other, the one in 1947, the other in 1951.

The irrepressible Anne Hubbard Davis had still another major gift to make to the American Friends Service Committee. This was money to build a house for the executive secretary of the committee. For the site, a committee of the AFSC board chose land immediately adjacent to Pendle Hill, the Quaker study center in Wallingford, Pennsylvania, west of Philadelphia. Clarence and Lilly Pickett were active in working with the architect. In order to allow for the overnight entertainment of guests, in addition to providing for the Picketts' two children, the house had five bedrooms and as many bathrooms. A study for Clarence was also included. Clarence and Lilly moved in from Moylan on 12 June 1937, naming the house "Waysmeet." This was the name on a plate sent to the Picketts as a gift by English Friend Joy Hodgkin, widow of Henry Hodgkin who had come to the United States in 1930 to be the first director of Pendle Hill.

Mrs. Davis first visited the Picketts in their new home ten days later. Waysmeet, the gift of Anne Hubbard Davis, who was short in physical stature but ten feet tall in generosity, not only became the home base of Clarence Pickett and his family, but also a crossroads of the world.

NOTES

1. Clarence Pickett journal, 2 Jan. 1935.

2. Homer Lawrence Morris, *The Plight of the Bituminous Coal Miner* (Philadelphia: Univ. of Pennsylvania Press, 1934).

3. *The Washington Post*, by the Associated Press, 26 Apr. 1935.

4. William Wistar Comfort, *Just Among Friends: The Quaker Way of Life* (New York: MacMillan, 1941).

5. Lilly P. Pickett, "Eleanor Roosevelt As I Knew Her," undated and unpublished typescript, family papers, courtesy of Carolyn Pickett Miller.

6. Pickett journal, 27 Jan. 1936.

7. Pickett journal, 24-25 May, 1937.

8. Pickett journal, 24-25 May, 1937.

9. Pickett journal, 24 July 1937.

10. Pickett tape-recorded account of his life, 1964.

11. Pickett journal, 11 Sept. 1937.

12. Joseph P. Lash, *Eleanor and Franklin: The Story of Their Relationship Based on Eleanor Roosevelt's Private Papers* (New York: Norton, 1971), 563.

13. Emergency Peace Campaign papers, AFSC archives.

14. *The American Friend* 24 (new series), no. 23 (12 Nov. 1936): 471.

15. Admiral Richard E. Byrd, *Alone* (Covelo, CA: Island Press, 1938).

16. Pickett journal, 3 Feb. 1936.

17. J. E. Brenda Bailey, *A Quaker Couple in Nazi Germany: Leonhard Friedrich Survives Buchenwald*, (York, England: Sessions, 1994), 46.

18. Clarence Pickett to Eleanor Roosevelt, 13 Nov. 1936, AFSC archives.

19. Bailey, *A Quaker Couple,* 167.

20. Pickett journal, 9 Nov. 1936.

21. Pickett journal, 10 Nov. 1936.

22. Pickett journal, 12 Dec. 1936.

23. Pickett journal, 8 July 1937.

24. Pickett journal, 8 July 1937.

25. Pickett journal, 5 Mar. 1936.

26. Clarence E. Pickett, *For More Than Bread* (Boston: Little, 1953), 65.

27. Pickett, *Bread*, 66.

28. Pickett, *Bread*, 66.

29. Stephanie Mansfield, *The Richest Girl in the World: The Extravagant Life and Fast Times of Doris Duke* (New York: Putnam, 1992).

30. Pickett journal, 27 Nov. 1937.

31. Mansfield, *The Richest Girl*, 142.

32. Pickett journal, 29 Nov. 1937.

33. Taped interview, Mildred Young, 21 June 1993.

34. Excerpt from diary of Anne Hubbard Davis as quoted at a memorial tea given in her honor at Davis House, Washington, DC, 2 May 1982, AFSC archives.

35. Margaret Jones, 2 May 1982 at memorial tea in honor of Anne Hubbard Davis.

Chapter 11

THE APPEAL TO THE GESTAPO

*The great problem is emigration:
it dominates everything else*

THE YEAR 1938, which included, in December, the visit of three Friends to the Gestapo in Berlin, can rightly be seen as a period of sustained growth in the life of the American Friends Service Committee. Chairman Rufus Jones, in the annual report for the year, claimed that the work of the committee had been "heavier than during any year since the peak of child-feeding in Germany, and there has been no year in its history when it has been called upon to face a greater variety of momentous tasks."[1]

Jones was thinking especially of the suffering of displaced people in Europe, but his thoughts were within the context of the committee's growing efforts to understand and deal with the complex social and economic problems at home. During the year, two hundred young women and men, under the guidance of the Social Industrial Section, studied these problems by living, working, and entering into the social life of communities in areas of tension and conflict in the United States. It was largely through summer workcamps that such opportunities were available. Similarly, the Peace Section expanded its outreach, taking over the Student Peace Service from the Emergency Peace Campaign. About two thousand persons were involved in the ten Institutes of International Relations strategically located all across the country. The programs at these ten-day institutes were designed to help build an informed and responsible public opinion directed toward the achievement of world peace.

With these two sections of the AFSC capably administered by veteran staff, Clarence Pickett's role in respect to these projects was largely interpretative, both in raising money for them and in speaking to participants. His style was to allow committees and staff to have a wide scope in decision-making. He was now addressing in his speaking engagements a broad variety of groups, from Quaker meetings to major audiences numbering in the thousands, on the average of once a week. His topics ran the gamut, from the relevance of the Old Testament prophets and the teachings of Jesus in respect to current social problems to the full range of issues being focused upon by the Service Committee. He and chairman Rufus Jones were the two leading Quakers on the speaking circuit. Thousands of members of the Religious Society of Friends, as well as persons of other faiths, were strongly identifying in spiritual and practical ways with these two leaders.

No set of problems in 1938 was as demanding for Clarence Pickett as those arising from the dominance of Adolf Hitler and the Nazi Party in Germany. Senior representatives (referred to within the intimacy of Quaker circles as "seasoned Friends") were posted by the American Friends Service Committee and the Friends Service Council in London to the centers in Paris, Berlin, Frankfurt, Vienna, and Geneva.

While the reports to Philadelphia from these Quaker embassies gave details of grim human stories behind the events of this period, the events themselves in broad outline were openly, albeit sometimes superficially, known to the general public. Prior to the outbreak of World War II on 1 September 1939 the major American newspapers had representatives in Germany and elsewhere, not free to undertake any investigative reporting but nevertheless able to keep their American readers abreast of major developments. For example, fully reported in the American press were the infamous Nuremberg Laws of 15 September 1935, which deprived Jews of German citizenship, confining them to the status of "subjects" and forbidding marriage between Jews and Aryans. In the next few years decrees supplementing the Nuremberg Laws would outlaw the Jew completely.

As journalist and historian William Shirer notes, "Already by the summer of 1936, when the Germany which was host to the Olympic Games was enchanting the visitors from the West, the Jews had been excluded, either by law or by Nazi terror—the latter often preceded the former—from public and private employment to such an extent that at least half of them were without means of livelihood."[2] By 1938 Jews were not permitted to practice—or were forced out of—the professions of law and medicine.

Early in 1938 the AFSC board of directors decided that its executive secretary and his wife should make an extensive trip in Europe, to consult fully with English Friends regarding relief and refugee matters, to have a vacation in the English countryside, and to visit with Friends and Quaker centers in Holland, Germany, Austria, Czechoslovakia, and Switzerland. Clarence and Lilly Pickett could scarcely have imagined how their itinerary on the Continent would coincide with what became known as "the Munich crisis."

Shortly after Germany forcibly annexed Austria, Pickett talked with Joseph Hyman, secretary of the American Jewish Joint Distribution Committee (JDC). The Committee had had word that five thousand Jews had left Vienna and were simply on the road somewhere and that there had been a wave of suicides. The next month Pickett was again talking with Hyman about the problem of the refugees from Austria and Germany. The JDC secretary was very discouraged, principally about a meeting he and other leaders had recently had with President Roosevelt on refugee matters. The president talked in generalities, noted that there was likely to be an international committee on which the United States would have a representative, "that the government is not likely to receive any great number of refugees, but that it may be willing to express its sympathy and interest in the voluntary efforts to bring refugees to this country."[3]

Indeed, just a day later, Mrs. Roosevelt told Clarence Pickett of her feeling that too much was being said about the refugee problem and that expectations beyond what was possible had been created. Clarence agreed with her and expressed the hope that the president might in some press conference or somewhere, more accurately define just what he conceived to be likely to happen. She wanted him to give her a memorandum on that point so that she could talk it over with the president.[4]

Pickett promptly sent a memorandum to Mrs. Roosevelt. Noting that the unsoundness of the present world dated back to the Versailles Treaty, he set forth a plan: "Why should not the president of the United States summon a conference of outstanding civilians of all nations for the purpose of drafting the international policies demanded if the world is to function successfully?" Realizing that this suggestion would probably not be acceptable, he closed the statement with the following in parentheses: "In an unstable world the only North Star for guidance is necessarily an ideal. A plan cannot be discarded therefore because it appears idealistic."[5] Mrs. Roosevelt returned the memorandum with typed responses on the bottom of the two pages, adding, "The president says he will keep the suggestion in mind."[6]

One bright spot in the AFSC picture was the decision of a Philadelphia Quaker, Howard Elkinton, to resign from the Philadelphia Quartz Company, a family firm, to make himself available for service in Germany. "He is in possession of his soul again,"[7] wrote Clarence, referring to Elkinton's freedom from internal pressures within the family company.[8] In April the Foreign Service Section appointed Howard and Katharine Elkinton to represent the committee in Berlin and approved establishing a hostel for refugees coming to the United States. The following month Clarence took the Elkintons to see the German ambassador. "He was most cordial; asked us whether we had been interfered with by the Party in Berlin; also wanted to know specifically what we did in Berlin. That was not easy to tell him."[9]

It was not easy, because it was politic not to divulge the extent to which the center knew about Germans seeking refuge abroad. It was clearly of first importance to obtain the necessary visas for the Elkintons (and their two children) to enter Germany. A few months earlier, former U.S. ambassador to Germany, William E. Dodd, had told Clarence, "that frequently he had had occasion to call in Gilbert MacMaster or Albert Martin [the two Quaker representatives in Berlin] to ask them to do things which the embassy could not do, because when the embassy acts they have to make an official approach to the proper officials of the government and that means that a simple and direct approach cannot be made. He appealed to us to maintain our center there."[10] The absence of any discussion of the refugee question with the German ambassador also reflected the lack of the AFSC's organizational preparedness in dealing with refugees. To move even one hunted and haunted family across the various international boundaries to some place of final settlement with a minimum of social and spiritual dislocation was no slight task.

In late July 1938 Clarence and Lilly Pickett and their daughter Rachel sailed third class for Europe on the *Europa*. They arrived in Cherbourg, France, in the early morning of 1 August, then in Southampton, England, in the afternoon. Beginning the next day and continuing for just a month, Clarence Pickett was plunged into committee meetings with English

Friends, these days interspersed with some holidays with Lilly in the English countryside.

On 8 August Clarence Pickett met in London with Myron Taylor, the former chairman of the U.S. Steel Corporation whom he had known in connection with the solicitations for Penn-Craft, and Robert T. Pell, a foreign service officer of the U.S. State Department. Taylor had been the principal representative of the United States at the refugee conference in July at Evian-les-Bains on the French shore of Lake Geneva to which thirty-two nations had sent high-caliber representatives. The conferees were present at the invitation of President Roosevelt, an initiative taken following the invasion of Austria by German troops. The invitation specified that no country would be expected or asked to receive a greater number of immigrants than is permitted by its existing legislation. It was this restriction regarding immigration that inevitably was to be the major hurdle to providing aid to refugees on a massive scale.

In part through the untiring efforts of Myron Taylor, the participants in the Evian conference established the Intergovernmental Committee for German Refugees, with permanent headquarters in London. When the committee convened in London on 4 August 1938, Myron Taylor stated, according to historian Arthur D. Morse, that "it was necessary to find new homes for 660,000 persons still living in Germany and Austria. Of this total, 300,000 were Jews; 285,000 were Christians of sufficient Jewish ancestry to fail the Nuremberg racial tests; and 75,000 were Roman Catholics."[11] Taylor was emphasizing the need for German cooperation in this effort. It was precisely in respect to this point that Clarence Pickett met with him and Pell. Pickett believed that what was needed were arrangements with the German government to allow emigrants to bring out property.

Following some weeks of vacation punctuated by consultations with English Friends, Clarence and Lilly crossed the channel, first to stop at the Quaker Student Hostel in Amsterdam, then to visit the Quaker school for refugee children in the centuries-old Eerde Castle in Ommen, Holland. As Lilly Pickett described the visit in her diary: "Clarence and I just stopped here in passing four years ago last May. Then the school had just opened, and there were eleven children in attendance. Now there are 120 children. Eighty of them are German, and the others Dutch, English and American. German is the language of the school."[12]

Howard and Katharine Elkinton were also in Ommen, prior to taking up their responsibilities at the Berlin Center, to place their two children, Dody and Peter, in the school for the year. Another student just arriving was a Jewish boy from Hansberg, Germany. Wrote Lilly: "Word has come of his father's death. Another one of the hundreds of suicides in that suffering land."[13]

The Picketts then crossed over into Germany to visit their dear friends, the Menschings, in Petzen. Wrote Lilly Pickett: "Their lives have been so much of tragedy, and fear, and there may be more at the hands of the present German government. Pastor Mensching is being asked again this month to sign away his soul in an oath of allegiance to Hitler. He has refused before, and will refuse again, and he fears this time he may be compelled to give up his church where he has been the pastor since his release from [an English] prison following the World War. The only reason he has been left so long is because he is so deeply loved by all his parishioners, who are absolutely loyal to him. If he is thrown out, he plans to go again to Africa as a missionary."[14]

On one of the days of their visit with the Menschings, Clarence and Lilly journeyed to Bad Pyrmont, thirty miles away, to meet with German Friends in the only Quaker meetinghouse in Germany. It had been built five years earlier using materials from what remained of a disused meetinghouse erected in 1800. Bad Pyrmont was the location for the annual gatherings of German Yearly Meeting with its membership of close to three hundred. By the time of the Picketts' visit, no German Friend was unaware of the evils being perpetrated by Hitler and his followers. Faced with conscription and no exemption for conscientious objectors, each individual Friend had to decide what his or her stand would be. Some were sheltering and assisting Jews and non-Aryans at great risk to themselves. By the end of the war, about eighty-two Quakers are known to have been either imprisoned or put into concentration camps, and some were shot or died there.[15]

Clarence and Lilly Pickett were to see and talk with a number of German Friends at their next destination, the Conference of European Friends in Vallekilde, Denmark. Then on 13 September the Picketts left Vallekilde by automobile with Howard and Katharine Elkinton for Berlin. They spent the night at Kolding, Denmark, near the German border, and the next morning the papers had in bold headlines, "Hitler Sends Ultimatum to Benes [of Czechoslovakia]." The Picketts and

Elkintons had a very brief family conference as to whether they should keep to their itinerary or remain in a neutral country. They decided quickly that if war came, Americans would be in a position to be of particular use in Germany.[16]

The Picketts and the Elkintons crossed the border Wednesday morning, 14 September 1938, without difficulty. Their American passports were sufficient for entry. "The drive to Berlin was over beautiful roads," said Pickett, "almost all of the way lined with trees planted in [Kaiser] Wilhelm's time . . . Part of the way we drove on one of the new autobahn roads, a regular highway laid out with almost as much engineering care as a railway bed."[17] That very same day, unknown to the Quaker travelers, the British prime minister, Neville Chamberlain, with the urging of Prime Minister Edouard Daladier of France, offered to meet with Hitler to find a peaceful solution to the Czechoslovakia crisis, going by air to Munich and then by train to Berchtesgarden as it finally developed.

With only the completely controlled German press to rely on, Clarence Pickett had no way of knowing what was happening in respect to Germany and Czechoslovakia, and the extent to which the Czech government was being pressured to cede German-speaking Sudetenland to Germany to avoid war. "Most of the time there we went along quite normally," he reported. "Only now and then did the imminent threat of impending war protrude. This was partly because of the press. It always implied that Germany was set on peace, but was the worst possible press in that atrocity stories and attacks on Benes were almost constant first page stuff. It could hardly have been worse."[18]

Pickett and Elkinton visited the American ambassador, Hugh Wilson. They also saw Raymond Geist, the American consul general, who had a long tale of woe. The preceding Saturday three thousand people had applied for visas for America. The consular office was simply deluged with people who had heartrending tales of woe—Jews or non-Aryans. They could get no work—were thrown out of their apartments—had property confiscated—lawyers had lost clients—doctors must all quit practice on 1 October. The large consular office was swarming with people when Pickett and Elkinton were there, and that, Geist said, was a comparatively quiet day.[19]

Clarence Pickett had long sessions with the staff of the Quaker Center, but any consecutive meeting was very difficult. When it became known that an American Quaker visitor was on hand, hope of help came to people who had to get out immediately. Realizing the shortness of his stay and the need to do many things, he did his best to keep clear of individual cases. But he did see close to a dozen persons. Fifteen years later, Pickett would remember vividly those days in Berlin: "Our hearts went out in agony over the suffering of these people. We were seeing also the corrosion, deformity, and subjection of thousands of Germans, and this was equally destructive of the inner resources of the life and spirit."[21]

On one occasion during his stay in Berlin Pickett was able to have an interview with a high-ranking official of the Nazi government and talked frankly with him of what lay in his heart, not only as to what was happening to the Jews but what was happening to all Germans. He told the official that he wanted to see Hitler. The official replied "that Hitler was a tyrant, was not quite normal, that certainly he would pay no attention to our protest if we were able to get to him, that such an effort might result in every vestige of our work being thrown out of Germany, and possibly even vengeance being taken on German Quakers."[22]

Pickett was deeply impressed by the spirit of German Friends—and "friends of Friends"—to whom he spoke one evening. How could they help prevent war? they asked. How could they let Czechoslovakian people know that they loved them? How could they be actually helpful to Jews in need? In the end, they drafted a most touching message to Czechoslovakian Friends, which the Picketts carried to them in person. Then the Sunday meeting for worship "can never be forgotten," wrote Clarence. "Several spoke—young and older—all with profound concern for the spirit of their countrymen who sought conquest, and ardent prayer for their own guidance and purity of motive."[23]

Clarence and Lilly Pickett left Berlin Monday evening, 19 September 1938, after consulting American Express as to the possibilities of getting into Prague. They knew that the meeting of Chamberlain and Hitler had taken place at Berchtesgarden, but knew nothing of subsequent international events. Clarence decided that one small contribution amid the tensions and uncertainties of the hour was to adhere to his itinerary. They stopped overnight at Breslau and stayed in a hotel near the station since they had to leave for the border early the next morning. During much of the night soldiers marched by the hotel, and at six the next morning they awoke to hear and see cavalry marching by toward the border. Crowds of people were along the streets, but were showing no enthusiasm for the event.

The Picketts found Prague dazed at what had so suddenly come upon them. The Czechs felt betrayed by France and England. Everyone expected war. Though believing in peace, the little group of Friends had not been able to see the pacifist testimony as possible in the extremity of the hour, and so all of the men were accepting military service. Broadcasts hourly brought news of developments and caution to be quiet. In this atmosphere the Picketts met with the little Quaker group—about a dozen, in a home, Tuesday evening, 20 September. After quite a period of silence Clarence brought greetings sent by the International Conference at Vallekilde and by German Friends. He spoke as he had done in Berlin, of the family of God, a conception of life so prominent in early Christianity, and again an idea so greatly needed. There was a spirit of deep worship and prayer throughout, he observed.

The next day Clarence and Lilly Pickett visited the social welfare department of the government, including Red Cross president Alice Masaryk, whose father, Tomas Masaryk, had been the first president of prosperous and politically stable Czechoslovakia, serving from its formation in 1918 until 1935. It was through the social welfare department that the Quaker child feeding in Sudetenland had been conducted for two years. "Alice Masaryk partakes of the courageous and statesmanlike spirit of her father," reported Clarence. "She is a kind of Jane Addams person, and must be a tower of strength in these trying periods."[24]

On 21 September, the Picketts went on to Vienna. The departure scene made an indelible impression on Clarence:

As we waited for our train at the station, two train loads of Germans (Social Democrats) and Czech refugees from Sudetenland came in. Old men and women, wives and children—hundreds of them, with a few articles packed on their backs; now and again a dog, a beautiful quilt, or whatever they most prized. There was no brass band to meet them. As they walked along the platform, peasants leaving their homes and for the first time being in the city—fearing they would never again see their homes—almost all wept. It was movingly sad. I can even now hardly write about it calmly. It was so unnecessary and so brutal. They were led by guides to the great public stadium, where they were being provided at public expense with beds of a kind, and food, awaiting transfer to a colony in the country or to some farm home near Prague, where farmers were willing to take them in.[25]

The journey to Vienna was uneventful. Much had happened since Clarence's previous visit in May of 1934. Now in September 1938, following the Anschluss in March, Pickett found the Quaker Center to be the only place in Vienna where an estimated one hundred thousand non-Aryans might get any counsel and help in getting out of the country. Pickett noted that there were eight workers, each conducting close to eight interviews every day except Saturday and Sunday. In some cases it was working out plans for immigration, in most cases it was only to offer encouragement and sympathy for those who could not leave. He considered the drain on the workers to be almost unbearable.[26]

On the Sunday of their visit there were sixty-five persons at the meeting for worship held at the Center. Many of them were Jews, or Christians classed by the new government as Jews and cast off by the Catholic and Protestant churches. These were friends of the Friends, finding a spiritual haven in the company of the Quakers. Pickett determined from conversations with leaders of the Protestant and Catholic churches that these churches were bearing no testimony regarding the treatment of Jews. "On the other hand," he wrote, "one found here and there brave souls who were going straight ahead with their Jewish friendships and risking their own standing, if not their safety, in doing so."[27] He also learned that, while official acts of persecution were bad enough, unofficial ones committed by hoodlums under Party guise were often worse.

The Picketts left Vienna early Monday morning, 26 September. Again their departure was spiritually traumatic: "As we drove away from the Center, at least one hundred and fifty people were lined up in a queue awaiting their number for interviews the following week. It could be three hundred or four hundred by 9:30 when the doors opened. We sighed, but drove on, hoping we could do more by being elsewhere, but we left with heavy spirits."[28]

Carrying out the itinerary entirely as planned in Philadelphia, the Picketts were heading by train for Innsbruck, thence for Geneva. Along the Danube they could see heavily armed troops, pontoons at every bridge in case the bridge was destroyed, and miles of tanks and guns, concealed only by a thin disguise of brush or canvas covers. Arriving in Innsbruck in the late afternoon, they decided to stop off and spend the night there so as to drink in the beauty of the surroundings, and to take the rest of the journey by daylight.

Internationally, "the road to Munich" was still in progress. Neville Chamberlain met with Adolf Hitler in Godesberg, 22 and 23 September. Detailed proposals worked out by France, England, and Czechoslovakia for starting an orderly ceding of Sudetenland to Germany, the demand made by Hitler at Berchtesgarden, were now unacceptable to the Fuehrer. The Sudeten area, he demanded, must be occupied by Germany at once. Chamberlain returned to London on 24 September. General mobilization took place in Czechoslovakia, a partial mobilization in France. Not well known to the international community were the extensive military preparations within Germany. Negotiations continued, but war seemed inevitable.

On the evening of 26 September, Hitler spoke at the jammed Sportsplatz in Berlin, "shouting and shrieking in the worst paroxysm I had ever seen him in," wrote American journalist William Shirer.[29] Clarence and Lilly Pickett could not fail to hear it: all over Innsbruck there were loudspeakers, so that no one could fail to hear Hitler's speech. Clusters of people formed around each loudspeaker to listen. The bus drivers stopped their busses to listen. Clarence and Lilly moved slowly about from group to group to see what was happening. Loud cheers interrupted the Fuehrer as he spoke in the Sportsplatz in Berlin. "Not a word—not a whisper came from the listeners in Innsbruck," wrote Clarence. "And so it was all over Germany, so far as our experience went."[30]

The Picketts crossed over into Switzerland the next morning, just one day before the closing of the border. After a couple of days of consultations at the Geneva Friends Center, they then traveled by train and ferry via Paris to London, arriving just in time to see the outburst of praise for Chamberlain's third meeting with Hitler (and Mussolini and Daladier) in Munich on 29 and 30 September. "I believe it is peace in our time," said Chamberlain. "We have sustained a total, unmitigated defeat," said Winston Churchill in the House of Commons debate.[31]

Clarence and Lilly Pickett were in England until 12 October. Life was a dizzy round of conferences at Friends House, now besieged by refugees from Germany, relief problems in Spain, and the newly emerged relief areas of Czechoslovakia. They left for New York on the *Ile de France*. On board, Clarence dictated for his journal some general observations about the countries he had visited. He viewed many of the problems as a true and legitimate offspring of the World War. Sixty years later this conviction was echoed in the review of a significant piece of World War I literature: "The First World War is the original sin of our dreadful century, the blood-polluted source of all our sorrows. From its oozing wounds issued the triumphs of Bolshevism, and Fascism; world-wide depression; and military innovations like large-scale bombardments, chemical warfare, and the soldierly conviction that mass annihilation is the best route to victory."[32] Then Clarence Pickett in his confidential report asked a question that he frequently asked of himself: "What can be done, especially by the American Friends Service Committee? That is hard to discuss briefly. Relief is still important. We may feel penitent for our part in the vicious Versailles Treaty and war settlement. But the Jews are the ones on whom now the burden for that war settlement falls hardest. We can do no less than give every aid possible to help those who come to us to make a new and fruitful start. This is and will be our chief relief work for some time."[33]

This is and will be our chief relief work for some time. Despite this prescient judgment, Clarence Pickett could not have guessed that the American Friends Service Committee would spend $4.5 million in aid to refugees by the time its refugee program was closed in 1949. Even though AFSC work with European refugees was carried on without regard to—or record of—the race or religion of those helped, it can be assumed that the greater part of the figure related to Jewish refugees.

Multiple administrative tasks and commitments faced Pickett upon his return. But nothing could sidetrack his concerns about events in Europe. At the end of October the American Friends Service Committee held its general meeting at the Cambridge (Massachusetts) Friends Meetinghouse. The attendance outgrew the meetinghouse in the evening and meetings had to be held in the Agassiz Theater on the Radcliffe College campus in order to have room for the crowds. Rufus Jones and Clarence Pickett spoke in the evening, Jones on "South Africa and China," reporting on his trip to those countries, and Pickett on "Problems in Europe."[34]

On 9 November Clarence Pickett went to Hyde Park to have lunch at the Roosevelt home. Pickett sat alongside the president during the meal and had his full attention. He reported quite fully to him on what he had seen in Germany, Czechoslovakia, and Austria. The president was very keen to know the attitude of the German people during the period preceding the Munich settlement. Pickett told him of the very deep appreciation which some people felt for the president's second statement on 27 September, suggesting an immediate conference of all nations directly interested and implying that, if war broke out, the world would hold Hitler responsible.

On the disarmament question, Clarence Pickett told the president that it seemed to him a mistake not to take Hitler seriously when Hitler spoke of his willingness to consider disarmament. Even though it might not be said sincerely, the German people thought it was, and Clarence viewed them as sincere in their desire for disarmament. One of the very best ways to give them the chance of expression is to take seriously the statement of their leader. FDR agreed in principle to this.

Clarence Pickett said that he kept wishing that Roosevelt were across the table from Hitler instead of Chamberlain. The president said that there was just one way that that could be brought about, and that was for both of them to travel to the Azores, and that he was not unwilling to consider a meeting with Hitler under those circumstances. "It seems fantastic," observed Clarence, "and yet it's worth giving thought to."[35] Clarence Pickett's conversation with President Roosevelt was to have some unexpected and controversial consequences a year and a half later.

Wednesday, 9 November. Just a few hours after Franklin Roosevelt and Clarence Pickett conferred in Hyde Park (Pickett returned to New York that evening) the worst pogrom that had yet taken place in the Third Reich occurred. It followed the shooting on 7 November of the third secretary of the German embassy in Paris, Ernst von Rath, by a seventeen-year old German Jewish refugee whose father was among the ten thousand German Jews deported to Poland in boxcars. Wrote historian Arthur Morse:

> On the afternoon of November 9 Ernst von Rath died of his wounds. At 2 o'clock the next morning a wave of arson, looting, murder and arrests began which stunned even a world by now immune to Nazi excesses. The "spontaneous" demonstration had been organized on teletyped orders from Reinhard Heydrich, who commanded the Security Service organization under Heinrich Himmler. In the ensuing orgy some 195 synagogues were burned, more than 800 shops destroyed, and 7,500 looted. The streets of Germany were littered by the shattered shop windows and the disaster became known as "the night of broken glass," or the Kristallnacht. Twenty thousand Jews [all men] were arrested and taken to concentration camps.[36]

As he left New York for Philadelphia on Friday morning, 11 November, Clarence Pickett saw the headlines marching in large type across the front page of *The New York Times:* NAZIS SMASH, LOOT BURN JEW-ISH SHOPS AND TEMPLES UNTIL GOEBBELS CALLS HALT. And there were reports from *Times* correspondents in Berlin and Vienna.

Late in the afternoon on Monday, 14 November, just before leaving his office, Clarence Pickett received a phone call from Paul Baerwald, chairman of the American Jewish Joint Distribution Committee, to say that messages had come to the committee from various cities in Germany to the effect that Jews were being denied permission to buy at gentile shops. Their own food shops were closed, and the feeding centers in various cities where the Kultusgemeinde (Jewish community organizations) were feeding had been closed. Baerwald asked whether AFSC channels for feeding could be opened up. Clarence cabled at once to Vienna and Berlin to get further facts."[37]

"Everyone here," scribbled Clarence to Lilly, who was in Caldwell, Idaho to be with her ailing mother, "is terribly shocked and saddened, and some embittered. Of course, I keep remembering the agony of some thousands of Germans who are suffering agony of soul but can say nothing. . . . Today came five cables from German families urging haste in helping them emigrate. But I am well and need lots of guidance to see how to be free from fear and prejudice in such a time."[38]

Tuesday, 15 November. Clarence Pickett consulted Philadelphia Quaker businessman Robert Yarnall, who, with his wife Elizabeth, had worked for two months during the previous summer at the Vienna Friends center. Then Clarence Pickett had lunch with Rufus Jones. Wrote Pickett in a tribute to Jones ten years later: "The proposal to visit the German government and to see if its policy concerning Jewish immigration [*sic*] could be modified grew out of a conversation at the lunch table. I merely made a slight comment, wondering whether something of this sort could be done, and before lunch was over, Rufus Jones's mind was clear that it should be undertaken forthwith, no matter what the obstacles."[39] It was agreed that a first step was to see the German ambassador. Pickett was successful in making an appointment for noon the following day.

Wednesday, 16 November. Pickett, Jones and Yarnall met with Ambassador Hans Dieckhoff. Hans Thomsen, the counselor to the embassy, was also present. The three Friends stated specifically what they had come for: that they had reports of serious distress among Jews and wished permission now to do group feeding in Germany. After

GRAY WOLVES. One of many species threatened by White House plans to expand oil and gas development in Greater Yellowstone and other unspoiled wildlands.

The Bush-Cheney energy plan would turn some of America's last wild places into polluted industrial zones. Please join NRDC today and help save _your_ natural heritage!

—John Adams

NRDC
THE EARTH'S BEST DEFENSE

NATURAL RESOURCES DEFENSE COUNCIL

40 W. 20th Street, New York, NY 10011 • www.nrdc.org

many inquiries, the ambassador agreed to inform the government of the Quaker request.[40]

Following the interview at the German embassy, the Friends then reported on their visit to Assistant Secretary of State George Messersmith, having seen him prior to going to the embassy. Messersmith and his associate, Pierrepont Moffatt, chief of the Division of European Affairs, strongly advised the Friends Service Committee to send a delegation to Germany at once, to try to arrange for mass feeding, to see Hitler, and to push for an orderly way for the emigration of Jews and non-Aryans.[41]

That evening, at Rufus Jones' house on the Haverford College campus, about twenty key Friends then and there set up a refugee service committee which had already been authorized in principle by the Foreign Service Section, the board of directors and the general committee, with Yarnall as chairman.

Thursday, 17 November. Clarence Pickett arranged for about twenty-five persons to hear Myron Taylor outline the refugee problem. The Foreign Service Section minuted its approval of the establishment of the Refugee Service Committee and decided that three Friends should be sent to Germany. On the same day a letter signed by Rufus Jones and Clarence Pickett went to every Friends meeting in the United States and Canada (to be read after meetings for worship on Sunday, 20 November), reporting on actions being taken by the AFSC but without mention of the proposed delegation. The gravity of the situation was stated succinctly in the opening paragraph: "Abundant evidence has come to the office of the American Friends Service Committee during the past few days revealing a profound shock to our spiritual life by the Jewish and non-Aryan persecutions in Germany. Cables from Germany indicate that American newspaper reports have not exaggerated the tragedy."

Then the letter spelled out the types and scale of assistance needed to bring refugees to the United States: affidavits guaranteeing support for the immigrants; housing and feeding of refugee families; and individual and meeting financial contributions. The balance in the general fund at the beginning of the month was only $2,500; at the end of September there had actually been a deficit of $1,000 in the unrestricted account. The letter concluded: "While the Service Committee will do everything in its power as a centralized channel for service, it is of the utmost importance that all Friends shall seek freedom from the spirit of bitterness and hatred and will be the channels for the expression of understanding and good will within their own communities."[42]

Friday, 18 November. The Service Committee as a whole met to discuss how the AFSC should respond to the crisis in Germany. In the evening the board of directors met and determined who should be asked to go to Germany. "I got home rather late tonight," wrote Clarence, "and was extremely tired."[43] On Saturday Clarence reported on developments in a letter to Lilly: "The German plot thickens. Now Dieckhoff is re-called [in retaliation for the summoning home by President Roosevelt of U.S. Ambassador to Germany, Hugh Wilson], but I will see him again before he leaves, I hope. It now looks as if Rufus, Alfred [Scattergood], and Bob Yarnall would sail in a few days to Germany to try to establish mass feeding and to see if we can arrange for orderly emigration. They will try to go directly to Hitler. They asked me to go but I can't feel I should leave here now."[44]

The following week Clarence Pickett's life was again dominated by the refugee problems in Germany. On Wednesday in New York he reviewed AFSC plans with Jewish leaders. Then on Friday he had a follow-up appointment at the German embassy in Washington, this time with Hans Thomsen, *chargé d'affaires* in the absence of the ambassador. Pickett had some questions: What were Thomsen's personal views about the Quaker delegation? Who would he suggest they see? What did he think of the delegation attempting to see Hitler or Goering? Have you had any recent word about the problem of distress among Jews?

Clarence Pickett, in confidential notes he wrote following the visit, observed that Thomsen was somewhat on the defensive regarding the idea of attempting to see Hitler or Goering, and his reply to the question regarding news of distress among Jews was startling, yet understand-able: "I have had no word but what I read in the American papers."[45] The interview with Thomsen was followed by a conversation with Pierrepont Moffatt at the State Department. Moffatt was one hundred per cent in favor of the delegation, and noted that Myron Taylor would soon be sailing for London to go further into the question of an orderly method of emigration.

The composition of the three-person delegation to Germany went through some changes. Clarence Pickett persuaded George Walton, prin-cipal of George School, to go in place of Alfred Scattergood, who was unavailable. It is interesting to note that the delegation members almost studiously represented the divisions within the Religious Society of Friends: Rufus Jones with strong ties to pastoral Friends; Robert Yarnall, prominently identified with Orthodox Friends in Philadelphia; and George Walton, a leader among Hicksite Friends.

On 1 December there were final meetings with the delegation subcommittee appointed by the board of directors, and also with the delegation members themselves. At 1:30 p.m. all of the AFSC staff and all board members, with as many husbands and wives as could come, met with the delegation in the 12th Street Meetinghouse for a meeting for worship. "It was a most impressive occasion," Clarence observed.[46] The delegation sailed the following day on the *Queen Mary*.

Despite the number of Friends who knew about the Quaker delegation, every effort was made to avoid newspaper publicity. But on Monday morning, 5 December, the *Philadelphia Record* had big, screaming headlines and a long story about the delegation, based in part on a "ship-to-shore" phone conversation the reporter had with Rufus Jones on board the *Queen Mary*. Clarence Pickett poured forth his frustration and anger in a letter he wrote to Lilly, still in Idaho:

> It [the story] may entirely spoil the chances of the delegation being able to do anything in Germany, but it may not. I called the German embassy, and they consented to see that no account of it was carried in the German press. That at least is one advantage of the controlled press—you touch the center and you control all. All day long I was hectored by the press wanting more stories. I called Mr. Stern, owner of the *Record*, and told him I thought this was a newspaper crime of the first order—when we were trying to do something for his race—he deliberately, for the sake of a headline, spoiled it. He seemed a little strimped [?] but he needed it as strong as it could be. It tends to make me feel anti-Semitic until I recall that *The New York Times* knew the story (I told them Saturday) and they kept it.[47]

Two weeks later David Stern came in to see Clarence Pickett, bringing in his apology. Pickett thought that Stern had come in because of a very critical report on the incident in *Time* magazine on 19 December. Then just at the very end of the year a lawyer for the *Philadelphia Record* came in to talk with Pickett to see whether "I would see that Rufus Jones and David Stern got together about a statement which would relieve David Stern of personal liability for the statements made in The *Record*. . . ."[48]

The *Philadelphia Record* revealed Quaker mission to Berlin, December 1938

Two English Quakers came aboard the *Queen Mary* at Plymouth to
accompany the American delegation to Cherbourg. They told the Americans of sensational headlines about the mission appearing in English
newspapers and on the radio. What none of the Friends knew at the time
was the publication of a satirical article in Goebbel's newspaper, *Der
Angriff*, which dubbed the Americans as "the three Wise Men, advising
loyal readers to be courteous and to quake with the Quakers."[49]

More important than these revelations were the preliminary reports
of the four English Friends who had been traveling throughout Germany on behalf of their Germany Emergency Committee. For example,
the report of William Hughes, after visiting in Saxony for three weeks,
emphasized the deeply tragic nature of the situation:

> I came away overwhelmed by the impression made by continual meet-
> ings with women, weeping and frightened, deprived of their husbands
> and sons, not knowing when another attack might be made on their homes,
> and all raising to us the same cry, "Help us to get out, and quickly!"
>
> ... It is not to be wondered at that a great many of the sufferers were
> constantly considering suicide. I was continually told this, and the

Jewish doctor in Berlin said to me that hardly a day passed on which he was not consulted about the easiest method. . . . I seemed always to be meeting people who were just off to attend a funeral.[50]

Hughes had visited the concentration camp at Buchenwald, where ten thousand arrested Jews were being held. "The conditions were very bad," he reported. "At first many men had not only to stand all day in the open, often at attention, but also to sleep in the open, or without beds. Sanitation and water supply were quite inadequate. Thirst was one of the major causes of suffering."[51]

During the transatlantic crossing, Rufus Jones prepared a statement that was to be used in interviews with German officials. It emphasized the close and friendly relations American Quakers had had with the German people and how unhappy they had been over the conditions of the Versailles Peace Treaty. He noted that, in the time of the blockade after World War I, Friends had fed German children, reaching at the peak no less than a 1.2 million children per day. "We have come now," the statement continued, "in the same spirit as in the past, and we believe that all Germans who remember the past, and who are familiar with our ways and methods and spirit will know that we do not come to judge or to criticize, or to push ourselves in, but to inquire in the most friendly manner whether there is anything we can do to promote life and human welfare and to relieve suffering."[52]

This was the statement (translated into German) that the three Friends took to the offices of the Geheime Staatspolizei (the Secret State Police), Gestapo for short, in Berlin. It was Raymond Geist, the American consul general, who was largely responsible for arranging the meeting with two high-level officers of the Gestapo, Standartenfuehrer Erlinger and Regierungerat Lischka, chosen by Minister of Security Reinhard Heydrich to discuss the Quakers' concerns.

Rufus Jones, as head of the delegation, with Geist as interpreter, asked the two officers to read the statement before they began discussions. Reflecting almost a decade later on the meeting, Jones wrote in part: "They read the document slowly, carefully and thoughtfully. It plainly *reached* them and we noted a softening effect on their faces, which needed to be softened. Then followed a prolonged conference in which we presented our plans and pleaded our cause, answering many questions. Finally the leaders said, 'We are now withdrawing to consult with the chief Heydrich, and in about twenty-five minutes we shall report the decision.'"[53]

As they waited, the three Friends settled into a time of silent worship. They learned later that the room was wired, so that anything they might have said would have been recorded. Upon their return, the officers reported that Heydrich had promised to telegraph every police station in Germany stating that the Quakers had been given "full permission to investigate the sufferings of Jews and to bring such relief as they see necessary."[54]

It is unlikely that the message was ever actually sent. The Quaker commissioners sailed home from Europe on the day before Christmas. While it had been possible to communicate with the home office through the United States embassy in Berlin, their cable from Paris the day before their departure best summarized their activities, findings, and recommendations:

> The great problem is an emigration problem. It dominates everything else. It is the settled purpose of the German government to drive out Jews. The events of November 10th were to hasten that purpose. Until a plan of rapid emigration, especially for young, effective persons is established, the authorities consider the problem unsolved, and further outrages are likely to occur, bringing greater suffering and injustice. . . . Plans for emigration of 50,000 a year for three years would probably prove a solution of the problem and reduce the virulence of persecution among those remaining.[55]

Having seen the previous summer the long lines of Germans and Austrians wanting to talk with staff at the Quaker centers about emigration, and knowing that the U.S. consulates in those countries were overwhelmed with would-be refugees, Pickett talked with Avra Warren, head of the Visa Division of the State Department, about a suggestion coming from the AFSC's Refugee Service Committee, to supplement the harried consulate staffs with German-speaking young Americans recruited and paid for by the American Friends Service Committee. Their role would be to do simple office tasks, such as opening mail, answering the phone, helping applicants to fill out forms. Warren, having himself just returned from visiting all of the consular offices in Europe, thought well of the idea.

It was midwinter, not the best time to recruit young college students for overseas work. Nevertheless, the report of the Quaker mission was percolating rapidly through Friends meetings, and many young people were ready to drop everything to respond to the need. A couple of weeks later, however, Pickett learned that Assistant Secretary of State George Messersmith had serious reservations about the plan. Messersmith felt that other organizations might wish to do likewise, and that there might in any case be a problem of divided loyalty on the part of the AFSC-paid employees.

A few weeks later both Clarence Pickett and Rufus Jones went to see the assistant secretary about the AFSC plan. But Messersmith was intransigent and could not see at all any possibilities for the Committee helping out by sending persons abroad to work in the consular offices. "It was an extremely unpleasant and unsatisfactory interview," said Clarence.[56] Rarely did Clarence Pickett admit to such negative feelings. In later years Pickett was to say that he was told "that the State Department could run its own affairs, and that if it desired to add to its consular staffs it could and would go to Congress and ask for an appropriation to do so. It was a hard blow."[57]

In the midst of his work in dealing with the complexities of how to rescue Germans, Clarence Pickett must have felt invigorated by an event at the Academy of Music in Philadelphia, Monday evening, 20 February 1939. The program called for an address by Mrs. Franklin D. Roosevelt, a concert by the Philadelphia Orchestra under guest conductor Georges Enesco, and the presentation of The Philadelphia Award, often called the Bok award because it was based on a fund created by Edward W. Bok in 1921. By tradition the award recipient was a mystery prior to the presentation. Leopold Stokowski had been the first winner. The award had always gone to a single individual, "who during the preceding calendar year shall have performed or brought to its culmination an act or contributed a service calculated to advance the best and largest interests of the community of which Philadelphia is the center."[58]

On this occasion the award of $10,000 for the first time was divided, to honor Rufus M. Jones, chairman of the American Friends Service Committee, and Clarence E. Pickett, its executive secretary. Jones and Pickett, both dressed in white tie and tails, received the medallions as the audience, filling virtually every seat in the great music hall, "arose in one vast wave to applaud and cheer," as one correspondent characterized the moment of the bestowal of the award.[59] Rufus Jones was the first to express appreciation. Clarence Pickett's response was characteristic of him. He said he wished that members of the AFSC staff, particularly those

*Rufus Jones, AFSC chairman, and Clarence Pickett, its executive
secretary, receive the 1938 Philadelphia (Bok) Award*

serving in Germany, were present and could be asked to stand up and be
recognized. He paid tribute to the "great host of Quaker and
non-Quaker citizens of this and other parts of our country who have done
the job and only we have been simple instrumentalities.[60]

In May 1939 the Service Committee released a pamphlet entitled
"Refugee Facts: A Study of the German Refugee in America." Using
U.S. Government records, the study revealed that over a six-year period
the number of immigrants admitted into the United States for permanent residence was actually (but only slightly) less than the immigrants
(previously admitted for permanent residence) who moved away. It noted
that in 1938 about one third of all refugees from Germany were Christians, and it stressed the extent to which, in most of the years since the
rise of Hitler, emigration from Germany did not even come close to the
quota allowed under the National Origins Law enacted in 1924 and
amended in 1929.

But the barriers to immigration of German refugees, especially Jews,
were deeply ingrained in the public mind. In business and other circles

there was a pervasive anti-Semitism, this often unspoken religious prejudice bolstered by extremists such as Father Charles E. Coughlin, a Detroit priest who defended German violence against Jews in his radio broadcasts. Clarence Pickett realized that there were these biases in many segments of American society. He also was aware of the deficiencies of the Roosevelt Administration in respect to the issue. While Franklin Roosevelt came to despise everything the Nazis represented, and almost from the start of the New Deal spoke out forcefully against the German government's persecutions, his objections did not reflect a troubled soul. Wrote historian Irwin Gellman, "The president drew attention to this emerging reign of terror in its infancy because it offended the sense of decency and fair play that had been preached to him and those of his social class since his days at Groton [boarding school]. Those who misread his sympathies as philo-Semitism were wrong. He deplored the brutality that Hitler heaped upon a vulnerable minority, nothing more."[61]

Paradoxically, Roosevelt for the most part had a prejudice against the tightly-knit foreign service fraternity in the State Department. Observed Gellman: "Many hailed from the East and had grown up with wealth, attended Ivy League schools, and entered the government to take their place as enlightened leaders in the service of their country. Built into the world view of the majority was adamant opposition to the communist menace and an unquestioning acceptance of their forbears' antipathy toward Jews, as a sly and untrustworthy race."[62] It was because of this view of career foreign service officers that President Roosevelt selected Senator Cordell Hull to be his secretary of state, a Tennessee Democrat who had virtually no qualifications in international affairs. Furthermore, Hull, consistently throughout his years in that key position, refused to become involved with Jewish matters and was regularly opposing government measures that might assist refugees. Gellman believes that this refusal did not stem from anti-Semitism, but rather that his wife's Jewish heritage, which he never once mentioned in his public life, "made him feel vulnerable to attacks from anti-Semites who would argue that his wife had forced him to support Jewish causes, and therefore that he had succumbed to un-American influences."[63]

In failing to get State Department support for AFSC-financed volunteers to help out in U.S. consulates abroad, Clarence Pickett was already encountering this wall of resistance to effective measures that might rescue Jews. But he was also soon to experience the resistance of the Congress to allowing twenty thousand German children, Jewish and non-Aryan, to come to the United States outside of the quota for German immigrants. The idea grew out of the realization by American Jews and others that thousands of parents in Germany were willing to part from their children given the terrible and dangerous circumstances under which they were living. Great Britain had already opened its crowded island to more than nine thousand refugee children.

Responding to a delegation of Roman Catholic and Protestant clergymen who had presented a petition to the White House calling upon the United States to open its doors to German children, Senator Robert Wagner of New York introduced a resolution in the Senate to implement the proposal, and Representative Edith Rogers of Massachusetts offered an identical measure in the House of Representatives. Known as the Wagner-Rogers Bill, or Child Refugee Bill, it proposed that a maximum of ten thousand children under the age of fourteen be admitted in 1939 and a similar number in 1940. They would be adopted temporarily by American families, with costs and responsibilities to be assumed by these families and by a newly-formed organization, the Non-Sectarian Committee for German Refugee Children. The migration of the children was to be supervised by the American Friends Service Committee. Clarence Pickett was named chairman of the Non-Sectarian Committee, with Catholic, Jewish, and Protestant co-chairmen.

Pickett tirelessly interviewed Congresspersons on a one-to-one basis. The subcommittees of the House and Senate Committees on Immigration held joint hearings in April. At the opening of the first set of hearings, a letter from Secretary of State Hull reminded the legislators that the Wagner-Rogers resolution opened the door to a departure from the quota system. Moreover, granting twenty thousand German visas, said Hull, in addition "to an estimated thirty thousand immigration visas now being issued annually in that country will inevitably necessitate increased clerical personnel, unfamiliar with the law and regulations, as well as additional office accommodations."[64] Clarence must have winced when he heard that. Spencer Coxe, who worked during the war in Washington for the National Planning Association and in that capacity often saw Pickett, recollected that Clarence was *outraged* by Hull's attitude regarding the plight of Jews in Europe. "Indeed, he held Hull responsible for the lack of decisive action by the United States in rescuing as many Jews as possible from the clutches of Hitler. Clarence was actually *bitter* on this point, his emotions being deeply stirred."[65]

On 1 July the Child Refugee Bill was finally reported out, with the proviso that the twenty thousand visas for children would be issued against the German quota, not in excess of the quota. Senator Wagner, appalled by the action in the House, withdrew the legislation from consideration by the Senate.

Later in July, Clarence and Lilly Pickett and both daughters left for a month's vacation at a weaving and craft school in Penland in North Carolina. This was a completely new experience for Clarence. "I wonder if weaving might not be a good old-age occupation," he wrote. "It occupies the mind enough to keep one from thinking of less valuable or more perplexing things, and has a good deal of lure to it."[66] "I must confess," wrote his secretarial assistant, Blanche Tache, to him, "I cannot picture you at work at a loom. I can't see you any other way than seated at a desk with stacks of mail, two secretaries hovering about you, and a Dictaphone."[67] It was a relaxing vacation in the mountains, with ample time for reading and for the writing of an article, "The Look Ahead," on German refugee children. He returned home refreshed at the end of August.

At daybreak on 1 September 1939, German armies poured across the Polish frontier and converged on Warsaw from the north, south, and west. As journalist and historian William Shirer would summarize the attack years later:

> Overhead, German war planes roared toward their targets: Polish troop columns and ammunition dumps, bridges, railroads and open cities. Within a few minutes they were giving the Poles, soldiers and civilians alike, the first taste of sudden death and destruction from the skies ever experienced on any great scale on the earth, and thereby inaugurating a terror which would become dreadfully familiar to hundreds of millions of men, women and children in Europe and Asia during the next six years, and whose shadow, after the nuclear bombs came, would haunt all mankind with the threat of utter extinction.[68]

Clarence Pickett and his associates in the American Friends Service Committee were now immediately faced with new and urgent demands for the relief of suffering in Europe.

NOTES

1. Preface to 1938 AFSC annual report.

2. William L. Shirer, *The Rise and Fall of the Third Reich: A History of Nazi Germany* (New York: Simon, 1960), 233.

3. Clarence Pickett journal, 14 April 1938.

4. Pickett journal, 15 April 1938.

5. Attachment to letter from Malvina Scheider, secretary to Mrs. Roosevelt, dated 5 Mar. 1938, holdings of the Franklin D. Roosevelt Library, Hyde Park, New York.

6. Attachment to Scheider letter, 1938.

7. Pickett journal, 18 Mar. 1938.

8. Letter to author dated 5 Aug. 1998 from Howard and Katharine Elkinton's son, Peter.

9. Pickett journal, 21 Apr. 1938.

10. Pickett journal, 21 Jan. 1938.

11. Arthur D. Morse, *While Six Million Died: A Chronicle of American Apathy* (New York: Hart, 1967), 218.

12. Lilly Pickett diary, trip to Europe (26 July-26 Oct. 1938), 52, family papers, courtesy of Carolyn Pickett Miller.

13. Lilly Pickett diary, 52.

14. Lilly Pickett diary, 54.

15. Ilse Ollendorff Reich, "Quakers Under the Nazi Regime," *Friends Journal* 40, no. 12 (December, 1994): 20.

16. Clarence Pickett journal, confidential summary report on trip to Europe, 28 Oct. 1938, 1, AFSC archives.

17. Confidential report, 1.

18. Confidential report, 2.

19. Confidential report, 3.

20. Confidential report, 3.

21. Clarence E. Pickett, *For More Than Bread* (Boston: Little, 1953), 124.

22. Pickett, *Bread*, 122.

23. Confidential report, 4.

24. Confidential report, 6.

25. Confidential report, 6.

26. Confidential report, 7.

27. Confidential report, 8.

28. Confidential report, 8.

29. Shirer, *Rise and Fall*, 397.

30. Confidential report, 9.

31. Shirer, *Rise and Fall*, 420.

32. Simon Schama, "Flaubert in the Trenches," a review of *Birdsong*, by Sebastian Faulks (New York: Random, 1996), *The New Yorker* 72 (23 Sept. 1996): 96-9.

33. Confidential report, 12.

34. Pickett journal, 29 Oct. 1938.

35. Pickett journal, 9 Nov. 1938.

36. Morse, *While Six Million Died*, 222.

37. Pickett journal, 14 Nov. 1938.

38. Letter dated 15 Nov. 1938, Pickett papers, AFSC archives.

39. Clarence E. Pickett, "In Heroic Enterprises," *The American Friend* 36 (new series), no.14 (8 July 1948): 223.

40. Pickett journal, 16 Nov. 1938.

41. Clarence Pickett to Lilly Pickett, 17 Nov. 1938, Pickett papers, AFSC archives.

42. Letter to one thousand Friends meetings and churches, dated 17 Nov. 1938, to be read on Sunday, 20 November, AFSC archives.

43. Pickett journal, 18 Nov. 1938.

44. Clarence Pickett to Lilly Pickett, 19 Nov. 1938, Pickett papers, AFSC archives.

45. Pickett journal, confidential memorandum, 25 Nov. 1938, AFSC archives.

46. Pickett journal, 1 Dec. 1938.

47. Clarence Pickett to Lilly Pickett, 6 Dec. 1938, Pickett papers, AFSC archives.

48. Pickett journal, 30 Dec. 1938.

49. George A. Walton, "Two Weeks in Berlin, December, 1938." *The Georgian*: George School Bulletin 10, no. 6 (June, 1939): 3-10.

50. William R. Hughes, Society of Friends Germany Emergency Committee, "Visit to Germany," 26 Nov. - 14 Dec. 1938, AFSC archives.

51. Hughes, "Visit to Germany."

52. Statement used by Quaker commission in interviews with German officials, December 1938, AFSC archives.

53. Rufus M. Jones, "Our Day in the German Gestapo," *The American Friend* 35 (new series), no. 14 (10 July 1947): 265.

54. Jones, "Our Day."

55. Telegram sent from Paris (for safety) 23 Dec. 1938, AFSC archives.

56. Journal, 1 Mar. 1939.

57. Pickett, *Bread*, 141.

58. Introduction, The Philadelphia Award, 1938, AFSC archives.

59. *Philadelphia Inquirer*, 21 Feb. 1939.

60. Stenotype copy of the proceedings of the presentation of The Philadelphia Award on the evening of 20 Feb. 1939, AFSC archives.

61. Irwin F. Gellman, *Secret Affairs: Franklin Roosevelt, Cordell Hull, and Sumner Welles* (Baltimore: Johns Hopkins Univ. Press, 1995), 17.

62. Gellman, *Secret Affairs*, 21.

63. Gellman, *Secret Affairs*, 98.

64. Morse, *While Six Million Died*, 257.

65. Spencer L. Coxe, Jr. interview, 16 Dec. 1996.

66. Journal, 30 July 1939.

67. Tache to Pickett, 23 Aug. 1939, AFSC archives.

68. Shirer, *Rise and Fall*, 597.

Chapter 12

THE ESCALATION OF RELIEF
AND REFUGEE NEEDS

For the ministry of the spirit as well as for
the alleviation of human misery

JUST A WEEK BEFORE THE GERMAN BLITZKRIEG against Poland, Germany and the Soviet Union had signed, on 23 August, a non-aggression treaty. The essence of the pact was that the Soviet Union agreed not to join Britain and France if they honored their treaty obligations to come to the aid of Poland in case she was attacked. While the pact itself was made public, contents of the secret protocol were not. They would become known only after the war with the capture of the secret German archives.

The protocol to the treaty spelled out the German and Soviet spheres of interest in eastern Europe, giving the Soviet Union a free hand to attack the Baltic states (Finland, Estonia, Latvia, and Lithuania) and identifying the demarcation line within a partitioned Poland in the event of a territorial and political transformation of the territories belonging to the Polish state. Indeed, following the German blitzkrieg the Russians quickly moved into their section of Poland, convincing the Germans that the Polish people should be denied any residual independent existence of their own whatsoever. "So, Poland, like Austria and Czechoslovakia before it," said William Shirer, "disappeared from the map of Europe."[1]

What remained after the Soviet Union seized her share of Poland in the east and Germany annexed her former provinces and some additional territory in the west was designated as the "General Government of Poland," to be under a German governor general. Wrote historian Hal Elliott Wert: "The population of the General Government —portions of Kilce, Krakow, Lublin, Lwow, and Warsaw districts—swelled to over 13,000,000 as refugees expelled by the Nazis from western and northern Poland crowded into Warsaw and the surrounding provinces. . . . The situation was compounded as Poles from the east made their way into the General Government."[2]

On Tuesday 5 September, the day after Labor Day and Clarence Pickett's first day at the office following his August vacation, Pickett spent every hour in conferences with members of the Foreign Service Section staff. The next day he cabled all AFSC workers in Europe: AFSERCO WISHES YOU TO EXERCISE COMPLETE FREEDOM REGARDING REMAINING OR LEAVING AND ADVISE FREQUENT CONTACT WITH AMERICAN CONSULATE AND AFSERCO OFFICE.[3] Early in the following week he and Rufus Jones convened a meeting of members of the board, the Foreign Service Section, and the Refugee Section, to consider what the AFSC might do in respect to Poland. The question before the committee was: should it simply support the present work in central Europe, or should it take a pro-active attitude, despite the difficulties, and expand programs? Clarence was very pleased with the view of the group, namely that the committee should respond aggressively to the needs in Poland. It was not certain whether the German government would allow Quaker workers into the distressed areas of Poland.[4]

As the point man for Quaker consultations regarding Polish relief, Clarence Pickett and both Paul Baerwald and Joseph Hyman of the Joint Distribution Committee conferred with Norman Davis of the American Red Cross on 20 September. The ARC was already funneling small amounts of money through the International Red Cross in Geneva to Poles who sought safety in neighboring countries. The next day the Polish commercial agent and consul in Philadelphia, in great distress because his wife and two small children were in Warsaw, came to see Pickett about the possibility of the AFSC finding a way to get food packages into Poland.[5]

The British blockade was a key obstacle. And one ingredient of President Roosevelt's commitment to the Allied war effort involved supporting the Continental blockade. According to Wert, "Privately, the president had confided to the British ambassador that, 'the restoration of Poland depended on the outcome of the war and not on the attempt to render aid. . . , however difficult it might be to resist the piteous appeal of the Poles and public opinion.'"[6] This was to be Roosevelt's position throughout the war.

A contradictory view came from ex-president Herbert Hoover. While he supported aid to Great Britain and France as the best way to keep America out of the war, he pressed for mass feeding programs for Polish refugees and the defeated Poles. He became the moving force behind the setting up of a consortium of relief agencies, the Commission for Polish Relief (CPR). On 1 October the secretary of CPR, Maurice Pate, urged the AFSC to obtain permission from the occupying powers to administer relief in Warsaw and other cities in what had been Poland.

Pickett agreed to try to visit the Russian and German embassies the next day to see what could be done. He was successful in making the appointments. He first consulted with Hans Thomsen at the German embassy. The *chargé d'affaires* agreed to cable his government about the Quaker request.[7]

Clarence then went to the Russian embassy: "I found out that [Constantine A.] Oumansky, the ambassador, had been recalled and is being purged," Clarence wrote. "I later found that this was because he was unable to prevent a series of articles critical of Russia from appearing in *The Saturday Evening Post*. Mr. [Dimitri Stepanovich] Chuvakhin is in charge. He is a young lad who speaks no English, and I had to talk through a young American girl who had studied Russian and who acted as an interpreter. The embassy was tragic in its ineffectiveness. One could hardly conceive of anything important happening through it."[8]

Pickett went to New York for a dinner engagement and later that evening reported to Maurice Pate on his consultations at the two embassies. Pate estimated that the CPR was in a position to raise millions of dollars for Polish relief. Clarence agreed to recommend to the AFSC board the following day the sending of one or two Friends to Warsaw very promptly. Homer Morris (already in England) and Howard Elkinton from the Berlin center were selected for this task, to be accompanied by William C. McDonald, a long-time Hoover associate with business interests in Poland. The next day Clarence was informed by the CPR that, according to their sources of information, Warsaw had been more than fifty percent destroyed, and there appeared to be about six hundred thousand homeless and foodless people. At the end of the week Herbert Hoover officially asked the Service Committee to administer relief in Poland on behalf of the CPR.

Negotiations began in mid-October in Berlin with the head of the Nationalist Socialist Welfare Agency (NSV), which quickly accepted the CPR-AFSC aid offer and promised to accompany the three representatives on an investigative tour of the General Government in Poland. No outsider had visited the territory since the Polish surrender of Warsaw on 27 September. On the day the cavalcade left for Warsaw, an accident occurred and injured Elkinton, who was taken back to Berlin. Deeply worried that the Quakers would be politically compromised if they rendered aid through the NSV, Morris wrote in his diary, "The accident was inexcusable because there was no car in sight [and] was on a perfectly straight, two-lane road. This whole thing is a symbol."[9] The incident remained a mystery. The German government offered to pay all hospital expenses, but it is not known whether Howard Elkinton agreed to accept the payment.

The CPR-AFSC representatives' itinerary was tightly controlled, but working through the U.S. consulate in Warsaw they circumvented some restrictions and formulated a reasonably accurate estimate of Polish food needs. They noted that the NSV was providing hot soup to about two hundred and fifty thousand residents and another three hundred thousand were receiving a bread ration. But the feeding program was selective. The NSV would not feed Jews. "McDonald and Morris concluded that the situation was critical, and that CPR [and the AFSC] would have to move quickly to prevent famine."[10] In making their proposal to the German government, they stipulated that the supplies would be shipped, controlled, and dispensed by U.S. workers and that aid would be distributed without discrimination.

After deliberating until mid-November, Germany concluded that all aid to Poland had to be provided through the NSV. Berlin strongly objected to the large staff that would be necessary to handle relief on so vast a scale. "The Nazis dreaded the prospect of U.S. [Quaker] relief workers being free to travel throughout Poland and report to the outside world," wrote Wert. "The Germans also objected strenuously to U.S. insistence on aid to Polish Jews."[11]

The German government had good reason to be concerned about outside visitors. On 12 October Hans Frank was appointed governor general of German-annexed Poland. "Himmler and Heydrich were assigned by Hitler to liquidate the Jews. Frank's job, besides squeezing food and supplies, and forced labor, out of Poland, was to liquidate the intelligentsia," wrote William Shirer. "'The men capable of leadership in Poland must be liquidated,' Hitler had said."[12]

It was within this morally reprehensible climate—and in the midst of an unusually severe winter in Poland—that negotiations continued, not only in Berlin but also in London, where permission to have relief supplies come through the British blockade needed to be secured. Despite the indecisive nature of these negotiations, the Service Committee sent off to Berlin and Warsaw two senior Friends, Edgar Rhoads, a successful businessman from Wilmington, Delaware, and Arthur Gamble, who had been a WPA organizer in Kentucky earlier in the decade and had served with the AFSC in Poland in 1919. If admitted, they would be responsible for the relief operation. Clarence Pickett continued to meet with officials of the CPR, the German *chargé d'affaires* Hans Thomsen, and Norman Davis, chairman of the American Red Cross. The Red Cross was negotiating independently with the German government, complicating the picture and making it necessary for Clarence to clarify relations between the Red Cross and the AFSC. The year 1939 ended with the collapse of the effort to provide substantial aid to the Poles.

But in February 1940 the Germans capitulated on the supervision issue and granted permission to the CPR/AFSC and American Red Cross to conduct a limited aid program in Poland. According to Wert, "shipments of canned milk and cod liver oil held at Gibraltar [by the Royal Navy] were released and landed in Italy before being transported north, but these supplies did not reach the Poles until late spring, since rail traffic was unable to move through the snowbound Alps."[13] Then, Germany's invasion of Holland, Luxembourg, Belgium, and France on 10 May, together with a tightening of the British blockade, brought to an abrupt halt even the limited aid that was getting through to occupied Poland.

In February and March 1940, in a trip west with Lilly, Clarence Pickett combined work on subsistence homesteads (now under the Farm Security Administration) with AFSC speaking engagements and family gatherings. The Picketts arrived in Los Angeles on 15 March, where he spoke at a public meeting. He was confronted with a Washington Merry-go-Round (Drew Pearson's syndicated column) disclosure that he was being considered for the ambassadorship to Germany.[14] Wrote Pearson:

"If and when new ambassadors are exchanged between the United States and Germany, as now seems probable, the man most likely to go to Berlin as U.S. envoy is a Quaker named Clarence Pickett ."[15] Three days later the Washington correspondent for the Los Angeles *Daily News* wrote that Pickett was "being seriously considered for appointment as American ambassador to Germany . . . with action upon the appointment being held in abeyance until Undersecretary of State Sumner Welles concludes his conversations with European statesmen and makes his report to the White House."[16] On 18 March Clarence Pickett spoke at the Whittier College Chapel, after which he and Lilly Pickett had lunch with a group at Whittier College president Mendenhall's home. "They discussed the question of my going to Germany if asked by the president . . . all said 'yes.'"[17]

Clarence and Lilly Pickett left Los Angeles the next day and arrived, via the southern rail route, in Washington the morning of 23 March. Clarence had an appointment at the White House to meet with the Arthurdale Committee. Rufus Jones must have known of the engagement at the White House and evidently thought it was an appointment to see the president. In a hand-written letter posted on 22 March and written on behalf of a group of Clarence's friends, Rufus reported the serious misgivings of the group regarding the possible appointment of Clarence as ambassador to Germany, first, on the grounds that it would take him away from the AFSC position, and secondly,

> . . . that it would be a dubious undertaking in this wartime atmosphere for any concerned Friend to be plunged into the diplomatic task of a militant nation. . . . The chance of accomplishing some great good end to offset the risks and sacrifices which would be involved was extremely slight. . . . The total effect of such a step on Quaker ideals and hopes and work in the world now and in the future needs very careful thought. . . . I pray for a wisdom from Above to guide thee to a right decision.[18]

It was only on 3 April that Clarence Pickett had an opportunity to explain to the AFSC board of directors his handling of the publicity concerning the ambassadorship. "No decision was taken or asked for," he wrote in his journal, "but the board did feel that we ought to assume additional responsibility if and when way opens."[19] While the minutes of the board meeting do not include any mention of this discussion, Clarence Pickett revealed many years later what had happened. When he returned from Germany in 1938, he had spoken with President Roosevelt about strengthening the United States embassy in Germany. He appealed to the president to consider placing the very ablest representation possible in Berlin in view of the critical relationships that were developing. Wrote Clarence:

> To my amazement, he turned to me and said that he was thinking of appointing me as ambassador—which was the kind of jest of which the president was capable. I said that of course he didn't really mean that; and I reiterated that I was concerned about choosing the most distinguished American in terms of this particular undertaking. He said that seriously he had given thought to the possibility of capitalizing on the long-standing reputation of Friends in Germany due to their relief work after the First World War, and that he had not spoken in jest. I reminded him that I would have to carry too many handicaps for the idea to be given serious consideration.
>
> After that, I dismissed the matter from my mind.[20]

There is no further reference to the matter either in his journal or in board minutes. Perhaps *Newsweek,* in an obscure column entitled "Political Straws," on 20 May gives the correct story: "The rumor is true, that Clarence Pickett, secretary of the American Friends Service Committee, was offered the ambassadorship to Berlin shortly before the Reich's newest offensive [10 May]; no appointment now seems likely."[21]

In June 1940 Clarence Pickett, in a public address to the biennial gathering of Friends in Cape May, New Jersey had an opportunity to reflect upon his deepest religious convictions. His reflections were within the context of a period when millions of Americans were becoming conscious of Friends, more as a social service agency than as a religious society. Pickett was aware of the need to express in words, as well as in deeds, basic Quaker tenets. He found that easy to do. "Ours is an elementary confidence in God and in human beings. . . . The primary fact of human beings is that they are the children of God and are of inestimable worth. . . . [Friends have] a basic confidence that the great realities of life are the supreme value of a consciousness of God and of the beauty that lies in the depths of human love."[22]

Clarence Pickett was faithful in attending meetings for worship on Sundays, not so much from a sense of duty as from a need to have that hour of quiet and sharing. It is clear from his journal, and from the accounts of those who also worshipped at the Providence Friends Meeting in Media, Pennsylvania, that he frequently was one of those who spoke in meeting, often expressing spiritual dimensions of some recent events in his life. "Most of Clarence's messages," observed a veteran AFSC staff member, Bronson Clark, "had a light sense of humor about them. He left you uplifted because he was not speaking in a depressed way."[23]

To be sure, there were many Friends who *hoped* Clarence Pickett would be present, just as Haverford College students and others leaned on Rufus Jones's presence in meetings for worship at the Haverford meetinghouse. Within the democracy of a traditional Quaker meeting for worship, there are inevitably those with special gifts in the ministry. Indeed, right into the twentieth century, some unprogrammed Quaker meetings formally recognized some members as "recorded ministers." They were encouraged to sit on the "facing benches" in order to be better heard by others.

Of great importance to Clarence Pickett in 1940 was the growing search within the three historic peace churches—Mennonites, Church of the Brethren, and Friends—for what might be termed a solution for conscientious objectors if conscription once again came into force. Early in 1937 Clarence Pickett had expressed to Mrs. Roosevelt his hope that a delegation from the historic peace churches might have an opportunity to meet with the president. She arranged for a delegation to see the president in his study at the White House in February. A representative of each of the historic churches left with him a one-page statement explaining their principles in respect to war. The Friends' letter concluded with these words:

> Insofar as they are true to these principles, Friends will make heavy sacrifices to transmit their spirit of love and faith, but they cannot, as followers of Christ, endorse war methods or support them, or be themselves a voluntary part of a system engaged in making war. We feel an obligation to make this conviction a matter of record with our Government now, in peacetime, not only in behalf of members of the Religious Society of Friends, but for any others who, for religious or conscientious reasons, would take a similar position.[24]

As historian Albert Keim explained it, "By the mid-30s a loose consensus among COs emerged around the idea of a form of alternative humanitarian service in lieu of military service. The alternative service idea was attractive to many peace church people because, as loyal citizens, they wanted a way to discharge their citizen obligations in wartime. Citizenship required more than sitting out a war in prison, for example. Alternative service, they believed, was more desirable than prison as a witness against war; it offered a practical demonstration of how to behave in wartime."[25]

In the fall of 1939 the AFSC Peace Section formed a subcommittee to give special consideration to the problems of the conscientious objector to war and military training. Pickett was asked to arrange another appointment with President Roosevelt for some leaders from the peace churches. The meeting took place on 10 January 1940. Clarence had not intended to go, but when he rang up the executive office, they asked him to come and introduce the members of the delegation to the president. Roosevelt was under very heavy pressure, was most affable, and only spent a few minutes with the group. A proposal for the treatment of COs in case of war was given to him. "He agreed to read it with care," said Pickett, and "expressed appreciation at having thought put on this problem by those mainly concerned."[26]

There seemed in January of 1940 to be little chance of a military draft being enacted. To suggest such a course, President Roosevelt knew, was politically risky, especially in a year when he was seeking an unprecedented third term. Even the armed services were not favoring a draft law. But following the German invasion of the Low Countries and France in May, public sentiment began shifting from an isolationist to an interventionist stance. On 6 June Clarence Pickett, representing the Religious Society of Friends, Orie Miller, speaking for the Mennonites, and Dan West for the Church of the Brethren had a conference with Francis Biddle, solicitor-general in the Department of Justice, who expressed the view that the draft was imminent. On 20 June, the day the Germans reached Paris, Congress began consideration of conscription in the form of the Burke-Wadsworth bill.

The proposed bill had a clause identical to the World War I law which mistakenly assumed that most conscientious objectors would be willing to serve in noncombatant military positions. The three service bodies of the historic peace churches—the Mennonite Central Committee, the Brethren Service Commission, and the American Friends Service Committee—moved vigorously to change the CO clause. Paul Comly French, a Philadelphia Quaker with experience of working for the government in Washington and the author of *We Won't Murder*, an analysis of the CO experience in World War I, was placed on the payroll of the AFSC's War Problems Committee.[27] He was sent to Washington to help defeat the conscription bill or, failing in that, to modify the Burke-Wadsworth bill to include an alternative service provision.

During the summer French, together with Mennonites, Brethren, and other Friends, worked tirelessly to bring into the draft bill reasonably acceptable provisions for conscientious objectors of all religious faiths. Slowly the efforts of the spokespersons for the peace churches bore fruit. But then in August, while the bill was being debated in the House and Senate, the CO clause, so carefully constructed in July, began to change form. The most unfortunate change was to take registration and hearing procedures out of the Justice Department and place them in the hands of local draft boards. This in effect meant that the management of CO matters would be handled by the new Selective Service Administration, an agency essentially operated by the armed forces for the purpose of conscripting men for military service.

Clarence Pickett, with his close ties to the Roosevelts and to other administration officials, was called into the negotiations on an emergency basis on the morning of Friday, 13 September. He attempted to get in touch with the president during the day, but was not successful. He did talk with an assistant attorney general who agreed to do what he could to straighten out the difficulties. Then in the evening, in Washington, he met with the official who was drawing up the registration questionnaire that COs would have to complete. "We had dinner together, and I found that he was an old friend of Tom and Esther Jones [and] formerly a professor of sociology at Fisk [University, where Thomas Jones was president]. He showed me the questionnaire as it was developing and also offered to allow us to help draft the regulations of the execution of the Draft Act."[28]

On 14 September Congress passed the draft bill, with decisions and hearings in respect to COs squarely in the hands of local draft boards, and two days later the president signed the new Selective Training and Service Act into law.

While Clarence was involved in repeated interventions regarding conscription in Washington and was regularly meeting with the War Problems Committee in Philadelphia, the greater priority for him in 1940

was the plight of European refugees. Significant sectors of public opinion viewed the Quakers as the dominant organization in the fields of
relief and refugee immigration—and expressed this view with generous
donations to the Friends Service Committee. But the facts of organizational life in respect to these needs were far more complicated. There
had to be coordination among interested agencies. Pickett was frequently
at the heart of these relationships. He particularly related to leading
American Jews and Jewish organizations.

A new organization, the U.S. Committee for the Care of European
Children, grew out of a surge of American interest in bringing English
children to the United States. The miracle at Dunkirk—the successful evacuation of over three hundred thousand British and French soldiers from
Belgium—was hailed as a great victory. But Winston Churchill reminded
the House of Commons that "wars are not won by evacuations."[29] Churchill
knew that the Luftwaffe bombers were based but five or ten minutes
away across the Channel and that sooner or later the Germans would attack
Britain. It was imperative that children be moved out of the cities.

It was always important to work out with interfaith and nonsectarian
agencies the proper role of the American Friends Service Committee.
There was great pressure upon the Service Committee, both from within
the Religious Society of Friends and from the public at large, to move
promptly to relieve distress, especially in those parts of Europe where the
committee had field staff. On 10 May the invasion of Holland, Belgium,
and Luxembourg clogged the roads in France with 3.5 million frightened
civilians. They came in railroad coaches and crowded cattle cars, in
vans, on bicycles, even on foot, hurrying, always hurrying south. Quaker
workers moved around, in accordance with the greatest needs, to set up
centers in Toulouse, Bordeaux, Montpellier, Angouleme, and Poitiers. In
great canteens they fed thousands daily, in public halls where straw mat-
tresses were spread in long rows on the floor, they gave shelter.

Clarence Pickett's job as executive secretary was immeasurably
strengthened by the appointment of James Vail, a highly respected Quaker
chemist, to head up a new European Relief Committee within the AFSC.
Later in the year this committee, the Refugee Section, and the Foreign
Centers Committee were merged into a Foreign Service Section with
James Vail as secretary. Vail's first responsibility was to visit with
Clarence, the French ambassador and the heads of U.S. Government
agencies tangential to the objective of shipping relief supplies to France.

Clarence Pickett's consistent view regarding "America's Food and Europe's Need," was eloquently stated in an address he delivered before the American Academy of Political and Social Science in Philadelphia in October 1940. "It may not be amiss to suggest," he said, "that the Germany which Britain now faces, and of which she so heartily disapproves, is in no small degree the product of the vicious weapon of blockade used during and following the [First] World War. . . . There is yet to be shown an illustration where the starvation of populations has been proved to be a permanent instrument of peace."[30] Based on the evidence coming from Quaker workers, Pickett reported that Germany was not taking food from unoccupied France. He shared his conviction that pledges made by the German government in respect to relief could be relied upon. He noted that the United States had a surplus of food. "The greatest danger facing the world today, in my judgment," Pickett claimed, "is that we shall fight to preserve civilization by methods which in themselves seek to destroy the very values which we profess to cherish."[31]

Shortly after his vacation on Cape Cod, Clarence was once again repeatedly in Washington to arrange for the shipment of food surpluses to unoccupied France. He conferred with Norman Davis, chairman of the American Red Cross, and Ernest Swift, vice president of the ARC, about joining together in an effort to secure British blockade exemption. He talked with William C. Bullitt, U.S. Ambassador to France, who was anxious to have food supplies shipped to unoccupied France.

Notwithstanding Ambassador Bullitt's convictions and initiatives—and the strong support of prominent persons both in and out of government—the ships did not sail. There was opposition at many levels of society, including religious leaders, to sending food to Europe. Pickett continued to press the case and took advantage of his many contacts, indeed friendships. Two days before Thanksgiving, he saw the president and informed him about the plan for sending a Christmas ship to France with food. Roosevelt approved of the idea but encouraged the ship to be large enough to be divided with cargo for both Spain and France. He asked Pickett to see Norman Davis the next day and to work out plans with him for the Christmas ship. Pickett told him he needed his help to get a uniformity of response, so the president wrote out a note to Norman Davis, asking him to talk with Pickett about plans for the boat.[32]

On 20 December, with no progress made in respect to a Christmas ship, Pickett had breakfast with Mrs. Roosevelt:

I told her of my distress that the Christmas ship had not yet been approved by Britain. She agreed to talk with the president and have him put pressure on the Red Cross. This she did at once, by talking with him in his bed, and he called the Red Cross. They insisted that they had done everything they knew, so I asked her to ask the president if he would consider calling Churchill and ask him to let the boat pass. I made it quite clear that after January 15 we know of no way of having milk for the thirty-five thousand children we are now feeding in southern France.[33]

Then, in the same conference with Mrs. Roosevelt , Clarence Pickett told her of the AFSC plan to send a delegation to Germany and England. She in turn discussed the matter with the president, who heartily approved of their going but did not want to be quoted as saying so in Berlin. It is likely that this presidential seal of approval was influential in AFSC board deliberations about a Quaker delegation. On 30 December, with no Christmas ship afloat, the AFSC board decided to move on the delegation.

Clarence Pickett's appointment calendar was always multi-faceted and crowded. Yet he found time to be responsive to individual concerns. Furthermore, he had that great ability that some busy executives have to make a visitor feel as if there was nothing on his docket other than listening to and conversing with you. Several persons interviewed for this biography specifically mentioned that feature of his character. It revealed a genuine interest in people. Sometimes, however, if a visitor stayed in his office longer than seemed appropriate, he would press a button under his desk top that would be a signal to Blanche Tache, his secretary, to interrupt the conversation and advise him about some other responsibility to which he needed to attend.[34]

In early October Clarence was in Northampton, Massachusetts to speak in Sage Hall at Smith College. Just as he was leaving for the train back to Philadelphia, Mrs. Stuart Burgess called him in great anxiety about her son, David, who was one of the twenty young men at Union Theological Seminary planning to refuse to register for the draft even though they would be exempt as ministerial students. This is what was known as the "absolutist" position, a refusal to cooperate in any fashion with a conscription system designed to procure men for the armed forces. By the end of the war there were just over six thousand men who were

imprisoned for their refusal to participate in any form of service—
military, non-combatant service within the military, or alternative
civilian service.[35] Of these, close to forty-five hundred were Jehovah's
Witnesses, whose refusal was based primarily on their claim of ministerial exemption. These statistics reveal a tiny but select group of men
who chose prison rather than the alternative service available for conscientious objectors.

Clarence sent David Burgess a wire suggesting that they meet in the
morning at Grand Central Station in New York. Burgess was there when
Clarence got off the sleeper and with him were nine of his co-objectors.
Pickett and the seminarians had a two-hour session, and they asked him
if he would stay over until evening so that others of the CO group could
talk with him. He agreed to meet them at nine o'clock.

Pickett saw them as scheduled. There were fifteen of the original
twenty present, but they had picked up six recruits who were more or
less on the fence. He noticed that they had done considerable thinking
during the day for, while they felt that the dramatic quality of their protest demanded that they act as a body, more and more they were coming
to see that they did not agree on all points. Clarence encouraged them to
act, each according to his conscience, because in the last analysis, he
thought, each had his own decision to make.

As the protest at Union finally evolved, most of the men did register,
but eight of them stuck to their absolutist convictions. True to form,
Clarence Pickett kept in touch with the men. At the end of October he
wrote to Malcolm Lovell, one of the eight non-registrants: "I want to
express my personal satisfaction that you have found a clear sense of
what should be done, and that you have maintained the right spirit in your
dealings with the court. I hope it may seem right to the judge to give a
suspended sentence, but in any case the maintenance of your inner
integrity and your loyalty to your religious conviction was the most important thing of all. Whatever happens, I shall not lose interest or
confidence in you. In our effort to rid the world of war, there will have to
be many methods of attack used, and for certain people the instrument
which you are using will probably be their fullest contribution."[36]

Throughout his lifetime, Clarence Pickett fully supported both those
conscientious objectors who accepted alternative service within the
Selective Service System and those who chose to object to conscription
itself. He saw that some young men were not prepared spiritually and

psychologically for the ordeals of imprisonment. In an apparently unpublished review of A.J. Muste's pamphlet, "Of Holy Disobedience," (Pendle Hill, January 1952), he criticized Muste for implying that there was only a minor place for the Civilian Public Service stand.[37] But Pickett was deeply moved by the story of the young Austrian farmer's refusal to comply with Hitler's draft despite the counsel of his family, priest, and bishop, resulting in the CO's execution, as told in Gordon Zahn's *In Solitary Witness: The Life and Death of Franz Jägerstätter.*[38]

At the close of the year Clarence Pickett received a letter from Elton Trueblood, who had been a student at Penn College when Clarence was pastor of the Oskaloosa Friends Meeting, and who, like Clarence, had gone on to Hartford Theological Seminary for a B.D. degree. Trueblood then obtained his M.A. and Ph.D. from Harvard University and at the time of writing was professor of philosophy and religion at Stamford University. Trueblood, widely known and respected in Quaker circles, was urging the American Friends Service Committee to reprint for distribution his article entitled "The Quaker Way" that appeared in the December 1940 issue of *The Atlantic Monthly.* The six-page piece was a careful analysis of the moral dilemmas faced by Quakers in both opposing oppression, as in the case of slavery during the Civil War, and refusing to participate in war. Elton Trueblood in his handwritten letter expressed his high regard for Clarence Pickett, noting his appreciation for Clarence's leadership in Oskaloosa.[39]

Clarence Pickett's reply, sent the day after Christmas, was illuminating, particularly for its self-criticism. He said that he considered the article to be a very good description of the frame of mind of a great many Friends, but he did not consider it a prophetic statement of vital religious pacifism. Pickett felt that what Trueblood had said in the *Atlantic* was a good description of the state of mind of persons who live in the present social and economic order and "make sufficient adjustments to it so that life moves on reasonably undisturbed. I find that is pretty much a description of my own tendency at times," he wrote, "to find a modest and middle class comfortable way out, but my own best judgment is that we are in the midst of the greatest social revolution the world has seen, and that it will require far more searching thinking and action than is at all characteristic of the Religious Society of Friends if we are to be a prophetic group, setting sufficiently loosely to position and possessions to glimpse the forms of association in life that must come."[40] Here was Clarence Pickett expressing, in just one long sentence, his deepest, most radical convictions. He was quite aware that he himself was not living up to what he glimpsed as needed, connected in his mind with what the earliest Christians had most valued.

In the same reply to Elton Trueblood, Clarence Pickett said that Anne Morrow Lindbergh's *The Wave of the Future* came very close to an intimation of the new life he was envisioning. "Are we afraid of paying the price of peace?" she wrote. "For peace has a price as well as war. The price of peace is to be a strong nation, not only physically but also morally and spiritually."[41]

Just three months prior to the correspondence with Elton Trueblood, Clarence Pickett, Rufus Jones, and John Rich, secretary of publicity for the AFSC, had had lunch with Charles and Anne Lindbergh at the Cosmopolitan Club in New York. Anne Lindbergh asked the three Friends if the AFSC would be willing to accept all of the royalties from the publication of her next book, *The Wave of the Future*. They agreed to accept the royalties, "and to have it publicly announced, because we are so strongly in sympathy with their [the Lindberghs'] position and are willing to be unpopular with them if necessary."[42] In a letter to her mother, Anne Lindbergh said, "I want to give the proceeds of it—*if any!*—to the Quakers, as they seem to be the only ones living up to the reality of the word *mercy*."[43]

On Christmas Eve of the year 1940, responding to Clarence Pickett's request, Anne Lindbergh read a speech on the radio, urging that food be sent to Europe.

As the year 1941 began, Clarence Pickett was giving a high priority in his schedule to negotiations relating to the shipment and distribution of food to occupied areas of Europe and to the food needs and refugee emigration problems in unoccupied France. It was for the purpose of addressing those issues that the AFSC board of directors decided to send Harold Evans and James Vail to Germany and Henry Cadbury and Robert Yarnall to England. Pickett obtained the necessary authorizations from the State Department for these Friends. All four of them sailed on 11 January, proceeding to their destinations through Lisbon, Portugal. Cadbury and Yarnall carried with them the first of AFSC's monthly remittances of $10,000 to the Friends Service Council in London for the relief of suffering in England.

On 9 June, Clarence Pickett and Burns Chalmers, recently returned from Quaker service in France, went to see Assistant Secretary of State Breckenridge Long, Chalmers to tell him of his experience with the consular office in Marseilles. Fortunately, Chalmers was able to speak very favorably of the consul there. Then Pickett discussed with Long the new, considerably more restrictive provisions for granting visas to refugees. The ruling applied to prospective immigrants from Germany and all of the occupied countries. The order immediately affected some three thousand refugees awaiting transportation from Lisbon (the last remaining neutral port on the Atlantic) to the United States. Long, unenthusiastic under any circumstances about aid to Jewish refugees, had convinced the president that spies had infiltrated the refugee stream. As a consequence, the State Department laid a bureaucratic minefield across the paths that refugees were using to come to the United States. The ruling had a direct negative impact on the work of the AFSC's office in Lisbon which had been opened in February 1941.

Clarence Pickett noted that the new procedure would highly centralize the granting of visas and slow up the process. "Although one can see the reason for this step," he wrote, "it is one more item in the process of regimentation and controlling people and is in my judgment a doubtful step."[44] Doubtful step! Once again an understatement, masking feelings of frustration and disappointment. Furthermore, he and others had no way of knowing that the toughening of State Department policies coincided with the decision of the Nazi leadership on 31 July 1941 to move forward with what was ominously referred to as "the final solution of the Jewish question."[45] Concentration camps now became extermination camps.

The publicity surrounding the Service Committee's position and actions in respect to refugees and to food for Europe was producing a greater public awareness of the Religious Society of Friends with its membership in the United States of only 100,000 members. Articles about Quakers, with an emphasis on their principles and programs, began appearing in prominent magazines. The *Readers Digest* published an article written by one of its own editors entitled "They Call Themselves Friends." *The Saturday Evening Post* published a long article. In December 1940 a very complimentary, colorfully written, and generously illustrated article appeared in *Fortune* magazine (with no by-line) entitled "The Lord's Battalions." The subtitle was "Quakers won't fight but they're great at cleaning up the mess that comes of fighting. With 'irresistible good will' they bind Europe's wounds."[46]

As helpful as the favorable publicity about the Friends Service Committee may have been, Clarence Pickett had no cause for satisfaction as international events in 1941 unfolded. Added to his concerns about refugees and about food for occupied and unoccupied areas of western Europe were his meetings with a group discussing the possibility of relief in Russia (as a consequence of the German invasion in June) and with the United China Relief Committee. James Dunn, economic advisor to the European division of the State Department, urged Clarence Pickett to explore the possibility of a Quaker relief operation in Greece. The British embassy was encouraging the Service Committee to resume a relief program in Spain. The needs of earthquake victims in Mexico were on Clarence's heart and mind.

On 27 May 1941, the AFSC board of directors approved a "Call to Persons of Good Will" to be issued over the signatures of chairman Rufus Jones and executive secretary Clarence Pickett. This impassioned, lengthy appeal, circulated, as it turned out, just before the German invasion of the Soviet Union on 22 June, read in part:

> The time has come for those who see clearly what is happening to the world, who feel its present tragedy and who, at the same time, have a firm grasp of the divine possibilities of this human life of ours, to speak a sober, solemn word in this hour of crisis. More important even than the question of convoys, or of American isolationism, or of unlimited national emergency, is the question whether there is not some way, in this universe that God has made, for the deeper life of humanity to have its turn of consideration, and for this gigantic tide of destruction to be brought to an end. We are being swept on by a cyclone of hate and fury into a world-wide barbarism and an animalism that have had no parallel in the records of the race.[47]

On 11 July 1941, Clarence Pickett's, brother-in-law, Gilbert Bowles, soon to be moving to Honolulu, wrote a letter on Tokyo Friends Center letterhead to Admiral Kichisaburo Nomura, the Japanese ambassador in Washington, introducing Clarence to the ambassador. "It gives me great pleasure to believe that my brother-in-law is to have the privilege of meeting your excellency. If not at this first meeting, I hope in the near future that he may be favored with the opportunity of conferring unhurriedly with you over vital questions of common interest."[48]

There was no opportunity for Clarence Pickett to see Ambassador Nomura that summer or autumn. Then on Friday, 5 December Pickett had a session at the State Department with Undersecretary of State Sumner Welles concerning the possibility of conscientious objectors going to Mexico to do reconstruction work. As he came out from Welles' office Ambassador Nomura and Saburo Kurusu, a special emissary from Japan, came out from the office of Secretary Hull, where they had just delivered the Japanese government's reply to the memorandum of the State Department concerning Indochina and Thailand. "There was great excitement on the part of the newspaper- and camera-men," wrote Clarence. "The ambassador is a big, husky man, while Kurusu is a little, insignificant looking person."[49]

On Sunday morning, 7 December over three hundred Japanese war planes descended upon Pearl Harbor, where the pilots found most of the Pacific Fleet anchored, unprotected and unprepared. Within two hours eight battleships were destroyed or badly damaged, and some two hundred aircraft destroyed. More than twenty-three hundred soldiers, sailors, and civilians were killed. Like most other Americans, Clarence spent much of the day and evening by the radio, listening to reports of Japan's declaration of war and the attacks on Hawaii, the Philippines, Hong Kong, and Malaysia.

Then the next day he and his colleagues listened to President Roosevelt call on the Congress to declare that, since "the unprovoked and dastardly attack by Japan on Sunday, 7 December, a state of war has existed between the United States and the Japanese Empire."[50] The whole atmosphere of cheering and hilarity on the part of the Congresspersons Clarence found disturbing. He felt that the president's speech was dignified and to the point. The one dissenting vote was pacifist Jeannette Rankin, a Republican member of the House from Montana, who on 4 April 1917, as the first woman in Congress, had voted, along with fifty other representatives and six senators, against the U.S. declaration of war resolution.

Quakers and others who had Japanese friends in the United States were immediately active in checking on the welfare of these newly-designated enemy aliens. Some Japanese were promptly interned— in part for their own protection. The Foreign Service Section of the AFSC quickly set up an Alien Enemy Committee. During a visit to New York,

Clarence Pickett sought out the Japanese consul, Shinichi Kondo. Clarence found him in the Japanese consulate with one other staff member, since the consulate was closed Monday and the door was guarded by a big, burly policeman and four FBI men. When Pickett told them who he was and what he wanted, he was allowed to go in and see the consul, who felt he had been treated as well as they could expect. Mr. Kondo was being allowed to go home every night, with a policeman to protect him. Pickett told Kondo that he would be glad to have the consul's wife and children come and stay at Waysmeet for as long as was needed.[51]

On 11 December Hitler and Mussolini declared war on the United States and the following day, in response to a written request from the president, the United States Congress unanimously recognized that "a state of war exists between the United States, Germany and Italy."[52] During these same days Clarence Pickett was calling together committees of the AFSC to confer about the enemy alien problem and to discuss alternatives to those procedures in the civilian defense program to which pacifists might object.

At the end of the week Pickett had an opportunity to converse at some depth with Dr. Heinrich Bruening, the former chancellor of Germany, who was not hopeful about the future of Europe, stating that basically the difficulty was a breakdown of the moral and ethical standards of life. Concluded Pickett:

> One came away from the experience feeling more certain than ever that the significant things that are being done and will be done in the next months and years will probably not be the great sweeping gestures related to the prosecution of the war, but the releasing of ideas and acts based on a right spirit which changes people's attitudes and gives them a sense that human life has value in itself and is not just a political pawn.[53]

It was within this perspective that Clarence Pickett would face the enormous challenges of an America at war.

NOTES

1. William L. Shirer, *The Rise and Fall of the Third Reich* (New York: Simon, 1960), 632.

2. Hal Elliott Wert, "U.S. Aid to Poles Under Nazi Domination, 1939-1940," *The Historian* 57, no. 3 (spring, 1995): 513.

3. Minutes, AFSC board of directors, 6 Sept. 1939.

4. Clarence Pickett journal, 12 Sept. 1939.

5. Pickett journal, 21 Sept. 1939.

6. Wert, "U.S. Aid to Poles," 512.

7, Pickett journal, 2 Oct. 1939.

8. Pickett journal, 2 Oct. 1939.

9. Wert, "U.S. Aid to Poles," 514.

10. Wert, "U.S. Aid to Poles," 516.

11. Wert, "U.S. Aid to Poles," 516.

12. Shirer, *Rise and Fall*, 662.

13. Wert, "U.S. Aid to Poles," 522.

14. Pickett journal,, 15 Mar. 1940.

15. Washington Merry-Go-Round, 14 Mar. 1940, Drew Pearson papers, Yale University Library.

16. Los Angeles *Daily News*, 18 Mar. 1940.

17. Pickett journal, 18 Mar. 1940.

18. Jones to Pickett, 22 Mar. 1940, Haverford College, Haverford, PA: Magill Library, Quaker Collection.

19. Pickett journal, 3 Apr. 1940.

20. Clarence E. Pickett, *For More Than Bread* (Boston: Little, 1953), 167.

21. *Newsweek*, 20 May 1940.

22. Clarence E. Pickett, "Worship and Works: How Are They Related?" *Friends Intelligencer* 97, no. 33 (17 Aug. 1940): 527-28.

23. Taped interview with Bronson Clark, 18 Aug. 1993.

24. Clarence Pickett to President Roosevelt, 11 Feb. 1937, AFSC archives.

25. Albert N. Keim, *The CPS Story: An Illustrated Story of Civilian Public Service* (Intercourse, PA: Good Books, 1990), 14.

26. Pickett journal, 10 Jan. 1940.

27. Paul Comly French, *We Won't Murder* (New York: Hastings House, 1940).

28. Pickett journal, 13 Sept. 1940.

29. *Winston S. Churchill: His Complete Speeches, 1897-1963*, ed. by Robert Rhodes James, Vol. VI (New York: Chelsea House, 1974), 6231.

30. Summary of address as published in The Fellowship of Reconciliation's journal, *Fellowship* 6, no. 9 (Nov. 1940): 135-37.

31. Summary of address, *Fellowship,* 1940.

32. Pickett journal, 26 Nov. 1940.

33. Pickett journal, 20 Dec. 1940.

34. Letter to author from Blanche Tache, 1 Nov. 1995.

35. Keim, *The CPS Story*, 8.

36. Letter, Pickett to Lovell, 26 Oct. 1940, AFSC archives.

37. Undated, Picket papers, AFSC archives.

38. Gordon Zahn, *In Solitary Witness: The Life and Death of Franz Jagerstatter* (New York: Holt, 1964), as reviewed by Pickett, *Friends Journal* 11, no. 6 (15 Mar. 1965), 141.

39. Trueblood to Pickett, 16 Dec. 1940, AFSC archives.

40. Pickett to Trueblood, 26 Dec. 1940, AFSC archives.

41. Anne Morrow Lindbergh, *The Wave of the Future: A Confession of Faith,* (New York: Harcourt, 1940), 38.

42. Pickett journal, 25 Sept. 1940.

43. Anne Morrow Lindbergh, W*ar Within and Without: Diaries and Letters of Anne Morrow Lindbergh, 1939-1944* (New York: Harcourt, 1980), 145.

44. Pickett journal, 9 June 1941.

45. Arthur D. Morse, *While Six Million Died: A Chronicle of American Apathy,* (New York: Hart, 1967), 304.

46. *Fortune* 20, no. 6 (Dec. 1940).

47. American Friends Service Committee, "A Call to Persons of Good Will," June 1941, AFSC archives.

48. Gilbert Bowles to Baron Nomura, with copy to Pickett, Haverford College, Haverford, PA: Magill Library, Quaker Collection.

49. Pickett journal, 5 Dec. 1941.

50. *The New York Times,* 8 Dec. 1941.

51. Pickett journal, 9 Dec. 1941.

52. Doris Kearns Goodwin, *No Ordinary Time: Franklin and Eleanor Roosevelt, The Home Front in World War II* (New York: Simon, 1994), 298.

53. Pickett journal, 12 Dec. 1941.

Chapter 13

CONFRONTING AN AMERICA AT WAR

*Where politics stand pretty squarely across the path
of the best services to human beings*

WHILE CLARENCE PICKETT'S DOMINANT INTERESTS were reflected in
his unflagging efforts to get food to, and refugees out of, Europe and
toward these objectives was demonstrating unmatched leadership, he
was nevertheless the executive secretary of the entire American Friends
Service Committee, with its three major program sections—foreign
service, social-industrial, and peace—and administrative offices—finance, publicity, and personnel. And now, beginning with the passage
of the Selective Service Act, a whole new and complicated program of
alternative services for conscientious objectors came under Pickett's
general administrative oversight. At every critical step in the designing
of what became known as Civilian Public Service (CPS) Pickett was
involved. He was fortunate to have as "secretaries" (directors) of the
Friends CPS program, serving successively, two Quakers who had lived
through the CO problems of World War I with him: Thomas Jones,
until he returned to Fisk University in January 1942 and then Paul
Furnas. They brought experience and vision to the task. Pickett worked
well with both of them.

Plans for alternative service projects—work camps, refugee, and relief activities at home and abroad—needed to be drawn up and presented to the new director of Selective Service, Clarence Dykstra. This
was done through what became known as the National Service Board
for Religious Objectors (NSBRO), with Paul Comly French as executive

secretary. Basically, the proposal was to have men who were classified by their local draft boards as conscientious objectors "by reason of religious training and belief" assigned to camps under the direction of the service agencies—the Mennonite Central Committee, the Brethren Service Commission, and the American Friends Service Committee. Under this arrangement the men would do "work of national importance" as the Selective Service Act stipulated, such as working for the U.S. Forest Service and the Soil Conservation Service.

The government was initially expected to provide funds to operate the camps and pay the men, but, especially after President Roosevelt reacted negatively to the whole alternative service idea, there was general recognition, both by government proponents of the plan and by the church agencies themselves, that to ask Congress for funds to operate the camps would expose CPS to hostile scrutiny and might scuttle the entire program. So the fateful decision was made: peace church service agencies would finance the program. Each man would receive $2.50 a month.

When President Roosevelt, having backed away from his initial negative reaction to the whole idea of Civilian Public Service, signed Executive Order 8675 on 16 February 1941, the unique church-state partnership was born. As historian Albert Keim has noted, "It began as a six-month experiment. It lasted through a year of uneasy peace, four years of total war, and two years of demobilization. . . . The actual relationship of the religious agencies to Selective Service was vague."[1] It was this undetermined, at times confusing, relationship—along with the vociferous complaints of some COs in the camps—that drew Clarence Pickett repeatedly into negotiations with his Mennonite and Brethren counterparts and, through the NSBRO, with Selective Service.

Clarence Pickett, throughout the existence of the Civilian Public Service program, pushed the government to expand its definition of "work of national importance." As Albert Keim was to observe, "From the vantage point of an idealistic young conscientious objector, many of the tasks assigned to CPS men seemed irritatingly superfluous in a world suffering horribly from global war."[2] It was out of this conviction that Pickett, on the very day, 5 December 1941, that the Japanese emissaries were seeing Cordell Hull, had a long session with Undersecretary of State, Sumner Welles, to gain permission for COs to serve in the earthquake zone of Mexico. The project had the support both of Mrs. Roosevelt and the U.S. ambassador to Mexico Josephus Daniels.

But both Hull and Welles disapproved of the plan. "I came away [from the appointment]," wrote Clarence, "feeling it was a case of where politics stand pretty squarely across the path of the best services to human beings."[3] The State Department also rejected the proposal that American COs work side by side with English Quakers in their Friends Ambulance Units.

Clarence Pickett was particularly impressed with the arduous and dangerous services being performed by the Friends Ambulance Unit in China, the men driving trucks to carry medical supplies up the Burma Road from Rangoon into China, the road infested with war lords, thieves, bandits, bogus, and legitimate tax collectors, and with COs refusing to carry any weapons of defense. Here was a good example in Clarence's view of William James' "moral equivalent of war." In early November 1942 the AFSC board strongly urged Clarence to find a way whereby properly-trained CPS men would be allowed by the U.S. government to serve in China. Pickett was already talking with the presidents of Quaker colleges about a plan to provide CPS men with training for overseas relief and reconstruction work. He was firmly against any arrangement in such colleges under which the armed services would have a unit on campus.

Clarence Pickett's calendar of engagements in the autumn of 1942 was happily interrupted by the marriage of his youngest daughter, Carolyn, to G. Macculloch ("Cully") Miller, whom she had met at Antioch College. The wedding took place at the Providence Friends Meetinghouse in the afternoon of 14 November with about one hundred and fifty people present. As is customary in Quaker weddings, there was no minister involved. The bride and groom made their vows directly to each other. Wrote Clarence: "It was a lovely, simple affair with no one asked to speak, but with Rufus Jones, Agnes Tierney, Annette Way and Passmore Elkington speaking, all very acceptably. Carolyn and Cully spoke their vows clearly and distinctly."[4] Following the reception in the social room of the meetinghouse, Clarence and Lilly Pickett hosted a dinner for twenty-four family members and others at Waysmeet.

Undaunted by government bureaucratic obstacles, in January 1943 Clarence Pickett drew up a letter to put before President Roosevelt requesting him to secure from the secretary of war permission for the AFSC to send a unit of CPS men to China. At the same time Pickett was discussing with his staff colleagues a proposal to draw two hundred men from CPS camps for training in Quaker colleges for post-war relief and reconstruction. Later that same month Mrs. Roosevelt made an appointment for herself, Clarence Pickett, and Rufus Jones to talk with Secretary of War Henry Stimson (formerly secretary of state during the Hoover presidency) at the newly-built Pentagon. The interview went well, although Clarence came away from it impressed by "the gold braid trappings and manifestations of luxury and arrogance around the new War Department building . . . the center for an enormous machine dedicated to destruction."[5] Stimson was quite convinced that COs ought to be used in relief and reconstruction work and agreed to support the AFSC's request for a China unit. A month later Clarence Pickett received a letter from President Roosevelt giving his approval of the plan.

While, through the White House, Clarence Pickett had access to high Administration officials, no such influential connections existed in the Congress. And it was within this body—the House of Representatives to be specific—that the whole scheme of using conscientious objectors in relief abroad received a *coup de grâce*. Congressman Joe [*sic*] Starnes of Alabama had heard of the plans, thoroughly disapproved of them, and inserted into the appropriations bill for the Army (which included funds for Selective Service) a carefully-worded rider prohibiting the use of any funds for the assigning of COs to work abroad. As Clarence Pickett was to view this calamity many years later:

> Much of the war fever of hatred was turned vigorously against young men to whom Selective Service had granted conscientious objector status. The bill with its rider passed in spite of all that could be done by the opposition. Seven of the eight men en route to China had to be notified when they reached South Africa to return as soon as possible to the United States and to Civilian Public Service camps. Because the eighth man was not within Selective Service jurisdiction, he was free to continue on his way.[7]

The Starnes amendment was a major setback for the three peace church agencies and for CPS men interested in service abroad. It was an especially hard blow for Clarence Pickett, who had skillfully gained the support of the Roosevelt Administration. The sought-for broadening of assignments, however, took place on the domestic scene, with COs volunteering for significant short-term human guinea pig experiments and with hundreds of COs going on a "detached service" basis to serve as attendants in mental hospitals. What kept impressing Clarence as he visited CPS camps and units was the maturing of the individual COs, in what was seen by some as a "laboratory of conscience," portending a new generation of leaders in the Religious Society of Friends and in other denominations.

In early March 1942 Clarence Pickett became involved with what the American Civil Liberties Union was to call "the single most wholesale violation of civil rights of American citizens in our history."[8] This referred to the evacuation, by an executive order prepared for the president by the War Department, of over one hundred thousand Japanese residents and Japanese-American citizens from the West Coast to inland "relocation camps" (regarded as concentration camps by those rounded up) one third of these being Issei (Japanese who were not eligible to become citizens), and two-thirds American-born Nisei.

While the Service Committee had offices on the West Coast, it was not the AFSC that took the major initiatives in respect to the crisis. "Our committee's contribution with the whole problem was so intertwined with the work of the Federal Council [of Churches] and other organizations," wrote Pickett years later, "that it would be impossible to make a separate story of it." However, there was one piece of the work that became the special responsibility of the Friends Service Committee. Milton Eisenhower (youngest brother of Dwight Eisenhower), director of the War Relocation Authority, called Clarence Pickett to ask whether the Service Committee would undertake to organize the transfer of Japanese students from West Coast universities and colleges to inland institutions. He said that he was prepared to give as much sanction as was required to the Committee if it would undertake the job. He felt that the job ought to be done by an agency that had complete freedom from government connections, and hence was asking the AFSC to undertake it.[10]

Clarence was immediately positive about the suggestion. He met with Milton Eisenhower the following week on a day when Eisenhower had been subjected to severe criticism about the plan from a Congressional committee. "His attitude," wrote Clarence, "was for me to go right straight [sic] ahead, and said that he himself would handle the Congressional committee. I was once again deeply impressed with his spirit and ability."[11] Pickett lost no time in seeking funds from foundations for the relocation program, observing that "the more one sees of the possibilities of the student relocation, the more one is inclined to feel that this may be one of the chief means of preventing the relocation [from the West Coast] from becoming a major and national catastrophe in our national life, because otherwise we would probably have a deeply-embittered minority for many years."[12]

Ten years later Clarence Pickett would say, "Few undertakings have ever been more completely satisfactory to me. About four thousand young people were aided in locating in more than six hundred colleges in various parts of the country, many of them never returning to the West Coast. Almost all of these students did very well academically, a high proportion winning special honors, and so far as I know there were no disciplinary cases among them."[13]

Of great interest to Clarence Pickett all during the war years was his involvement in the National Planning Association (NPA). This entirely voluntary and independent organization, founded in 1934, drew together leaders from the fields of government, business, labor, and the professions, leaders who were concerned to look at social and economic problems and then, during the war, to focus on postwar problems and opportunities. For example, in September 1941 a small group of prominent bankers, including Russell Leffingwell, vice president of the Morgan Bank in New York, and J. Stewart Baker, chairman of the Bank of Manhattan Company, met at the Engineers Club in New York. Each man spoke about the thinking being done within his respective banking institutions. Clearly, Pickett's assumed role was to lift the sights of others in the group. There seemed to be fairly general agreement to a proposal he made that it might be well to study world standards of living and to propose for the world what the president had proposed for the United States, that we determine that no one in the world should be allowed to live below a given standard.[14]

Early in 1942 Clarence Pickett urged the board of directors of the NPA to publish a series of popularly-written pamphlets about relief and reconstruction needs following the war. For this task he recommended to John Coil, executive director of the NPA, that the Association obtain the services of a young Philadelphia Quaker, Spencer Coxe, who was a conscientious objector in the AFSC's Ashburnham, Massachusetts CPS camp. Pickett then persuaded Selective Service—"pulled strings," according to Coxe—to "detach" Coxe from the camp for service as a writer working under John Coil and the NPA board of directors.[15] Apart from detached service for individual COs to work in the office of the

National Service Board for Religious Objectors or in the offices of the three service committees, this arrangement was a most unusual one— and continued for the duration of the war.

Clarence Pickett was increasingly realizing that two very divergent views were developing within the National Planning Association with regard to the U.S. role in postwar relief and reconstruction. One group of persons with representation in industry, in the Army, and in other government agencies wanted to take the present opportunity to maintain a large army in almost every corner of the world to police especially the less-developed countries, while the U.S. exploited them. Another group was determined to use the United States' new and additional power to help those countries come to self-realization, not on an imperialistic basis. "This struggle looks as if it might go on for some time," wrote Clarence, "and it represents a crucial time in our national development."[16]

Pickett's journal reveals how stimulating meetings of the National Planning Association were in his busy life. He was a member of the board of trustees from 1943 to the time of his death. Clearly he relished the opportunity to find common ground with Americans of differing viewpoints and to look ahead, with them, to the postwar years. His experiences with the Association, leading to an increasing number of acquaintances in the business, government, and academic arenas, were one of the pipelines through which he was able to enrich and challenge his colleagues in the American Friends Service Committee, and indeed the Quaker constituency as a whole.

No account of Clarence Pickett's life during these war years would be complete without an attempt to describe the scope of his undertakings as AFSC executive secretary of what by 1943 was close to a $2 million enterprise. An administrative staff of sixty-five was based in Philadelphia; thirty-six field staff members in seven countries; thirty-five peace and social-industrial field staff persons across the United States. Sixty-two directors served in fifteen Civilian Public Service units. There were one hundred and fifty summer work campers led by sixteen directors. Peace service volunteers in international seminars, peace caravans, and Mexican units, numbered one hundred and seventy. Members of the many AFSC committees totaled five hundred. It was Clarence Pickett who was at the center of this dynamic and growing organization.

The record shows that he was frequently away from the offices of the AFSC at 20 South 12th Street in Philadelphia. Typically, on any given day out of the office he would be engaged in multiple appointments and tasks. Take, as a good example, Monday, 12 April 1943: Appointment at the State Department regarding French refugees who had crossed the border into Spain and were in great need of clothing; talk with Alabama Senator John H. Bankhead to report on a visit Clarence made to the Birmingham area for the Farm Security Administration; tea with Jonathan Daniels, newly-appointed U.S. ambassador to Mexico, to talk about the proposal to train two hundred COs for overseas relief work.

During the day, via his Philadelphia office, Pickett received an invitation from the First Lady to have dinner at the White House that evening. He accepted, and took the opportunity to raise with Mrs. Roosevelt the question of feeding in countries occupied by Germany. She brought it up at once with the president, and it became a matter of rather prolonged conversation. When Mrs. Roosevelt left to attend a meeting, the president asked Clarence Pickett to come over and talk to him at his side of the table. This Pickett did, learning that the president "felt terribly frustrated about this whole question of food, that he had tried, and was still trying, to find some formula that would work, but thus far saw no light."[17]

During the war years Clarence Pickett became increasingly aware of issues of color, both within the United States and in the international arena. Often during his visits in Washington he would meet with Will W. Alexander, an African American who was the administrator of the Resettlement Administration and Farm Security Administration of the U.S. Department of Agriculture. Especially after Pearl Harbor and the action of the U.S. government in relocating Japanese Americans from the West Coast, Alexander was concerned that the war might metamorphose into a whole new set of alliances, with countries with peoples of color arrayed against white nations, with violent implications for the United States given its sizable population of African Americans. It was on the occasion of one such conversation with Will Alexander in January 1942 that Clarence deemed it "extremely unfortunate that the planning [for the future] that is going on should be carried on by two men, Churchill and Roosevelt, without the participation of any person of color."[18]

Clarence Pickett's actions and decisions in respect to race relations, both as an individual and within the scope of the American Friends Service Committee itself, were consistent with his lifelong religious commitment to equality, his disdain for violence, and his belief in personal persuasion as a path to social change. In May 1942 he was a member of a delegation to visit the editor of *The Evening Bulletin*, Philadelphia's afternoon newspaper, "to talk over ways in which the paper could assist in preventing race and religious discrimination."[19] A year later Pickett and others visited the owner of the *Philadelphia Record* to urge the dropping of specifics in respect to religion, race, and color in classified advertisements. Pickett by this time was already active in the Fellowship Commission of Philadelphia, a coalition, founded in 1941, of nine city-wide agencies concerned with minorities denied equal rights in the metropolitan area. In 1949 he became its third president, serving until 1956, then became honorary president until the time of his death.

There was a feeling that perhaps the American Friends Service Committee might have a special role, even on a national level, beyond its relatively quiet contribution in consistently conducting work camps on an interracial basis, even in racially sensitive regions of the country. "There is, I believe," wrote Clarence Pickett years later, "considerable justification for this kind of oblique approach. It still seems to me that the best way to bridge gulfs of prejudice and fear is perhaps not so much to tackle them directly as to bring the various groups together in common work, recreation and worship."[20]

Nevertheless, the Committee, along with the rest of the country, had become increasingly aware of the seriousness of the racial tensions in the United States. A more direct approach was called for. Consequently, in January 1944 a Committee on Race Relations under the Social-Industrial Section of the AFSC was organized, its initial responsibility being the designing of the self-help program at Flanner House, a black community center in Indianapolis.

In March 1944 the Julius Rosenwald Foundation and Marshall Field invited one hundred leaders, including Clarence Pickett, to meet in Chicago for a weekend conference on race relations. All the leading African Americans were there, according to Pickett. He singles out in his journal, educator and author W.E.B. Du Bois, Lester B. Granger (executive secretary of the National Urban League), P. L. Prattis (executive editor of *The Pittsburgh Courier*), and Judge Hubert T. Delany of New York. Lillian Smith, a white woman from Clayton, Georgia, author of *Strange Fruit*, was also there. "I was much impressed with Lillian Smith," said Clarence, "who, through her little paper called 'The

South,' says exactly what she thinks and gets away with it. It is partly her charm and depth of character that carries her message."[21]

The conference decided that an obvious step was to set up a clearing house for information about what was being done in the field of race relations across the country. The group committed itself to complete unwillingness to accept segregation, but on the whole was not concerned to pass resolutions. "There was considerable inclination on the part of the Negro group," wrote Clarence, "to feel that the white members of this group were too passive, and not sufficiently aware of the crisis nature of the race problem in the country and in the world. My own judgment is that they were probably right, and that it is very healthy to have their emphasis."[22]

Two months later Clarence Pickett was in Chicago, again at the Sherman Hotel, to follow up on the initial conference. After a day's discussion it was decided to set up the American Council on Race Relations, to locate it in Chicago, and to design it as a research project, sharing experienced personnel where special race tensions existed, and cooperating fully with existing agencies.

The next morning, a Sunday, when Clarence regretted not being able to attend a local Friends meeting for worship, presentations and discussion continued. At the conclusion of the session the group appointed officers and "to my regret," he wrote, "I was asked to chair the gathering for the present."[23] In fact, he was to continue as president of the Council for a number of years, traveling to Chicago (or occasionally to New York) almost every month for executive board and committee meetings.

In early February of the same year, 1944, Clarence Pickett responded to an invitation to meet with John W. Pehle, assistant to Treasury Secretary Henry Morgenthau, Jr. and director of the newly-appointed War Refugee Board, consisting of the Secretaries of War, State, and Treasury. The purpose of the Board was to clear the official channels for action in respect to visas and transportation for refugees. Clarence told Pehle that he thought there was no use making a pronouncement unless, in addition, the U.S. offered to take considerable numbers of persons who might be released by Germany and put them in decent camps or colonies, pending the time when they could either return to their former homes or have permanent settlement elsewhere.[24]

Indeed, they appreciated his comments to such an extent that Secretary Morgenthau telegraphed Rufus Jones, as AFSC chairman and personal friend, appealing to him to do everything in his power to get Pickett to accept an important post with the War Refugee Board for at least a few months.[25] Rufus Jones's reply pointedly revealed the climate of opinion within the AFSC:

> In answer to your telegram I would say that it is inconceivable that we could willingly give up Clarence Pickett for anything that would take him away from his present work. He is made in Heaven for the far-reaching constructive Quaker tasks. There is unfortunately no one who could, in any degree, replace him. And I have a feeling that he is so completely dedicated to this work that he would hardly be likely to leave it for anything else, but he is away from home, and I cannot consult him.
>
> Unfortunately, his health is very precarious, and we find it necessary to send him off for occasional periods of rest in order to stave off a breakdown.[26]

It is doubtful that Clarence Pickett was on the verge of a breakdown. He was at Earlham College in Indiana for a series of lectures and meetings. He phoned John Pehle directly to express his regrets at not being available. But four days later he and Lilly Pickett did leave for a month's vacation in Florida.

As the United States' role in regard to relief operations increased—not only through the State Department's Office of Foreign Relief and Rehabilitation (OFRRO) but also the President's War Relief Control Board (the panel charged with the responsibility of licensing private relief groups) and the National War Fund from which grants for relief were available—it was becoming obvious that non-governmental organizations needed to achieve some unity in dealing with government. Clarence Pickett was prominently active in the founding of the American Council for Voluntary Agencies for Foreign Service, which at its height of effectiveness included fifty voluntary agencies. Joseph P. Chamberlain of Columbia University became the first chairman of the Council, with Pickett as vice chairman, beginning in June 1944. One of the first actions of the Council officers was to talk with the appropriate government administrators about a national effort to solicit used clothing for foreign relief, a form of aid in which the AFSC had had many years of experience.

Clarence Pickett concluded the year 1944 with a whirlwind visit to England and unoccupied France. It was his first transatlantic crossing by air, on a propeller-driven seaplane with fourteen passengers in all, leaving from La Guardia Airport (Long Island Sound) at 2:00 p.m. on a

Sunday and landing the next morning on the Shannon River at Foynes, Ireland. While the trip by air was a great saving in time for Clarence Pickett, it may have been at the cost of some damage to his heart. It was the opinion of his physician, Dr. Wayne Marshall, commenting on the trip over fifty years later, that increasingly in his senior years Pickett was suffering from coronary heart disease, which was aggravated by the heavy load of work he pushed himself to carry.[27]

Clarence Pickett was fortunate to be the guest of Barrow Cadbury of the Cadbury chocolate company and was placed in the Euston Hotel in London just across the street from Friends House. "It has what is called in England central heat," he recorded in his journal, "although the radiators were never very hot. There was hot water, which is a great asset. I slept wonderfully and today spent the day at Friends House getting acquainted."[28]

For the next two weeks Pickett was involved in a marathon of meetings with the Friends Service Council (FSC), Friends Relief Service (FRS), Friends Ambulance Unit (FAU), and their respective committees, bringing into these appointments AFSC Foreign Service Section traveling field staff members John Judkyn (posted to England) and Margaret Frawley (posted to France). Then, with English Quaker leaders, Pickett visited personnel at the American Embassy, the new French embassy (which grew out of the French government-in-exile headed by Charles De Gaulle), and British officials, both government and nongovernmental, concerned with relief services.

Every Sunday Clarence attended a Quaker meeting for worship in a different meetinghouse. He was impressed with the low age level of the members of the meetings. In mid-November he noted in his journal that during the previous night five "doodle-bugs" (pilotless jet-propelled German aircraft, later known as the V-1, or buzz bombs) came over from the Continent together with a number of V-2 rockets. Clarence was saddened to learn that Hugh Crosfield and his wife, leading English Friends, had been killed when their home was hit. Pickett was among two dozen prominent Americans who, the previous July, had appealed to the Germans not to engage in the wanton cruelty of robot bombing.

At the end of November Clarence Pickett and Margaret Frawley traveled by air to France. Here he came face to face with some of the recent effects of the war. The airport at the edge of Paris had been seriously bombed. His first night he was billeted by the Air Force Command in a hotel with Joseph Schwartz of the American Jewish Joint Distribution Committee, both sleeping in the same bed. "There was no heat, hot water, towels or soap, but apart from that the accommodation was not bad," he noted. "We went out for an evening meal about 8 o'clock and found an American army canteen where they gave us a good meal free. No Paris restaurants were open."[29]

The next morning Pickett was able to get in touch by phone with Henry van Etten of the Friends Center. They met at the American embassy, where Clarence knew Paul Warberg, the liaison officer between the embassy and SHAEF (Supreme Headquarters, Allied Expeditionary Force). Pickett hoped that Warberg would find suitable lodging for him and Joseph Schwartz. SHAEF found a place for them at the Ritz Hotel. "I was a little concerned about being the guest of the Army," said Clarence, "but it was the only way of getting transportation or billeting that was at all satisfactory, so I accepted it for this short time."[30]

For all of one week Pickett met with relief personnel (of six different nationalities) who had been working under Secours Quaker, the French Friends organization, in the south of France during the occupation. When Germany seized the unoccupied portion of France in November 1942 the eight American Quaker representatives working in southern (Vichy) France were interned in Baden-Baden, Germany. They were repatriated on 15 March 1944. Now, on the occasion of his visit with the staff of Secours Quaker, he learned that the agency had just been allowed to visit political prisoners. There were about one hundred thousand French citizens who had been arrested as collaborationists. Secours Quaker was given permission to visit these prisoners, to go into their cells and talk freely, and to visit the relatives when they come out. They carried in some parcels, but mostly it was a spiritual and social service to the prisoners and their families.[30] Clarence was impressed with the importance of the program.

While minimal progress was made in respect to delivering food to malnourished and starving millions in Europe's occupied areas during the war, Clarence Pickett was encouraged by steps being taken regarding postwar relief. In the autumn of 1943, with Roosevelt's encouragement, Secretary of State Hull, at the Conference of Foreign Ministers' meeting in Moscow, "engineered a four-Power declaration pledging the United States, Great Britain, the Soviet Union, and China to continue cooperation in a great international organization to be established at the earliest practicable date." It was Roosevelt himself who, during one of Churchill's visits to the United States, thought of the term "United Nations" to describe those countries fighting the Axis powers. Then, in early November, the President hosted a ceremony at the White House "to commemorate the signing of an international agreement for a United Nations Relief and Rehabilitation Administration [UNRRA] to feed, clothe and house the world."[33] It supplanted OFFRO of the U.S. State Department, and Herbert Lehman, as its director, shifted from the one to the other.

Upon his return from France to England, Clarence Pickett continued to focus on the coordination of relief services between English and American Friends. In mid-December Pickett made his last farewells at Friends House, had dinner at the Euston Hotel, and at midnight took a train to Greenock, the seaport just outside Glasgow, arriving there twelve hours later on the first leg of what was to be a long and wearying return home by boat. There were about four thousand passengers on the boat, and all but one hundred and fifty of these were British, American, Canadian, Australian and New Zealand troops, some hundreds of wounded men among them. There were eighteen men in Clarence's stateroom, and they slept in double deck bunks. "While all of them were very nice people, civilian government officials for the most part," wrote Clarence, "there was some snoring and almost complete lack of privacy. We had one chair and one table in the stateroom."[34]

It was only when Clarence Pickett returned home that he realized how tired he was. Having shaken off two head colds during the trip, he was now, on Christmas Day, down with another cold. He and Lilly Pickett received nearly seven hundred Christmas cards. "It is a big job, really, to take time to read what our friends have sent us," he said. "We are taking it in easy stages so that it does not become a monotonous job, but rather a little visit with each of our friends."[35]

It was Emily Cooper Johnson, chairman [sic] of the Peace Section Committee, who some years later expressed the devotion for Clarence Pickett that these friends of his felt: "Thee held every one of us, staff and board and committees, right up to our best attitudes and spirits. Thee has constantly kept us alert to be sure that what we do is done in humility and simplicity, honestly and courageously."[36]

Clarence Pickett and his friends could hardly have anticipated how pivotal events in 1945 would impact upon the work of the American Friends Service Committee.

With Rufus Jones, chairman, Clarence Pickett reports to a public meeting in January 1943 at the Race Street Friends Meetinghouse in Philadelphia

NOTES

1. Albert N. Keim, *The CPS Story: An Illustrated History of Civilian Public Service* (Intercourse, PA: Good Books, 1990), 30.

2. Keim, CPS Story, 43.

3. Clarence Pickett journal, 5 Dec. 1941.

4. Pickett journal, 14 Nov. 1942.

5. Pickett journal, 25 Jan. 1943.

6. Clarence E. Pickett, *For More Than Bread* (Boston: Little, 1953), 218.

7. Pickett, *Bread,* 219.

8. Doris Kearns Goodwin, *No Ordinary Time: Franklin and Eleanor Roosevelt, The Home Front in World War II* (New York: Simon, 1994), 321.

9. Pickett, *Bread,* 158.

10. Pickett journal, 2 May 1942.

11. Pickett journal, 8 May 1942.

12. Pickett journal, 1 June 1942.

13. Pickett, *Bread,* 159.

14. Pickett journal, 15 Sept. 1941.

15. Interview with Spencer Coxe, 16 Dec. 1996.

16. Pickett journal, 22 Oct. 1942.

17. Pickett journal, 12 Apr. 1943.

18. Pickett journal, 5 Jan. 1942.

19. Pickett journal, 12 May 1942.

20. Pickett, *Bread,* 376.

21. Pickett journal, 21 Mar. 1944.

22. Pickett journal, 22 Mar. 1944.

23. Pickett journal, 6 May 1944.

24. Pickett journal, 9 Feb. 1944.

25. Telegram dated 14 Feb. 1944, from holdings at the Franklin D. Roosevelt Library, Hyde Park, NY.

26. Jones to Morgenthau, 15 Feb. 1944, Haverford College, Haverford, PA: Magill Library, Quaker Collection.

27. E. Wayne Marshall, M.D., letter to author, 30 June 1998.

28. Pickett journal, 23 Oct. 1944.

29. Pickett journal, 26 Nov. 1944.

30. Pickett journal, 28 Nov. 1944.

31. Pickett journal, 29 Nov. 1944.

32. Goodwin, *No Ordinary Time,* 470.

33. Goodwin, *No Ordinary Time,* 470.

34. Pickett journal, 21-28 Dec. 1944.

35. Pickett journal, 25 Dec. 1944.

36. Emily Cooper Johnson to Clarence E. Pickett on the occasion of his retirement as executive secretary in 1950, family papers, courtesy of Carolyn Pickett Miller. ("Chairman" rather than "chairperson" is used throughout the text inasmuch as during the years covered by this biography "chairman" was current usage irrespective of whether the office holder was male or female.)

Chapter 14

THE NOBEL PEACE PRIZE

I think there was a general feeling of unworthiness

IN THE FIRST WEEKS OF 1945, Clarence Pickett—"conscious that I am overtired and when there are so many calls on my time"[1]—focused on reports and issues arising from his trip to England and France, and on problems within the AFSC that had come up during his absence. Central to the work in January and February was Pickett's hope that the liberation of the Nazi-occupied countries and of Germany itself, once that had been achieved, would quickly open the way for relief services, governmental and non-governmental, in the form of food and clothing. As chairman of the American Council of Voluntary Agencies (ACVA), his advice was pivotal to building a working relationship between the ACVA member organizations and the United Nations Relief and Rehabilitation Administration Agency (UNRRA). He was accepting speaking engagements near and far. He was urging the public to accept voluntary rationing of food in order to make more food available for Europe.

On 12 April 1945—a day Americans of his generation would long remember—Clarence Pickett was in Washington, DC, for a round of appointments. He had breakfast with Joseph Everett of the National Housing Agency, which had inherited the remaining responsibilities for subsistence homesteads. There were early morning meetings with Conrad Van Heining and Fred Daniels of UNRRA. These were followed by an appointment with Attorney General Francis Biddle, Pickett informing him that the Service Committee heartily endorsed the proposal in his annual report to Congress concerning the administration of conscientious objector units under any new draft.

Clarence Pickett met at the Cosmos Club with Comfort Cary, a Philadelphia young Friend who was assistant director of the International Student House. They talked about the possibility of her joining the staff of UNRRA to work with displaced persons in Germany. He encouraged her to do so and explained to her his discussion that morning with Conrad Van Heining.

Clarence Pickett then had lunch with Francis Sayre, special assistant to the secretary of state, with particular responsibility for foreign relief and reconstruction operations. "He feels deeply concerned," wrote Pickett, "that we [the Quakers] should get into Germany as soon as possible, because he feels that the crushing blows that are now falling on her are really condemning Europe to a generation of poverty, since the full economy of Europe is so tied up with Germany. He also feels that the restoration of fellowship is the greatest problem."[2]

Pickett's next appointment that day was with Wilder Foote, administrative assistant to Secretary of State Edward Stettinius. The secretary of state was completely occupied with preparations for the San Francisco Conference (25 April to 26 June) where the charter of the United Nations was to be drawn up. Clarence wanted Stettinius to know how very important he viewed the secretary of state's position at this point in history.

Clarence Pickett concluded his appointments at the State Department by meeting with still another assistant secretary, this time about passports for representatives of private agencies appointed to work in foreign countries. They finished talking at five o'clock, and Clarence went back to the Cosmos Club to rest a little. Wrote Pickett:

> I went to the library and slept from 5:30 to a quarter after 6. Then I went downstairs, and the telephone girl announced to me that President Roosevelt was dead. My first words were, "Harry Truman!" . . . All evening long and throughout the night I felt limp and stunned. We had become so accustomed to working with this present administration that one wonders what the changes might mean.
>
> My mind turns even more to Mrs. Roosevelt, whom I have always felt is a truly great person because of the rare quality of her spirit and unwillingness to be daunted, and her concern for the deeper and more abiding values in our society. I think she probably will be even more useful and perhaps greater in her new role than as First Lady.[3]

Just ten days later, a Sunday, Clarence and Lilly received a phone call from their son-in-law, Cully Miller, to tell them that they were grandparents. Deborah Breese Miller was born at 4:30 in the morning. "It is a little difficult yet," wrote Clarence, "to comprehend that we are grandparents. It seems a very short time since I was present at Carolyn's birth at the Reed Memorial Hospital in Richmond [Indiana] in 1922."[4] A second granddaughter, Jennifer Joy Miller, arrived on 25 October 1947.

Early in the morning of 7 May 1945, Clarence went to New York to attend the annual meeting of the United States Committee for the Care of European Children. He was walking along 18th Street on his way to the meeting when he was stopped by a Greek shopkeeper who told him that Germany had surrendered unconditionally. Almost immediately confetti, toilet paper, and telephone books began floating from offices, and this continued all during the forenoon as he and others sat in the United States Committee office. While Clarence shared in the sense of relief that hostilities in Europe had ended, he could not let himself get too enthusiastic, considering the continuing war in the Far East.[5]

The next opportunity for Clarence Pickett to visit Mrs. Roosevelt was at her New York City apartment, on 19 May: "She talked freely about the president's passing. She said that she still had a feeling that he was off on a long trip and would return, and that she missed him terribly, especially at breakfast time, as they breakfasted together and talked over family affairs. She had a new freedom because she is not in the White House, when it came to writing her column, but she missed the information which she could always call on from the president when she was trying to understand the background of the events that were happening."[6]

Two days later, Clarence Pickett, board member Harold Evans, and Paul Furnas, executive director of Civilian Public Service, had an appointment with President Truman. Their talk with the president was quite satisfactory. They explained that they had had a good deal of contact with his predecessor due to programs which the AFSC was carrying out, and that they wanted him to know something about the committee and the Religious Society of Friends. They told him what Quakers had done during and after the last war, and what Friends were currently doing in Europe, and that the AFSC hoped to do relief work in Germany. The president quickly said that he certainly wanted Germans fed and hoped that the AFSC would go ahead with its plans and even suggested that his

Clarence Pickett solicits a question at a 1945 AFSC meeting at the Race Street Friends Meetinghouse

visitors see Assistant Secretary of War John McCloy about permissions to enter Germany.

Clarence Pickett told the president about programs in Civilian Public Service and his feeling that COs were not being used at all to their full capacity. Truman said that he had felt this was the worst failure of the Army and that he had tried to get them to be more careful about the use of manpower but had not succeeded very well. "He was a good listener, asked good questions," wrote Clarence, "and when we expressed our concern for him and his very difficult new undertaking, he said that he hoped we would pray for him, which I think was a very honest request on his part."[7]

In July Clarence Pickett got a phone call from Dwight Eisenhower, the general responding both to a telegram he had received through Milton Eisenhower from Pickett, and to a letter received from Mrs. Roosevelt. General Eisenhower indicated that there would be acute need, especially among civilians, in defeated Germany. He urged Pickett to submit a proposal for services to him at his headquarters in Frankfurt.

Clarence was deeply exercised over the possibility of peacetime conscription being enacted in the United States. The Selective Service Act provided for the dismantling of conscription six months after the end of the war. Already there were American leaders advocating universal military training. Many reasons were being put forth in support of a continuing draft: national security, a means of reducing unemployment, beneficial effects in discipline and physical health from the training.

The AFSC's statement, "Permanent Conscription," rejected all of these arguments, point by point: "We dread especially the psychological effect of conscription on our national thinking. It will intensify the spirit of violence and our readiness to resort to force, leading us into further wars. It will create a false sense of security based upon arms while spiritual and cultural factors in national defense may be neglected."[8]

All through the year Clarence Pickett was finding opportunities to speak out on the issues that were on his heart and mind, principally the moral obligation to provide food for Europe. Quite apart from reports to Quaker meetings, Pickett gave sixty public speeches in 1945 to a wide variety of audiences, four of these commencement addresses.

Clarence and Lilly Pickett were vacationing at home when the atomic bomb was dropped by the U.S. Air Force on Hiroshima on 6 August. And then Nagasaki was bombed on 9 August. Clarence was sickened by what he heard on the radio about the destruction and the loss of lives. He followed carefully the radio reports on the negotiations between the United States and Japan in respect to a formal ending of the war. Following the signing of the surrender document on the *Missouri* on 2 September, he sent an open letter to President Truman and General MacArthur urging that the occupation of Japan be undertaken in a spirit of reconciliation rather than revenge. It was AFSC staff member, Elizabeth Gray Vining who wrote the letter, and who, a year later, would begin to have a unique relationship with Japan.

One of Clarence Pickett's foremost characteristics was his persistence in respect to social issues. Such was clearly the case in regard to racial intolerance and discrimination. He knew that, generally speaking, American Quakers, despite some historical achievements relating to matters of race, were by and large as racially prejudiced as most Americans. This realization led him to see Quaker race relations programs as doubly effective: good for the wider community and good for the Religious Society of Friends itself. His view was ably set forth within the statement of purpose of the AFSC Race Relations Committee: "To continue in our times the Friends' ministry to those who suffer from intolerance and strife between men—in the knowledge that intolerance and injustice brutalize both the perpetrators and those who are victims, and stunt the human personality."[9] Within this perspective Pickett was pleased with the appointment of James Fleming in November 1945 as

*Clarence Pickett and Hans Simon, president of the New School
for Social Research, New York, NY, 1945*

secretary of the Race Relations Committee. Fleming was an African
American who had been director of the Philadelphia Fair Employment
Practices Commission.

What is evident from his journal entries is that Pickett was himself
growing in his own understanding of racial problems. In November he
had an opportunity to see in New York "Deep Are the Roots," a play
about a decorated African American soldier who returns to the South
after the war. "It is the frankest discussion of the race question that I
have ever seen in a play," he wrote. "It is terrifically strenuous to go
through, but it is very well done and most impressive."[10]

What struck those who worked with Clarence Pickett, especially in
the field of race relations, was his clarity in identifying certain practices
as socially corrosive—indeed, as evil—and, in the words of one of his
associates, Barbara Moffett, he demonstrated "a marvelous simplicity
in his way of handling complex challenges."[11]

One such challenge was in September 1946 when the British Army
and British Red Cross refused to accept the inclusion of Jean Fairfax,
dean of women from Tuskegee Institute and an African American, in a

group of ten AFSC relief workers assigned to work in the British zone of Germany. Wrote Clarence at the time: "We are not inclined to send anyone if we have to kowtow to this objection."[12] This was also the view of the group itself. Ten days later he attended the Foreign Service Section executive committee meeting specifically because of his interest in the Jean Fairfax case. Again he notes in his journal: "We cannot accept that turn-down."[13]

Yet, clear as he was about the issue and despite the strong support of that view by Race Relations Committee secretary James Fleming (his opinions on the matter were detailed in a three-page memorandum) and others, Clarence had to deal with complex organizational factors, principally the overall relationship between the American Friends Service Committee and the British Friends Relief Service. With a firm underlying commitment to work together in relief operations, as had been the case since 1917, the two Quaker bodies frequently needed to bring the deepest springs of spiritual energy and sensitivity to bear upon mutual problems. There was always the danger of the better-financed American organization being overly aggressive.

A key problem in the Jean Fairfax case was that the AFSC was not dealing directly with the decision-maker in the field, in this case the British army, and there were two organizational layers screening the AFSC from this direct contact, the British Red Cross in the field and Friends Relief Service in London. The difficult determination which Clarence Pickett made in this case, after transatlantic consultation with Julia Branson, associate secretary of AFSC's Foreign Service Section who was temporarily based in England, was to assign Jean Fairfax, with her agreement, to become a member of AFSC's Austrian team based in Vienna, where she became an able and popular worker, referred to by Viennese young people as their "brown angel of mercy."[14] Many years later, in an interview with the author of this biography, Jean Fairfax praised Clarence Pickett for the manner in which he had personally handled the complex and delicate situation, while expressing deep regret that British Friends had not taken a firmer stand.[15]

With the war in Europe over, reports were coming in to London and Philadelphia about surviving German Friends. Each had had to struggle with her or his conscience in respect to the issue of conscientious objection. Clarence Pickett was fully aware of the compromises many European Quakers felt compelled to make. He did not fault them. He was aware that some Friends in German-occupied territories had joined in varying degrees of participation in the Resistance movements, and in respect to such movements he expressed unconventional views in a major address to Friends in July 1946:

> To maintain the integrity of national honor and citizenship, people banded themselves together in a movement which was willing to use deceit, lying, undercover methods, anything that would mislead and deceive the occupying enemy. Germany itself was, during that period, an occupied country, occupied by the kind of administration which developed a strong, vigorous, resistance movement. This in itself bred the same kind of deceit. And who shall say that we, ourselves, have not been to some extent in the same position.
>
> All of these things have left their deep scar of moral and spiritual tragedy and infection, which we in our generation have to live with. In a Christian community, if it is to be a colony of Heaven, integrity, uprightness of word and deed, straightforwardness of conduct, never have been so much needed. Hat honor, plainness of dress and speech, arose out of just such a determination to grow persons of complete integrity in a world that had adjusted itself to deceit and fraud. Again, as with our forebears, we must develop those strict and vigorous disciplines of integrity and honor if we are to be colonists of Heaven in a world that has had the experience of the resistance movement.[16]

In the spring of 1946 Clarence Pickett was involved in what was considered by many to be a modern and international variation on the Cinderella story. Subsequent to a proposal made by the Japanese minister of education after the end of the war, an American Education Mission, consisting of leading educators and headed by Dr. George Stoddard, president of the State of New York University, visited Japan "to advise and consult with General Headquarters and with Japanese educators on problems relating to education in Japan."[17] In the course of a reception of the mission members at the imperial palace, the emperor suddenly turned to Dr. Stoddard and asked him, through an interpreter, if he could find an American to tutor his twelve-year-old son, the crown prince, in English.

Elizabeth Gray Vining, a forty-four-year old Philadelphia Quaker and a published writer working at the American Friends Service Committee, was encouraged by some associates to apply for the position. She did so reluctantly, not seeing herself as qualified. It was Clarence Pickett who wrote to Dr. Stoddard, listing briefly Elizabeth Vining's education, travel, books, and personal characteristics. He closed his letter with these words:

> I have mentioned this matter to her, and of course she says that it is a complete surprise to her to think in these terms, since she had in mind withdrawing from our staff to do some further writing in the near future. Also, she insists that she would not lift a finger to seek the appointment, but I think she would be willing to consider it if, knowing as much as it is possible to know about her, there was a united judgment that she would be useful in that capacity. If you think she is worth considering, I should hope that she might go to Albany and have a talk with you.[18]

The rest is history. Elizabeth Gray Vining was chosen by the imperial household from among two candidates submitted by the American Education Mission to be the tutor in English of the Japanese emperor's heir apparent, Prince Akihito. Years later she learned that she was chosen in part for her convictions in respect to peace and reconciliation and because of her experience with sorrow in the death of her husband, Morgan, in an automobile accident after less than five years of marriage. The story of her four years in Japan on this assignment is charmingly told in her book, a best-seller, *Windows for the Crown Prince*.[19] Clarence Pickett was understandably extremely pleased with his role in the appointment. On the occasion of a report she made during a home leave to personal friends and Friends at the end of her first year in Japan he wrote: "I am deeply confirmed in my feeling that she is exactly in the right place and that there could hardly have been any American who would have suited that undertaking more perfectly."[20]

In this same spring of 1946, on a beautiful Sunday afternoon—cool, fresh, and sunny all day—the Picketts' oldest daughter, Rachel, and Armand Stalnaker were married at the Providence Friends Meetinghouse. Once again Clarence was impressed with the manner in which the couple made their vows to each other. There were about four hundred guests present for the ceremony and the reception. The Picketts hosted thirty-four family members and others for a sit-down supper in the evening.

Clarence Pickett, secretary of the International Institute of Education, on deck at the July 1947 inauguration of the AFSC's Boat Seminar Program for students

One of the lasting contributions of Civilian Public Service during the war was the reform movement that developed as a result of close to two thousand conscientious objectors volunteering to be ward attendants in mental hospitals. Selective Service had approved these assignments because the staffs of mental hospitals were decimated by the onset of the war, as notoriously ill-paid hospital employees moved on to better-paying jobs in the war economy. For example, Philadelphia State Hospital in 1941 had one thousand employees. By October 1942 only two hundred remained. Designed for twenty-five hundred patients, the hospital held six thousand. There was an average of one attendant for three hundred patients (the minimum set by the American Psychiatric Association was ten), some of them violent, others incontinent.[21]

Clarence Pickett began to learn, as others did, that the success of the COs as mental health attendants grew out of their effort to put nonviolence into practice. "It would be wrong to say that all objectors performed admirably under trying conditions," writes historian Albert Keim in his *The CPS Story*.[22] Furthermore, the reforms and new emphases of the CPS men were not always kindly received by their fellow workers, who were typically impersonal and violent in their dealings with patients.

Directly stemming from this service of COs in mental hospitals was a movement called the Mental Health Hygiene Program. Pickett followed the movement with great interest, based as it was in part on the Friends unit at the state hospital, Byberry, in Philadelphia. The program in May 1946 became the National Mental Health Foundation. Clarence

Pickett agreed to serve on the board of directors and attended its first meeting in October of that year.

Clarence Pickett's interest in the field of mental health did not arise solely because of his support of what clearly became a publicly-recognized accomplishment of the Civilian Public Service program. He knew of the depression Rufus Jones had suffered following a concussion in 1914. Clarence knew of AFSC worker Alice Davis' severe nervous breakdown in November 1935, his immediate reaction being to invite her to come and live in the Pickett home. He was also acquainted with the nervous breakdown Henry Cadbury suffered, during which Cadbury sought and received psychiatric assistance. Clarence and Lilly Pickett visited him and his wife, Lydia, in April 1942 at the Westtown Farmhouse while he was recovering from depression. Then, just a year later, Clarence noted in his journal that he had had breakfast in Washington with English Friend Bertram Pickard, who told Clarence of his serious nervous break.

But even closer to home was the experience with Lilly's sister, Letha. In the very months that the National Mental Health Foundation was established, Letha Peckham came from her parental home in Idaho to live with the Picketts at Waysmeet. Clarence's journal entries frequently mention her. "Letha Peckham isn't very well, and I feel I have to be with Lilly as much as possible."[23] "Clifford [Peckham, on a visit from Idaho], Lilly and I paid a visit to Letha, who is now in the hospital in Germantown."[24] "The fact that Letha is not very well leaves us all with a certain degree of anxiety . . . ."[25]

Clarence was actively seeking out information about mental health institutions. In July he visited the Louden Knickerbocker Hall in Amityville, New York. He corresponded with the Friends-related Sheppard and Enoch Pratt Hospital in Baltimore. It is not clear from the record just what the diagnosis was, and in fact Letha Peckham began to feel better in late July and went to stay for an extended period of time with her brother Errol and his wife at Penn-Craft in western Pennsylvania.

Then a crisis developed in May 1949; Letha Peckham was refusing to speak. As a devoted member of the Christian Science church she was accepted for residence at Tenacre in Princeton, New Jersey. Two years later she returned to Caldwell, Idaho, lived with and cared for her parents, taught voice and piano, and sang in churches and her brother's funeral chapels. Said Carolyn Pickett Miller about her Aunt Letha: "Hers was a tragic story. She had a voice which presumably showed promise and went to New York City to study voice. While there she fell in love with a man; her father absolutely refused to let her marry this man; and that broke her spirit. . . . Her career never went anyplace. In 1955, one winter night, she left the house and took her own life by jumping into the Snake River."[26]

As a follow-up to the outstanding work performed by conscientious objectors in the mental health field during the war, the American Friends Service Committee established institutional service units, providing an opportunity for both women and men to work in mental hospitals. By 1950 Clarence Pickett was noting that "one out of eight persons in the U.S. spends some part of his life in a mental hospital."[27] In January 1951 he spent several hours with three hundred psychiatrists who were members of the professional association, Group for the Advancement of Psychiatry. The question before them was, "Do the principles that we use in our work with individuals have any application in international affairs?"[28]

The membership of the AFSC executive board (the term "board of directors" was discontinued in May 1946) provided for impressive continuity in respect to the committee's policies. But in 1946, in order to provide for the counsel and inspiration that would come from new appointees, members with six or more years of service were required to move off the board, with the possibility of being reappointed after a sabbatical year. "It meant a number of old standbys had to go off," noted Pickett, "and that is very sad. Bob Yarnall, Harold Evans, Edward Evans, and a few others had to go off, and I hope some of them, at least, will come back on after their year of vacation."[29] Harold Evans had been on the board every year since 1932; Edward Evans since 1938; Robert Yarnall since 1940. Prior to those years they were active on AFSC committees.

With Pickett's far-flung organizational affiliations and his propensity to be out of the office frequently, it was of signal importance to him and the Committee that except for one year, ever since his appointment as executive secretary there had been, as chairman of the Committee and its executive board, one of two Friends, Rufus Jones, professor emeritus of philosophy at Haverford College, and Henry Cadbury, Hollis Professor of Divinity at Harvard Divinity School. Indeed, Jones, Cadbury and

Pickett could be viewed as an AFSC troika, forging ahead harmoniously with an enviable degree of unity.

Another important change at this time was the recognition by the Committee that certain positions, especially overseas, required some depth of familiarity with the country being served, and a considerable degree of expertise in the language. At an all-day meeting of key staff and board members in April 1947 there was consensus about the need for selected Friends to make a career out of service with the Committee, this recognition in no way to downgrade the importance of the two- or three-year assignments or the priority of providing for very short-term opportunities in Quaker workcamps and other such units. Clarence Pickett was personally feeling conflicted on the issue. Earlier in the year he had shared his view that the Service Committee's basic weakness in foreign service was the lack of persons who could speak the language. That fact made him feel all the more the importance of getting more young people trained, both in their having something to say and having the languages through which to say it in various parts of the world. "I often feel that I would give up everything I own, except wife and children," he confessed, "if I had real facility in two or three foreign languages. I might really amount to something."[30]

This very candid assessment of the importance of being fluent in a foreign language (as noted earlier, it was in the learning of French and German that he was relatively weak at Penn College) led him to agree to having AFSC employees in differing tiers of service. But he was uneasy about it. He did not want the American Friends Service Committee to become a professionalized agency. He felt that the committee might lose its distinctive Quaker character—the use of the volunteer person who is a non-professional and offers freely of himself or herself to help meet need.

Quite apart from this issue, which was to continue throughout his lifetime, Clarence Pickett was now being increasingly candid about what he saw as two societies of Friends in the world. He was not referring to the Orthodox and Hicksite branches. Rather, he was recognizing that there was, on the one hand, a sect, including "many devout, informed, dedicated and effective persons who represent the richest and best of spirit and life which has been developed by this religious body."[31] Alongside this sect, in his view, was the Religious Society of Friends as a movement involving hundreds and thousands of persons with whom the most devout Friend could find warm, full, and understanding fellowship, "but who might have no association with any religious body, or who may be active in one of the Protestant churches, the Roman Catholic church, the Jewish group, and even religions of other traditions."[32]

Into the American Friends Service Committee were coming many of these persons, who chose to maintain their religious affiliations, but who considered themselves a part of the Quaker movement. Clarence Pickett, while himself active in the sect and seeking to nourish it, welcomed into the Service Committee persons who, while not Friends, understood the meaning of spiritual strength. "The power of convincing, the eloquence of the selfless deed, the concern for meeting human suffering," he said. "This is the language of the spirit, understood in almost any part of the world."[33]

The distillation of his convictions in respect to the Religious Society of Friends as a sect had been set forth in a landmark address to Quakers a few years earlier in an effort to define a significant religious society: "Obviously such a definition cannot be in terms of size of membership or political influence, nor in terms of completeness and logic of theological dogma. It may be an oversimplification, but I should like to suggest that a significant religious society is one which builds and preserves persons and also one which is successful in motivating society toward creative ends."[34]

Pickett then cited the experience of Christians during their first three hundred years. He saw that they had been held together by the strong bonds of fellowship and had assumed that membership in the community involved one in the refusal to participate in war. "I imagine that we, like the early Christians," he concluded, "will find our significance as a religious society not so much in terms of talking about the peace testimony of the Religious Society of Friends as of growing a quality of spiritual life which simply makes it impossible for those who are members of this fellowship to support a society based on destruction of other lives."[35]

Two very heartwarming events for Clarence Pickett occurred in the spring of 1947. Although technically the thirtieth anniversary of the establishment of the AFSC was on 30 April, it was decided to celebrate the event on Saturday, 10 May at Haverford College. By that date a number of national magazines had carried stories about the upcoming celebration. In a major piece in its religion section, *Newsweek* chronicled the accomplishments of the AFSC: expenditures since its founding totaling $60 million, distribution of material aids valued at $10 million, and approximately sixty million people directly assisted in twenty-two countries. *Newsweek* characterized Rufus Jones as "the man behind the [Quaker] movement, responsible for a large part of the AFSC success."[36] Wrote Pickett following the Haverford event :

> I spoke in the afternoon, and we closed with a meeting for worship. It was one of the best day's discussions I have ever attended in my life. We definitely looked forward and not backward, and it didn't pay too high a deference to patterns of service that had been developed in the past. There were altogether in the neighborhood of five hundred people there.[37]

Clarence Pickett accepted an honorary degree on 7 June, commencement day at Haverford College. He had twice refused such degrees, but decided that the degree was a vote of appreciation for the Service Committee. Gilbert White, the College's new president and recent assistant executive secretary of the AFSC, persuaded him to accept the degree. His acceptance led to a trail of other honorary degrees, the next one in the same month at Earlham College.

On 31 October 1947, when Clarence Pickett returned from having lunch, he found his office full of newspaper people and photographers who had heard from the wire services that the American Friends Service Committee and the (British) Friends Service Council had jointly received the Nobel Peace Prize. Clarence wanted to make sure that the photographs were not entirely focused on him. In one widely-used photograph he was showing the cablegram from Norway to his secretarial assistant, Blanche Tache. In still another he was flanked, all beaming, by James Read, secretary of the Foreign Service Section, and Ray Newton, secretary of the Peace Section. Some papers published side by side individual photos of Rufus Jones, Clarence Pickett, and Henry Cadbury.

It was a difficult enough task to handle, in time for afternoon and evening news deadlines, requests for information about the AFSC and the Friends Service Council. More difficult to explain was the real intent of the Nobel Committee in Oslo: to award the prize to the Religious Society of Friends, the Nobel Committee only seeing the two service organizations as representative of the Society. Indeed there was no mention of either of the Quaker service bodies in the address of Gunnar Jahn, chairman of the Nobel Committee, at the presentation of the Nobel Peace Prize in Oslo on 10 December 1947. Rather, it was a historical account of the origin of the Quaker movement in England, the principles of Friends, and their activities relating to peace and social justice issues. Then Gunnar Jahn stated succinctly why he thought Quakers deserved the peace prize: "It is the silent help from the nameless to the nameless which is their contribution to the promotion of brotherhood among nations, as it is expressed in the will of Alfred Nobel."[38]

Looking back on the event, Clarence was to say, "I think there was a general feeling of unworthiness. The award, insofar as it is deserved, is given to a long procession of Friends and like-minded persons stretching over three hundred years, who have tried by the gospel of the deed to make real the love of God for His children, and while it falls upon those who at this time are banded together in various labors of love, to enjoy this honor, it also lays upon all of us a high calling to more intelligent and dedicated personal and group life. . . . Our prayer may well be that we ourselves may be more fully 'a prepared people' for this high calling."[39]

In these heady and challenging weeks involving the Nobel Peace Prize award, Clarence Pickett could hardly have guessed that after the turn of the year he would be prominently involved in Middle East issues.

NOTES

1. Clarence Pickett journal, AFSC archives, 1 Jan. 1945.

2. Pickett journal, 12 Apr. 1945.

3. Pickett journal, 12 Apr. 1945.

4. Pickett journal, 22 Apr. 1945.

5. Pickett journal, 7 May 1945.

6. Pickett journal, 19 May 1945.

7. Pickett journal, 21 May 1945.

8. "Permanent Conscription," a statement by the American Friends Service Committee, minutes of AFSC board of directors, 3 January 1945.

9. AFSC 1945 annual report, 14.

10. Pickett journal, 10 Nov. 1945.

11. Barbara Moffatt taped interview, 3 June 1993.

12. Pickett journal, 10 Sept. 1946.

13. Pickett journal, 23 Sept. 1946.

14. Clarence E. Pickett, *For More Than Bread* (Boston: Little, 1953), 386.

15. Telephone interview, 4 June 1993, and letter, 12 Aug. 1997.

16. Clarence E. Pickett, "The Quaker as Citizen," *Friends Intelligencer* 103, no. 29 (20 July 1946): 423-24.

17. Elizabeth Gray Vining, *Quiet Pilgrimage* (Philadelphia: Lippincott, 1970), 190.

18. Vining, *Quiet Pilgrimage,* 195.

19. Elizabeth Gray Vining, *Windows for the Crown Prince* (Philadelphia: Lippincott, 1952).

20. Pickett journal, 5 Oct. 1947.

21. Albert N. Keim, *The CPS Story: An Illustrated History of Civilian Public Service* (Intercourse, PA: Good Books, 1990).

22. Keim, *The CPS Story,* 71.

23. Pickett journal, 8 May 1946.

24. Pickett journal, 18 May 1946.

25. Pickett journal, 4 July 1946.

26. Excerpts from letters to author from Carolyn Pickett Miller, dated 8 April and 29 Aug. 1994.

27. 1950 AFSC annual report, 16.

28. Letter, Clarence Pickett to Gilbert MacMaster, 12 Mar. 1951, Haverford College, Haverford, PA: Magill Library, Quaker Collection.

29. Pickett journal, 8 Jan. 1947.

30. Pickett journal, 11 Jan. 1947.

31. Undated, typewritten statement by Clarence Pickett, AFSC archives.

32. Undated statement.

33. Clarence E. Pickett , "And Having Done All, To Stand," 1951 William Penn Lecture, The Young Friends Movement of the Philadelphia Yearly Meetings, Philadelphia, 26.

34. Clarence E. Pickett, "Toward a Significant Religious Society," *Friends Intelligencer* 99, no. 32 (8 Aug. 1942): 507-09.

35. Pickett, "Toward...Society," 1942.

36. *Newsweek*, 28 Apr. 1947, 85-86.

37. Pickett journal, 10 May 1947.

38. Elmore Jackson, *Middle East Mission: The Story of a Major Bid for Peace in the Time of Nasser and Ben-Gurion* (New York: Norton, 1983), Appendix I, 108.

39. Clarence E. Pickett as quoted in article entitled "Friends Receive the Nobel Prize for Peace," *Friends Intelligencer* 104, no. 45 (8 Nov. 1947): 599.

Chapter 15

THE TRUCE OF GOD

That deep communion in which all of us are one family

FROM THE VERY DAY OF THE FOUNDING OF THE UNITED NATIONS (UN) in April 1945 the American Friends Service Committee took steps to support the organization. Clarence Pickett saw the world body as a reconciling force and as the base for multilateral aid to both the war-devastated countries and to what were known at the time as the underdeveloped nations. In these first years the UN was located in Flushing Meadows (Long Island), New York and referred to as "Lake Success." The AFSC established its office in 1947 in New York ("Quaker House") close to the expected site of the new UN buildings, and by 1948 had staff at work monitoring issues and interceding as a recognized nongovernmental organization (NGO).

It was in respect to tensions and developments in Palestine that Pickett first became prominently involved in the United Nations. Early in 1946 Great Britain determined that it could not continue to administer Palestine in accordance with the terms of the mandate approved by the Council of the League of Nations in 1922. Under the terms of the mandate Britain was responsible for promoting the establishment of a national home for the Jewish people in Palestine, with the understanding that nothing would be done to prejudice the civil and religious rights of non-Jewish communities. With Jewish immigration (some of it illegal in the view of the British government) increasing and with growing tensions in Palestine and adjoining Arab countries, Great Britain decided to refer the Palestine problem to the United Nations.

To deal with this referral the United Nations set up a Special Committee on Palestine composed of eleven member states. Its report and recommendations were published in August 1947. The Jewish Agency accepted the recommended partition plan, the Arab governments and the Arab higher executive rejected it. Early in 1948 the UN Palestine Commission reported on the organized efforts by Arab groups, both inside and outside Palestine, to prevent implementation of the so-called Partition Resolution passed by the General Assembly the previous year. Armed violence was increasing throughout Palestine. A state of civil war developed.

On Sunday, 8 February 1948 Francis Sayre, diplomatic advisor to Herbert Lehman, director general of UNRRA, and formerly assistant secretary of state, and Benjamin Gerig, deputy representative of the United States in the UN's Trusteeship Council and former professor at Haverford College, both well-known to Clarence, called on Rufus Jones at his home on the Haverford College campus. Clarence Pickett came over from Waysmeet to share in the discussion of how Jerusalem, a city precious in the heritage of three major world faiths, might be spared from the destruction of war.

The idea of a kind of "peace of God" in Jerusalem developed. Rufus Jones agreed to try to get together the highest-ranking persons of Catholic, Protestant, Jewish, and Mohammedan faiths at Quaker House in New York on Tuesday, 17 February, and he was successful in doing so. Subsequently, on 21 March, an appeal written by Rufus Jones as honorary chairman of the American Friends Service Committee and signed by a number of world Christian leaders, was sent to Isaac Hertzog, chief rabbi of Palestine, and Amin Berg Abdubhabi, head of the Supreme Moslem Council, calling for a "truce of God" in Jerusalem.

Believing that the appeal should be supplemented by personal approaches, the AFSC and its British counterpart, Friends Service Council, sent James Vail, secretary of the Foreign Service Section, from Philadelphia and Edgar Castle, a successful educational administrator, from London to Jerusalem for direct discussions. Their cable to Clarence Pickett on 26 April reported on a tragedy in the making:

> Saw Jerusalem disintegrating before our eyes into physical and moral chaos. Situation close to anarchy. Destructive house-to-house

conflict demolishing homes and civic buildings. Murder to secure weapons commonplace. Fear and suspicion disrupting civic life already approaching standstill. Unless fighting ceases before 15 May Jerusalem faces destruction. Cutting of water, fuel, electricity imminent. Disease will spread and multiply present suffering. Serious refugee problem inevitable. Immediate appointment successor civil authorities Jerusalem vital.[1]

The two Quaker representatives were significantly instrumental in securing Arab League, Jewish Agency, and Christian acceptance of the truce. They strongly urged the United Nations to appoint a commissioner for Jerusalem, to be supported by a neutral force of disciplined police. The UN quickly rose to the challenge. On 7 May Andrew Cordier, administrative assistant to the director general, Trygve Lie, phoned Clarence Pickett. What Cordier wanted to find out was whether the AFSC had anyone to suggest to be commissioner for Jerusalem. After they talked a while, it was clear that the UN wanted Clarence to accept the position—that the Arabs and Jews had united on his name and that the UN wanted to forward his name to the high commissioner in Jerusalem, who in turn would forward it to the British Foreign Office.

Pickett told Cordier that he couldn't make up his mind so promptly, and went home. But as soon as Clarence Pickett got home, Andrew Cordier called again to say that Trygve Lie and the United Nations Assembly president had both been consulted about the appointment since speaking to him earlier. They both heartily agreed and were very eager to forward Clarence's name so that he could be on the ground by 15 May, just one week away. "This seemed to me to be moving pretty fast," wrote Clarence. "I asked him to give me two hours to talk with some of my friends. I called up Reed Cary, Harold Evans, and tried to call one or two others who were away. Of course, Lilly and I had quite a weighty conference about this also."[2]

At 8:30 that same evening Pickett called Cordier back to say that it seemed unwise for him to accept the appointment, given his continuing involvement in assessing a request from Leo Szilard (one of the scientists involved in the manufacture of the atom bomb), Beardsley Ruml (chairman of the board of R.H. Macy & Company), and the columnist Samuel Grafton, that the AFSC sponsor a peace conference to discuss major issues between the United States and the Soviet Union. Clarence also cited cautions issued that very morning by his doctor, Wayne Marshall. Wrote Clarence: "He [Marshall] sees nothing wrong at all except my blood pressure is a little too high—which I already know. He gave me quite a talk about slowing down, ordered me to quit at four in the afternoon, take a nap after lunch, and in general to slow down. . . . Jerusalem, of course, is not the place where one would go for quiet repose."[3]

Clarence then suggested executive board member Harold Evans, after getting Evans' willingness to submit his name for the delicate mission. But Cordier wanted to leave the door open to the possibility of Pickett himself taking on the assignment. "It was a very tough evening," said Clarence, "because the wires were pretty busy all evening trying to clarify our minds on this very difficult matter."[4]

The pressure on Clarence Pickett to accede to the request came from several sources. There was his basic commitment to the United Nations. He had respect for the individuals who saw him as indispensable in the situation. AFSC colleagues were urging him to undertake the mission because the invitation had been to him personally, largely because of his standing among Jewish groups.

The pressure was also coming from deep within himself. These UN officials could not have struck a more resonant chord in Clarence's mind and spirit. They seemed to be saying, "We want the kind of interest you have in the power of spiritual resources brought to bear on this problem, and therefore we come to you expecting help."[5] And he saw that if the world could be turned toward reconciliation in this situation, it might point the way toward further use of the spirit of understanding in contrast to the use of arms in the settling of further disputes.

There was a very brief hiatus in the consideration of the request while Andrew Cordier and others at the UN looked elsewhere for a municipal commissioner. But on Monday Cordier phoned Pickett with a request that he and Harold Evans come to New York on Tuesday for consultations with key players in the negotiations. A special AFSC board meeting was scheduled for the next day. The weight of opinion in the board and within a smaller group of four Friends appointed by the board was that Clarence should take the position, but it was left to him and Harold Evans to make the final decision. "After about an hour and a half of sweating it out [with the four Friends], I said I would go home and talk the matter over with Lilly and would report later in the evening."[6]

Clarence and Lilly went out to dinner that evening and then went home to talk about the UN request. Little is known about that conversation, except that Clarence decided he could not under any circumstances take on the assignment. An indication of the crisis nature of the decision is contained in this unusual journal entry the next day: "I haven't been very much good today because of the experience yesterday and last night of trying to decide what I ought to do about going to Jerusalem."[7] Harold Evans agreed to go, and James Vail, just recently returned from Palestine, was persuaded to accompany Evans.

By the time the two Friends left the United States the latter part of May, the situation in Palestine had altered drastically. On 14 May 1948, the State of Israel Proclamation of Independence was published by the Provisional State Council, the forerunner of the Knesset, the Israeli parliament. The British mandate was terminated the following day, as planned, and regular armed forces of Transjordan, Egypt, Syria, Lebanon, and Iraq entered Palestine and began an open assault on Israel. After some initial successes by Arab arms, the Israeli forces rallied, broke the siege of Jewish west Jerusalem, and occupied substantial areas both in the north and the south of Palestine.

In Cairo, Harold Evans and James Vail were warmly welcomed by the newly appointed UN mediator, Count Folke Bernadotte of Sweden, and his associates. They all proceeded to Jerusalem where they participated in a number of conferences aimed at a truce in the overall conflict in Palestine. The plan for a municipal commissioner lost support at the regional level, especially on the part of Transjordan, which was not a member state of the United Nations. Evans and Vail soon returned home, reporting to AFSC staff at the end of June.

In the midst of the pressures of these events, Clarence Pickett was finding time, always on a Sunday afternoon, to visit Rufus Jones who had suffered a coronary occlusion, resulting first in hospitalization and then confinement to his home on the Haverford campus. On 16 June he died peacefully in his sleep. The wider circle of Friends and the Christian community as a whole thereby lost one of its most distinguished members. The memorial service was held at the Haverford Friends Meetinghouse on Sunday afternoon, 29 June. Clarence was one of those who spoke. Later, at the graveside, he read at the request of the family some of Rufus Jones' favorite poems and Bible passages. Mary Hoxie Jones, his daughter, wrote a letter of deep appreciation to Clarence for his contributions that afternoon.

A second great loss—this one international in scope but nevertheless very personal to Clarence Pickett—was the assassination of Count Folke Bernadotte by Jewish extremists on 17 September 1948. The tragedy vividly called to Clarence's mind the agonizing evening he and Lilly had spent making the decision that he should not go to Jerusalem either as commissioner or as counselor to the commissioner. He had the feeling that, but for the grace of God, it might have been him. He admitted to a feeling of depression the next day. Then, very characteristically, he expressed deep concern that the general public might blame the assassination on the Jews as a whole. "Very few Jews carry responsibility for this," he wrote, "although I suppose the actual gun firing was done by members of the Stern Gang in Jerusalem, but the stigma, I am afraid, will still rest there, unjust as that may be."[8]

In Clarence's view the great international loss was somewhat mitigated by the promotion—and subsequent excellent service—of Ralph Bunche, the African American who was deputy mediator for Palestine. Observed Pickett: "That the leadership passed into the hands of Dr. Ralph Bunche was one of those blessings all too rare in political history."[9]

Earlier in the year the executive committee of the AFSC board of directors met, at Clarence Pickett's request, to consider the need for some administrative changes in light of Clarence becoming sixty-five years old in 1949. He wished to remain active but without the administrative burdens of the executive secretary. While Henry Cadbury would continue to be AFSC chairman until January 1960 and would be succeeded by Harold Evans, it was clear that a new generation of Quakers, some of them veterans of Civilian Public Service, were beginning to provide leadership for the Committee.

Overshadowing Clarence Pickett's involvement in the Middle East crisis in 1948 were his tireless efforts to bring together for face-to-face conversation prominent Americans and Russians, principally at the United Nations headquarters in Flushing Meadows on Long Island, New York, but also at other international gatherings. These efforts were part of a three-pronged approach that the American Friends Service Committee was making to defuse the "cold war" that had developed between the United States and the Soviet Union. The other two components of this approach were, first, to urge leading Americans to formulate proposals for the settlement of outstanding issues between the two super-powers and, second, to strengthen the United Nations itself.

A full-page ad, under the heading, ". . . Not by might, nor by power, but by my spirit. . . ." appeared in major newspapers across the country in 1948. It stated in part:

> The world is aghast at the dread prospect of the United States and Russia competing for military supremacy. This need not be; this must not be. War, or militarism to forestall war, means ultimate ruin for all. The American Friends Service Committee believes that peaceful relations are possible between the United States and Russia. We do not minimize the issues that now exist between the two countries, but neither do we believe that war would settle these issues. It would only intensify them. We call for a faith that other means can be found which could lift us to a new level of life in which war is outmoded.[10]

A coupon at the bottom of the ad invited readers to indicate approval or disapproval of the statement. The committee was flooded with responses of approval, some with contributions.

To understand the context of Clarence Pickett's dominant interest following World War II, one only has to recall some of the crises between the Soviet Union and the United States: the installation by the Red Army of pro-Soviet regimes in Poland, Romania, Bulgaria, and Hungary following Germany's defeat; the proclamation of the Truman Doctrine in March 1947, providing for economic and military aid to nations, such as Greece and Turkey, seeking assistance against Communist aggression; the proposed merging of the American, British and French zones in conquered Germany into a West German Federal Republic; in June 1948 the land and water blockade of Berlin by the Soviets to demonstrate their disapproval of the proposed West German state; the airlift into Berlin by U.S. and British air forces to supply the city with food, coal and other goods; and then in September 1949, President Truman's announcement that the Soviet Union had developed and tested an atomic bomb. These were times of severely increased tensions between the two countries, a rivalry that raised the specter of nuclear war.

It could be said that Clarence Pickett's personal and direct interventions in respect to the relationship between the United States and the Soviet Union began with a meeting he had in February 1948 with Andrei

Clarence Pickett greets Andrei Gromyko,
USSR ambassador to the United Nations in 1948

Gromyko, the USSR ambassador to the United Nations. But a precursor
to the private meeting with Gromyko was Clarence Pickett's decision,
at the invitation of the Soviet Counsel General in New York, to attend a
social occasion in celebration of the thirtieth anniversary of the Russian
Revolution. Several hundred persons—Soviet officials, some UN officials, and many friends of the USSR—were present at the buffet supper.
Pickett was able to have brief conversations with Andrei Vyshinsky,
Deputy Minister of Foreign Affairs for the Soviet Union, Andrei
Gromyko, the Soviet's representative on the United Nations Security
Council, and Kuzma Kiselev, chief delegate to the UN from Byleorussia.
Kiselev told Pickett of the deep impression, simply by his presence, that
the American head of UNRRA, Richard Scandrett, had made, not only
upon officials but also upon the public at large in Byleorussia.[11]

Given the tendency of Americans to assume that any person attending an occasion to celebrate the Russian Revolution must be a communist or "fellow traveler," Clarence Pickett felt it appropriate to report on the event in writing to the AFSC board of directors. He said that he had no feeling whatever of any need to express any attitude toward communism or the Russian government. "It seems to me important that we should keep the whole enterprise entirely above any effort to express approval of things political in Russia in order to gain favor," said Pickett, "for I am quite clear that all dealings with them should be on a strict humanitarian basis."[12] Notwithstanding public criticisms, Clarence Pickett would hold to this position throughout the rest of his life, accepting invitations to social gatherings sponsored by the Soviets at the United Nations or at their embassy in Washington.

On a weekend in February 1948 Clarence Pickett, with the assistance of William Lancaster, chief counsel for National City Bank of New York, had an opportunity to have lunch with Andrei Gromyko at Gromyko's residence in New York. After the meal, seated with other guests around a big table in Gromyko's living room, Clarence Pickett had an opportunity to submit his proposal for the holding of a conference in Europe the following summer, to bring together people in the fields of religion, science, and culture for the purpose of determining whether progress could be made in producing a new climate in which political decisions were made. It proved very difficult for Gromyko to see the value of such a gathering. Clarence felt "pretty inadequate" in making the proposal concrete. It was the first occasion at which he suggested using the Nobel Peace Prize to further peace between the United States and the Soviet Union. He was exhausted when he returned home: "This kind of thing may not seem to take very much, and it may look very pleasant on the outside, but it really is very demanding of thought and energy."[13]

Immediately upon his return from a month's vacation in Florida, he assessed the status of the initiatives taken in respect to the Soviets. "I found that our discussions with the Russian officials have matured somewhat while I was away, but I shall have to get very busy to have another interview with Mr. Gromyko soon. . . . Of course, relations between Russia and the United States have deteriorated a great deal during this month."[14] Clarence was, undoubtedly, referring in part to the widely publicized report of a subcommittee of the House Foreign

Affairs Committee which stated, that "Communists and the Russian government have only one goal—world revolution."[15]

In mid-April Pickett led a delegation of three Friends to meet with President Harry Truman, urging him to avoid the use of violence as a threat. The president did not agree with them on that point. The Quakers left the appointment realizing that they could not expect imaginative thinking from the president in respect to the Russian-American situation."[16]

At the very end of the month Pickett gave a major address at a Yale University seminar on "The Politics of Time and the Politics of Eternity," and publicly announced that the AFSC would use the Nobel Peace Prize money to improve Russian-American relations. Listing some of the many current crises in international relations and the manner in which these questions were absorbing and interesting, and "freighted with the stuff of which political destiny" is made—"the politics of time"—he noted how their very gravity tended to make people consider forfeiting those abiding values," which he termed "the politics of eternity," to assure a temporal victory.

Pickett was particularly concerned about America's increasing reliance on military preparations and the possible use of the atomic bomb. "Following that path would mean our downfall,"[17] he stated. The politics of eternity to which he was referring were those individual and organizational actions that reflect a belief in justice, in the power of love, and in the sacredness of the individual. He saw these actions as instruments of political change: "Individuals, small groups, voluntary associations, dedicated men and women, who determine to experiment in all avenues of life with the best but potent forces of understanding and sacrificial devotion—they are the ones who will turn the tide. And if it is turned, it will be done in the heat and struggle of difficult situations, not in quiet cloisters. Hardly ever has there been such a clear and significant call to a generation of men and women."[18]

Slipped into the text of this weighty address were two lines that, like a picture taken with a telephoto lens, revealed two constants in Clarence Pickett's life: "I do believe that there is no cause for ultimate and final despair," and this: "Just because we are at one of those balancing moments of history, it is a great time to be alive."[19] It was this inner spiritual quality that enabled him to move with relative ease and much energy into his daily round of commitments and responsibilities.

Another important speaking engagement in the spring of 1948 was an address at the annual dinner of the American Russian Institute in New York. According to the invitation, Clarence Pickett was to be a subordinate speaker, with Andrei Gromyko the principal one. But, on the very day of the dinner at the Waldorf Astoria, with a registration of a thousand guests ("pretty much the Social Register of New York" as Clarence saw it), Gromyko informed the Institute that he would be unable to speak at the dinner. Gromyko had intended to deliver an address reiterating the Soviet desire for peace and security, but he canceled it lest the speech be interpreted to mean that the Soviet Union was pleading for peace from a position of weakness, an impression he did not wish to give.[21] Coincidentally, just the previous week the Institute had been placed on the U.S. Attorney General's list of subversive organizations in the country. Pickett found neither one of these developments a deterrent and decided to stick closely to the already-typed text of his talk, originally restricted to twelve minutes. He introduced his plea for some kind of exchange of ideas and points of view between Americans and Russians (with the expenses of the program to be covered by Nobel Peace Prize funds), with these words:

> I speak to you tonight on the subject of cultural relations with Russia, as a Quaker. With apologies to Mr. Gromyko, I feel compelled to make my position clear, that I am not a communist. . . . I feel compelled to say, furthermore, that I *do not* believe in dictatorship. I *do* believe in freedom of thought and discussion, and in the international exchange of ideas.[22]

At the end of June, with William Lancaster as intermediary, Clarence Pickett had a second meeting with Andrei Gromyko. Pickett told Gromyko that the U.S. Department of Commerce had granted the AFSC's request for a license to ship $25,000 worth of streptomycin to the Russian Red Cross and Red Crescent for use in the treatment of tuberculosis. He also raised the possibility of three persons from the AFSC visiting Moscow in the near future. Gromyko was cordial, but Pickett realized that to make any permanent change in relationships between the two countries would take a long time and "a very great dedication and diligence."[23] In July the Service Committee received word from the Russian government that it would not, for the present, issue visas to AFSC visitors to enter Russia. While understanding how American-

Russian relations as a whole influenced almost every decision of the
Soviet Union, Clarence Pickett was deeply disappointed in the decision. One road of personal diplomacy was now blocked, and it was not
until 1955 that American Quakers, six in number and headed
by Clarence Pickett, were able to visit the USSR.

Clarence Pickett in mid-October spent two days at the home of Marshall
Field in Huntington, Long Island, New York, meeting with other trustees
of the Field Foundation. It was during a lunch that Clarence learned, in a
phone call from Lilly, that their daughter Rachel had given birth to a baby
boy. "We hadn't expected the baby before nearly another month," Clarence
said, "so she [Rachel] was caught a little short on preparations, and they
haven't yet picked out a name, in case the baby should be a boy."[24]
He was subsequently named Timothy Lee Stalnaker. A second grandson,
Thomas Allen Stalnaker, was born two days before Christmas in 1950.

With Pickett's strong encouragement, and the endorsement of
several persons prominent in public life, there developed within the
Service Committee a commitment to set forth, for public distribution
and discussion, proposals reflecting its belief that war between the United
States and the Soviet Union, and the resultant global catastrophe, were
not inevitable. In July 1948, under the direction of the AFSC's
Russian-American Committee, Robert Frase began a six-months' study
in the search for constructive proposals to create better relations. Frase
had served as chief of the UNRRA mission to Byleorussia in 1946, and
in 1947 had prepared a prospectus for a study on the international
control of atomic energy. He was also the recipient of a Guggenheim
Foundation fellowship which was extended to allow time for the preparation of a background paper on the East-West conflict.

 With Frase's background paper as the basis for study, early in 1949 a
"working study group" of fifteen Friends began meeting, with Gilbert
White, president of Haverford College, as chairman and Stephen Cary,
one of Pickett's two assistants, as secretary. Pickett himself was not
directly involved in the writing of the report, but provided leadership in
channeling it to opinion-makers, both in and outside government, for
suggestions. Following widespread comment and some editing, the
report, The *United States and the Soviet Union*, was published as a hard-
cover booklet by Yale University Press in November 1949.

A new and major appeal for assistance from the United Nations was the principal reason Clarence Pickett did not have time to be an active member of the study group on Soviet-American relations. Once again the request related to the Middle East, in this case following a series of armistice agreements between Israel and neighboring Arab states. Under these agreements Transjordan annexed the West Bank, including the eastern sector of Jerusalem, becoming in 1949 a new state, the Hashemite Kingdom of Jordan; Israel absorbed Jewish West Jerusalem, the Negev to the south, and parts of Galilee; and Egypt assumed a kind of protectorate over the Gaza Strip, a sliver of territory in southwest Palestine twenty-five miles long and eight miles wide. The United Nations placed upon Clarence Pickett and the American Friends Service Committee an unprecedented emergency appeal for aid on behalf of two hundred thousand of the scattered half million Palestinian refugees who had fled from their villages.

The pleas for AFSC's cooperation began with another phone call, this one from Paris, to Clarence Pickett on 28 October 1948, from Andrew Cordier in his same capacity as administrative assistant to the director general. Cordier urged Pickett very strongly to come over for a few days to talk with him and other UN staff members.[25] Fortunately, Elmore Jackson, one of Clarence's assistants, was due to arrive in London on that very day. Clarence asked Elmore to proceed immediately to Paris while he, Clarence, consulted with colleagues in Philadelphia.

The role of the AFSC in respect to refugees in Palestine did not come into full bloom overnight. The committee already had as a Quaker emissary in Israel Clarence's close friend, Moses Bailey, on leave from Hartford Theological Seminary. The dual purpose of Bailey's explorations was refugee relief and resettlement. A modest program was initiated with a staff of four based in the Old City of Acre. Given the limited resources available to the Committee for work in Israel and neighboring countries, Philadelphia AFSC staff in conversations with the UN thought in terms of expanding the type of program brought into place by Moses Bailey, with an emphasis on the resettlement of refugees, both Jews and Arabs.

But the United Nations staff had other ideas. The UN plan, as it finally evolved, was to launch a nine-months' emergency program, pending more permanent arrangements, at a cost of $32 million. The

International Committee of the Red Cross was asked to be the distributing agency in the main area of Palestine and in Israel, the League of Red Cross Societies in Arab states outside Palestine, and the American Friends Service Committee in the Gaza Strip.[26] Stanton Griffis, United States ambassador to Egypt and acquainted with Quakers because of AFSC relief operations in Poland, was appointed director of the overall program, named the United Nations Relief for Palestine Refugees.

Clarence Pickett was, from the outset of AFSC discussions with the UN, in favor of undertaking a sizable program if a request came from the United Nations. The official invitation came to him from UN director general Trygve Lie on 7 December 1948. The AFSC board at its meeting on 1 December had already given extensive consideration to the anticipated proposal. "They seem to be united in undertaking this service," wrote Clarence, "although there were questions which could not be answered."[27] Principally there were questions about leadership and personnel; Clarence was giving attention to this matter of competent leadership virtually every day.

On all matters of personnel he had the enthusiastic and capable assistance of his newly-appointed personnel secretary, Elizabeth Marsh Jensen, who had worked with him at the AFSC from 1930 to 1935. In her later years Elizabeth stated in an interview that at the time of the need for the estimated fifty volunteers for the operation in the Gaza Strip there were eighty-three vacancies within the AFSC, most of them in the United States, that needed to be filled.

Clarence Pickett believed that volunteers, American and British, would come forward for the Gaza Strip program. He was right. Many of them were conscientious objectors who had not been permitted to serve overseas during the war. But there were also Quaker veteran workers willing to go, and by the end of December the first Quaker workers were in the field. Clarence Pickett was being urged by the executive committee of the AFSC's board to go to Cairo and the Gaza Strip to work with the various governmental and UN authorities related to the relief program. Dr. Wayne Marshall gave his approval for air travel. Lilly Pickett was persuaded to accompany Clarence.

Clarence and Lilly Pickett left for Switzerland Wednesday evening, 7 January 1949. With stopovers in Gander, Newfoundland, in Shannon, Ireland, and Paris, they arrived in Geneva at four in the afternoon of the next day. They were met at the airport by Howard Wriggins, AFSC's representative in Geneva for the Arab refugee program and previously the head of the French mission. Bertram and Irene Pickard, British Friends in charge of the Friends Center, had flowers and oranges to greet the Picketts in their room.[28]

The flight to Cairo had to be postponed because of a cold and ear infection Clarence developed. But the delay provided time for him to visit with friends and international figures. Clarence Pickett was finally cleared by the Swiss doctor attending him to fly to Cairo, again an overnight trip, this time with stopovers in Rome and Athens and with an early-morning landing at the Cairo airport. He and Lilly were met by two AFSC workers and a representative of the American Embassy. Customs officials had been alerted by Egyptian authorities and quickly passed them through. An embassy car drove them to the Shepheard Hotel, giving them their first introduction to Egyptian life. "It is colorful, to say the least," wrote Clarence. "Dress represents everything from smart New York costume to men in flowing robes—to most abject rags."[29]

The next day Clarence was hard at work, meeting with Stanton Griffis, the U.S. ambassador and director of the Palestine relief program, and with Abdel-Ahim Halin Mahfooz, head of the Red Crescent. Griffis arranged for a special UN plane to take him, the Picketts, and some others to Gaza the next day for an initial one-day visit. They were up at dawn—for security reasons there was no flying in and out of the Cairo airport at night. "It was interesting though dreary," reported Clarence, "to fly for one and a half hours and see no vegetation—only sand— except along the Suez Canal. Emmet Gulley [of the AFSC staff] met us in the pasture at Gaza which serves as an airfield. He certainly looked prosperous in the new maroon Ford with "Quakers" written on it in Arabic and English."[30]

The quick visit was largely an impressionistic one for Clarence, although he did authorize the rental of an available rest house when he saw how crowded the living quarters were for the Quaker staff. He had time to visit some of the refugee camps. He knew that upon arrival in December the Quaker contingent had found refugees, two hundred thousand of them, living in abandoned buildings, former prison cells, Samson's Tomb, caves, holes in the sand, and mosque courtyards. Most of the refugees had brought with them from their villages no more possessions than the clothes they wore. What financial resources they had were soon expended for food. "Here was the heart of our visit for me," wrote Clarence. "They looked thin but mostly not diseased. The Egyptian army has been helping them out more than I had realized, both for some food and for tents. But even so they are a sorry lot."[31]

Returning to Cairo—flying through a sandstorm and arriving just five minutes before the airport curfew—Clarence spent the next week successfully negotiating with various officials, Egyptian and international, to speed up the flow of personnel, particularly doctors and nurses, and food to the Gaza Strip. Then on 26 January he made the ten-hour trip from Cairo to Gaza by rail, the long train of fifteen cars almost entirely filled with soldiers. From the very slow-moving train Clarence saw the lush green farms fed by the Nile—"more beautiful oranges, tangerines, cauliflower, cabbage and alfalfa I've never seen,"[32] he observed. But after crossing the Suez Canal at Ismalia, the countryside was barren, punctuated by no more than a half-dozen settlements with indescribably bad housing. "This project is incredibly difficult," commented Clarence, "tragically needed, and absorbingly interesting."[33]

At the end of January, the day before he returned to Cairo, Clarence Pickett personally met at the Gaza airstrip the member of the United Nations truce-observer team who was flying in to head a convoy of vehicles to Faluga in the Negev, a pocket of Palestinian Arabs and Egyptian troops cut off by Israeli forces. The trucks carried in twelve tons of food for the three thousand civilians, and the Egyptian army sent in food for an equal number of trapped Egyptian soldiers. Quaker workers, Emmet Gulley and Lee Dinsmore, went with the convoy representing the AFSC. They crossed the Egyptian-Israeli lines not more than two miles from Gaza. All mines had supposedly been cleared from a fully mined road, but one was missed and exploded under Emmet's car, doing no damage. They found a great welcome in Faluga, which had just reached the end of its supplies.[34]

As it developed, several members of the Quaker contingent cooperated with the Egyptian army in the weekly distribution of supplies. Colonel Gamal Abdel Nasser (to become prime minister of Egypt in 1954 and then president in 1956) handled the negotiations on behalf of the army and was administratively in charge of the distribution of food. A relationship of confidence developed between Nasser and the Friends, resulting, as Elmore Jackson, former head of the Quaker UN program, would in 1983 reveal in his book, *Middle East Mission*, "several long evenings in which Colonel Nasser and the Quaker convoy team sat around darkening campfires discussing the differences and similarities between Quaker and Islamic thought, especially in the field of social ethics, those areas in which religious tenets, personal philosophy, and the need for social and political action intersect."[35]

A direct outcome of this relationship was Elmore Jackson's secret shuttle diplomacy in 1955 between Cairo and Jerusalem, including confidential conversations with President Nasser of Egypt and Prime Minister David Ben-Gurion of Israel. The mediatory efforts were regrettably undermined by *fedayeen* attacks from the Gaza Strip into Israel, by Israeli retaliations, and finally by the Egyptian decision in September of that year to obtain eastern European arms on a barter basis from Czechoslovakia.

Back in Cairo after the brief visit to the Gaza Strip, Clarence Pickett was engaged in a round of appointments, increasingly complex since so many people needed to be seen by him, and many wanted to see him. In a key, two-hour meeting with Azzam Pasha, secretary of the Arab League, Pasha expressed the view that repatriation of hundreds of thousands of refugees was crucial to any peace settlement. The return of Palestinian refugees to their home villages or their resettlement in Arab lands—any measures that would free them from the camps—quickly became a principal issue between the state of Israel and neighboring Arab countries. Pickett could hardly have imagined that right to the end of the twentieth century the American Friends Service Committee would be assisting refugees in the Gaza Strip and would be publishing and promoting its views on the conflicts in the Middle East and on how peace might be achieved.

The series of appointments in Cairo and the meetings with Quaker workers en route to the Gaza Strip or based in Cairo, stretching over a week's time, ended with Clarence Pickett having a talk with Egypt's Premier Mahmoud Fahmy Pasha. Pickett was quietly but very cordially received. The premier spoke of the great satisfaction it was to have a chance to aid a truly humanitarian effort as contrasted with the usual political appeals. He said he envied the Friends. "We were quite moved by his evidence of sincerity and understanding of the religious motivation which he felt prompted us,"[36] wrote Clarence.

Clarence and Lilly Pickett's visit in the Middle East was not confined to Cairo and the Gaza Strip. They also traveled via Beirut and

Haifa to Jerusalem for talks with a range of religious and other leaders. Clarence was able to make a side visit to the Old City of Acre where just a few months earlier, as a result of Moses Bailey's mission, the AFSC had initiated a refugee relief program. Pickett's most inspiring ("priceless" was his word) meeting in Jerusalem was with Martin Buber. Clarence Pickett viewed him as a man of deep discernment, an elderly seer, a prophet in the tradition of Isaiah, Jeremiah, Amos, and Hosea. "I shall always remember him sitting in the rather solitary grandeur of the King David Hotel lobby," wrote Clarence, "looking forward to the day when, hopefully, political struggles will sufficiently subside so that he may again be permitted to teach oncoming generations in Hebrew University from whose buildings he is now excluded because it is located in the Arab part of Jerusalem."[37]

In the meeting with Martin Buber Clarence Pickett seems to have found confirmation of his growing, basic conviction about the Middle East. He wrote several years later:

> The need for a fundamentally religious viewpoint, if this part of the world's terrifically complex problems are to be worked through, I found shared by persons of many faiths—Jewish, Protestant, Catholic, Quaker, Moslem. On the level of politics, history, psychology (all of them important) the problem seemed flatly insoluble unless there was brought to bear that deep communion in which all of us are one family. As I went about, talking with persons of the different faiths, it began to seem to me not impossible that the words of the great prophets would even yet prove to be the note which alone could bring peace within this great family of kindred peoples: the call of Allah in the Koran, "but I invite you to the Mighty, the Forgiving"; and of Micah in the Old Testament, "and what does the Lord require of thee, but to do justly, and to love mercy, and to walk humbly with thy God?"; and of Jesus in the New Testament, "Love your enemies . . . do good to them that hate you, and pray for them that do spitefully use you."[38]

In urging Clarence Pickett, accompanied by his wife, to go to the Middle East, the AFSC board of directors had virtually decreed that they take some vacation during their return. This they did in part by going by boat to France from Beirut, with ports of call in Alexandria (Egypt), Piraeus (Greece), Naples, Leghorn, and Genoa (Italy), enabling them to make side trips to Athens and Pisa. Docking finally in Marseilles, they then went by air to London for his appointments with English

Friends. "Evidently there is to be little leisure here,"[39] wrote Clarence. And from the very first day he had to contend with a cold which robbed him of his voice before he left England.

Upon arrival in the United States, apart from dealing with a myriad administrative questions, Pickett was immediately in demand for reports on the Middle East. In April the AFSC general meetings were held in Cambridge, Massachusetts. The Saturday evening session had to be shifted from the Friends Meetinghouse to the new lecture hall at Harvard University to accommodate all those who wanted to hear him. He was deeply moved by the interest shown in his report. But such occasions were taxing. Clarence's doctor, Wayne Marshall, ordered several weeks of rest because of high blood pressure. Reluctantly, Clarence obeyed the instructions.

In mid-May he and Elmore Jackson, now head of the Quaker United Nations Program, visited with Mrs. Vijaya Lakshmi Pandit, India's ambassador to the United States and sister of Prime Minister Nehru. Pickett and Jackson wanted to talk with her about her brother's approaching visit to the United States, hoping that Nehru, a great spirit and a world figure, coming from a country that was standing in between Russia and the United States as a neutral, might make a special contribution to the east-west controversy in his public addresses. But Nehru was to say in person to a sizable group of Quakers in October during his visit that he did not want to be too much in the role of giving advice, since he was a guest of the United States.[40]

Towards the end of June Clarence Pickett, Henry Cadbury in his role as chairman of the AFSC, and Elmore Jackson, spent an hour and a half in Washington talking with the Russian ambassador, Alexander Panyushkin, about a renewal of cultural relations between the U.S. and the USSR and to give him advance notice of the AFSC's upcoming book on Russian-American relations entitled *The United States and the Soviet Union*. They were to learn the following year that the report had been translated into Russian and selectively distributed in the USSR. The State Department was also given notice. Then at the end of November, Gilbert White, chairman of the study group, and Clarence Pickett personally gave a copy of the final report to Deputy Undersecretary of State, Dean Rusk.

The closing months of 1949 for Clarence Pickett were filled with multiple tasks in the Philadelphia headquarters of the AFSC and the usual obligations deriving from membership in various organizations and on the boards of several foundations. It would be his last full year as executive secretary of the American Friends Service Committee. But there was no thought of real retirement on anyone's mind.

In December 1949 Clarence Pickett, with the approval of the AFSC executive board, testified at the second trial of Alger Hiss in the federal court in New York. Speaking extemporaneously from notes prepared in advance, Pickett told the jury of Alger Hiss' involvement with the Service Committee as a resource leader at summer peace institutes, and stated that his contacts led him to believe that Alger Hiss was a very able, extraordinarily honest person of complete integrity.[41]

Clarence Pickett's support for Hiss was within the context of having talked with Whittaker Chambers shortly after Chambers, a confessed ex-Communist espionage agent and senior editor of TIME magazine, accused Hiss of having belonged to an underground Communist cell in Washington during the 1930s. At the time of the visit Chambers was a member of the Pipe Creek Friends Meeting in Maryland. Another Friend who was prominently involved in the controversy was Congressman Richard Nixon, raised in a Quaker family in Whittier, California. Pickett visited with him in connection with the case.[42]

When in January 1950 the jury brought in a verdict of guilty of perjury, Pickett referred to it at the AFSC staff meeting two days later. According to Stephen Cary, "Clarence made a very moving statement growing out of his long personal association with Alger Hiss, in which he indicated that the most tragic result of the trial to him was the fact that his confidence in the jury system was shaken, rather than the fact that Alger Hiss had been convicted."[43] And, on that same day, Clarence Pickett wrote Alger Hiss and his wife, Priscilla, saying in part: "I cannot understand the decision, but there it is. I want you to know that many of us in the AFSC staff and participants generally are doing our best to enter into sympathy and understanding with you in these extremely difficult times."[44]

Clarence Pickett kept in touch with Priscilla Hiss when Alger went to prison and then visited both of them shortly after Hiss' release. Clarence admired Alger Hiss for making his life in prison a positive, challenging experience. As Brock Brower noted in an article in *Esquire,* "When he [Hiss] went out of the gates on 27 November 1954, there were rousing cheers from the bleak prison windows. Hiss's success in prison derived from human qualities that would be hard to fake. Possibly for some days, or some weeks, but not for almost four years."[45] These were the qualities with which Clarence Pickett identified.[46]

NOTES

1. Clarence E. Pickett, *For More Than Bread* (Boston: Little, 1953), 264.

2. Clarence Pickett journal, AFSC archives, 7 May 1948.

3. Pickett journal, 7 May 1948.

4. Pickett journal, 7 May 1948.

5. Pickett journal, 7 May 1948.

6. Pickett journal, 7 May 1948.

7. Pickett journal, 13 May 1948.

8. Pickett journal, 18 Sept. 1948.

9. Pickett, *Bread*, 266.

10. *The New York Times,* 21 Apr. 1948, et.al., AFSC archives.

11. Pickett journal, 6 Nov. 1947.

12. Pickett journal, 6 Nov. 1947.

13. Pickett journal, 14 Feb. 1948.

14. Pickett journal, 21 Mar. 1948.

15. *The New York Times*, 1 Mar. 1948.

16. Pickett journal, 14 Apr. 1948.

17. Clarence E. Pickett, "The Politics of Time and the Politics of Eternity," Conference on the American Friends Service Committee, Yale University, 28-29 Apr. 1948, AFSC archives.

18. Pickett, "Politics of Time," 1948.

19. Pickett, "Politics of Time," 1948.

20. Pickett journal, 2 June 1948.

21. *The New York Times*, 3 June 1948.

22. Text of address made at dinner meeting of The Russian American Institute, 2 June 1948, AFSC archives.

23. Pickett journal, 22 June 1948.

24. Pickett journal, 12 Oct. 1948.

25. Pickett journal, 28 Oct. 1948.

26. Pickett, *Bread*, 267.

27. Pickett journal, 1 Dec. 1948.

28. Pickett journal, 8 Jan. 1949.

29. Pickett journal, 16 Jan. 1949.

30. Pickett journal, 18 Jan. 1949.

31. Pickett journal, 18 Jan. 1949.

32. Pickett journal, 26 Jan. 1949.

33. Pickett journal, 27 Jan. 1949.

34. Pickett journal, 28 Jan. 1949.

35. Elmore Jackson, *Middle East Mission: The Story of a Major Bid for Peace in the Time of Nasser and Ben-Gurion* (New York: Norton, 1983), 24.

36. Pickett journal, 6 Feb. 1949.

37. Pickett journal, 10 Feb. 1949.

38. Pickett, *Bread*, 282.

39. Pickett journal, 10 Feb. 1949.

40. Pickett journal, 14 Oct. 1949.

41. As also noted in letter, Pickett to Percy M. Thomas, Plainfield, Indiana, 13 Feb. 1950: AFSC archives.

42. There are no further references in Clarence Pickett's journal to other meetings with Richard Nixon in regard to this case or on any other subjects. However, several Friends who were interviewed for this biography had heard directly from Clarence or indirectly from Lilly Pickett that Nixon's mother had talked to Clarence in Whittier, California about her son's behavior following his election to the House of Representatives. She is purported to have said, "You know, he isn't living in the way in which we brought him up." Clarence Pickett evidently acceded to her request to make a pastoral call on Richard Nixon in what turned out to be, as Clarence put it, "the slipperiest conversation" he could recall ever having had. Then, in a letter dated December 30, 1952 to his good friend Gilbert MacMaster, following Dwight Eisenhower's election as president of the United States, Clarence said, "Thee asks whether I know Richard Nixon. I do know him quite well. I'm afraid his Quakerism does not go very deep. However, he has been elected vice

president, and we have fully in mind the obligation of keeping in touch with him, and perhaps deepening his sense of responsibility as a Friend in this responsible post."

43. Stephen Cary, memorandum to Stephen Thiermann, AFSC San Francisco regional office, 27 Jan. 1950: AFSC archives.

44. Pickett to Hiss, 21 Jan. 1940: AFSC archives.

45. Brock Brower, "The Problems of Alger Hiss," *Esquire*, Dec. 1960 (as quoted by Meyer A. Zeligs, *Friendship and Fratitude: An Analysis of Whittaker Chambers and Alger Hiss* (New York: Viking, 1967). See also Tony Hiss, *The View from Alger's Window: A Son's Memoir* (New York: Knopf, 1999).

46. A full treatment of the Quaker connections in this case may be found in the author's illustrated article, "Clarence Pickett and the Alger Hiss Case," *Friends Journal* 40, nos. 11 and 12 (Nov. and Dec. 1994): 9-13 and 12-15 respectively.

Henry Cadbury presents to Clarence and Lilly Pickett, at Haverford College on 20 May 1950, one of two albums of letters sent to Clarence on his retirement as executive secretary. Andrew Cordier, assistant to the United Nations director general, looks on.

The 1950 Quaker United Nations team: Gerald Bailey (UK), Clarence, Agatha Harrison (UK), Elsa Cedergren (Sweden), Heberto Sein (Mexico) and Elmore Jackson (US)

Chapter 16

STEPS TO PEACE

Searching for the heart of humanity

AT THE TURN OF THE YEAR IN 1950, Clarence Pickett's resignation and replacement as executive secretary of the American Friends Service Committee moved quickly. On 12 January the Committee issued a news release announcing that the AFSC executive board had agreed to accept Pickett's resignation, to be effective 1 April. In just over one hundred words, Henry Cadbury, chairman of the board, simply but eloquently summarized Pickett's contribution over the two decades of service:

> In looking back over the more than twenty eventful years during which Clarence E. Pickett has headed the staff of the American Friends Service Committee, the executive board voices its affectionate appreciation of the leadership he has furnished in interpreting within and without the Religious Society of Friends his spiritual ideals. He has embodied in his own person the tact and wisdom so necessary to express in practical deeds the Quaker alternative to international and internal strife.
>
> The confidence which he inspired in the staff and in the general public has won for the Committee widespread support. His services since 1929 have contributed enormously to the effectiveness of the Committee's ministry of reconciliation. We are happy that he has consented to continue on our staff in another capacity, relieved of the arduous duties of administration and serving as minister without portfolio.[1]

Said Clarence Pickett about his retirement: "The administrative responsibilities of the office of executive secretary are such that it has seemed to me desirable that they should be carried out by a younger person."[2] The very next day, a Saturday on which the general Service Committee sessions were taking place, the executive board announced the appointment of Pickett's successor, Lewis Hoskins, thirty-three years old, who had served as director of personnel since July 1949. Prior to that he had served with the Quaker unit of forty-five international volunteers in China for three years, part of that time as head of the mission.

Later that same day the board announced that Clarence Pickett had agreed to serve as honorary secretary, his assignments to be worked out with the incoming executive secretary and under the overall guidance of a new Consultative Committee on Foreign Affairs. The timetable for the changeover of administrative duties to Lewis Hoskins was subsequently moved from 1 April to 1 March. On Monday, 27 February Clarence Pickett, visibly choked up, explained to the AFSC staff that it would be the last time he would preside at the weekly meetings as executive secretary. Over the years he had established a firm tradition of beginning the 9:00 a.m. staff meetings exactly on time by being attentive to the striking of the hour on the huge clocks located on the City Hall tower, only two blocks from the meetinghouse, which was (and still is) crowned by the statue of William Penn. Punctuality was important to Clarence. The staff meetings always began with a brief period of silent worship.

Close associates and personal friends of Clarence and Lilly Pickett soon determined that there should be a special occasion to honor them. A "Clarence E. Pickett Testimonial Committee" was formed. The day decided upon was Saturday, 20 May, the place: Haverford College, on the Main Line west of Philadelphia. Invitations to attend the public meeting and to write letters for presentation to the Picketts were widely distributed.

The day of the celebration began with a meeting for worship in Roberts Hall, followed by a simple box luncheon in the gymnasium of the College, and in the afternoon by the programmed portion of the occasion, with AFSC chairman Henry Cadbury presiding. The reporter for the *Friends Intelligencer* estimated that there were close to eight hundred Friends and friends of Friends gathered for the event. The principal speaker was Andrew Cordier, executive assistant to the secretary general of the United Nations, the man who had personally tapped Clarence Pickett on the shoulder two years earlier to render service in the Middle East. Pickett himself gave an address with the title, "Retrospect and Prospect," expressing the hope, as Rufus Jones had phrased it, that the American Friends Service Committee would remain a "Quaker candle with a universal light."[3] Gilbert White, president of Haverford College, announced that Clarence Pickett had accepted an appointment to the Haverford faculty as lecturer in Christian ethics.

A central feature of the afternoon program was the presentation of a bound volume of letters of tribute from some three hundred friends from all over the world. The Picketts were to receive a second volume at a later date. Many of these letters were addressed to Clarence and Lilly as a couple. Only a few of their closest friends knew of the sacrifices Lilly was making in the furtherance of Clarence's career as an AFSC executive. In an interview with Margaret Bacon in 1972 when Lilly Pickett was ninety years old, Lilly spoke of both the satisfactions and the sacrifices.[4] Foremost among the satisfactions of her life with Clarence was the opportunity to meet a wide variety of prominent and interesting people. She always remembered the overnight stay of Eleanor Roosevelt, the First Lady, at Waysmeet who on her own initiative changed the sheets and made up her bed in the morning. And Lilly accompanied Clarence on ten trips overseas. She was proud of her husband for having the "talent to be close to people. He had a real gift to make friends with people," she said.[5] And Lilly's support of him was clearly important.

But the sacrifices were many. When the Picketts moved from Richmond to Philadelphia, Lilly Pickett was plunged into a routine of constant entertainment, according to Margaret Bacon. Daughter Carolyn remembers her father's frequent absences from home. She recalls the "tremendous number of overnight guests" and the burdens this placed on her mother. Her mother told her that in one single year, there were overnight guests on two hundred and fifty days. [6] All this company led to additional persons for meals and to mountains of laundry. By Lilly's own account the resentments she felt about these circumstances were outweighed by the satisfactions she experienced in coming to know men and women from all over the world and "in seeing the response everywhere to the gentleness and love in Clarence."[7]

Also presented to the Picketts that Saturday afternoon was a cardboard replica of the house that would be built for them on the edge of the Haverford campus from contributions to the Service Committee designated for that particular purpose. The Hoskins family would be moving into Waysmeet since its donor, Anne Hubbard Davis, had specified that the house was for whomever was the executive secretary of the AFSC.

As the associate editor of the *Friends Intelligencer* was to describe the whole occasion: "The day was a succession of shared happinesses. In contrast with impressive phrases like 'a beacon in a divided world sensitive to the hopes of frustrated men,' 'one of the great statesmen of our time,' and one who 'leads the quest of men's souls to moral integrity,' was the unassuming quality of Clarence Pickett himself, in part a would-be denial of this almost overwhelming praise, yet in that very quality lay proof positive."[8]

Clarence was persuaded by the editor of the AFSC's *Bulletin* to write a swan song. Reflecting on the life of the Service Committee, he admitted that "one might well conclude that we have been almost wholly unsuccessful in these thirty-three years of effort. But victories are won not only in the great mass movements of men but primarily in the hearts of individuals. . . . We shall let our voice be heard in opposition to what seems to us the mistaken course which our country takes. We shall depend even more on the method of demonstration and on the kindled spirit to show the effectiveness of love, good will and reconciliation through the lives of increasing numbers of people."[9]

Following Clarence Pickett's progression from AFSC executive secretary to honorary secretary, working with the Consultative Committee on Foreign Affairs (advisedly "consultative," since Pickett, broadly speaking, was preeminently the Quaker leader in international affairs), there was no diminution in his schedule of appointments and speaking engagements. In addition, at the outset of the change, he was asked to continue his membership on the boards of the Independent Aid and Field Foundations and his personal solicitation of high-level contributors to the AFSC.

He was encouraged to continue his concerns in the race relations field. During much of 1950 he was acting chairman of the State of Pennsylvania Committee for the Fair Employment Practices Commission, and in April he moved up to the presidency of the Fellowship Commission in Philadelphia. His relationship to the American Council on Race Relations ended when that organization closed down, for financial reasons, in November 1950.

Clarence Pickett was studiously careful to relinquish his executive secretary responsibilities, although it was understandable that staff members would look to him for advice. There was no effort on his part to exercise control of that office. Indeed, Lewis Hoskins wished he had had more counsel from his predecessor: "It would have been helpful if

Clarence had invited me out to the Waysmeet barn to go over the responsibilities, but he didn't. Probably he did not want to give more counsel because he was afraid it might be heavy-handed—this is the way you do things."[10] It is of interest to note that Hoskins, as he undertook the position of executive secretary, was directly and indirectly responsible for a staff of two hundred persons in the Philadelphia office, one hundred in the regional offices (each office having its own regional secretary and multiple committees), and close to one hundred in foreign service. The AFSC family also included nearly six hundred board and committee members.

Whatever may have been the reasons for the lack of greater attention to the transfer of duties, clearly there was no lessening of commitments on Clarence Pickett's calendar. He was traveling to Washington for engagements with government officials and some congresspersons and to New York for foundation and committee meetings, and for conversations with leaders of voluntary organizations active in the fields of race relations, social and technical assistance (dubbed "the Point Four program" because it was the fourth point in the Presidential inaugural address on 20 January 1949), control of atomic energy, displaced persons in Europe, and China famine relief.

On 4 June Clarence Pickett left for another trip to the West Coast, again to combine meetings arranged by AFSC regional offices with visits to Pickett relatives. Inasmuch as Clarence Pickett's siblings were so much older than he, he was now relating to a large number of nieces and nephews and *their* children. Still his commitment to family was strong. He was always especially pleased when a family member showed up at one of his speaking engagements. Similarly, he was deeply disappointed on his return trip from the West that, because of a failure in communications, he was not able to connect with his sister Mary Ward.

During the night of Pickett's return home from Chicago on 24 June 1950, Secretary of State Dean Acheson phoned President Truman in Independence, Missouri to report that the North Koreans had invaded South Korea. Just three days after Clarence Pickett's return to Philadelphia his Consultative Committee on Foreign Affairs met from lunch until five o'clock, spending a great deal of time over the new and tragic events in Korea. "We decided to assemble [before issuing a statement]," said Pickett, "as much information as possible from mission boards who have operations in Korea and from the government."[11]

The crisis on the Korean peninsula gave added impetus to Clarence Pickett's concern about Russian-American relations. Many Americans were convinced that behind the North Korean invasion across the 38th parallel lay the power of the Soviet Union. Anti-communist sentiment in the United States was increasing, with Senator Joseph McCarthy of Wisconsin contending that the Department of State was riddled with communist sympathizers.

In May Secretary of State Acheson had announced that the United States would supply military aid to France and its colonies in Indochina to assist in the fight against communist insurgents. In July President Truman called for a partial mobilization and asked Congress for an additional $10 billion for rearmament. These and other developments conspired to produce among many Americans a fear that the world was moving ever closer to World War III.

Quite apart from the trip to the West Coast, Clarence Pickett was, on the average, giving three public speeches a month, most of them to Quaker groups. A noted one was the Quaker Lecture which he gave at the annual sessions of Western Yearly Meeting of Friends in mid-August. His chosen subject was "The Meaning of Membership in the Religious Society of Friends," responding in part to a growing public interest in the Society. He urged Quakers to "sit loose to technical membership. Real inclusion in this fellowship of the dedicated is a matter of the inner life and not of outward form."[12] Then he made this significant statement, not only setting forth the lineage of the Religious Society of Friends but also reaffirming his view of Jesus:

> It is clear that our religious body grew out of the mystical stream of religious thought: Isaiah, Jeremiah, Amos, and Hosea. Those great proponents of spiritual religion as contrasted with formalism and dogma are the forebears of the life and ministry of Jesus. They found religion in an inward experience which was not limited, as they felt, to people of one nation, sect or class. The references Jesus makes to the Old Testament indicate his warm sense of kinship with these great explorers of the Spirit. He stepped into the eternal stream of vital consciousness of God in human life, he collected such as were drawn to him in a warm fellowship, and he trusted the vitality of this transforming experience to create its own forms and bring its own reforms. He gave very little attention to forming a church.[13]

The ever-worsening state of relations between the two superpowers, the United States and the Soviet Union, was never far out of the reach of

Clarence Pickett's mind and heart. Quite suddenly in September, and once again with the assistance of William Lancaster, chief counsel for National City Bank of New York, Clarence Pickett was directly involved in arranging for Yakov (called by Westerners "Jacob") Malik, Gromyko's successor as the USSR's permanent representative to the United Nations, and Dean Rusk, at the time assistant secretary of state for Far Eastern affairs, to meet for completely off-the-record conversations at the Lancaster home in Manhasset, Long Island, New York. With Pickett the principal intermediary, the meeting took place in the evening of Sunday, 1 October. Only Lancaster was present with the two officials.

Monday morning Lancaster reported to Clarence Pickett that the Malik-Rusk conference had been friendly in every way. Rusk pointed out the feelings engendered on the part of Americans by the Berlin blockade, the rigid control of Russia over the satellite countries, and the support of the attack in Korea. Malik said that they were constantly embarrassed by America's backing such governments as Bao Dai in Indochina, the reactionary government in Greece, and nationalist China. The entire conference was held in good humor, with both maintaining a certain official reserve. Lancaster felt that Rusk's reserve was more obvious, that Malik was more outgoing, but actually just as reserved. No specific proposals were arrived at, but Malik told Lancaster that he would be glad to come again for a similar experience. Malik drove Rusk to the station when he had to take the 10:38 p.m. train to New York.

During the very evening that Dean Rusk and Jacob Malik were meeting at the Lancaster home, Clarence Pickett, upon his return to Quaker House, met for a planning session with those Friends who had been brought together to serve as a short-term Quaker United Nations team during the meetings of the fifth UN Assembly. They were Agatha Harrison, an English Friend with close ties to India's leaders; Gerald Bailey, secretary of the East-West Committee of London Yearly Meeting; Elsa Cedergren from Sweden; Heberto Sein from Mexico; Elmore Jackson, now the full time representative at the United Nations for the AFSC as a non-governmental agency recognized by the Economic and Social Council; and Clarence Pickett.

Working as part of the Quaker United Nations team, Clarence Pickett's days were chock-full of appointments with UN delegates at Lake Success and off the record meetings with delegates at Quaker House. Sandwiched between this marathon of interviews was a follow-up con-

versation with Dean Rusk at his office in Washington and a major
address at the Academy of Music in Philadelphia on "Prospects for
Peace." The other speakers were Benegal Rau, head of the Indian
delegation at the UN, Roy Reuther of the United Automobile Workers,
and James P. Warburg, former banker and author of *Faith, Purpose and
Power: A Plea for a Positive Policy.*[14] Said Pickett in part, revealing how
blunt he could be:

> We discuss freely the atheism of the communists. We haven't suffi-
> ciently evaluated our own atheism. If there is a God, and if He is a god of
> love, if all men are His children, then I can see no way that we can
> actually believe in Him and at the same time prepare to squander our
> substance on preparations to blow His children to bits. It is not the
> atheism of others but the atheism of ourselves which is our real threat.[15]

At the time of the Dean Rusk-Jacob Malik confidential meeting Malik
indicated his desire to meet a few representatives of American business.
Following up on that lead, Clarence Pickett, in consultation with Joseph
Willits of the Rockefeller Foundation and his own Consultative Com-
mittee on Foreign Affairs, decided to contact Chester Barnard, presi-
dent of the foundation and formerly, for thirty years, president of the
Bell Telephone Company of New Jersey; Henry Ford II, president of
Ford Motor Co.; and Charles E. Wilson, chairman of the board of
General Electric Co. (not to be confused with Charles E. Wilson, a top
executive at General Motors who became secretary of defense under
President Eisenhower). Chester Barnard was already acquainted with
Clarence Pickett and immediately agreed to the meeting with Malik.

Next on Clarence's list was Henry Ford. Seeking to arrange an interview with Ford for Pickett was Rowan Gaither, Jr., a lawyer closely
associated with the Ford Foundation. On a Friday afternoon in late October, Pickett was informed that Ford would be willing to see him the
following morning in Grosse Pointe, Michigan. Clarence canceled engagements and plans and went to Detroit in the evening by train from
New York.

Arriving in Detroit at eight the following morning, Clarence was
picked up by a chauffeur to go out to Ford's beautiful home on the Lake
Michigan shore. For two and a half hours Ford and Pickett talked about
the plans for a conference of businessmen with Jacob Malik. Ford knew
very little about the Service Committee. As to the conference with Malik,

Ford wanted to know if such a gathering was looked upon with favor by the State Department. Wrote Clarence: "I thought Henry Ford himself should have direct confirmation. So I called Dean Rusk and had him talk directly with Henry Ford."[16] Clarence Pickett found Ford not at all opinionated, quite inclined to learn, and not overestimating his own contribution. Ford arranged transportation for Pickett by air back to New York, enabling him to be home late that evening.

Charles Wilson, whom Clarence already knew, responded eagerly when the suggestion for the conference was presented to him. He expressed the view that nothing was more important than establishing relations with the Russians outside of political circles. He encouraged Clarence to include Frank Abrams, chairman of the board of the Standard Oil Company of New Jersey since 1945, so that "it would not seem that these two foundations [Rockefeller and Ford] were joining in some great secret peace effort."[17]

The conference of the four businessmen and Clarence Pickett with Jacob Malik took place on Sunday, 19 November, again at the home of Mr. and Mrs. William Lancaster in Manhasset, only twenty minutes away from the Soviet residence on Long Island. Mrs. Lancaster served lunch entirely alone in order that servants could not give unwanted publicity to the meeting. The Americans arrived at the home at noon to consult before Mr. Malik's prompt arrival at one o'clock. "He brought with him," wrote Pickett, "the son of the first USSR ambassador, Alexander Troyanowsky, who [that is, the son] as a boy went to the Friends school in Washington. Malik speaks English fairly well, but we suspected that he wanted to have an interpreter (since the interpreter took down notes on what he said) so as to have a record of his own comments. Throughout the meal and thereafter, from 1:00 to 4 o'clock, we talked."[18]

Clarence Pickett felt that the businessmen did a good job in being very frank with Mr. Malik, at the same time maintaining a completely friendly attitude throughout. Malik evidently expressed great appreciation that the four men had taken off a Sunday to talk with him. Pickett helped Malik with his coat, when he excused himself at four o'clock, and raised the question as to whether Malik would like to meet with other such groups. The response was in essence noncommittal. Clarence Pickett took upon himself the responsibility of reporting the gist of the conference to the State Department. This he did in a conversation with Dean Rusk two days later.

In early December a third meeting took place at the Lancasters' home in Manhasset. This time the guests were Clarence and Lilly Pickett, Elmore and Beth (his wife) Jackson, Mr. and Mrs. Jacob Malik, and Mr. and Mrs. Semyon Tsarapkin from the Soviet mission to the United Nations. "From one o'clock to four we spent the time," wrote Clarence, "just visiting, talking about customs and habit and matters of general, common interest in this country and in Russia. . . . As the group was leaving, Mr. Malik took me aside to say that, if the four gentlemen who met two weeks ago at this same place wished to pay a visit to Russia, they would be granted visas if they should apply at the embassy. . . . This, of course, lays upon them, and upon Mr. Lancaster and myself, a very heavy responsibility."[19]

A week later, Pickett had an appointment with Dean Rusk at the State Department. Pickett told him of the invitation from Malik to the four businessmen to visit the Soviet Union, but not on a reciprocal basis as proposed by Charles Wilson, and not with a large group representing various segments of American society. Clarence Pickett argued, however, that the State Department should consider the significance of even four distinguished American businessmen visiting Russia, that such a mission might relax the tension between the two countries. This was Clarence Pickett's repeated argument, namely that there was a place and value in such direct personal approaches. And yet any such visits needed to have the approval of government. His next move was to encourage one or more of the businessmen to talk in person with Rusk.

The People's Republic of China, not recognized by the United Nations, was invited to send a mission to Lake Success in order to participate in discussions relating to Formosa and Korea. Members of the Quaker United Nations team noticed that the Russians were the only delegates who were approaching the Chinese delegates in the corridors and lounges at Lake Success. As members of a recognized nongovernmental organization and as such allowed to circulate in the halls and lounges, these six Friends decided that common decency alone dictated a friendly attitude toward the Chinese. "We are very anxious that they shall not come into a cold climate," Pickett said.[20]

An opportunity soon presented itself. In the delegates' lounge, Agatha Harrison and Clarence Pickett observed that General Wu, leader of the delegation from the People's Republic of China, was sitting alone, and apparently unoccupied. So they introduced themselves to him and had a brief conversation. Clarence wanted particularly to have him know about the Quaker unit in China of twenty men and that the unit was having difficulty in getting permission to move about. Since they were conducting mobile clinics for children who had kala-azar (an insect-spread parasitic disease ninety percent fatal at the time if untreated), the inability to travel was proving to be a great deterrent to the unit's effectiveness. Genereal Wu knew very little about the unit, although he knew something about Quakers.

Clarence was quite interested that at the very moment he and Agatha Harrison stepped up to speak to General Wu, three cameramen came and began to take photographs. Following the conversation, a whole crowd of newsmen swarmed about Clarence and wanted to know whether he was making a peace proposal. He assured them that he was not, and told them the business that he was talking with General Wu about, and gave them substantially the text of the conversation. "But it does indicate how hungry they are for news of any kind about the attitude of the Chinese delegates," observed Clarence.[21]

Interwoven with the Quaker team's involvement with political issues—and the growing awareness of the need for civilian relief in Korea—was a concern hatched by Agatha Harrison that there be a meditation room at the Lake Success UN headquarters. In the process of lining up support for this idea both within the UN administration and the delegations, Clarence Pickett learned from Muhammad Zafrulla Khan, chief delegate from Pakistan, that Khan found it necessary to say his prayers during the day in a telephone booth.

Clarence Pickett and Elmore Jackson moved quickly, first getting the support of Andrew Cordier and through him Trygve Lie, and then approaching delegates from a number of countries. Space for the meditation chamber was carved out of a committee meeting room. The inclusion of a meditation room was already on the architectural drawing boards for the new United Nations headquarters to be located on the East River in New York.

In mid-November Clarence Pickett agreed to debate on the American Forum of the Air on 17 December (both radio and television) with Earle Cocke, national commander of the American Legion, issues centering on universal military training (UMT). Clarence notes in his journal that he undertook the assignment with trepidation. The broadcast was on a Sunday afternoon in Washington, DC.

Clarence started off the discussion, broadening it out to point out that UMT was simply one of a series of major items in preparedness for war, and that he thought he and Mr. Cocke should discuss the whole question of war itself. Clarence pointed out that the United States and other countries had fought in World War I to preserve democracy, yet there was probably less democracy as a result. World War II was fought to kill German and Japanese militarism, but the United States was currently considering rearming those countries. He noted that there were more dictatorships in the world than prior to World War II. Therefore, it seemed to him, that the major question was, "Is war an instrument that can bring the kind of security that we are seeking through preparedness in the military sense?"[22]

On the occasion of this debate Clarence Pickett was asked by a member of the audience the proverbial question put to pacifists:

> Mr. Pickett, if a member of your family was walking down the street a hundred yards from you and you saw a ruffian spring at her, would you resort to prayer, or would you attack the ruffian in order to protect the child?[23]

It is important to hear his reply in his own words. It reveals once again the strength of his mother's influence:

> That is usually put in the form of what would you do if your grandmother was attacked. That is a common question, and I think a glib and easy answer to that is never very much good. It is a very real question. I have never had that kind of test. I do not know what I would do. I do know, however, this—unfortunately my grandmother died before I ever saw her—that my mother would have said she would rather die than to have her son become a murderer. I know that is the output of the kind of life that she taught me to try to live, and that is about the only kind of answer I feel is adequate. I do not want to be glib and say I would of course kneel down and pray. I probably would not do any such thing. I might lose my temper. I might do many things, but I do know what the one who is most precious to me in my childhood would have wanted me to do.[24]

The extent of Clarence Pickett's isolation on issues relating to the buildup of armaments was pointedly illustrated when he attended in

January a meeting of the American Council on Education, made up of about six hundred of the college and university presidents of the country. They were discussing the question of universal military training (UMT). Apart from Thomas Jones, president of Earlham College, Clarence Pickett was the only one who took issue with the principle of military conscription. "I was interested," wrote Pickett, "that there was very generous applause when I finished my presentation, and not that it was any tribute to me, but I think they were genuinely glad to have someone speak out frankly in opposition to universal military training on principle."[25] It was heartening that evening, in a meeting with the board of managers of Haverford College, for Clarence to learn that the College was unwilling to lend itself to any form of military training on its campus.

In respect to UMT, Clarence Pickett undertook special assignments. One of these, in February, was a half-hour broadcast on the issue with Mrs. Roosevelt, with whom he firmly differed regarding UMT. Then in that same month he asked Robert Hutchins, president of the University of Chicago, to speak on the radio in opposition to James Conant, president of Harvard University, on the same issue. Hutchins agreed to the request, already differing sharply with the Administration's point of view on preventing war by military preparedness. This conversation paved the way for Clarence Pickett and Lewis Hoskins to have a two-hour conversation in Chicago in March with Hutchins, a member of the board of trustees of the Ford Foundation, regarding a sizable contribution to the Friends Service Committee from the foundation.

With encouragement from Robert Hutchins and from Paul Hoffman, director of the foundation—the Ford Foundation was initially headquartered in Pasadena, California, where coincidentally Hoffman's son, Hallock, was a leading staff member of the AFSC's Pasadena regional office—the Committee moved into high gear to submit a grant request over the joint signatures of Lewis Hoskins and Clarence Pickett. In mid-April the foundation approved a grant of $500,000 "toward the general objectives of reducing world tensions and improving international understanding."[26] In June, the foundation made a second half-million dollar grant. It is quite evident that Clarence Pickett's extensive acquaintances in the world of big business were partially responsible for these initial broad-based grants from the Ford Foundation, given at a time when the new foundation itself was identifying its program priorities.

As chairman of the American Council of Voluntary Agencies for Foreign Service, Clarence Pickett was involved early in 1951 in the setting up of American Relief for Korea. The initial emphasis was clothing—new and used—with shipping primarily from West Coast ports. Pending permission for private agency personnel to be in the field, distribution of clothing was being made by military authorities. Pickett was successful in persuading the actor Douglas Fairbanks, Jr. to accept the chairmanship of American Relief for Korea, with himself as vice-chairman.

On Sunday, 18 March Clarence Pickett was one of two guests of honor (David Sarnoff, chairman of the board of the Radio Corporation of America, was the other) at a dinner in the ballroom of the Waldorf Astoria Hotel in New York City. The occasion, with an attendance of one thousand persons, was arranged by the Jewish Theological Seminary of America. Sarnoff gave the main speech of the evening. Pickett received the Seminary's first World Brotherhood Award for his "indefatigable and devout humanitarian service to his brethren at home and abroad, regardless of color, nation or creed."[27]

At the end of March Clarence Pickett gave the prestigious William Penn Lecture sponsored by the Young Friends Movement of the two Philadelphia Yearly Meetings. It was the custom to have the text in pamphlet form available for distribution at the close of the lecture. Clarence spent a good deal of time the previous day going over his speech so that he would not have to pay too much attention to the manuscript.

The lecture was given in the historic Friends meetinghouse at 4th and Arch Streets in Philadelphia. The meetinghouse was absolutely packed with some two thousand Friends. Pickett's title was, "And Having Done All, To Stand," a quotation from Ephesians. "I put a good deal of emphasis," he observed, "on the importance of doing everything we could do to influence public action before we find ourselves in the position where we finally have to take a stand against the public and that really what makes standing in opposition effective is having done everything we can beforehand."[28] He touched on issues that were extant in the lives of contemporary Quakers, both young and old. "As men depend more on the power of external force," he said, "we should learn better the arts of the spirit."[29] He spoke for fifty minutes and held the attention of the audience throughout the lecture. Consistent with Quaker practice at the time, a period of silent worship was observed at the conclusion of his address.

Ever since the "retire-
ment" gathering in May of
1950, Clarence and Lilly
Pickett were involved in the
designing and building of
their house on the edge of the
Haverford College campus.
All through the spring of
1951 they would visit from
time to time to see how the
work was progressing. They
also had to make preparations
to move from a large house
not their own to a relatively
small one, this time their
own. The house, sometimes
referred to by Clarence and
Lilly as a "cottage," was
a rambling, white-stucco
rancher with blue trim. A
patio looked out on what was
to become a lovely garden

*In his study, carved out of the Haverford
house attic, Clarence visits with
a neighbor boy*

dominated by a giant oak and a tulip poplar. There was a guest wing
with a separate entrance. Carved out of the attic space was a study for
Clarence Pickett, giving him the assurance of some privacy. Finally the
day, 27 April, for the move arrived. Wrote Clarence: "Movers came at
8:30 this morning, and it was five o'clock before two of the vans were
packed, and six o'clock before we arrived at Haverford, and 9:30 before
we were unloaded. It was an exhausting day. I hope I will never have to
move again; it's too strenuous an undertaking."[30]

Although the American Friends Service Committee report, *The United
States and the Soviet Union,* had little impact on American policy, it did
attract a good deal of public interest. Clarence Pickett was impressed
with the "dissatisfaction in the minds of many people of broad scope
and experience about our [the U.S.] going into a major armament program."[31] Given this response, the Committee decided to raise its voice
again in an examination of American foreign policy. Clarence Pickett

Clarence's study upstairs in the Haverford house gave him some privacy, 1951

was one of fifteen Friends on the so-called working party. The end result of this effort was a sixty-page pamphlet, *Steps to Peace: A Quaker View of U.S. Foreign Policy,* issued in April 1951. The study sought to identify why American policies were failing and how an alternative program might succeed.

It was Clarence's responsibility to circulate *Steps to Peace* to some of the leading Americans with whom he was acquainted. Committee meetings of the National Planning Association provided one such opportunity for feedback. One member, businessman Frank Atschul, said that his faith would not quite rise to the requirements demanded by the pamphlet. "Several others spoke with warm appreciation. Beardsley Ruml took me off to a private room to talk more fully about the nature of the report, its assumptions, etc."[32]

Throughout the year of 1951 there was never a month when Pickett was not exerting himself to arrange for the "visit to the east" of prominent American businessmen. Now that some progress had been made in gaining permission from the Russians, the task was focused on U.S. government officials. Step one was for Clarence Pickett and Elmore Jackson to visit with Philip Jessup, a Friend and at the time special ambassador to the United Nations. He warmly supported the idea and agreed to speak to Secretary of State Acheson. But Charles Wilson, now a cabinet member, reached the secretary first. Wilson's report to Clarence was disheartening: Acheson was not enthusiastic about the proposed visit but had no objection to the issuance of passports for the travelers. Pickett agreed to call together Abrams, Barnard, Ford, and Lancaster, to talk through the question as to whether the visit should really be made.[33]

On 16 October Clarence and Lilly Pickett left for the meeting of the UN General Assembly in Paris. As on previous occasions, the visit to the Continent was preceded by a two-week stopover in England. The Picketts were housed at the Great Western Royal Hotel in London as guests of Paul Cadbury, who, the previous summer, with other English Friends, had visited Russia. Cadbury, with Clarence's assistance, had recently reported in the United States on that trip to a number of prominent Americans.

Relations with the Soviets were at the top of Clarence Pickett's agenda, and he was particularly pleased to have a visit in England with Sarvepalli Radhakrishnan, the Indian ambassador to Moscow and a scholar of distinction. "He has made the unusual arrangement," wrote Clarence, "of teaching for about five months at Oxford [as Spalding Professor of Eastern Religions and Ethics], spending one month in India, and six months in Moscow. He has made friends with and understands the people with whom he has to deal, I think, better than any other ambassador in Moscow. He apparently is deeply appreciated there, although he is anything but in political agreement with them. He has found, as I think all people who deal with Russians do find, that complete frankness is the thing they most want, and he has been completely aboveboard with them. He also is not a diplomat, and that probably is to his advantage."[34]

In Paris, Clarence and Lilly were housed in a little apartment at the Friends Center. The other members of the Quaker United Nations team, also housed at the Quaker Center, were: Percy Bartlett, Agatha Harrison, and Gerald Bailey from Great Britain, Heberto Sein from Mexico, and Elmore Jackson. The next day the six Friends spent the whole morning going through the sixty items on the assembly agenda to determine what issues were the most important to them as a Quaker delegation. On the top of their list was disarmament.

Prior to the opening of the Assembly on 8 November, Clarence Pickett, Elmore Jackson, and Gerald Bailey (who was also among the English Friends who had recently visited Russia) attended a crowded reception at the Soviet embassy. They were able to talk briefly with Jacob Malik, Semyon Tsarapkin, and Andrei Vyshinsky, USSR foreign minister. Vyshinsky "seemed deeply appreciative of the visit of the

English Quaker group to Russia, and said that they had been very frank in their comments, both favorable and unfavorable, as to what they had seen in Russia."[35]

The sixth session of the United Nations Assembly opened on Thursday, 8 November. Secretary of State Dean Acheson was the first principal speaker. Pickett saw it as "a polished address that had in it definite proposals for disarmament. . . . But what disturbed us all [the Quaker delegation] was a long list of charges against Russia, alluding to her and nobody else. While they were not given in a bitter tone of voice, they were set forward in ways that one could see would cut very deeply into the spirit of the Russians, who sat very near the front of the auditorium where Mr. Acheson was speaking."[36] In the afternoon Vyshinsky spoke. "He made about an hour and a half speech," said Clarence, "all of it an attack on what Mr. Acheson had said, and, as Mr. Acheson had made the Russians the devil, so the Russians made the United States the devil. . . . When our delegation got home, we were all almost completely exhausted from having listened to these vigorous attacks from one side and then the other."[37]

The next day the Quaker members, still deeply discouraged by the way in which the UN was being used as a place for two nations to abuse each other, put their minds to what might be done. "The fate of the world, in a sense, is at stake," wrote Clarence. "There is a real possibility that the United Nations may be wrecked by this continual batter [sic] of bitter denunciations."[38] The Quaker delegation decided to fan out to encourage representatives of countries not aligned with either of the two power blocs to speak out against the use of the assembly for propaganda purposes. Another initiative taken was the delivery of a note to British Foreign Secretary Anthony Eden, encouraging him to see his opening speech as an opportunity to lift the basis of discussion from recrimination and accusation to a higher level. Whether it was in response to the message or not, the fact is that Eden rose magnificently to the challenge. "He did it with a sense of earnestness and humility that I am quite sure impressed the audience," wrote Clarence.[39]

The Quaker UN team followed the practice of inviting assembly delegates to the center for dinner and off-the-record conversations. One such evening that Clarence Pickett found especially useful was when Benegal Rau, chief delegate from India, and Kavalam Madhava Panikkhar, who had been the Indian ambassador to China from 1948 to

1952, came to dinner. "He [Panikkhar] does not pretend to defend China," Clarence wrote, "but he does help one to understand how things look to them, and the amount of misunderstanding of the Chinese by us as Americans is perfectly appalling."[40]

At the end of November, Clarence Pickett, Elmore Jackson, and Gerald Bailey spent a long evening with Jacob Malik at the USSR embassy in Paris. The subject was disarmament. Pickett's highly confidential report on those three hours of conversations makes fascinating reading. As was the case with Mr. Gromyko, Malik expressed the Soviet conviction that American industrialists favored heavy armament expenditures because it was good for business. Because Clarence Pickett had heard this argument many times before and was convinced that it was not simply a propaganda line, he answered it with considerable vigor, pointing out that "the more intelligent American industrialist does not want war, or even major war preparations."[41]

Toward the end of the visit, Malik said, "Why can't Quakers do more about the impasse into which we in the political arena seem to get all the time?" Pickett took the occasion to tell Malik of the basic and abiding approach of the Friends Service Committee, how Quakers had gone into a situation of great suffering only to help people in their distress, with no expectation of trying to affect the political scene or to win customers for American business, but simply to help people needing help. Clarence reported on the tremendous response there normally was, with the keyed up bitterness that arises in time of war often soon evaporating. He used Germany after World War I as an illustration.

He then told Malik that whatever status Friends had in talking with delegations at the United Nations arose out of that kind of background and motivation. He posed the question, "Could not that same point of view be accepted by the politicians? Was it not feasible to think of a political leader suggesting that things be done even at loss and expense to the stronger powers merely because they ought to be done and not because they would win allies or some form of economic benefit?"[42]

To this Jacob Malik responded, "That is a truly noble conception." Malik made no qualifications. He said he had the highest respect for Friends and that point of view and for the way in which Friends had tried to work it out. Pickett was interested to see that Malik did not say it would never work in politics. "We sat in silence a considerable time after that," said Clarence, "and I felt that perhaps it was the high moment of our interview."[43]

At the conclusion of the UN General Assembly, the Picketts went home on the *America*, arriving in New York on 24 December. They spent Christmas day with their daughter Carolyn and her family in Moorestown, New Jersey. Blanche Tache, his secretarial assistant, had everything in good order at the office. Clarence was now looking forward to completing work, with help from two staff members, on the autobiographical account of his years as AFSC executive secretary. But, with no end of ongoing commitments, he was not able to cloister himself for sustained attention to this task. With the leading title being *For More Than Bread*, the book would be published in 1953 by Little, Brown and Company.[44]

NOTES

1. News release, 1 Dec. 1950, AFSC archives.

2. News release, 1950.

3. Mildred A. Purnell, "A New Chapter," *Friends Intelligencer* 107, no. 21 (27 May 1950): 315-16.

4. Lilly Pickett oral history, Margaret Hope Bacon, 1972 tape and transcript, courtesy of Margaret Bacon.

5. Lilly Pickett oral history, 10.

6. Interview with Carolyn Pickett Miller, 26 Apr. 1993 and telephone conversation, 3 June 1999.

7. Margaret Hope Bacon, "Lilly Pickett," 1972 (unpublished), courtesy of Margaret Bacon.

8. Purnell, "A New Chapter," 1950.

9. AFSC *Bulletin*, March 1950, 2.

10. Taped interview with Lewis Hoskins, 2 Oct. 1993.

11. Clarence Picket journal, 26 June 1950.

12. Clarence E. Pickett, "The Meaning of Membership in the Society of Friends," given at Western Yearly Meeting of Friends, 15 Aug. 1950, p.12, AFSC archives.

13. Pickett, "Meaning of Membership," p. 4.

14. James P. Warburg, *Faith, Purpose and Power: A Plea for A Positive Policy* (New York: Farrar, 1950).

15. Advance copy of speech to be given by Clarence E. Pickett at the Academy of Music, Philadelphia, Friday, October 13, 1950, AFSC archives.

16. Picket journal (confidential), 28 Oct. 1950.

17. Picket journal (confidential), 20 Nov. 1950.

18. Picket journal (confidential), 19 Nov. 1950.

19. Picket journal (confidential), 3 Dec. 1950.

20. Clarence Pickett to Gilbert Bowles, 21 Nov. 1950, AFSC archives.

21. Picket journal, 30 Nov. 1950.

22. Picket journal, 17 Dec. 1950

23. From the proceedings of the American Forum of the Air, National Broadcasting Company, 17 Dec. 1950, AFSC archives.

24. Proceedings, 1950.

25. Picket journal, 19 Jan. 1951.

26. Letter dated 8 May 1951 from The Ford Foundation.

27. From the text of the award, AFSC archives.

28. Picket journal, 25 Mar. 1951.

29. Clarence E. Pickett, "And Having Done All, to Stand," William Penn Lecture, The Young Friends Movement of the Philadelphia Yearly Meetings, Philadelphia, 1951, 26.

30. Pickett journal, 27 Apr. 1951.

31. Pickett journal, 6 Apr. 1951.

32. Pickett journal, 28 May 1951.

33. Pickett journal, 19 Jan. 1951.

34. Pickett journal, 26 Oct. 1951.

35. Pickett journal, 7 Nov. 1951.

36. Pickett journal, 8 Nov. 1951.

37. Pickett journal, 8 Nov. 1951.

38. Pickett journal, 9 Nov. 1951.

39. Pickett journal, 9 Nov. 1951.

40. Pickett journal, 13 Nov. 1951.

41. Pickett journal (confidential), 30 Nov. 1951.

42. Pickett journal (confidential), 30 Nov. 1951.

43. Pickett journal (confidential), 30 Nov. 1951.

44. Clarence E. Pickett, *For More Than Bread* (Boston: Little, 1953).

Chapter 17

SPEAK TRUTH TO POWER

To me, it seems abundantly clear that there is one moral order and purpose

A REVIEW OF SOME OF CLARENCE PICKETT'S APPOINTMENTS in the single month of January 1952 brings to light the remarkable scope of his religious concerns and undertakings at 68 years of age. After spending New Year's Day at home, Pickett was "back at the office on the regular beat . . . getting a little start on catching up on correspondence. Lewis Hoskins was in for an hour conference, and then we had lunch together."[1] In the evening, Clarence took the train to Washington, DC.

Much of the following morning and afternoon was spent with Harold Snyder, director of the AFSC's Washington Seminars Program, and Gordon Allport, professor of psychology at Harvard University, who was to be the resource leader at the seminar that evening on the subject, "What Youth Around the World is Thinking," drawing on a survey Allport had made in thirteen countries. As usual, Clarence presided at the seminar. He was pleased with the attendance, which included Dorothy Fosdick of the State Department, Luther Evans of the Library of Congress, and Roland Sargeant, director of the Voice of America.

Back in his Philadelphia office the next morning, Clarence pulled together once again the threads of the concern to assemble a delegation of prominent American businessmen for a visit to the Soviet Union. He reported by phone to William Lancaster in New York on the interview he had had the previous afternoon in Washington with Charles Wilson. At noon, Pickett presided at a meeting of one hundred and sixty-five persons who had agreed to work on the financial campaign for the Fellowship Commission and House Fund. Present were a newly-elected member of the Philadelphia City Council, the newly-elected city solicitor, and the newly-elected mayor, Joseph Clark.

Typically, Clarence would spend Saturday at home, catching up on reading and correspondence. Then Sunday morning he and Lilly attended the meeting for worship at their own Providence Meeting in Media, their first since the return from Paris. They were warmly welcomed, and in Clarence's view it was a meeting of real depth.

Monday morning he reported to the AFSC staff on his experiences in Paris, needing to leave halfway through in order to attend, as chairman of the Fellowship Commission, a meeting of the City's Civil Service Commission. In the afternoon he met with two members of the Society of Brothers from Paraguay. He was well acquainted with, and sympathetic to, the Hutterites, whose roots went back to the time of the Radical Reformation of early sixteenth century Europe, when thousands of so-called Anabaptists left the institutional church to seek a life of simplicity, brotherhood, and nonviolence in communal villages or Bruderhofs. He arranged for his visitors to have interviews in New York with appropriate staff members of the Rockefeller and Ford foundations. Later in the year he was instrumental in obtaining a grant for the Society's medical outreach program in Paraguay from the Doris Duke Foundation of which he continued to be the chairperson.

Pickett agreed the following day to be in touch with possible speakers for the annual Fellowship Commission dinner in March, including Clement Attlee, the former British prime minister, and Muhammad Zafrulla Khan from Pakistan. "What we want to do," Pickett said, "is to make a real impact on the community of Philadelphia to understand something of the importance of race in the world today."[2] On Wednesday Clarence reported to the AFSC executive board on the UN Assembly in Paris. The following day he spent several hours with Joseph Willits, director for the Social Sciences of the Rockefeller Foundation, talking over the memorandum Pickett had prepared in response to Willits' request for suggestions as to what were the central reasons for a decline in moral values in the national life and how a foundation could help with the process of restoring those values. In that paper, entitled, "Morals and Modern Life," Pickett made a number of suggestions based on the assumption that there had not been in the past fifty years a growth in the application of moral standards to life comparable to the amazing growth in the impact of science upon our life.[3]

Pickett's specific suggestions included support for the fledgling organization, the Society for Social Responsibility in Science; a study of the material being accumulated in the hearings in the Senate, under the chairmanship of Friend Paul Douglas, on moral standards and political practices; and the sponsorship of a series of addresses in the United States by Albert Schweitzer. Joseph Willits was not entirely satisfied with Pickett's suggestions, evidently feeling that there was "a shortage of saints." "Just how the Rockefeller Foundation can stimulate the production of saints," wrote Clarence, "is not easy to see."[4]

Refreshed from a Sunday spent at meeting for worship and at home, he was confronted on Monday by a request from a group of visitors that he be a candidate for president of the United States, independent of the two major political parties and of the Progressive Party. They thought of him as a peace candidate. He told them he did not see himself as made in the mold of a politician, and he knew that Wayne Marshall, his physician, would not permit him to undertake such a demanding assignment.

The following Tuesday he attended an all-day meeting of the board of the Field Foundation, distributing $325,000. Clarence was particularly interested in the request from the Japanese-American Citizens League for their legal fund to get reimbursement for those who suffered financial losses during the relocation period in the war. Clarence was pleased to note that board members thought they should encourage this group which had stood with so much character during this trying period of relocation and now reestablishment in their homes. This effort on the part of Japanese Americans would not bear fruit until Congress passed (and President Ronald Reagan signed into law) the Civil Liberties Act of 1988, providing for an official apology and monetary reparations to surviving internees. Payments in the amount of $20,000 to more than eighty thousand Japanese Americans began in 1990.[5]

There was little rest the final weekend of the month. On Saturday Clarence attended the annual meeting in Philadelphia of the Friends Social Union, which embraced both Orthodox and Hicksite Friends, to hear a talk by Norval Webb, pastor of the East Main Street Friends Church in Richmond, Indiana. In the afternoon Clarence went to Atlantic City to be one of several Americans to address, at the Dennis Hotel, a group of young German doctors. All involved in the gathering were guests of Howard Buzby, the Quaker proprietor of the hotel.

On Monday, 28 January Clarence was in the office all day, then in the evening spoke at a Parent-Teacher Association meeting of the Moorestown Friends School and public school; Tuesday, in the office and a speech at the Philadelphia Peace Chest luncheon; Wednesday, packing for Florida vacation; then, with Lilly, to Washington for an interview with Charles Bohlen, counselor to Secretary of State Acheson, regarding the businessmen's visit to the East. At 6:45 p.m., Clarence and Lilly Pickett, in the midst of a severe cold snap, took the Seaboard Air Line Railroad's "Silver Meteor" south.

Upon his return from three weeks' vacation in Florida, Clarence was soon at work on the proposed businessmen's visit to the Soviet Union. While the State Department was ready to issue the necessary permissions for the trip, it was unwilling to endorse the visit publicly. Clarence noted that he found himself again carrying the load in respect to the mission. In early April he met with William Lancaster, Charles E. Wilson, and Chester Barnard to think through strategy once again. Later in the month he was unsuccessful in arranging a visit with the newly-appointed ambassador to the USSR, George Kennan. He journeyed to Detroit again to talk with Henry Ford, but the train was two hours late, seriously cutting into the time he had with Ford. But he talked for three hours with Charles Moore, Ford's public relations director, who turned out to be well-acquainted with Friends and was willing to share information with Clarence about Ford and his family.

At the end of May Clarence and Lilly spent another Sunday afternoon at the home of Mr. and Mrs. Lancaster in Manhassett, with Mr. and Mrs. Malik as guests in what was only a social occasion. In June there was a strategy meeting in New York with Lancaster and Wilson. In mid-July Lancaster and Pickett had a two-and-one-half hour session with Malik at the Soviet residence in Glen Cove, Long Island, prior to Malik's return home with his wife and daughter. "We both told him," wrote Clarence, "that we did not believe the present administration would approve of such a visit [by leading American businessmen], that we were prepared to raise the question early in any new administration that might take over January 20 [1953]. . . .[6] Clarence unsuccessfully attempted to get an appointment with Republican vice presidential candidate Richard Nixon to discuss the proposal. Pickett and his Consultative Committee on Foreign Affairs shifted their attention entirely to the idea of a Quaker delegation visiting Russia.

In 1952 Clarence Pickett gave no less than fifty public speeches. Many requests were turned down. The variety of audiences to which he spoke is an indication both of his popularity and of his conviction that these appearances provided an important opportunity to spread his view on critical public issues which he always saw in a broad religious context. And there is no doubt that he experienced a sense of fulfillment from these occasions. He always noted in his journal the estimated number of persons present, whether they were receptive and had good questions. He was almost without fail at his best under these circumstances—articulate, conveying an optimistic spirit even when dealing with depressing and intractable problems, leaving the audience with some ideas as to what might be done about them.

A principal theme, whenever Clarence in these years dealt with international affairs, was to point out the self-defeating discrepancy between private codes of conduct and public principles. In his life and thought he repeatedly emphasized this very central conviction. To hundreds of Quakers gathered at the end of June 1952 for a biennial conference in Cape May, New Jersey, he elaborated on it. It is important to hear just how he put it:

> When there is a difference between the standards of moral conduct we teach in our homes and schools, on the one hand, and the demands made by the state, on the other, we can but suffer cynicism and moral callousness. . . . There cannot be two standards of ethics, one for private dealing and another for public policy. . . . It is not we who have to solve all the problems of the world; the heart of the Eternal is touched by the tragedy of events that are going on. It is the direction in which His spirit tries to move people that we should seek.[7]

In October 1952 Clarence Pickett gave the third annual Ward Lecture at Guilford College in North Carolina. His subject, once again, was "Friends and International Affairs," bringing together his knowledge of the three hundred-year history of the Religious Society of Friends and his deep involvement in current international happenings. Here in this forum he challenged members of his own Quaker faith to see the danger of a new isolationism. "It is the isolation that comes from being the

Elmore Jackson, director of the Quaker United Nations Program, and Clarence Pickett talk in 1952 with Mrs. Vijaya Lakshmi Pandit, president of the UN Eighth General Assembly

privileged, wealthy landowner in the big house on top of the hill who looks down in every direction on poor people who owe him money. And it is difficult to prevent this from isolating him in spirit and sympathy from the rest of the world."[8] Again Pickett called attention to the dichotomy between private and public codes of conduct. "I do not see how a Friend can ever accept this double standard judgment. God does not keep double entry bookkeeping, one entry for states and the other for individuals."[9]

In September 1952 a whole new opportunity came to Clarence Pickett. One of President Truman's secretaries, William Lloyd, phoned to see if Clarence would be willing to serve on the Commission on Immigration and Naturalization just then being appointed by the president. Pickett agreed to serve. The first meeting was in mid-September at the White House, including a short interview with the president. Clarence was impressed with the genuine eagerness that Truman showed to see that something comparable to America's inner strength and idealism be done about immigration and naturalization.[10]

Clarence Pickett agreed to participate as one of several commission members in hearings scheduled for New York, Minneapolis, Chicago, Atlanta, and possibly St. Louis. It was a demanding schedule. The president wanted to submit the commission's report to Congress before it reconvened on 3 January 1953. Typically, commission hearings would take one or two days, with a meeting of the commission itself sandwiched into the end of the first day. Following the two days of hearings in Chicago, Clarence offered a tentative opinion: "I don't see how we can come out of this experience of hearings without feeling there is a strong desire on the part of many people in the country for a more liberal policy than that decided upon by the Congress in its 1952 legislation [the McCarran-Walters Immigration and Nationality Act passed on 27 June over the president's veto]."[11]

The Seventh General Assembly of the United Nations opened on 14 October 1952. There was a preliminary dedication of the new UN headquarters on the East River in New York City. The more formal dedication would come later. The building included a small chapel on the first floor, suitable to all faiths, but a bit more publicly located than Clarence might have hoped. The Quaker United Nations team consisted of Gerald Bailey (UK), Agatha Harrison (UK), Elmore Jackson (U.S.), Sigrid Lund (Norway), Heberto Sein (Mexico), and Clarence Pickett. Many of the same issues discussed at the previous assembly were on the agenda: the working out of an armistice in Korea, the relationship of southwest Africa to South Africa, the need for multilateral disarmament. With Quaker House located just a few blocks from the UN building, the international Friends team strongly emphasized off-the-record meetings at the house with delegates and others.

There were some particular nations to which the Quaker team looked for leadership within the international community. India was one of these. Clarence

Pickett's increasingly close relationship with Prime Minister Nehru's sister, Mrs. Vijaya Lakshmi Pandit, represented a rich resource for the Quaker UN team. At the Seventh UN Assembly she headed the Indian delegation. The following year she would become president of the assembly.

Clarence never missed an opportunity to visit with Mrs. Pandit. On one evening of the seventh assembly the Quaker team was invited to her apartment for supper, which she herself cooked. "Mrs. Pandit was just lovely," he wrote, "talking about her experiences here and the reactions she always has to American life. She told us something about her visit with President-elect Eisenhower."[12] Clarence Pickett believed that it was unlikely that anyone representing Mahatma Gandhi's native country at the United Nations would profess to be in every sense a follower of Gandhi, yet, he felt, "there is in the plea of that delegation the same resounding call to moral values, to spiritual forces, to the deep in human life, and for this one is profoundly grateful."[13]

The report of the President's Commission on Immigration and Naturalization was issued on schedule at the very end of 1952. Clarence Pickett was pleased to see that *The New York Times* on 2 January gave almost four columns to the report, published a full page of excerpts from the report, and editorially endorsed the proposals. Among the Commission recommendations was the abolition of the quota system based on national origin and the substitution of a unified quota system without regard to national origin, race, creed, or color. Senator Patrick A. McCarran of Nevada severely condemned the report and singled out for criticism commission members Clarence Pickett and Earl G. Harrison, dean of the University of Pennsylvania law school and a former U.S. commissioner of immigration, McCarran noted that the two were sponsors of organizations considered by some to be communist fronts. These criticisms were promptly refuted in the press by Eleanor Roosevelt.[14] Coincidentally, the next week, Mrs. Roosevelt made a first-time overnight visit to the Picketts' Haverford home in conjunction with a speaking engagement at Haverford College.

While Clarence himself did not take charges of connections with alleged communist front organizations seriously, the American Friends Service Committee could not afford to brush them aside without careful documentation of Pickett's multiple affiliations, because the publication, *Counterattack,* reflecting the continuing McCarthyism of the period, was being widely circulated and was filled with inaccurate information. Given his strong views on the armaments buildup and the need for U.S./USSR reconciliation, Pickett became a perfect target for anti-communist ideologues.

The accusations were to pursue Clarence Pickett in one form or another for the rest of his days. Indeed, in early June 1953 when he was asked to speak on the subject of immigration at a hearing set up by a subcommittee of the House Judiciary Committee, Pennsylvania Congressman Francis Eugene Walter, the co-sponsor of the McCarran-Walter Act and soon to become chairman of the Un-American Activities Committee, jumped up as Clarence Pickett was seating himself.

He wanted to know if Clarence Pickett was a member of the board of the American Committee for the Protection of the Foreign Born (an organization which Clarence thought was doing worthwhile work). Pickett told him that he understood that Senator McCarran had made that statement in public, but that he had no record of ever having been on the board or even a sponsor, and that he had written to the organization and asked them to search their files. They had done so and had found no such record. Walter said that that record was in the Un-American Activities Committee's files, and Pickett appealed to him to be good enough to get it removed from the files as an incorrect statement, and also expressed the hope that more sense of public responsibility might be assumed by those who put material in those files.[15]

Following a series of other questions, including "Are you a communist?" to which Pickett answered, "No," Congressman Emmanuel Celler from New York, who was presiding at the hearing, intervened, saying that this questioning was all foolishness since he knew Clarence Pickett and the American Friends Service Committee. "I was interested," wrote Clarence, "to see how exercised, nervous and red in the face Congressman Walter was. I would think that he must lead a very unhappy life."[16]

A year later, confronted by a similar accusation of membership in organizations on the attorney general's list of alleged communist fronts, Clarence was more outspoken: "This time it seems to be three committees, one of them I have never heard of, and none of them have I ever belonged to. This system of being accused secretly is a vicious and abominable practice, just like the kind of thing that Germany did in Hitler's time, and we shall have to hit it square on the head one of these times. I hope I can choose the right time to play my part in exposing the viciousness of the system."[17] Pickett did indeed play a part in fighting the libelous practice. He became, in 1962, chairman of the Ad Hoc Committee to Abolish HUAC (the House Un-American Activities Committee) and then òne of the three honorary chairman of the National Committee to Abolish HUAC. Clarence Pickett also became at this time an active member of the National Committee to Repeal the McCarran Act.

A far more congenial event in Washington early in the year was the presentation to Clarence Pickett by Heinz Krekler, the *charge d'affaires* of the Federal Republic of Germany, of the Order of Merit—Grosses Verdienstkreuz—bestowed upon Pickett the previous November by the president of the republic, Theodor Heuss. The citation read in part:

> In conferring upon you this decoration, my government wishes to express its profound appreciation of the work which you, as executive secretary of the American Friends Service Committee, carried out to fight hunger and hopelessness among the German people in one of its darkest days. . . . It wishes to honor you, and through you the Society of Friends, and all those who support it.[18]

Krekler said that as a young boy he had been fed by the Quakers after World War I.

At the very beginning of July 1953 Clarence and Lilly Pickett sailed from Hoboken, New Jersey, to Europe, Clarence's seventeenth crossing, Lilly's ninth. The purpose was to vacation, to visit Quaker centers in Amsterdam, Berlin, and Geneva; to attend a Quaker conference and German Yearly Meeting in Berlin; and to participate in two conferences, organized by the AFSC, in Clarens, Switzerland, for younger officials assigned to their countries' foreign offices in Europe.

Upon the Picketts' return from Europe, the principal item on Clarence's agenda was the session of the United Nations Eighth General Assembly. Again, Pickett headed the Quaker international team, which every Wednesday morning at 9:00 held a Quaker meeting for worship in the UN meditation room. Principal issues of concern to Clarence Pickett were the plight of Palestinian refugees in the Middle East, the strains between India and the United States, racial segregation in South Africa, and the peaceful use of atomic energy.

In early October the Washington seminars over which Pickett presided resumed under the administrative leadership of Harold Snyder. Clarence Pickett was now also presiding again over Fellowship Commission meetings in Philadelphia in his capacity as president. It was to this organization that he was now making his primary contribution in the field of race relations.

In mid-January 1954 Clarence and Lilly took off for another trip to the West Coast, again traveling entirely by train. Apart from an all-day stopover in Chicago during which they visited with members of the new Lake Forest Friends Meeting, they went directly to Caldwell, Idaho to visit with Peckham relatives, forty-strong as it turned out, and for Clarence to fulfill two speaking engagements, one at the local Methodist church and the other at the chapel of Greenleaf Academy. After the five days in Caldwell, the Picketts traveled to the West Coast, their schedule now to be in the hands of the AFSC regional offices in Portland, Seattle, San Francisco, and Pasadena. The record shows that Clarence Pickett gave a dozen public addresses, two press conferences, two radio broadcasts, had speaking engagements at eight Friends meetings, and was a resource leader at an institute of international relations. After a week of vacation at Laguna Beach, California, the Picketts went on to San Antonio and Austin, Texas and to Richmond, Indiana, Clarence again fulfilling engagements made by AFSC offices in those cities.

The Picketts arrived home from the West in time for sessions of the two Philadelphia Yearly Meetings, now, through the work of joint committees, moving towards an ending of the great 1825 Separation in the Religious Society of Friends. Of primary concern to Philadelphia Quakers was the explosion of the hydrogen bomb earlier in the month at Bikini Atoll in the Marshall Islands. With a yield of fifteen megatons, the bomb was a thousand times more powerful than the bomb dropped on Hiroshima. An appointed committee including Clarence Pickett and Elizabeth Gray Vining determined that an interview with President Eisenhower should be sought. The American Friends Service Committee, Brethren Service Commission, and Mennonite Central Committee jointly placed an advertisement in *The New York Times* with the heading, "No Man Can Serve Two Masters," with the message reading in part

> Today the cross of Christ stands in the shadow of the cross of hydrogen. Two crosses: one standing for redemptive love and forgiveness, for the acceptance of suffering, for hope, for life; the other for hatred and massive retaliation, for the infliction of suffering, for fear, for death. One proclaims that evil is overcome by good, the other that evil can only be met with evil. . . . "Not by might, nor by power, but by my spirit, saith the Lord."[19]

Early in the summer Clarence Pickett and twelve other Friends began work on the fourth AFSC pamphlet in the series of studies on possible ways to ease tension and move toward international peace. The "working party" included pacifists with somewhat differing points of view, but all believed it was time to present an alternative to an American foreign policy based on military strength. Chairman of the panel was Stephen Cary, who had been prominently involved in the development of the three previous studies, *the United States and the Soviet Union, Steps to Peace,* and *Toward Security Through Disarmament.* Clarence Pickett's participation in the writing of the fourth pamphlet, entitled *Speak Truth to Power: A Quaker Search for An Alternative to Violence,* was to demand many hours of his time for the balance of the calendar year.

Clarence and Lilly Pickett began their summer vacation by spending a weekend at the Buck Hill Falls colony, Clarence lecturing Sunday evening on the specialized agencies of the United Nations. Then they drove to Woodstock, Vermont, for a week with their friends, the Thomas Harveys and another week at the Lake Mohonk Mountain House in New Paltz, New York. Owned and operated by the Smileys, a Quaker family, the hotel is embraced by seventy-five hundred acres of woodlands, with a full measure of trails. The Picketts were guests of the Smiley family, Clarence's only obligation being to speak at the Sunday morning church service. Observed Pickett: "They are accustomed to having a sermon and being a little bit impressed with it, but not getting excited about it."[20]

In mid-August Clarence Pickett went to the federal court in Philadelphia to explain to the judge the point of view of the Religious Society of Friends concerning its young men who refused to register or to have anything to do with the draft. The young man before the court was Vail Palmer, a member of the Friends Meeting at Fourth and Arch Streets in Philadelphia. Palmer was taking the "absolutist" position and had already served a year and a day in a federal prison. Clarence found the judge eager to understand Palmer's position. At the end of the proceeding the judge sentenced Palmer to three years in prison, but paroled him at once, saying that he saw no good purpose in returning him to jail. He was fined $500. Under the advice of his lawyer, who saw the proceeding as an important test case, Palmer appealed the decision, considered "fair" by Pickett, to the Third Circuit Court of Appeals (in Philadelphia). The court upheld the conviction by a 4-3 vote. The U.S. Supreme Court declined to review the decision of the Circuit Court.

Responding to an appeal from Clarence Pickett and George Walton,who also had appeared in court on Vail Palmer's behalf, a number of Friends quickly came forward with funds to pay the $500 fine and to help defray costs of printing legal briefs."[21]

Whether at his office in Philadelphia or at home, Clarence was frequently on the phone. "How time-consuming telephone calls can be!" he said. "Today I have been working on getting Senator [William] Fulbright [of Arkansas] to come for lunch with the trustees of the New Hope Foundation, getting Senator [James] Duff [of Pennsylvania] to speak at the Fellowship Commission, the mayor [of Philadelphia] to join us in a party to honor Norman Thomas, and writing an article for *The Friend*. It hasn't been a very busy day, but these telephone calls mean that you have to be on the alert, and I find when the day is over that I am a little tired."[22]

It was not always Pickett who was taking the initiative to see government officials. He was at a meeting on technical assistance at Haverford College one day when Lilly Pickett phoned him to say that Congressman William G. Bray of Indiana had come to see him at the house unannounced. Bray was very much disturbed over tensions in the Formosa Straits. President Eisenhower had received full authority from Congress to take whatever military action he deemed necessary to repel a Chinese Communist assault on Chiang Kai Shek and his Nationalist army on Formosa (Taiwan). On 22 January the President ordered three aircraft carriers from Pearl Harbor to join the Seventh Fleet which was patrolling the Formosa Straits. Wrote Clarence:"[We] worked out a way by which he can share his concern with someone in the State Department. Ordinarily it seems that Congressmen have very little, if any, access to the Department. . . . He seemed a great deal relieved after our two or three hours' conversation, although I didn't feel we had actually gone very far in finding a solution to the problem he faces, but he wants to talk, and that in itself may be a help."[23]

On 1 April the Picketts were the subjects of Edward R. Murrow's weekly "Person to Person" television program. Clarence mentions in his journal how there were fifteen CBS workmen who arrived at noon with three cars, two trucks, two cameras, and twenty floodlights. It was Lilly this time who wrote an eight-page single-spaced typed report about the event: "If you want to have for yourself a peck of surprises regarding the wonders of modern science in general and television in particular, just wait until Edward R. Murrow asks you if you would be willing to appear with him on his "Person to Person" television program in your own home."[24] Well in advance of the day of the program, additional telephone lines were installed, and an electrical crew installed a cable to tap into Haverford College circuits.

Lilly Pickett's well-written account of the great event, with children and grandchildren and hordes of neighbors watching, is a period piece, capturing the early days of television production before the use of sophisticated cameras and satellite transmissions. Murrow, who never left his studio in New York during the interview, was pleased with the Picketts' performance, which was followed by a segment with Marlon Brando on the West Coast. Clarence felt that it was "an incredibly short time," with one question that had been planned being left out. Edward Murrow estimated that twenty-five million people had watched the program. At midnight, as the CBS crew was still gathering up equipment, Clarence left for Chicago.

Toward the end of April Clarence Pickett was engaged in one of his marathon-like trips to the Midwest. Following a day of discussions about disarmament with representatives of the Quaker lobby, Friends Committee on National Legislation, Pickett left for Iowa City via Chicago. In the evening he spoke to a community meeting on the role of voluntary agencies at the United Nations. The next morning he was at Penn College, where he spoke at the chapel. In the afternoon he visited the AFSC Des Moines office and talked with the editor of the *Des Moines Register* who had taken a leading part in arranging for a visit of some Russian farmers to Iowa and some Iowa farmers to the USSR.

Then Clarence went on to Minneapolis where he met for lunch with a small group of professionals and businessmen, U.S. foreign policy being the topic. The following morning, a Sunday, Clarence spoke at the local Friends Meeting and in the evening lectured there on "Friends and International Affairs." Then he took the sleeper for Chicago, and from there another sleeper for Buffalo. Following an evening and well-attended meeting at the Collins Friends Meeting south of Buffalo, he took the train to New York. The next morning he and Lewis Hoskins met with Jewish leaders to consider the possibility of the American Friends Service Committee administering the Hadassah Hospital in Jerusalem.

Clarence reached home in time for an engagement at Haverford College, but the next morning was off to New York again, first for a long meeting with the secretary of the Doris Duke Foundation and then in the afternoon a meeting at Quaker House, "thinking further about next steps concerning the Gaza-Israel situation." The following morning he had a conversation on the same subject with Ralph Bunche; then "back to Philadelphia where Lewis Hoskins and I met with Leo Szilard. He is one of the atomic scientists who helped create the bomb but is now very anxious to prevent its use."[25]

The executive committee of the AFSC board proposed to Clarence Pickett in March that he relinquish the post and title of honorary secretary at the end of April and "retire from active responsibility to the Committee as executive secretary emeritus."[26] While Pickett would then, as of 1 May, shift over to pension income, an office and secretary (Blanche Tache on a part-time basis) would still be provided. The executive board approved of this new arrangement, minuting its appreciation once again for Clarence Pickett's life and witness:

> Trusting people himself, he has brought them to trust one another. He has made it his business in life to help people understand and to share his faith that it is not by might but by God's spirit that men and nations have greatness. His own clarity of mind and integrity of soul have been an inspiration to all who know him.[27]

It seems fitting that, quite coincidentally in the last week of his service as honorary secretary, Clarence Pickett called on Mrs. Ruth B. Shipley on the final day of her twenty-seven years as chief of the Passport Office of the State Department, to thank her for her many kindnesses to the Service Committee and to wish her well in her retirement. As for himself, the new emeritus status would not result in any diminution of his undertakings. Indeed, he would be accepting wholly new tasks and challenges.

NOTES

1. Pickett journal, 2 Jan. 1952.

2. Pickett journal, 8 Jan. 1952.

3. Clarence E. Pickett, "Morals and Modern Life" prepared for Rockefeller Foundation, 28 Jan. 1952, AFSC archives.

4. Pickett journal, 28 Jan. 1952.

5. Information based on a letter dated 28 Feb. 1996 from George Oye, a Friend and former internee.

6. Pickett journal, 16 July 1952.

7. Clarence E. Pickett, "Religious Concern and International Action," *Friends Intelligencer* 109, no. 35 (30 Aug. 1952): 492-93.

8. Clarence E. Pickett, "Friends and International Affairs," Ward Lecture, Guilford College, North Carolina, 22 Oct. 1952, 21, family papers, courtesy of Carolyn Pickett Miller.

9. Ward Lecture, 1952, 22.

10. Pickett journal, 17 Sept. 1952.

11. Pickett journal, 9 Oct. 1952.

12. Pickett journal, 8 Dec. 1952.

13. Undated article for *United Nations World,* AFSC archives.

14. Eleanor Roosevelt, "Pointed Penn," *Philadelphia Inquirer,* 15 Jan. 1953.

15. Pickett journal, 10 June 1953.

16. Pickett journal, 10 June 1953.

17. Pickett journal, 21 May 1954.

18. An address by Dr. Heinz L. Krekler, charge d'affaires of the Federal Republic of Germany, at the presentation of the Order of Merit to Mr. Clarence E. Pickett on 16 January 1953. AFSC archives.

19. *The New York Times,* 16 Apr. 1954 (Good Friday) AFSC archives.

20. Pickett journal, 8 May 1954.

21. Letter to author from Vail Palmer, 14 Apr. 1999.

22. Pickett journal, 28 Dec. 1954.

23. Pickett journal, 5 Feb. 1955.

24. Lilly Pickett, Edward R. Murrow's "Person to Person" program, Columbia Broadcasting System, 1 Apr. 1955, family papers, courtesy of Carolyn Pickett Miller.

25. Pickett journal, 21 Apr. 1955.

26. Memorandum, Lewis Hoskins to Clarence Pickett, 24 Mar. 1955, AFSC archives.

27. Minute signed by Henry J. Cadbury, chairman, 4 May 1955.

Chapter 18

EXECUTIVE SECRETARY EMERITUS

*The fresh growth of the Spirit coming out of the fertile soil
of a lifelong dedication to service*

IN THE MIDDLE OF MAY 1955 CLARENCE PICKETT LEFT NEW YORK on
the *Parthia*, first for brief stays in England, Sweden, and Finland, and
then, with five other American Friends, a month-long visit in the
Soviet Union. The visit was the culmination of efforts begun four years
earlier to gain permission, as the published report on the Russian visit
states it, "to seek out worshippers of God, to bring them greetings
and encouragement, and to share with them the fellowship of the
Holy Spirit."[1] The Americans followed in the footsteps of seven English
Quakers who, in 1951, visited the USSR on a goodwill mission. The
trip was organized through Intourist, the commercial Soviet agency for
handling tourists. They were not guests of any organization; the AFSC
paid all expenses.

Clarence Pickett was the senior member of the group with his broad
background of international experiences and contacts with Russians as
an observer at the United Nations. His Quaker compatriots were Hugh
Moore, AFSC finance secretary; Stephen Cary, head of the AFSC American Section; Wroe Alderson, a marketing economist; Eleanor Zelliot,
assistant to the editor of *The American Friend* based in Richmond,
Indiana; and William Edgerton, a specialist in Russian literature and
fluent in the Russian language. The group flew from Helsinki, Finland,
to Leningrad on 2 June. After checking in at the hotel, all of them went

immediately to a Baptist church service and, with William Edgerton interpreting, spoke to a sea of two thousand enthusiastic church members. "We felt very close to the worshipping Baptists," the report read, "and knew we were among, as Wroe Alderson put it, a cloud of witnesses. The singing and the handkerchief-waving noted by other visitors were very meaningful to us also."[2]

After two days in Leningrad the Quaker visitors flew to Moscow where their meetings with evangelical Baptists matched the experiences in Leningrad. At the Moscow Baptist Church, the only one in the capital city, Clarence Pickett preached to an estimated three thousand people, with still others unable to get into the jammed church. The text for his sermon was, "Blessed Are the Peacemakers," but unfortunately the Intourist interpreter was a Russian who knew nothing about the Bible and who, according to Quaker group member William Edgerton, translated "peacemakers" as "the partisans of peace, or freedom fighters."[3]

While contacts and meetings with religious groups in the Soviet Union were the primary focus of the visit of the six Friends, an equally important objective was to be exposed to a broad range of places, people, and institutions in the USSR and thereby to be able, upon return to the United States, to share impressions of Soviet life. The ninety-five page printed report, *Meeting the Russians: American Quakers Visit the Soviet Union*, stated the visitors' basic approach:

> We hoped that our journey might serve as a symbol to the Russians of the goodwill and the desire for peace that we believe to be deeply rooted in the hearts of Americans. . . . We were not unaware of the nature of communist beliefs and practices, and we were conscious of our obligation to make the journey not only with open minds and open hearts, but also with open eyes. In our contacts with Soviet citizens during our visit and in our reports to our fellow citizens after our return home, we were determined to try to maintain a single standard of honesty and goodwill, keeping both groups in mind whenever we spoke to either.[4]

This was an important statement. It especially reflected Clarence Pickett's long-standing principle of being open and even-handed about his views. While on many occasions he was accepting invitations to social events at the Soviet embassy and welcoming, indeed seeking, opportunities to talk with Soviet officials, he was quite frank about where he stood in respect to the Soviet regime. As early as 1933 he indirectly stated his view in a letter to Joseph Stalin, appealing to him "to use consideration and the deepest human sympathy for those who differ from you in their political and philosophic views."[5] At the annual dinner of the American Russian Institute in New York in June 1948, with Andrei Gromyko present, he had flatly declared his position regarding communism and dictatorships.

Throughout the visits, Clarence Pickett was seen and dealt with by the Russians as the senior member of the group. Stephen Cary tells how Intourist, despite Marxist egalitarian pretensions, would give Clarence favored treatment. In one case he was assigned a hotel room with a grand piano. Nevertheless, it was a fact of life that Clarence Pickett was the member of the mission who had wide personal contacts. When the group was in Moscow, it was he who led the way in calling on U.S. ambassador Charles Bohlen, whom he had known in Washington. It was Clarence Pickett who was usually the point of contact with the foreign press, such as Clifton Daniel of *The New York Times*, and William Worthy, correspondent for the *Baltimore Afro-American*.

And it was Pickett who was able to arrange for an interview with acting Soviet foreign minister Andrei Gromyko the day before the group (with the exception of William Edgerton) left the USSR. In that fifteen-minute interview Pickett gave Gromyko a copy of an AFSC statement on Russian proposals for disarmament. Clarence characterized the meeting as very satisfactory, finding the foreign minister cordial and responsive. In reply to a question about taking undeveloped film out of the country, Gromyko said that the Quakers' luggage did not need to be checked at all.

Clarence Pickett returned to the United States on the *Media*, following a stop in Berlin and London, arriving home Saturday night, 16 July, but in time to be able to attend meeting for worship at Providence Friends Meeting Sunday morning. Weary as he was from the trip to the Soviet Union, he was nevertheless in Washington the following Tuesday with Wroe Alderson to have lunch with seven members of the Senate Foreign Relations Committee, to see Walter Stoessel, who was responsible for Russian affairs in the State Department, and to meet with those attending two Washington seminars. "They asked good questions," said Pickett, referring to all of these meetings, "seemed very much interested, and we had no sense of hostility because we had visited a communist country."[6]

Throughout the rest of the year Clarence Pickett, along with other members of the Russian delegation, was booked solid with speaking engagements on the USSR trip. While a confidential journal had been duplicated and circulated to a small number of persons at the time of the journey, the printed report, *Meeting the Russians*, very much an interpretative piece, was not published until the next year. It seemed to the AFSC Public Relations Department that every Friends meeting in the country was wanting to have a first-hand report from a delegation member, particularly Clarence Pickett. Clarence did pick up on some of these Quaker invitations, but more often he was reserved for either private interviews or non-Quaker audiences. In September he reported on the visit to Soviet ambassador Georgi Zarubin. Later in the month he spoke with editors of the *Providence* (Rhode Island) *Journal*, and, in the space of three days, with students and faculty of three New England universities.

In August 1955 a whole new opportunity opened up for Clarence Pickett. He was asked by the nominating committee of Friends General Conference (FGC), the Hicksite national association responsible for biennial gatherings and the publication of educational literature, to be chairman of the conference. In that capacity he would preside at the biennial conferences, at meetings of the roughly one hundred member central committee, assembling once a year, and its smaller executive committee, meeting three or four times a year.

Pickett was drawn to the offer because earlier in the year, the divisions caused by the Separation of 1825 had ended, the two Philadelphia Yearly Meetings (Hicksite and Orthodox) had united into one body; the same step was taken by the two New York Yearly Meetings, and three yearly meetings in Canada united into one Canadian Yearly Meeting. These actions brought into Friends General Conference new members and new opportunities, developments in which Clarence Pickett was keenly interested. As a former pastor and executive in the Five Years Meeting of Friends, the national association of yearly meetings based in Richmond, Indiana, Clarence was already recognized as a sensitive ecumenical Friend.

His informal investiture as chairman of Friends General Conference took place on 1 October 1955. While Clarence Pickett was known for his work with the American Friends Service Committee, he was not personally very well known to many of the FGC leaders, some of whom, while liberal theologically, were quite conservative in respect to social and economic issues. Almost immediately Pickett was involved in plans for the 1956 biennial conference to be held the following June in Cape May, New Jersey, a week-long gathering traditionally attended by two thousand or more Friends including hundreds of children.

Clarence Pickett's involvement in the structural workings of the Religious Society of Friends during this period of his life was also reflected in the amount of time he devoted to attending the sessions of the Five Years Meeting of Friends held 23-26 October 1955 in Richmond, Indiana. Immediately following that gathering, Clarence headed to Germantown, Ohio for a week-long meeting of the Friends World Committee for Consultation, the worldwide body responsible for informally knitting together the disparate yearly meetings of the Religious Society of Friends. Writing about the occasion, Pickett noted that a good deal of emphasis was placed on the period for worship each morning. "This probably is a good thing," he said, "because there are matters to be decided of great importance to world Quakerism, and they need to be carried forward in a spirit of humility and devotion."[7]

On the very last day of the year, Clarence and Lilly Pickett left home for Hawaii, to be away for two and a half months. Of course, the visit to the West Coast before and after the vacation in Hawaii included speaking engagements for Clarence. The AFSC regional offices were always aggressive in arranging such opportunities. In Honolulu Clarence and Lilly were guests of his sister Minnie, now eighty-eight years old, and husband, Gilbert Bowles. Clarence gave twelve public addresses while on vacation, most of them about the Russian visit.

With Lilly Pickett detouring to Caldwell, Idaho for a visit with relatives and friends, Clarence arrived home in time for sessions of the united Philadelphia Yearly Meeting. At one of the sessions the Meeting decided that a delegation of three Friends should travel to Montgomery, Alabama to visit the mayor and other city leaders and to meet African American leaders. It was almost nine months to the day since the seamstress, Rosa Parks, had refused to move to the back of a city bus in order to release a place for a white man, her arrest precipitating a bus boycott by African Americans. Many Friends in the yearly meeting were deeply supportive of the Gandhian approach Martin Luther King, Jr. was taking in the leadership role thrust upon him in the crisis.

It is interesting to note how the yearly meeting's decision to send three members to Montgomery developed. On the occasion of the report of the Peace Committee, the committee proposed that "the Yearly Meeting send a letter to the citizens in Montgomery, Alabama, who are involved in an acutely difficult interracial situation."[8] Consideration of the proposal by the hundreds of members, each with an equal right to participate, proved to be inconclusive, and the presiding clerk suggested that the concern be carried over to the next morning's session. That delay gave George Hardin, the dynamic secretary of the Peace Committee, an opportunity, on his own initiative, to be in touch by phone with Martin Luther King, Jr., who welcomed the idea of a delegation of Friends; with Thomas Thrasher, minister of the Episcopal Church of the Ascension, who also welcomed the visit; and with W. A. Gayle, mayor of Montgomery, who said, "You all don't need to bring your guns down here. We are a civilized people and will welcome your efforts to get rid of this here boycott business."[9]

These initiatives were reported to the morning session on 27 March with the proposal that "as soon as possible Clarence Pickett and one or two other Friends go to Montgomery in the spirit of compassionate love and under a sense of Divine guidance."[10] The meeting approved the proposal. The two other Friends, selected at a later time, were Dorothy Steere, a well-known and respected member of Radnor Friends Meeting, west of Philadelphia, and George Hardin.

They left by train at midnight on 12 April, arriving in Montgomery the evening of the following day. En route, the three Friends talked at length about the upcoming visit, Clarence Pickett emphasizing that it should be "a team venture." The written statement of purpose read in part:

> We are aware that there is no simple, easy answer to the problems with which you are faced. We come in humility, to learn as much as we can from both sides, and to give support and encouragement to the creative potentialities we believe exist in both groups toward bringing about a solution which does not compromise basic human dignity.
>
> We bring Christian greetings to both parties of this conflict, holding you in our hearts as you search for answers, and for that spirit of God which is in all men.[11]

Together the three Friends met some of the principals on both sides of the conflict. Since Mayor Gayle was out of town, they met with Joseph Azbell, city editor of the Montgomery *Advertiser* who, according to Clarence, "took great pains to tell us the whole story of race relations in Alabama, and, with a good deal of understanding and sympathy, told us both sides."[12]

In the evening of their first day, delegation members met for a pot-luck supper with white moderates, who were finding themselves con-sidered as radicals by segregationists. On that occasion the three Friends learned that negotiation in respect to the narrow issue of bus seating was no longer acceptable to Montgomery African Americans. They were now interested in freedom and full citizen rights.

The next morning, a Sunday, the Quaker group first went to the Sun-day school at the (white) Dexter Avenue Methodist church, and then to the Dexter Avenue Baptist Church, of which Martin Luther King, Jr. was the pastor. The sermon was delivered that morning by an African American minister from Chester, Pennsylvania. Clarence Pickett was asked to speak briefly about the concern under which the Quaker group had come to Montgomery. In the afternoon the Friends attended a biracial meeting called by the Alabama Human Relations Council. That afternoon the mayor's office arranged for Clarence Pickett to see the commissioner of police, Clyde Sellers. Said Pickett: "I was well received. I said to him, as I went into his office, 'I suppose you're saying, what right does this man, Pickett, have to be butting into our affairs down here?' 'No,' he said, 'we know what is going on is of public interest. We have had a lot of visitors. Glad to have you.'"[13]

Clarence Pickett described Sellers as an agreeable person who seemed "not unappreciative" of the call and who described himself as a reli-gious man. Sellers noted that he and the mayor had joined the White Citizens Council and that their political influence had resulted in a ma-jor increase in the council membership. Clarence felt that Sellers was determined to prevent any break in the line that would yield to the Afri-can American side of the debate. Clarence praised the police commis-sioner for the order he had issued to all police to abstain from any acts of violence in connection with the boycott.[14]

It was the experience of talking with Martin Luther King, Jr., first after the service at the Dexter Avenue Baptist Church and then the following day with him and his wife, Coretta, at their home, that re-sulted in the most lasting impressions for the three Friends. George Hardin recalled in later years how he examined the screen door from which the bomb thrown at the King home on 30 January had bounced back into the yard before exploding: "That gave me a new feeling and mind-set to the journey. We're dealing with the real thing, with limited time for discussion and prayer."[15]

What most impressed Clarence Pickett was that prior to the bomb-throwing the Kings had been receiving some twenty to thirty anonymous hostile calls a day threatening them, but since that event when King returned to the house and appealed successfully to a crowd of angry, armed "Negroes" [*sic*] to return home, saying that they must meet hate with love, only one hostile call had been received. King "felt that the attitude he took showed the redemptive quality of such a position in a time of stress."[16]

In the evening of their last day in Montgomery the three Friends attended a mass meeting at one of the large Baptist churches, with about seven hundred or more persons filling the church when they arrived, with more in the basement and in the street listening through loudspeakers. There was "real singing" when the meeting began. Then Martin Luther King, Jr., who had returned from a two weeks' vacation, was welcomed back and later made an announcement of gifts that had come in for the bus boycott and of the purchase of a number of new station wagons to increase the amount of available transportation.[17]

Clarence Pickett brought to the audience the greetings of Philadelphia Friends. Wrote George Hardin: "He did a splendid job! Loud, and clear, and affirmative, and you would have enjoyed his handling of the Biblical reference of 'the man who talketh with his feet,' and how the walkers were speaking to the whole world! And when he drew his ten minutes to a close, there was an explosive standing ovation and great applause! And I found a tear running down Dorothy's [Steere] cheek, and found one on mine, too."[18]

"This has been an exhausting evening," wrote Clarence, "but very rewarding."[19] The three Friends took the train home the next morning, Clarence going directly to New York for a meeting of the Field Foundation; then, the following day, to speak at noon to the Burlington, New Jersey, Rotary Club and in the evening to preside at one of the Washington Seminars. The week concluded with a round of appointments at the AFSC offices in Philadelphia and board and committee meetings at Pendle Hill.

During the entire last week of June Clarence Pickett, as chairman of Friends General Conference, presided at the evening sessions of the biennial Cape May conference with an attendance of close to twenty-five hundred Friends. The evening lectures reflected the prestige he brought to the chairmanship. He was instrumental in bringing to the gathering Douglas Steere, professor of philosophy at Haverford College, to speak on "The Christian Approach to Other World Religions;" his long-time friend Alexander Purdy, dean of the Hartford Theological Seminary, to address from a New Testament perspective the subject, "Many Members, One Body;" and Gaganvihari Mehta, ambassador of India to the United States, to answer the question, "How Shall We Wage Peace?" Clarence himself gave the address on the first evening of the conference, speaking on "How Inclusive Is Love and Unity?" He also participated as a resource leader in the morning round table on "Pacifism in Practice."

In accordance with a long-standing plan, Clarence Pickett was hospitalized for several days in the first week of July for a thorough physical examination. The checkup was mainly for the purpose of determining whether his health would permit a possible around-the-world trip with Lilly and another Quaker couple. Clarence's physical ailments were largely confined to times of high blood pressure which triggered an urgent need for rest, attacks of gout which began in 1949 and could be countered by medication, and, last but by no means least, recurring head colds for which massage therapy and rest were the needed remedies. He was, year by year, losing some weight, a problem which he viewed as a family trait. He did not believe in taking undue risks with his health and was attentive to what doctors ordered.

In the summer of 1956 the Picketts did not take their usual vacation on Cape Cod. They did spend more time than usual with their daughters and their families in Moorestown, New Jersey and Fanwood, New Jersey. Over the Labor Day weekend Clarence attended the Friends Conference on Race Relations at Wilmington College in Ohio, with one hundred and thirty Friends present, and was one of four principal speakers. He chose as his topic the impact of racial segregation in the United States upon U.S. relations with nations of color. His closing comments captured the thrust of his address:

> Our goal is to see as far as we can that relations of understanding, of fellowship, of belief in the sacredness of the life and spirit of men and women of all shades of color exist. No more important and searching statement can be made than that the lightest of the white and the darkest of the black are children of a common heavenly father. No more

important quest can be entered upon by ourselves as Christians and Americans than to see that we recognize men and women for what they are, not dividing them into superior and inferior.

The mills of the gods move with precision. The nature of the quality of men of color will be acknowledged whether we do it or not. Let us not stand in the way. Let us find our place in the forefront of those who look upon people as people, with the eye of vision of what they may become, and what in the eyes of an Almighty Creator they now are.[20]

A week later Clarence Pickett left by train for Chicago. For many months the AFSC regional office based in that city had been requesting from the national office assistance in dealing with racial segregation and discrimination in housing. Specifically, the regional office staff wanted an interracial delegation of Friends to investigate the intimidation African American residents were experiencing in the Trumbull Park Homes low-income public housing project, part of the South Deering community in South Chicago. The six-person delegation, three from Philadelphia and three from Chicago, began its work within a month after the third anniversary of the Trumbull Park disturbances, which followed the moving into the all-white project of the first black family. At the time of the Quaker delegation's visit, there were twenty-five African American families residing in Trumbull Park Homes.

The formal report of the delegation vividly described the situation:

> The teenagers and young men with nothing else to do, simply roam the streets, gathering in gangs to intimidate Negroes or those who would express friendship for Negroes. Not even the young, white Methodist minister is safe from their abuse and vandalism. Firecracker bombing, window-breaking, automobile mutilation, tormenting small Negro children, and obscenity are the pastimes of the larger boys and the "vigilante" elders. . . . Negroes in the project are not free to walk the streets of South Deering [which surrounds the project] day or night, without fear of physical attack or hurled epithets.[21]

Delegation members visited with eight of the black families, the pastor of the Methodist church, a South Deering business leader, officials of the Chicago Commission on Human Relations and the Chicago Housing Authority, and with Chicago mayor Richard Daley. They were not able to secure appointments with leaders of the South Deering Improvement Association, a principal source of hatred and agitation.

Clarence Pickett was particularly impressed with the quality of the African American citizens, who had to be escorted by the police to and from their homes and who had a feeling of despair, almost as though they were in prison. In conversation with Mayor Daley, he and his associates suggested "that the police, instead of being concentrated in one spot, and sitting there in their cars in the Negro neighborhood trying to prevent things from happening to the Negroes, should patrol the entire community in the normal way and allow the Negro citizens to try walking on their own. . . ."[22]

The delegation recognized that "the exercise of freedom will require courage and forbearance on the part of Negro residents to an even greater degree than has already been shown [and] we believe that in white residents there must exist the capacity for [friendly] action only waiting to be released."[23]

At the AFSC executive board meeting on 4 April 1956, the idea of having Clarence and Lilly Pickett and another Quaker couple make a world trip under AFSC auspices was included in the report of the executive secretary, Lewis Hoskins. Sumner and Lela Mills of Western Yearly Meeting (Sumner an AFSC board member and the recently-appointed presiding clerk of the Five Years Meeting of Friends) were invited to travel with their personal friends, the Picketts. Their itinerary called for travel by train to the West Coast, by ship to Honolulu, and after a few days' rest in Hawaii, on the *President Wilson* to Japan, arriving in Yokohama on 24 October. There they were met by Philadelphia Friend Esther Rhoads, who, among other assignments in Japan, had been AFSC's representative after the war in LARA (Licensed Agencies for Relief in Asia) and by Clarence's niece Jane Bowles, whose husband, Gordon, was assistant director of International House, built by John D. Rockefeller, III. The four American Friends stayed at the international center during their three weeks' visit in Japan. "While the weather was chilly," wrote Clarence, "the house was heated, a luxury not available that early in the autumn to most visitors. Did we miss something by having such privilege? I expect so. Though it did help health-wise, and I hope was not too much of a barrier between us and our less privileged Friends."[24]

Among the many engagements Clarence Pickett had during his stay in Japan, perhaps the most moving was a luncheon program held at the

Foreign Press Club in Tokyo for fifteen young women, the so-called Hiroshima Maidens, who had been among those Japanese who had survived the bombing but had been grossly disfigured by the atomic blast. These women had been in the United States for a year and a half to receive plastic surgery under a program initiated and promoted by Norman Cousins, editor of the *Saturday Review of Literature,* and the Hiroshima Peace Center Association of New York.

Cousins himself was present for the Press Club event. "How can we adequately express our appreciation for the graciousness and the spaciousness of spirit which these girls have brought into our lives?" he said.[25] He thanked Quakers for arranging hospitality in American homes for the Japanese women. Raymond Wilson, visiting Japan on a leave of absence as executive secretary of the U.S. Quaker lobby, the Friends Committee on National Legislation, reported on the occasion, writing in part, "I doubt if any of the two hundred guests present today will soon forget the gripping power of love and goodwill expressed throughout the program today. The whole ceremony might have been a theatrical circus. It was very much of a holy benediction."[26] Many years later Clarence Pickett, reflecting on the significance of simple, single gestures of good will, noted the profound effect Norman Cousins' project had had on a nation embittered toward the United States because of the atomic bombings: "The care and love given to the girls made a vast and lasting difference in the attitude of the Japanese people toward us."[27]

Another memorable occasion for the Picketts, and especially for Clarence, was a brief visit to the imperial palace grounds to call on Crown Prince Akihito. For Clarence Pickett the visit had special meaning because of Elizabeth Vining's tutorial connection with the prince after the war. The interview lasted only fifteen minutes because Prince Akihito had to go to the university for a lecture. Observed Pickett: "He wore a tweed suit, and his house, while comfortable, was not elaborate or expensive. He is now twenty-three, and rumor has it that a diligent search is under way for a suitable wife for him. One feels, in such a visit, quite reassured of his ability and character, but also the real handicaps to normal development because of the restrictions put on royalty."[28] In November 1958 the Imperial Council approved the engagement of Crown Prince Akihito to a commoner, Michiko Shoda. They were married in April 1959. She would become the first empress of Japan who was not a member of the nobility.

In Kyoto Clarence Pickett called on Keiji Hisamatsu, one of the few Zen *koji*, a title given to an accomplished Zen scholar whose personality represents the Zen spirit. Wrote interpreter Yuki Takahashi Brinton four decades later:

> It seemed quite natural for these two sages to be talking together in a Kyoto house. The house was old, simple and small, but seemed spacious as there was hardly any furniture. The only decoration was a flower in a vase. The fragrance of incense added to the atmosphere. We sat on the tatami floor, with a padded cushion under our legs. I wondered if it was the first time for Clarence to sit on the floor. But he did it without fuss, though it was not easy for him.
>
> First the host served tea, green powdered tea with hot water, blended with a tiny bamboo whisk. A small bite of sweet cake is offered to the guest before the tea is ready to be served. Until the guest finishes drinking the tea, no words are spoken. It is rather a ritual.[29]

Wrote Clarence: "I asked him questions—his evaluation of meditation, his idea of God, his attitude as a Zen toward humanitarian service. Each question brought from him an encompassing lecture on the whole nature of Man and God as Zen Buddhists see it—and, with a concern for his health and my own cold feet, and Yuki's attempts to translate abstract words, my understanding left a good deal to be desired."[30]

A principal objective of the world trip was an opportunity for the Picketts and Millses to spend a month in India. It was Clarence's first visit, despite his many years of keen interest in the country, going back to the soul-stirring contacts in England and the United States with Rabindranath Tagore in 1930 and his deep identification with Mahatma Gandhi and the independence movement. At the time of the visit the American Friends Service Committee and the Friends Service Council, based in London, working closely with some Indian Friends, were jointly sponsoring a Friends center in Delhi. Programs included arranging for the exchange of Indian and Pakistani students and the holding of meetings for diplomats who were alumni of AFSC conferences.

When the Millses and Picketts were visiting the Delhi center an invitation came to them to attend the first general meeting of Friends to be held in India, this time in Rasulia (where a rural center supported by British Friends was located) near Hoshangabad in the central India state of Madhya Pradesh. It was truly "general." There were present those who had found help in the Friends of Truth movement, which includes a good many persons who still think of themselves as Hindus, some Indian and Western Friends who, while loyal members of the Religious Society of Friends, still draw sustenance from other prophets of religion as well as from Christ, and some whose allegiance was wholly to Christ as the only Savior.[31]

There were a hundred persons attending the three-day conference, eighty of them Indians. Clarence was impressed with the Spartan arrangements, the cost being thirty-five cents a day per person for food and lodging. He also envied the adeptness of the Indians and some few Westerners at sitting on the floor indoors or on the ground outdoors. He was among those at the gathering who needed a chair. A full morning session was given to small-group discussions, one to consider the religious faith of Friends, a second to discuss Quaker social testimonies, and a third to consider Friends and politics. "When reports of these discussions were given," wrote Clarence, "the wide range of theological outlook again became evident."[32]

These differing views were vigorously defended in good spirit. For Clarence Pickett, it was T. R. Addison, a member of the Preston Patrick Friends Meeting in northwest England, who lifted the discussion to the desired plane. Addison had come as a farmer to Rasulia in 1913 and had helped to develop a sizable farm community. "Out of his work with growing plants and the soil, somewhat reminiscent of Jesus' parable, [Addison] brought us back from what could have become threshing theological straw to the fresh growth of the Spirit coming out of the fertile soil of a lifelong dedication to helping earth, sunshine and rain produce better farm crops."[33]

The Millses and Picketts paid a visit to the rural development project in the village of Barpali in the state of Orissa on the west coast of India. Here they visited with the staff of eleven American Friends, including three medical doctors and an equal number of trained Indian workers. The demonstration project had already been in existence for five years. It was now making significant strides in health education, vegetable gardening, and the establishment of a cooperative to enable Barpali weavers to buy their supplies at a saving and sell their products in a wider market, including the United States.

At the end of January 1957 Clarence and Lilly Pickett and Sumner and Lela Mills had a thirty-minute interview with Prime Minister Jawaharlal Nehru. Nehru had recently returned from the United States where he and President Dwight Eisenhower, during a visit to the president's farm in Gettysburg, talked almost continuously for twelve hours. The topic most on Eisenhower's mind was the Middle East. Nehru revealed to his American guests that he had spoken out strongly against the "Eisenhower Doctrine," the policy of the United States whereby military and economic aid was provided to non-communist countries, even those ruled by persons who represented the rich landowners and who had little desire to improve the lot of their own people internally.

Leaving Bombay by ship at the end of January 1957, the Millses and Picketts sailed for Mombasa, Kenya, with brief stopovers in Karachi, Pakistan, and Mogadiscio, Somalia. The stop in Kenya provided them with the opportunity to visit with East African Friends. Then they sailed to Cape Town, South Africa, for a visit with South African Friends, and again by boat up the west coast of Africa, with a stopover in Dakar, Senegal, to Naples and Genoa, Italy. Finally they traveled by train to England for a week's stay in London. They sailed for home on 8 March on the *United States*, arriving in New York on 13 March.

Clarence Pickett's journal entries following his return from the round-the-world trip show evidence of the long absence interrupting to some extent the flow of his usual engagements. He does indicate that he was in great demand to speak about various aspects of the world trip, indeed, eighty times in the next twelve months.

Among these engagements was his address to the Southeastern Friends Conference in Orlando, Florida on 8 March 1958. It was one of the very few major Pickett addresses that was tape recorded on a reel-to-reel machine. Listening to it at the end of the century reveals why Clarence Pickett was such an outstanding speaker even at age seventy-four. The title of his address was "Looking at Ourselves Through Asian Eyes," but he ranged well beyond the confines of the recent trip. Speaking as he was to an audience of Friends, he focused on the relevance to political thinking of the central Quaker belief in God as resident in everyone. He referred to his own experiences in dealing with Soviet ambassadors at the cost of being labeled a communist. "We must never lose the human being in politics," he said. "It is through right personal relations that we earn the right to disagree."[34]

Why was it that Clarence Pickett was in such demand as a public speaker? He brought to his audiences rich life experiences that were pertinent to current issues. He was an appealing and deeply respected person. Based on sketchy notes, his delivery was flawless, forceful, and with uplifting interest. There were no emotional flourishes or theatrical effects. He was aware that public speaking was taking more out of him than in previous years. But, he observed, "it keeps me alert to ways of saying what we have seen and felt; I hope the talks have been helpful— at least they have kept me open and alert." [35]

The Washington Seminars were increasing in scope and participation. Clarence Pickett continued to welcome the responsibility of presiding at these semi-monthly meetings. In the calendar year of 1958 the Seminars involved three hundred and forty participants, most of them from the executive and legislative branches of government, and thirty consultants. Among the themes were "Implications for U.S. Policy of Recent Scientific Developments" and "Next Steps to Disarmament."

Upon his return from the world trip, Clarence Pickett also resumed his responsibilities as chairman of Friends General Conference. Planning for the 1958 biennial week-long conference in Cape May, New Jersey began early, and once again Clarence was instrumental in obtaining for the evening program some impressive speakers. One of these was Norman Cousins, editor of the *Saturday Review* (the magazine renamed because it was no longer focusing exclusively on the review of literature). To a jammed auditorium in a dynamic address entitled "The War Against Man," Cousins denounced the testing of nuclear weapons and flatly rejected these weapons as necessary for national security. "I believe that American security begins with a statement to the world," he said, "that we would rather die than use these weapons on other people."[36]

The Cape May pier auditorium was even more packed the following evening, Friday, 27 June—with adults and children and with African Americans from southern New Jersey—when Martin Luther King, Jr. addressed the conference on "Nonviolence and Racial Justice." It was an electrifying experience for an audience already predisposed to his pacifist convictions. There was a standing ovation when King concluded in his by-then characteristic fashion:

> Let us continue, my friends, going on and on toward that great city where all men will live together as brothers in respect to dignity and worth of all human personality. This will be a great day, a day, figuratively speaking, when "the morning stars will sing together, and the sons of God will shout for joy."[37]

Clarence Pickett had an opportunity that evening to renew his acquaintance with King that had begun with the visit of the three Philadelphia Quakers to Montgomery, Alabama in the spring of 1956. As president of the Fellowship Commission in Philadelphia, Pickett had also been present in April 1957 when King received the Commission's annual award and was cited as the person who had made an enduring and abiding contribution to improvement of human relations in America. Pickett was drawn to the African American leader in part because of King's adherence to Gandhian principles within a Christian context. In his *Stride Toward Freedom*, published in late 1958, King would say that "Christ furnished the spirit and motivation, while Gandhi furnished the method."[38] Early in the next year the American Friends Service Committee arranged for King and his wife, Coretta, to spend four weeks in India, for the most part visiting with followers of Mahatma Gandhi.

The year 1959 would bring to Clarence Pickett, as a charter member of the controversial Police Review Board of the City of Philadelphia, a whole new responsibility and experience.

NOTES

1. *Meeting the Russians: American Quakers Visit the Soviet Union,* American Friends Service Committee, Philadelphia, 1956, 15.

2. Report from the Quaker group visiting the USSR, June 15, 1955, AFSC archives.

3. Interview with Stephen G. Cary, 12 Apr. 1993.

4. *Meeting the Russians*, 15.

5. Pickett to Stalin, 27 June 1933, AFSC archives.

6. Clarence Pickett journal, 19 July 1955.

7. Pickett journal, 28 Oct. 1955.

8. Minute 36, 1956 Philadelphia Yearly Meeting, 18, Haverford College, Haverford, PA: Magill Library, Quaker Collection.

9. Letter to author from George Hardin, dated 29 Dec. 1993.

10. Minute 65, 1956 Philadelphia Yearly Meeting, 29.

11. George Hardin, Clarence Pickett, and Dorothy Steere, "Three Quakers in Montgomery," *Friends Journal* 2, no. 18 (5 May 1955): 280-81.

12. Pickett journal, 14 Apr. 1956.

13. Pickett taped interview with Edwin Randall, 30 May 1956, AFSC archives.

14. Pickett journal, 16 Apr. 1956.

15. Hardin, letter to author, 29 Dec. 1993.

16. Pickett journal, 16 Apr. 1956.

17. Pickett journal, 16 Apr. 1956.

18. Hardin, letter to author, 29 Dec. 1993.

19. Pickett journal, 16 Apr. 1956.

20. Clarence E. Pickett, "A Broad Look at Color In the World," as condensed in *The American Friend* 44 (new series), no. 19 (30 Sept. 1956): 296-98.

21. "Quakers Look At Trumbull Park," a report by the delegation (Clarence E. Pickett, Helen Baker, Lucy P. Carner, R. Ogden Hannaford, G. Nicholas Paster, George Watson), American Friends Service Committee, Chicago Regional Office, October 1956, pp. 4, 6, AFSC archives.

22. Pickett journal, 12 Sept. 1956.

23. Trumbull Park delegation report.

24. Pickett journal, 24 Oct. 1956.

25. E. Raymond Wilson, "America-Japan Society Welcomes Hiroshima Maidens," Japan journey letter #18, 28 Oct. 1956, 3.

26. Wilson, "Hiroshima Maidens."

27. Fellowship profile: Clarence E. Pickett , *Fellowship Commission News*, 22 Sept. 1962.

28. Travel report of Clarence E. and Lilly P. Pickett (1 Oct. 1956 - 13 Mar. 1957) Tokyo, 9 Nov. 1956, AFSC archives.

29. Letter, Yuki Takahashi Brinton to author, 19 May 1998.

30. Pickett travel report, Kyoto, 12 Nov. 1956.

31. Clarence E. Pickett, "General Meeting of Friends in India," *Friends World News*, #52, April, 1957, 9-10.

32. Pickett, "General Meeting," 1957.

33. Pickett, "General Meeting," 1957.

34. Clarence E. Pickett, "Looking at Ourselves Through Asian Eyes," address given at Southeastern Friends Conference, Orlando, Florida, 8 Mar. 1958, family papers courtesy of Carolyn Pickett Miller.

35. Pickett journal summary, Mar. 1957 - Mar. 1959.

36. Norman Cousins, "The War Against Man," *Friends Journal* 4, no. 29 (9 Aug. 1958): 465-67.

37. Martin Luther King, Jr. "Nonviolence and Racial Justice," *Friends Journal* 4, no. 28 (26 July 1958): 442-44.

38. Martin Luther King, Jr., *Stride Toward Freedom: The Montgomery Story* (San Francisco: Harper's, 1958), 85.

Left to right: adults, Armand Stalnaker, Rachel Pickett Stalnaker,
Lilly Peckham Pickett, Clarence Pickett , G. Macculloch Miller,
Carolyn Pickett Miller; children, Timothy Lee Stalnaker,
Thomas Allen Stalnaker, Deborah Breese Miller,
Jennifer Joy Miller. Thanksgiving, 1956.

Chapter 19

THE LAST TRIP WEST

How firm were his roots, yet how questing his spirit!

CLEARLY ONE OF THE MOST CHALLENGING COMMITMENTS Clarence Pickett made at this stage in his life, at age seventy-four, was his willingness to be a member of the Police Review Board of the City of Philadelphia (later, at the behest of the Police Commissioner, named the Police Advisory Board). The board, largely as a result of initiatives taken by the Greater Philadelphia Branch of the American Civil Liberties Union, was established in October 1958 by an executive order of Democratic mayor Richardson Dilworth after an ordinance to create such a board failed to pass City Council.[1]

The purpose of the board was to investigate and make recommendations on complaints of police misconduct in respect to private citizens. "Misconduct" included abusive language, false arrest, unreasonable or unwarranted use of force, unreasonable searches and seizures, and discrimination because of race, religion, or national origin. Complaints could be brought by citizens, civic groups, and public officials and employees. While New York City had established a civilian Complaint Review Board in 1953, it was a mechanism within the police department. Philadelphia was the first city in the United States to have a board entirely composed of representatives of various community groups and interests, all serving on a volunteer basis. In its second year a part-time executive director was appointed. As one historian has expressed it:

> Too few Philadelphians recall the day when their city was the national leader in community-police relations. It was called the Police Advisory

Board, and it was the most revolutionary thing to come out of the city since the Revolution itself. Civilians judging policemen, blunting the force of potential abuse of authority—it was our forefathers' idea of democracy. It had never been done before . . . .[2]

Given the pioneering nature of the board, it is not surprising that Clarence Pickett was willing to serve as a member. As president of the Fellowship Commission for seven years, 1949 to 1956 (and honorary president, 1956 to the time of his death), he knew well of widespread objectionable police practices, such as disrupting interracial social gatherings, accosting interracial couples on the street, and generally displaying brutality in respect to African Americans. It is of note that Clarence was elected vice chairman of the Board of five members (enlarged to eight in 1961). The rules and procedures governing acceptance of complaints, investigations, and dispositions were formulated by the board itself. What was particularly congenial to Pickett's outlook were the alternatives to a formal investigation and hearing of complaints developed by the part-time executive director, Martin Barol. Said Pickett in a newspaper interview: "He [Barol] went over all the cases ahead of time. He attempted to settle cases and relieve the Board of that work. It was a grueling job. I would say he settled about half the cases."[3]

The alternatives to a formal investigation and hearing included holding a conference with both parties in attendance, explaining the actions of the police officer to the aggrieved citizen, obtaining a letter of apology from the accused officer, and recommending to the police commissioner that the complainant's arrest record be expunged. While Clarence Pickett's journal often gave some sketchy information about the formal hearings, always with the complainant accompanied by counsel and with the police officer backed by an attorney supplied by Philadelphia Lodge No. 5 of the Fraternal Order of Police, no formal records of the proceedings were kept. The board sessions could be lengthy and contentious. Noted Clarence on one occasion: "Police Review Board hearings, all day, three very difficult cases, where one is distressed to see pretty clear discrimination against Negroes."[4]

The Fraternal Order of Police year after year objected to the existence of the board. And, when Clarence Pickett became chairman in 1964, the John Birch Society stepped up its attacks on him by inviting the public to phone for a tape-recorded message denouncing him as a dangerous communist sympathizer. Said Clarence: "We know that on the whole the police don't like us, and haven't wanted us. But in spite of the fact that they prefer we don't exist, they cooperate very well with us. The police represent the strong arm of the city. We represent citizen concern—for common decency to be observed in the community. The citizen should not regard the police as his enemy. My own feeling is that the more we reflect citizen concern that the police shall restrain themselves, the more citizens will not regard the police as their enemy."[5]

Clarence Pickett served on the Police Advisory Board up to the time of his death in 1965. The author of this biography asked Martin Barol, the former executive director of the Board, whether Clarence Pickett ever raised any questions in respect to the fact that police carried firearms. Barol did not recall any such discussion. Pickett saw no inconsistency in being a pacifist and in accepting a proper role for the police even when armed.

In May 1959 Matsuo Tanaka, consul general of Japan in New York, visited Clarence Pickett and invited him to become honorary consul general of Japan "at Philadelphia." Being assured that the position would not require much work, Pickett accepted the assignment, sending to the consul general a detailed curriculum vitae. The appointment was officially made by the office of the Ministry of Foreign Affairs in Tokyo, effective November 21, 1959. A few days later Clarence attended the opening of the Japanese trade fair in Philadelphia's convention center where the appointment was publicly announced.

In January 1960 acting Secretary of State Douglas Dillon certified the appointment. Pickett then received from Japan a carefully-crafted document covering his functions and "matters for which the honorary consul is incompetent [*sic*]."[6] Included in the permitted functions were the issuance of visas, the welcoming of Japanese luminaries to Philadelphia, and participation in special events related to Japan. On one occasion he and Lilly Pickett attended a reception dinner in New York for Crown Prince Akihito and his wife. Clarence would always be on hand to welcome Japanese trade missions and to be present at the annual Japanese Trade Fair. He served as a consultant to a local karate organization.

Clearly the appointment as honorary consul general at Philadelphia was a recognition of Clarence Pickett's sustained interest in Japanese

Clarence Pickett, as consul general at Philadelphia for Japan, 1959

Americans beginning with the infamous relocation of West Coast Japanese to what Clarence called on occasion "concentration camps."[7] Coupled with this concern was the relief work of the American Friends Service Committee after World War II in Japan itself. Treasured by Clarence was the Certificate of Appreciation given to him by the Japanese American Citizens League in September 1957, followed several years later with a testimonial from the same organization. Pickett was also the recipient of a Certificate of Merit and Token of Gratitude in November 1960 from the Association for Japan-United States Amity and Trade in commemoration of the one hundredth anniversary of the exchange of the ratifications of the treaty of amity and commerce between the two countries. In this same year, 1960, Clarence Pickett received three honorary degrees: a Doctor of Literature from Brandeis University in Waltham, Massachusetts and from Drexel Institute in Philadelphia; and a Doctor of Humane Letters from his alma mater, William Penn College.

When Norman Cousins addressed Friends at their 1958 Cape May Conference, Clarence Pickett was already cochairman of the National

Committee for a Sane Nuclear Policy. SANE, as it came to be called, was established to achieve the permanent cessation, internationally, of nuclear weapons tests; general disarmament with inspection, complete down to police levels of small arms; a strengthened United Nations with a permanent peace force to discourage aggression; and arms control measures to prevent the spread of nuclear weapons to new nations. At the outset its program focused on publishing advertisements in major newspapers in order to influence public opinion. One of the first such advertisements had the headline: "We are facing a danger unlike any danger that has ever existed," referring to the destruction that would result from a nuclear war. The statement, with a coupon that could be mailed to President Dwight Eisenhower, was signed by close to fifty prominent Americans including Eleanor Roosevelt.

In the relative calm that followed the breakup of the Soviet Union as the twentieth century ended, it is easy to forget that a nuclear war between the two superpowers was a distinct possibility, with some scientists monitoring a "doomsday clock" with a calculation of "midnight," the time of mutual annihilation. SANE brought together pacifist and non-pacifist proponents of initiatives that would pull back the world from the abyss. It called largely for multilateral measures as compared to U.S. unilateral moves. As executive director Homer Jack said in 1962: "We are not pacifists, and we are not for unilateral disarmament. We are not fellow-travelers, and we are not soft-headed. We know the problems the President [Kennedy] faces. We try to be constructive."[8]

In bringing together, under one organizational umbrella, persons of differing persuasions and faiths, SANE inevitably had internal stresses and strains. But, as was his practice in other organizations, Clarence Pickett stayed at his post despite difficulties. It was not until the end of 1963, a year after Norman Cousins completed his cochairmanship, that the national board elected Benjamin Spock, the famous pediatrician, and Stuart Hughes, a Harvard University professor, as cochairmen of SANE. Pickett continued as one of several honorary sponsors from as many as a dozen countries. And in May 1963 he received from the National Committee for a Sane Nuclear Policy the Eleanor Roosevelt Peace Award at a dinner in his honor with three hundred and fifty persons present.

Early in 1959 Clarence Pickett accepted an invitation to give the annual Quaker lecture at the High Point Friends Meeting in North

Carolina in October, with the understanding that the speech would be published as a pamphlet. He decided to speak on "The International Responsibility of Friends."[9] It was one of the first times that Pickett chose to address the apparent conflict between pacifists like himself who were reasonably content to work with governments in respect to war and the causes of war, and those pacifists who believed increasingly that more radical actions, some involving civil disobedience, were needed to influence decision-makers and the public at large. In 1953, at the very conclusion of his autobiographical account of his work as executive secretary of the American Friends Service Committee, *For More Than Bread*, Clarence Pickett stated his most fundamental conviction:

> To live in that state of tension which enables us to be at the same time critic and friend of government, to study its workings sufficiently to be able to help religious insight become political action, remains part of our duty and call. And withal, and beyond all, to maintain an abiding faith in the power of good to overcome evil, to live in that way of loving service for which we all most deeply yearn: nothing less than this kind of energetic commitment of our whole lives can satisfy the inner sanctuary of the human spirit.[10]

By the time of his address to North Carolina Friends, members of the Religious Society of Friends were becoming aware of some new and unusual expressions of their peace testimony. Perhaps the most spectacular of these actions was the sailing of the thirty-foot ketch *Golden Rule* from San Pedro, California on 25 March 1958, to Honolulu, Hawaii, en route to the U.S. nuclear test zone in the South Pacific to protest continuation of weapons experiments there.[11] The skipper was a Quaker by convincement and a former Navy commander, Albert Bigelow. Two other members of the four-man crew were also Friends. The crew was jailed on 1 May for trying to sail from Hawaii.

Clarence Pickett was helping his co-religionists to realize that "responsibility" had various dimensions, from the type of service in which he was involved at the United Nations to the more radical forms of witness which, in fact, mirrored some of the actions taken by the earliest Friends in the seventeenth century. They, too, were arrested and jailed. As Pickett put it,

> Many striking parallels could be cited between those whom we revere as our Quaker forefathers and those who now feel themselves directed to

unusual methods of expression. But these are exceptional times in which we live, and we may well expect unusual methods of speaking to our national and international need. . . . There is power in letting it be known that we do not allow ourselves to accept these massive preparations for destruction.[12]

Just a year later, in November 1960, a thousand Friends converged from across the United States for the Quaker peace witness in Washington, DC. The year was the 300th anniversary of the 1660 declaration to Charles II in England in which Quakers stated that war was contrary to the spirit of Christ and wrong in the sight of God. The pilgrimage to Washington encompassed two days, Sunday and Monday, with the central action being a march, two by two, across the Potomac River to the Pentagon, where Friends stood in a single line, with appropriate posters, facing the Pentagon on three sides. "On the vigil line," wrote Edward Behre, "we will stand quietly and expectantly in prayerful waiting for the Divine Spirit to make itself felt in and through us."[13] The pilgrimage included visits on Monday by selected Friends with government officials.

Clarence Pickett did not participate in the Washington witness. On the Friday evening of that weekend he presided at a SANE meeting in Philadelphia. On Sunday he spoke at a Germantown Friends Meeting adult class. It is not known to what extent he considered going to Washington for what proved to be the first such witness the city had ever experienced. The vigil included many senior Friends who had not previously engaged in that type of demonstration.

Clearly, Pickett had no objection to the witness. The previous May he and Norman Cousins, as cochairmen of SANE, had spoken to seventeen thousand persons inside Madison Square Garden in New York (with hundreds not able to get seats) who gathered to call for a nuclear testing ban. Eleanor Roosevelt was cochair of the rally with Harry Taylor, former president of Sarah Lawrence College. Late in the evening when the rally broke up, five thousand persons, led by veteran Socialist campaigner, Norman Thomas, marched with signs from 8th Avenue to Broadway and down to 42nd Street. *The New York Times* gave front page attention to the rally and march the next morning.

In the year 1962 Clarence Pickett himself participated in some walks and vigils for peace. In March he briefly participated in a walk around

City Hall in Philadelphia to protest the renewal of bomb testing. In mid-April he was in Chicago to walk with vigil groups from the suburbs for the final blocks to Orchestra Hall where he and others were the main speakers. The issue was the testing of nuclear weapons.

On Sunday, 29 April an unusual opportunity for Clarence Pickett to witness for peace presented itself. President and Mrs. Kennedy invited recipients of the scientific, literary, and peace Nobel prizes from the United States and Canada and their spouses to be guests of honor at a White House dinner. In all, there were one hundred and seventy-five guests. Clarence and Lilly Pickett represented the American Friends Service Committee, which, jointly with the Friends Service Council in London, had received the Nobel Peace Prize in 1947.

Earlier in the day Clarence Pickett—and Linus Pauling, an award-winner in chemistry and later in the year the recipient of the 1962 Nobel Peace Prize (the award having been delayed for a year)—joined the Quaker-sponsored vigil in front of the White House to draw the president's attention to the urgency of ending the nuclear arms race. When the president greeted Clarence Pickett prior to the dinner, he indicated that he knew of the vigil and was evidently appreciative of the humor and wider significance of having the White House "picketed" from the outside and from the inside on the same day. Kennedy also knew that Clarence Pickett had been appointed in 1961 to be a member of the National Advisory Council for the Peace Corps. It is significant that President Kennedy agreed to see six Quakers the following Tuesday morning, including Henry Cadbury, chairman of the AFSC, and George Willoughby, one of the crew members of the *Golden Rule.*

With the death of President Roosevelt, Clarence Pickett's contacts with Mrs. Roosevelt declined sharply, but never ended. On a number of occasions Clarence and Lilly would stop on their way to a vacation in New England to see Eleanor Roosevelt at her house, Val-Kill, in Hyde Park, New York. She was generous in responding to his requests that she see persons whom he could vouch for. On the occasion of her seventieth birthday, just a week before his own, he wrote a long letter of appreciation for their relationship. Said Clarence: "There is a very rich heritage in my life, in part of which Lilly joins, in our association with you."[14]

It was principally at the United Nations that Pickett would see and interact with her. In late December 1945 President Truman appointed

Eleanor Roosevelt one of the U.S. delegates to the United Nations. She served with distinction. She was appointed by the president to a four-year term on the UN's Human Rights Commission and chosen as chairperson by acclamation at its first plenary session in 1947. By the end of 1948 the General Assembly adopted the commission's landmark Universal Declaration of Human Rights.

On the occasion of her seventieth birthday, Eleanor Roosevelt is quoted as saying, "I think I have a good deal of my uncle Theodore in me, because I could not, at any age, be content to take my place in a corner by the fireplace and simply look on. Life was meant to be lived. Curiosity must be kept alive."[15] Clarence Pickett could see in himself the same reluctance, perhaps inability, to withdraw from active life in his senior years.

Eleanor Roosevelt died in early November 1962. On the occasion of her interment in the rose garden on the Roosevelt estate in Hyde Park, Clarence and Lilly Pickett were among the privileged guests who watched the last rites with sorrow and with gratitude. What deeply impressed Clarence was that "for a mile there was a mass of men, women, boys and girls, uninvited guests and neighbors, waiting to say good-bye as the funeral procession drove by. A great soul had left us. But to have known her had been a benediction."[16]

It was on one of Clarence Pickett's trips to the West Coast that he happened to meet a man who was much interested in talking with those who are no longer living. "To him it seems a great reality," Clarence observed. "To me, it is very unclear."[17] Yet a number of years later, just nine days after his 80th birthday on 19 October 1964, Clarence Pickett had a "sitting" with Arthur Ford, a Disciples of Christ minister. Ford's autobiography, *Nothing So Strange*, was, by the time of Pickett's visit, in its ninth printing. In the book he explains how a French-Canadian young man, Fletcher, who was killed in World War I, became his intermediary, his "control."[18]

Clarence Pickett went to the sitting in Ford's apartment in Philadelphia with Walter Voelker, an active member of Abington Friends Meeting, and another guest, William Rauscher. Ford did not know who Walter Voelker was bringing with him. "It was a normal living room such as yours or mine," wrote Voelker. "The only thing that was different was that when Arthur sat in his reclining chair he put a small silk handkerchief over his eyes to shut out the light."[19]

The seance, as was frequently the case, was tape-recorded, in this instance by Voelker. The transcript of the "sitting" reveals that a deceased Pickett relative was eager to communicate through Fletcher with Clarence: "There's a very nice lady here who has the name of Mamie or Minnie. Minnie, I think. And she hasn't been over too long, but she wants to speak to this man here [Pickett]. . . . She must have lived to be quite old, but she looks just like a young person in the spiritual body. Do you have a sister by the name of Minnie, sir?"[20] Clarence Pickett said, "Yes."

Then Fletcher indicated (through Ford) that he had Clarence's mother with him and was searching for her name. "It's a two-syllable name that starts with either H-e-l or H-i-l . . . . Did your mother have a name like that?" "Hulda," said Pickett. Then Fletcher: "Hulda, that's it. And she is very happy and sends her love. . . ." Messages were also received from Clarence's brother-in-law Gilbert Bowles, and from Harold Ickes, the secretary of the Department of Interior with whom Clarence had worked during the Depression. Then Fletcher, in a long conversation with Clarence, comes to the point of associating a lily with Clarence's wife and associating the 13th chapter of Corinthians with his children, Rachel Joy and Carolyn Hope.

Clarence Pickett takes note of the experience in his journal: "Went with Walter Voelker to see Arthur Ford, who is able to communicate with the dead. Very interesting and not a hoax, I think, but of secondary importance to me now."[22] Voelker remembered Pickett saying to him after the session, "What impressed me most was what Arthur Ford said about prayer before the "sitting" started."[23] A number of years earlier, on the occasion of the memorial service of a close colleague, Clarence Pickett spoke of death as an "experience of transition" in which a person leaves behind the physical "and, as he goes and hovers between the life of the body and the untrammeled life of the spirit, one catches a glimpse of something very precious. God seems to stoop down and make Himself very consciously present, so that to join Him in the new world is a welcome experience."[24]

On the first day of 1963, Clarence and Lilly left for a two months' vacation in Hawaii with stopovers, as usual, on the West Coast. Typically, Clarence would spend time walking, preferably in the sunshine, reading, answering mail forwarded to him, and writing book reviews. The Honolulu Friends Meeting also claimed his attention.

Upon his return hom, Clarence resumed his organizational commitments: Peace Corps Advisory Council, United States Committee for Refugees, Pendle Hill board and curriculum committee, Fellowship Commission, Japanese consulate, National Planning Association, Field Foundation (at one of the meetings the trustees made grants totaling $1 million), UNICEF (both nationally and locally), SANE, and the Police Advisory Board. Clarence continued chairing the AFSC Washington Seminars.

A new responsibility arose out of the October 1962 confrontation between the United States and the Soviet Union when the U.S. discovered that the Soviets were building offensive missile bases in Cuba. With Clarence taking a special interest in the crisis and the U.S. relationship with Cuba, his Advisory Committee on International Issues, with the approval of the AFSC board of directors, initiated plans to send a delegation to Cuba. Clarence was named chairman of the Cuba Committee and was asked to talk with Dean Rusk about the validation of passports for travel to Cuba. Authorization was not immediately secured, but several months later committee member John Hoover and Quaker doctor Joseph Stokes were given permission to travel to Cuba as journalists, only to be refused entry visas by the Cuban government. Following a hurricane disaster in Cuba in October, however, both governments authorized the sending of a plane load of relief supplies accompanied by four AFSC representatives.

Clarence Pickett's responsibilities within the national structures of the Religious Society of Friends continued. He was vice chairman of Friends General Conference and active on its committees. At the Midwest "Gathering" of the conference at Traverse City, Michigan at the end of June, he spoke, at the request of the general secretary (the author of this biography), about his own spiritual pilgrimage. A month later he gave a major address at the sessions of the Five Years Meeting of Friends held at Earlham College. And shortly thereafter he was back in the Midwest for a speaking engagement at Illinois Yearly Meeting held in the farming community of McNabb, Illinois.

Once again, in the 1963-64 winter, Wayne Marshall, Clarence's family physician, urged him to spend two months in a warmer climate because of his sensitive heart. Clarence and Lilly were invited by two Philadelphia Quaker couples to vacation at the Highland Park Club in Lake Wales, Florida. It was a winter haven frequented by a number of Friends from the north, and every Sunday there was a Quaker meeting for worship at the club. As Clarence described the setting: "Most club members are sixty or over, many in their early eighties, and one, ninety-four. The pace is slow, the food excellent, and there is a kind of general custom not to indulge in discussing controversial issues. I'm sure we differ widely and often with this predominantly Republican group, and there are a few more venturesome spokesmen once in a while."[25] On one occasion Pickett gave a public address.

As was his custom while on holiday, Clarence Pickett took with him a half-dozen books for reading and review. He had barely started in on a review of *The History of Earlham College* by Opal Thornburg when he came down with pneumonia and was hospitalized. The local doctor was worried about the effect of the pneumonia on his heart. Notwithstanding these health limitations, Clarence did finish reviewing all the books he had brought with him (and started on some additional ones) before returning home in March.

Pickett's organizational commitments remained much the same in 1964. One new development was the concern of Philadelphia Yearly Meeting about the African American church burnings in Mississippi. Clarence was prominently involved in arranging for a team of Friends to work on rebuilding the churches. In June there was the week-long Friends General Conference gathering in Cape May, New Jersey with an attendance of twenty-eight hundred Quakers.

Clarence Pickett's days were always well punctuated with special events and visitors. One such occasion was the Swarthmore College commencement where Burmese statesman U Thant, secretary general of the United Nations, received an honorary degree and where President Lyndon Johnson was the speaker. Among the more interesting visitors at his Haverford home was English Friend Horace Alexander, to talk about the continuing tensions between India and Pakistan. A Buddhist priest from Ceylon wanted to know how Quakers had developed their peace and social testimonies. On another occasion an Eastern Orthodox priest from Ethiopia consulted with Pickett about the same question.

In mid-July Clarence and Lilly again chose Cape Cod for a two weeks' vacation, enjoying the lovely weather, visiting with close friends, and worshipping at Yarmouth Friends Meeting. Clarence, probably restless for meaningful activity, went by train overnight to Washington for a meeting of the Peace Corps Advisory Council. He returned to Hyannis the following night by sleeper.

All the time he was away he was wrestling with a sore left knee and sore ankles, and with some shortness of breath. Dr. Marshall came out to see him at the house on Sunday morning, 2 August, after the Picketts' return from vacation and ordered him to rest completely for several weeks. He was released from house detention in time to tour, with the new secretary of the Police Advisory Board, William Gray, the sections of Philadelphia affected by two days of riots at the end of August. These were not race riots per se. Both black and white shops were raided and looted.

In September Clarence spent time on the writing of an article entitled, "Does the Tail Wag the Dog?" solicited by the editor, William Hubben, of the *Friends Journal*. The request reflected the criticism of some Friends that the widespread and well-publicized programs of the American Friends Service Committee were subordinating the activities of local meetings and yearly meetings. Pickett recognized that persons involved in AFSC projects often viewed the Religious Society of Friends as a service agency. "They miss the invisible roots of spiritual concern that lie behind the projects," he wrote, ". . . It is important that they learn otherwise."[26]

In early October a correspondent for the *Philadelphia Inquirer* interviewed Clarence Pickett for two hours in preparation for writing a story about him that appeared on the Sunday preceding his eightieth birthday on 19 October 1964. Clarence was impressed with the extent to which the reporter focused on philosophical and religious questions. The correspondent characterized Pickett as a "dedicated idealist and relentless foe of human greed, cruelty and apathy."[27]

Responding to a question, Pickett said that his most satisfying task had been his involvement in the relief program for the Arab refugees in the Gaza Strip in 1949. He remained optimistic about the human condition. Said Pickett: "As for giving up and letting the weight of the world's sins and cruelties weigh one down, I just am not built that way. I work on the theory that if you can find some spots of light, you can always work to let in more light."[28] Here was a reaffirmation of what he had said in his "Politics of Time and Politics of Eternity" address at Yale University in 1948.

Then Clarence Pickett revealed something that he had not publicly spoken about previously: "One of his greatest regrets, at eighty," wrote the *Inquirer* reporter, "is that Providence did not permit him to 'suffer enough.' He has led, he says, a full and fortunate life, free of major illness, any 'deep, deep disappointment,' and doing a job he both loved and was paid to do."[29]

Here was a disclosure quite in keeping with his sensitivity to suffering. There was the agony of spirit he had experienced on the many occasions when he witnessed and confronted distress, sometimes on a massive scale, as was the case in Germany and Austria during the rule of the Nazis. He had spoken eloquently in a nationwide radio broadcast in 1944 of the need "to live in the welter of the world's suffering and to retain an ultimate confidence in God and in man."[30]

In November, just before Thanksgiving, Clarence Pickett received a full physical checkup from Dr. Marshall. "Apparently I'm sound," said Clarence. But Marshall convinced him that he and Lilly should again spend their winter holiday in a warmer climate.

They chose Arizona, near Phoenix, where they had personal friends. Leaving on 23 December, they spent Christmas and the next week in St. Louis with their daughter Rachel, and her family. In Phoenix they settled into a small but comfortable rented house, with gas heat to supplement, when needed, the usually good weather. Christmas cards and other mail were regularly received from home and office. Clarence kept up with correspondence and read Richenda Scott's *Quakers in Russia* and other books. Above all, he did lots of walking, coatless and hatless on clear and warm days.

Always interested in and supportive of local Friends, Clarence went to both the pastoral and unprogrammed Friends meetings. He attended the regional AFSC executive committee meeting in Phoenix. Depressing for him was the proximity of military bases. "We never can escape from the roar of Army jets which fly over us almost all of the time, reminding us that we are on a powder keg. . . . Almost every day hundreds of planes fly overhead, wasting gas . . . to train men to kill."[31] But, on the whole, the month in Arizona was characterized by Lilly as restful.

At the beginning of February the Picketts went by train to Pasadena, California. There they were housed in a little apartment with a pullman kitchen. As expected, there were a few speaking engagements arranged by the AFSC regional office, and, as usual, there were many Pickett and Peckham relatives who came to visit and to take them out for meals. Clarence was regularly catching up on correspondence. On one occasion he visited the Center for the Study of Democratic Institutions, where some former AFSC staff members were employed.

From Pasadena the Picketts traveled to San Francisco where they stayed for a couple of days with Clark and Catharine Kerr, he being the president of the University of California at Berkeley; then by overnight train to Portland, Oregon, for just one day; and, again by overnight train, to Boise, Idaho, where they were to spend the weekend visiting with Peckham relatives.

It was on that leg of the trip, on 4 March, that Clarence Pickett became ill during the night. Lilly's brother Hubert, coming over from Caldwell twenty miles away, met the train as planned, and, after checking them in at the Downtowner Motel, took them directly to his doctor, Richard Vyeital, who sent them to Dr. Hugh Atchley, a heart specialist. Dr. Atchley immediately admitted Clarence into St. Adolphus Hospital in Boise. Clarence was able to walk to his room, but during the next twenty-four hours became increasingly ill, with his temperature going up to 104°. By now his condition was serious. By the second day, he was put on oxygen and given intravenous feeding. A second heart specialist was called in to act as consultant. Special nurses were on duty around the clock, in part to relieve Lilly of the task of being constantly at his bedside.

On the eighth day of his hospitalization Clarence's condition suddenly got much worse. Lilly Pickett phoned her two daughters to report that their father was grievously ill. Rachel was free to come to Boise and took the next plane; Carolyn was tied down by her employment. Wrote Lilly, "The next morning, when Rachel arrived, her father put his arms around her and gave her a kiss. The next two mornings he did the same and asked if she would have to go home that day. She assured him she would not, that she would wait until he was stronger. His response was a sweet smile, and they then visited for a time."[32]

On 17 March 1965 Lilly and Rachel talked with both the doctors and the nurse and were assured that Clarence's latest tests were all good. They urged Lilly and Rachel to go out for a ride with Hubert, promising that a nurse would be at Clarence's side the whole time, holding his hand to help him relax. Upon their return Lilly hurried into Clarence's room ahead of Hubert and Rachel and did not find the nurse there. Wrote Lilly:

As I went further into the room, so I could see around his curtain, I saw he was quiet now, but it was the stillness of death. The nurse saw me and hurried in to say that a few minutes before, as she sat beside him, he just relaxed and quit breathing. Hubert and Rachel came, and we all stood in silence by the bedside, benumbed that death had come unexpectedly so promptly after a favorable medical report. His great heart of love had stopped, having spent its last ounce of strength, and he was at peace.[33]

By one of those strange coincidences, the Peckham Dakin Funeral Home, founded by Lilly's brother Clifford Peckham, who had died in 1955, handled the arrangements for the casket to be shipped by train to Media, Pennsylvania, Lilly and Rachel accompanying it. The interment was on 22 March in the graveyard of the Providence Friends Meeting, the casket decked, at Lilly's request, with a beautiful sheaf of white lilies at the center of which was a nest of white roses. The immediate family, a few relatives and friends were present for the burial with Colin Bell, AFSC executive secretary, leading a brief service in which he associated Clarence Pickett's life with William Penn's dictum, "Let us then try what love may do." In the afternoon of the same day a memorial service was held at the meetinghouse for meeting members, family, and close friends.

Two days later a service for the AFSC family and others was held at the Friends Meetinghouse on Race Street. Two days later a memorial service for the general public, with eight hundred persons in attendance, was held at the Friends Meetinghouse at 4th and Arch Streets in Philadelphia. On this occasion Philadelphia mayor James Tate was present. So also were five police officers in full uniform, paying tribute to Clarence Pickett's service on the Police Advisory Board. And there were spokespersons for Japanese Americans, African Americans, the Mennonite Central Committee, the Brethren Service Commission, UNICEF, and the Fellowship Commission. Henry Cadbury introduced the memorial meeting by welcoming particularly those who were unfamiliar with a Quaker memorial meeting for worship and by explaining how the unprogrammed meeting would proceed. Twenty-five persons participated in the ministry of the meeting. Later in March memorial services were held in Quaker meetinghouses in New York, Washington, and elsewhere.

Literally hundreds of cables and letters poured into the AFSC from all over the world. Major articles on the life of Clarence Pickett appeared in a wide variety of newspapers and magazines. Almost uniformly these expressions of appreciation mentioned the close contacts he had had with influential persons in government, business, and academic circles. Yet, these articles noted, he never lost that humility of spirit that expressed itself in a deep concern for the disadvantaged. One Friend experienced Clarence as "infinitely charitable. There was an utter incorruptibility about him. He remained a transparently simple person. He did not glory in the contacts and connections that he had. He was not ambitious for power."[34] Another personal quality mentioned was his warmth and humor, gentle and ever-present. But, as his colleague Stephen Cary phrased it on an anniversary of Clarence Pickett's death, "First and foremost was his transparent faith in the immanence of a living God whose power to touch and redeem was beyond question or limit. . . . He lived as if this were true, and for him it bécame true.[35]

Within the American Friends Service Committee itself his loss was particularly felt. Quaker leader Douglas Steere, in one of the memorial meetings, reminded Friends how Clarence Pickett had built the committee "into a stethoscope to lay against the heart of the world to hear the heartbeat—to hear the needs that were there, to be obedient to the needs, and to be given the wisdom to meet them."[36] And it seemed fitting that a message from overseas, this one from Service Committee workers in Togo, West Africa, would capture the essence of this great soul and beloved Friend: "How fortunate we and the world have been to have had him with us thus long! How firm were his roots, yet how questing his spirit! His influence and the light that was so unusually clear in him will, of course, never die."[37]*

* There were two posthumous public recognitions of Clarence Pickett: the one, Pickett Hall, a men's dormitory at Wilmington (Ohio) College dedicated on 23 October 1965; the other, the Clarence E. Pickett Middle School, opened by the School District of Philadelphia in September 1970.

NOTES

1. Spencer Coxe, "Police Advisory Board: The Philadelphia Story," *Connecticut Bar Journal* 35, 1961, 138-55.

2. John Hetherington, "The Philadelphia Police Advisory Board: A Political Memoir." Unpublished manuscript, Urban Files, Samuel Paley Library, Temple University, Philadelphia.

3. "Pickett says Police Advisory Board won't brook political interference," *The Sunday Bulletin*, 31 Mar 1963.

4. Clarence Pickett journal, 21 July 1959.

5. Gertrude Samuels, "Who Shall Judge a Policeman?" *The New York Times* Magazine, August, 1964.

6. "Regulations concerning functions of honorary consuls-general and honorary consuls as amended," Ministry of Foreign Affairs, instructions No. 9, 1954.

7. Taped interview with Eleanor Stabler Clarke, 3 Nov. 1993.

8. "SANE—and Others," *Time*, 27 Apr 1962, 22-23.

9. Clarence E. Pickett , "The International Responsibility of Friends," High Point Friends Meeting, High Point, North Carolina, 18 Oct. 1959, AFSC archives.

10. Clarence E. Pickett, *For More Than Bread* (Boston: Little, 1953), 420.

11. Albert Bigelow, *The Voyage of the Golden Rule: An Experiment with Truth* (Garden City NY: Doubleday, 1959).

12. Pickett, "International Responsibility," 10.

13. C. Edward Behre, "The Vigil at the Pentagon," *Friends Journal* 6, no. 34 (1 Nov. 1960): 564-65.

14. Clarence E. Pickett to Mrs. Franklin D. Roosevelt, 31 Aug. 1954, AFSC archives.

15. *New York Herald Tribune*, 11 Oct. 1961, as quoted in Joseph P. Lash, *Eleanor: The Years Alone* (New York: Norton, 1972), 303.

16. Clarence E. Pickett, "Eleanor Roosevelt," *Friends Journal* 8, no. 23 (1 Dec. 1962): 504-05.

17. Pickett journal, 8 Mar. 1956.

18. Arthur Ford, in collaboration with Marguerite Harmon Bro, *Nothing So Strange* (New York: Harper, 1958), 32.

19. Letter, Walter Voelker to author, 4 Mar. 1994.

20. Transcript of sitting, 28 Oct. 1964.

21. Transcript, 28 Oct. 1964.

22. Pickett journal, 28 Oct. 1964.

23. Letter, Walter Voelker to author, 4 Mar. 1994.

24. From the record of Clarence Pickett's ministry at the memorial service for Leslie Shaffer, Providence Friends Meeting, 4 June 1950, AFSC archives.

25. Pickett journal, 31 Mar. 1964.

26. Clarence Pickett, "Does the Tail Wag the Dog?" *Friends Journal* 10, no. 23 (1 Dec. 1964): 545-46.

27. John R. Murphy, *Philadelphia Inquirer*, 18 Oct. 1964.

28. Murphy, *Inquirer*.

29. Murphy, *Inquirer*.

30. Text of Pickett's address, "Church of the Air," Columbia Broadcasting System, 23 Apr. 1944, AFSC archives.

31. Pickett journal, 11 and 18 Jan. 1965.

32. Pickett journal (this section written by Lilly Pickett), 16 Mar. 1965.

33. Pickett journal, 17 Mar. 1965.

34. Interview with Spencer Coxe, 16 Dec. 1996.

35. Stephen G. Cary, "The World Brightened When He Talked About It," *Friends Journal* 30, no. 15 (15 Oct. 1984): 8-9.

36. Excerpted from remarks made by Douglas Steere at the memorial meeting for worship held at Central Philadelphia Friends Meeting, 24 Mar. 1965, AFSC archives.

37. Ruth Smith, "Clarence E. Pickett, 1884-1965," *The Friendly Way* 72 (July 1965): 2.

INDEX

A

WITNESS FOR HUMANITY

was composed on a Macintosh 7600 desktop computer using Adobe Pagemaker 6.0 and typefaces from the Adobe Type Library: Times, Caslon Open Face, and Adobe Caslon. One thousand copies were printed in the United States by Printrcrafters, Inc., Philadelphia, Pennsylvania in October 1999. It was printed on 60# Gladfelter Supplee Recycled paper, 358 ppi.

In 1931, The Times of London commissioned the Monotye Corporation, under the direction of Stanley Morison to design a newspaper typeface. According to Morison: "The Times, as a newspaper in a class by itself, needed not a general trade type, however good, but a face whose strength of line, firmness of contour, and economy of space fulfilled the specific editorial needs of the Times." Times New Roman, drawn by Victor Lardent and initially released in 1932, was the result. The Linotype version is called Times Roman.

William Caslon released his first typefaces in 1722. They were based on seventeenth-century Dutch old style designs, which were then used extensively in England. Because of their incredible practicality Caslon's designs met with instant success. Caslon's types became popular throughout Europe and the American colonies: printer Benjamin Franklin hardly used any other typeface. The first printings of the American Declaration of Independence and the Constitution were set in Caslon. For Adobe Caslon, designer Carol Twonbly studied specimen pages printed by William Caslon between 1734 and 1770. Caslon Open Face was issued by the Barnhart Brothers & Spindler foundry in 1915. It was originally a reproduction of Le Moreau de Jeune, a type from France's G. Peignot foundry.

Book Design by
Eva Fernandez Beehler and Rebecca Kratz Mays